Soil Erosion and Conservation

SOIL EROSION AND CONSERVATION

R. P. C. Morgan
Silsoe College

Edited by
D. A. Davidson
University of Strathclyde

Copublished in the United States with
John Wiley & Sons, Inc., New York

Longman Scientific & Technical,
Longman Group UK Limited,
Longman House, Burnt Mill, Harlow,
Essex CM20 2JE, England
and Associated Companies throughout the world

Copublished in the United States with
John Wiley & Sons, Inc., 605 Third Avenue, New York, NY 10158

First published 1986
This is a revised and enlarged edition of
SOIL EROSION first published in the TOPICS IN
APPLIED GEOGRAPHY series in 1979
Reprinted 1988, 1990, 1991

British Library Cataloguing in Publication Data
Morgan, R.P.C.
  Soil erosion and conservation.
  1. Soil erosion
  I. Title   II. Davidson, Donald A.
  631.4′5   S623
  ISBN 0-582-30158-0

Library of Congress Cataloging-in-Publication Data
Morgan, R.P.C. (Royston Philip Charles), 1942-
  Soil erosion and conservation.

  Rev. and enl. ed. of: Soil erosion. 1979.
  Bibliography: p.
  Includes index.
  1. Soil erosion 2. Soil conservation.
I. Morgan, R.P.C. (Royston
Philip Charles), 1942–   Soil erosion.   III. Title.
S623.M683   1986   631.4′5   85–24035
ISBN 0-470-20671-3 (USA Only)

Set in 10/11 pt Linotron 202 Times
Produced by Longman Group (FE) Limited
Printed in Hong Kong

CONTENTS

FOREWORD

The need for greater as well as more reliable agricultural yields is a continuing and ever-increasing global challenge. A wide range of economic, social, environmental, demographic and political factors interact to cause the dire situation that exists in many countries. Environmental considerations can be grouped under the two related headings of climate and land degradation. Climatic stress can be applied through periods of more extreme temperature or precipitation patterns. Land degradation indicates a lowering of the fertility status of the soil by a reduction in nutrient level or by physical loss. Sometimes it is thought that land degradation is confined to tropical, arid or semi-arid regions but it is being increasingly realized that a range of insidious processes also exists in cool temperate regions. Current concerns focus around the reduction in organic matter levels in cultivated areas as well as on the effect on the soil of acid rain. The longer established view is that land degradation is frequently associated with soil erosion and its resultant disposition.

Although the significance of soil erosion has been widely appreciated for over 50 years, and despite the research of pioneers such as R. A. Bagnold, H. H. Bennett, W. S. Chepil, W. H. Wischmeier and A. W. Zingg, it is only during the last decade that there has been a major flourish of studies concerned with monitoring and modelling erosional processes. The first edition of Roy Morgan's book was published in 1979 in the series *Topics in Applied Geography*. It was a short volume which provided readers with a succinct yet comprehensive overview of soil erosion. This new and much enlarged edition reflects the output of international research in recent years; in addition, the second part of the book now focuses on soil conservation practices. The reader will be impressed by the extent to which Roy Morgan's own research experience is evident. His final plea is for recognition of the contribution which applied physical geographers can make to the prediction and management of soil erosion. His book is an excellent demonstration of such a contribution and it is hoped that it is widely read by all concerned with this important subject.

Donald A. Davidson

PREFACE

Soil erosion is a hazard traditionally associated with agriculture in tropical and semi-arid areas. In recent years, however, its importance has become apparent in areas devoted to forestry, transport and recreation. Moreover, erosion is increasingly being recognized as a hazard in temperate countries such as Britain, Belgium and Germany. Conservation measures depend upon a thorough understanding of the mechanics of the erosion processes. This book is the first text to concentrate on soil erosion, a subject which is usually covered only briefly in books on soil conservation.

The mechanics of erosion are reviewed in the first part of the book with emphasis on the extent of and deficiencies in current knowledge. Techniques of classifying land with respect to erosion risk are also examined and a simple working method is presented. A discussion of various approaches to modelling soil erosion focuses on the value of models for predicting rates of soil loss and planning conservation work. Strategies for erosion control are related to the changes that man can make to the soil, plant cover and slope of the land and the effect that these have on the mechanics of erosion. The themes developed in the first part of the book are integrated in a case study of erosion risk evaluation and conservation planning in Peninsular Malaysia. Here the application of erosion mapping, land classification, erosion modelling and conservation systems is described in practice. Attention is given to working with scarce data using remote sensing and detailed field survey.

The book is intended for undergraduate and postgraduate students studying soil erosion and conservation as part of their courses in geography, environmental science, agriculture, agricultural engineering, hydrology, soil science, ecology and civil engineering. In addition it provides an introduction to the subject for those concerned with resources survey and development, agricultural, recreational and rural planning, and for those working on soil erosion and conservation at research or experimental stations.

My thanks are due to the Director, Malaysian

Meteorological Service, for supplying many of the data used in the analysis of erosivity for Peninsular Malaysia; Messrs B. B. Lim and C. L. Woo for extracting data from the records of the Meteorological Station of the Department of Geography, University of Malaya; Mr H. H. Soh for assistance with much of the work carried out on the University of Malaya campus; Ing. Zoot. MS. L. Carlos Fierro and Ing. Zoot. J. Jabalera Ramos for help in the field in Mexico; and various students of the Department of Geography, University of Malaya and the National College of Agricultural Engineering, Silsoe who have assisted with both field and laboratory work. The data on soil erosion in Bedfordshire are derived from a research project supported by the Natural Environment Research Council. I am also grateful to my wife, Gillian, for help in the field, reading and improving the manuscript and providing encouragement at all times.

R. P. C. Morgan
Silsoe
September 1977

Considerable advances have been made over the last decade in our understanding of the processes of soil erosion, particularly in the areas of the interaction between raindrop impact and soil strength and the initiation of rills. A better understanding is also being obtained of the ways in which plant covers and crop residues affect both water and wind erosion. These increases in knowledge are changing current thinking on the approaches used to predict erosion and are providing the basis for a new generation of erosion models. The results of this recent work have been incorporated into this revised version by an expanded treatment of erosion processes and their controlling factors. Although this has necessitated an increase in length, the format of the first part of the book has not been altered except that the material on erosion risk evaluation in Peninsular Malaysia, formerly presented as a case study, has been brought forward to the appropriate sections of the earlier chapters.

The opportunity of writing a more comprehensive volume has enabled a fuller treatment to be given to soil conservation practices: this now makes up the second part of the book. Strategies for erosion control are first examined with emphasis on the integration of agronomic measures, mechanical controls and soil management. The following chapters discuss the range of measures that are available under each of these headings, paying particular attention to their design and, through a review of research findings, their effectiveness.

The objectives of the text remain unchanged and, to meet these, the sections on erosion control on grazing lands and in urban areas have been enlarged, and agroforestry is introduced. All the original diagrams have been retained and many new ones added. Although much work is still undertaken by agricultural engineers in the United States, important contributions are now being made by researchers in geography and soil sciences, especially in western Europe and Australia. There has been also a great increase in the amount of research carried out by local scientists in Africa, India, China and south-east Asia. The relevance of this upsurge of activity is reflected in the expansion of the reference list from just over 200 to just over 600 citations.

The text continues to be based on courses which I give at Silsoe College. Some of the material is taken from the research carried out by myself and my students. The contributions of the latter are referenced and much appreciated. Some of this research was supported by grants from the Agriculture and Food Research Council and the Natural Environment Research Council. I am grateful again to my wife, Gillian, and also to my son, Richard, for accepting the disruptions caused by the preparation of this book.

R. P. C. Morgan
Silsoe
May 1985

ACKNOWLEDGEMENTS

We are grateful to the following for permission to reproduce copyright material:

George Allen & Unwin for table 9.1 from table 1 *Geomorphology and Soils* by Richards, Arnett & Ellis (taken from Kolenbrander 1974); American Society of Agricultural Engineers for fig 5.1 from fig 1 (Meyer & Wischmeier 1969); Edward Arnold (Publishers) Ltd for figs 1.2, 5.4 & table 5.1 from figs 6.17 (pts B, D), 4.13a, table 5.1 (Gregory & Walling 1973) and fig. 4.11 from fig 1 p 36 (Morgan 1980b); B T Batsford Ltd for fig 2.1a from fig 3.10 (Withers & Vipond 1974) and table 10.7 from tables 7.3, 7.10 pp 116, 126 (Hudson 1981); B T Batsford Ltd and American Society of Agricultural Engineers for table 10.6 from table 1 p 1302 (Temple 1982) & table 8.2 p 137 (Hudson 1981); Catena Verlag for fig 2.5 from fig 1 p 141 (Savat 1982); Council of Europe for tables 3.1, 3.3 (Fournier 1972); East-West Environment & Policy Institute for fig 7.1 from fig 3 p 12 (Perrens & Trustrum 1984); Elsevier Science Publishers for table 5.3 from pp 312–313 (Zachar 1982); the editor for fig 1.5 slightly amended from p 386 (Wolman 1967); the editor for table 5.11 from table 6 (Morgan 1985); the editor for table 4.8 (Eyles 1970); Hedeselskabet for fig 10.7 from map & fig p 4 (Jensen 1954); Instituut voor Bodemvruchtbarheid for fig 6.5 from fig 5 p 11 (Knottnerus 1979); the editor for table 6.1 from table 1 p 375 (Morgan 1981b); the editor for fig 4.18 from figs 3, 4, 8, tables 1, 2, pp 136, 138, 143, 137, 139, 142 (Hannam & Hicks 1980); the editor for fig 5.3, tables 5.5, 5.6 from fig 5.1, tables 1, 2 (Morgan, Morgan & Finney 1984); the editor for fig 6.3a from fig 1 p 200 (Bollinger 1975); Prentice-Hall Inc for figs 2.4, 8.1 from figs 5.6, 8.8, 8.9 pp 126, 259, 261 (Troeh, Hobbs & Donahue 1980) (c) 1980 and table 4.3 modified (Stallings 1957) (c) 1957 renewed (c) 1985; Les Presses Universitaires de France for fig 5.2 (Fournier 1960); T C Sheng for fig 4.16, table 4.5 (Sheng 1972a); the editor for fig 8.2 from fig 2 p 37 (Brierley 1976); the editor for fig 4.17 from fig 1 (Morgan 1985b); U S Department of Agriculture for fig 4.5 from fig 1 (Wischmeier & Smith 1978); Universite Louis Pasteur, Laboratoire de Geographie Physique for fig 4.7 from p 17 (Pihan 1979); University Malaya Department of Geography for data in table 4.4 (Panton 1969); Van Nostrand Reinhold Co Inc for figs 10.3–10.6 from figs 7.10, 8.7, 8.8, 8.9, 8.11, 8.13, 8.14, 8.18, 8.19 pp 163, 182, 183, 184, 185 (Gray & Leiser 1982) Copyright Standard Scholarship; the editor for fig 4.8 from fig 2 p 166 (Smithen & Schulze 1982); John Wiley & Sons Ltd for figs 1.3 from 4.2 p 76 (Walling & Webb 1983), 1.4 from fig 1.6 p 14 (Kirkby 1980), 2.1b from 2.12 p 65 (Knapp 1978), 4.9 from fig 5.1 p 181 (Roose 1977), 6.3b from fig 1 p 296 (Morgan 1978), 8.3 from fig 11 p 472 (Jiang, Qi & Tan 1981), tables 7.1, 8.1, 10.2, 10.4, 10.5 from tables 8.3, 8.12, 8.7, 8.5, 8.6 pp 258, 285, 269, 265, 266 (Morgan 1980), table 9.2 from table 6.1 (Schwarb, Frevert, Edminster & Barnes 1966); the editor for figs 4.3, 4.14 from fig 1 & table 1 pp 94–95 (Stocking & Elwell 1973b).

Chapter 1
DISTRIBUTION
OF SOIL EROSION

The rapid erosion of soil by wind and water has been a
problem since man began cultivating the land. Although it is a
less emotive topic today than in the period immediately
following the 'Dust Bowl' in the United States in the 1930s, its
importance has not diminished. Soil erosion remains a
problem in the United States, in many tropical and semi-arid
areas and is increasingly recognized as a hazard in temperate
countries including Great Britain, Belgium and Germany.

The prevention of soil erosion, which means reducing the
rate of soil loss to approximately that which would occur
under natural conditions, relies on selecting appropriate
strategies for soil conservation and this, in turn, requires a
thorough understanding of the processes of erosion. The
factors which influence the rate of erosion are rainfall, runoff,
wind, soil, slope, plant cover and the presence or absence of
conservation measures. In Fig. 1.1 these and other related
factors are grouped under three headings: energy, resistance
and protection. The energy group includes the potential ability
of rainfall, runoff and wind to cause erosion. This ability is
termed erosivity. Also included are those factors which
directly affect the power of the erosive agents such as the
reduction in the length of runoff or wind blow through the
construction of terraces and wind breaks respectively.
Fundamental to the resistance group is the erodibility of the
soil which depends upon its mechanical and chemical
properties. Factors which encourage the infiltration of water
into the soil and thereby reduce runoff decrease erodibility
whilst any activity that pulverizes the soil increases it. Thus
cultivation may decrease the erodibility of clay soils but
increase that of sandy soils. The protection group focuses on
factors relating to the plant cover. By intercepting rainfall and
reducing the velocity of runoff and wind, a plant cover protects
the soil from erosion. Different plant covers afford different
degrees of protection so that, by determining the land use,
man, to a considerable degree, can control the rate of erosion.

The rate of soil loss is normally expressed in units of mass
or volume per unit area per unit of time. In a review of erosion

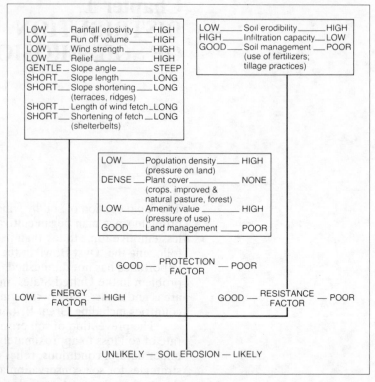

Fig. 1.1   Factors affecting soil erosion.

under natural conditions, Young (1969) quotes rates of the order of 0.004 5 kg m^{-2} y^{-1} for areas of moderate relief and 0.045 kg^{-2} y^{-1} for steep relief. For comparison, rates from agricultural land, in the range of 4.5 to 45.0 kg m^{-2} y^{-1}, are classed as accelerated erosion.

Theoretically, whether or not a rate of soil loss is severe is judged relative to the rate of soil formation. If soil properties such as nutrient status, texture and thickness remain unchanged through time it is assumed that the rate of erosion balances the rate of soil formation. Even relatively small changes in the plant cover can result in considerable increases in erosion. Comparing two otherwise identical drainage basins in the highlands of Peninsular Malaysia, Douglas (1967*a*) shows that in the Telom basin, with 94 per cent of its area under rain forest, the erosion rate is 0.21 kg m^{-2} y^{-1}, whilst in the Bertam basin, where only 64 per cent is under forest, the rate is 1.03 kg m^{-2} y^{-1}.

The effects of erosion are felt not only in the areas where top soil is removed by water and wind, the subsoil and bedrock exposed and the land entrenched by gullies, but also in the areas downvalley or downwind where the ground is covered with sand and silt deposits, ditches and canals are clogged with sediment and reservoirs silt up. Deterioration in the quality of cropping and grazing land as a result of erosion brings about reduced productivity and increased expenditure on fertilizers to maintain fertility. In extreme cases yields become so poor that land has to be taken out of cultivation. Siltation of reservoirs and rivers reduces their capacity, creating a flood hazard, and the sediment is a major pollutant, lowering water quality.

The severity of erosion varies in time and space. The sediment production resulting from an individual climatic event depends upon local topographic, soil and landuse conditions so that these factors cause regional variations in erosion. Since climate consists of a series of events of different intensities, it is a major factor explaining short-term temporal variations in erosion. However, climatic characteristics, especially rainfall volumes, rainfall intensities and wind speeds, vary regionally whilst landuse can change over time in relation to economic incentives and government policies. In addition, long-term temporal variations in erosion may arise from fluctuations in climate, such as runs of drought or abnormally wet years, or from changes in soil properties, such as the loss of organic matter, a trend often associated with continuous arable production on sands and sandy loams. Thus the interplay of spatial and temporal variations is rather complex. Despite this interrelation, it is helpful to consider the two separately.

1.1   SPATIAL VARIATIONS

On a world scale, investigations of the relationship between soil loss and climate (Langbein and Schumm, 1958) show that erosion reaches a maximum in areas with an effective mean annual precipitation of 300 mm. Effective precipitation is that required to produce a known quantity of runoff under specified temperature conditions. At precipitation totals below 300 mm, erosion increases as precipitation increases. But, as precipitation increases so does the vegetation cover, resulting in better protection of the soil surface. At precipitation totals above 300 mm, the protection effect counteracts the erosive effect of greater rainfall, so that soil loss decreases as precipitation increases. There is some evidence (Douglas, 1967*b*), however, to indicate that soil loss may increase again with precipitation as the latter and therefore the runoff reach still higher levels (Fig. 1.2). The availability of information on sediment loads in rivers has increased enormously over the last twenty years. Although the data relate only to the material carried in suspension because of the technical difficulties in measuring bed load and the relative paucity of observations on

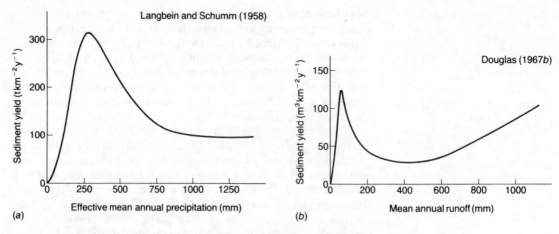

Fig. 1.2 Proposed relationships between sediment yield and (*a*) effective mean annual precipitation; (*b*) mean annual runoff (after Gregory and Walling, 1973).

solute concentrations, they can be used to provide a reasonably reliable assessment of the global pattern of water erosion (Fig. 1.3; Walling and Webb, 1983).

The major feature revealed by this assessment is the vulnerability to erosion of the semi-arid and semi-humid areas of the world, especially in China, India, the western USA, central USSR and the Mediterranean lands. The problem of soil erosion in these areas is compounded by the need for water conservation and the ecological sensitivity of the environment, so that removal of the vegetation cover for cropping or grazing results in rapid declines in organic content of the soil, followed by soil exhaustion and the risk of desertification. Other areas of high erosion rates include mountainous terrain, such as much of the Andes, the Himalayas, the Karakorams, parts of the Rocky Mountains and the African rift valley; and areas of volcanic soils, for example, Java, South Island of New Zealand, Papua New Guinea and parts of Central America.

Within any particular area there will be considerable variation in erosion rates but if the rates are grouped into those related to natural vegetation, cultivated land and bare soil, each group follows a broadly similar pattern of global variation (Table 1.1). One exception to this is the humid tropics. Measurements of soil loss from hillslopes in West Africa (Roose, 1971) ranging in steepness from 0.3° to 4° yield mean annual rates of erosion of 0.015, 0.02 and 0.003 kg m^{-2} under natural conditions of open savanna grassland, dense savanna grassland and tropical rain forest respectively. Clearance of the land for agriculture increases the rates to 0.8, 2.6 and 9.0 kg m^{-2} whilst leaving the land as bare soil produces rates of 2, 3 and 17 kg m^{-2} respectively. Thus removal of the rain forest results in much greater rises in

Table 1.1   Rates of erosion in selected countries (kg m^{-2} y^{-1})

	Natural	Cultivated	Bare soil
China	< 0.20	15.00–20.00	28.00–36.00
USA	0.003–0.30	0.50–17.00	0.40– 9.00
Ivory Coast	0.003–0.02	0.01– 9.00	1.00–75.00
Nigeria	0.05 –0.10	0.01– 3.50	0.30–15.00
India	0.05 –0.10	0.03– 2.00	1.00– 2.00
Belgium	0.01 –0.05	0.30– 3.00	0.70– 8.20
UK	0.01 –0.05	0.01– 0.30	1.00– 4.50

Sources: Bollinne, 1978; Browning, Norton, McCall and Bell, 1948; Fournier, 1972; Jiang, Qi and Tan, 1981; Lal, 1976; Morgan, 1981a; Rao, 1981; Roose, 1971.

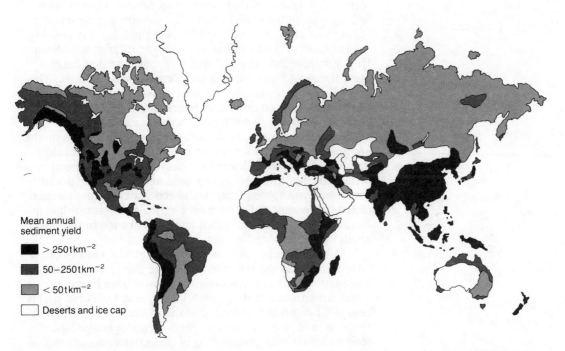

Mean annual sediment yield
- ▇ > 250 t km^{-2}
- ▓ 50–250 t km^{-2}
- ▒ < 50 t km^{-2}
- ☐ Deserts and ice cap

Fig. 1.3   A tentative map of global variations in suspended sediment yield (after Walling and Webb, 1983).

erosion rates than does removal of the savanna grassland. Where the land is cleared, erosion is highest in the rain forest areas whereas under natural conditions it is highest in the dense savanna areas. These measurements emphasize the high degree of protection afforded to the soil by the rain forest but also reflect the erosive capacity of the high rainfalls of the humid tropics when the protection is destroyed as well as the sensitivity of the rain forest ecosystem to disturbance. Given the present rate of removal of the tropical rain forest, a second area of high vulnerability to erosion is being created which, with the magnitudes of soil loss involved, is likely to prove as severe a problem as that of the semi-arid and semi-humid areas of the world.

A third area with high risk of erosion is not discernible from Fig. 1.3 but relates to regions where the landforms and associated soils are relicts of a previous climate. Although they may appear to be stable under the present climate, only a slight disturbance is needed to destroy this stability. Butler (1959; 1967), applying the principle of stratigraphy to soil mantles over a range of landscapes from hilly terrain to aggradational plains in southeast Australia, finds evidence for periods of stability, during which soils developed on the land surface, alternating with periods of instability when erosion and deposition took place. Since the erosion was clearly at accelerated rates, resembling in severity present-day gullying around Canberra or wind erosion on wheat farms near Swan Hill, Victoria, but occurred well before any settlement by man, the most likely cause is significant climatic change. This could be due to either increased aridity or greater seasonal storminess; both could create deterioration of the vegetation cover. Although it is not known whether explanations of this kind are more widely applicable, Richter (1980) uses a similar argument to account for recent erosion in the heads of the box-like valleys or *dellen* in Germany. These valley heads were formed by extension of the drainage network in periglacial conditions and subsequently stabilized under a more temperate climate. Clearance of the area for agriculture has resulted in increased surface runoff which has concentrated in the valley heads and reactivated erosion.

Care should be taken in interpreting data on rates of erosion because the rate varies with the size of the area being considered. Part of the sediment removed from hillsides, embankments and cuttings finds its way into rivers but part is deposited *en route* on footslopes and in flood plains where it remains in temporary storage. Since larger drainage basins tend to have larger proportions of these flatter areas suitable for deposition, erosion rates expressed per unit area are generally higher for small basins and decrease as the catchment becomes bigger. The proportion of the sediment eroded from the land surface which discharges into the river is known as the sediment delivery ratio. Surprisingly few studies have been made of this, considering it is fundamental to assessing sediment yield, but it varies from about 3 to 90 per cent, decreasing with greater basin area and lower average slope (Maner, 1958; Roehl, 1962; Renfro, 1975).

The relative importance of the factors controlling spatial variations in erosion is dependent upon scale. So far, greatest emphasis in this section has been paid to climate but this is

dominant only at a certain level in the hierarchy of scales at
which landforms and erosion can be considered. It is implicit
in the Russian work on landscape science that landforms are a
result of the interaction of a number of variables and that, in
decreasing order of importance, these are geological structure,
climate, hydrology, soils, vegetation, man and animal life
(Kalesnik, 1961). In passing from the macro- to the
micro-scale, gradual changes occur in the dominant variable.
As far as soil erosion is concerned, climate is dominant at the
macro-scale but, at the smaller scales, is fairly uniform over
the size of the areas being considered, and soils and vegetation
become important.

Some support for this scale-linked pattern of controlling
factors is provided by studies of drainage density (Gregory and
Gardiner, 1975; Morgan, 1973a). Since drainage density is an
expression of the distribution of streams in the drainage
system, it is a useful if somewhat crude indicator of runoff and
is often used as an index of the severity of erosion. Broad
variations in drainage density on a macro-scale are associated
with differences in climate. At the meso-scale, regional
variations can be related to differences in rainfall volume but
the pattern is complicated by variations due to lithology and
relief. At the micro-level, differences in lithology, normally
expressed through soil type, and the frequency and intensity of
individual climatic events become important. Studies of the
sediment yield of rivers (Fournier, 1960; Rougerie, 1967;
Diaconu, 1969) reveal a similar pattern for the effect of scale.
Measurements of hillslope erosion (Roose, 1971) show the
roles played by slope and landuse at the micro-scale.
Assembling the evidence from these various sources enables a
general scheme for the scale effects on factors influencing
erosion to be constructed (Table 1.2).

Table 1.2   Factors influencing soil loss at different scales

Scale of analysis			Evidence
Macro	Meso	Micro	
climate	lithology relief		Sediment yield of rivers
climate	lithology relief	micro-climate lithology (soil)	Drainage density
climate	altitude relief		Studies of erosion rates
climate		plant cover micro-climate	Studies of soil loss from hillslopes

1.2   TEMPORAL VARIATIONS

Most geomorphologists accept that most erosion takes place during events of moderate frequency and magnitude simply because extreme or catastrophic events are too infrequent to contribute appreciably to the quantity of soil eroded over a long period of time. Magnitude–frequency ideas were applied to studies of sediment transport in rivers by Wolman and Miller (1960). They found that the dominant event, the one responsible for most work, was larger in magnitude than the most frequent event but was by no means extreme, corresponding to the stage of bankfull discharge, an event with a return period of between 1.33 and 2 years.

A similar concept may be applied to erosion on hillsides. Experimental studies of Roose (1967) in Senegal show that between 1959 and 1963, 68 per cent of the soil loss took place in rain storms of 15 to 60 mm; these storms have a frequency of about ten times per year. Studies of erosion in mid-Bedfordshire, England (Morgan, 1981a), indicate that in the period 1973 to 1979, 80 per cent of the erosion occurred in thirteen storms, the greatest soil loss, comprising 21 per cent of the erosion, resulting from a storm of 57.2 mm. These storms have a frequency of between two and four times a year. Measurements of erosion near Ibadan, Nigeria, showed that half the annual soil loss can occur with between two and seven storms (Lal, 1976) whilst on tea estates in Kenya half of the annual soil loss is recorded with between three and six storms (Othieno and Laycock, 1977). In contrast to this evidence supporting a somewhat frequent dominant event for hillslope erosion, Hudson (1981a) emphasizes the role of the more dramatic event. Quoting from research in Zimbabwe, he states that 50 per cent of the annual soil loss occurs in only two storms and that, in one year, 75 per cent of the erosion took place in ten minutes.

A comparison of the studies of sediment transport on hillslopes with that in rivers indicates a more frequent dominant event for the former and suggests that the dominant event frequency may vary for different erosion processes. Further evidence for this is provided by research on shallow debris slides and mudflows on cultivated fields and grassland in the Mgeta area of Tanzania for which the dominant event has a return period of once in five years (Temple and Rapp, 1972).

Even though most erosion of soil from hillsides and transport of sediment in rivers occurs in these dominant events of relatively moderate magnitude, the effects of an extreme event can be very dramatic. This is because extreme events can have effects which are different in kind as well as degree and may well be longer lasting. For example, rainstorms with return periods greater than once in one hundred years may initiate headward erosion of gullies and the formation of new channel heads. A slow-moving equatorial storm disturbance within the northeast monsoon deposited 631 mm of rain on 28 December 1926 and 1194 mm between 26 and 29 December in the Kuantan area of Peninsular Malaysia, resulting in extensive gully erosion and numerous landslides. The scars produced in the landscape were still visible thirty-five years later (Nossin, 1964).

The significance of extreme events is also illustrated by Thornes (1976) in his studies of erosion in southern Spain. Extensive changes to hillslope and channel form occurred in the area around Ugijar during a storm of 198 mm between 17 and 19 October 1973 with 175 mm of rain falling on 18 October. The return period of this event is estimated to be in excess of 500 years. On the hillslopes there was widespread development of parallel, closely-spaced rills or *caracavas*, 300 to 700 mm deep, running straight down the slope and

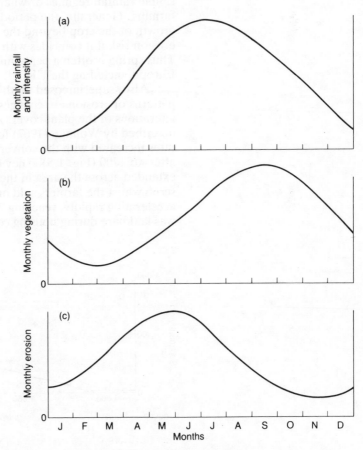

Fig. 1.4 Seasonal cycles of rainfall, vegetation cover and erosion in a semi-humid climate (after Kirkby, 1980).

extending headwards to the divides; numerous rotational deep-seated and planar shallow landslides; and extensive deposition of material on the terraces of the river valleys. The main effects in the river channels were scour and fill of extensive areas where, prior to the flood, the land was irrigated for production of beans, tomatoes and fruit.

In addition to the variations in erosion associated with the frequency and magnitude of single storms, rates of erosion often follow a seasonal pattern. This is best illustrated with reference to a rainfall regime with a wet and a dry season (Fig. 1.4). The vegetation growth follows a similar pattern but peaks later in the season than the rainfall. The most vulnerable time for erosion is the early part of the wet season when the rainfall is high but the vegetation has not grown sufficiently to protect the soil. Thus the erosion peak precedes the rainfall peak.

Somewhat more complex seasonal patterns occur with less simple rainfall regimes or where the land is used for arable farming. Generally, the period between ploughing and the growth of the crop beyond the seedling stage contains an erosion risk if it coincides with heavy rainfall or strong winds. Thus spring is often a peak time for erosion in western Europe, including the UK.

Also, superimposed on the frequency–magnitude patterns of erosion are changes brought about by man's alterations of the plant cover. A typical sequence of events is described by Wolman (1967) for Maryland where soil erosion rates increased with the conversion of woodland to cropland after AD 1700 (Fig. 1.5). They declined as the urban fringe extended across the area in the 1950s and the land reverted to scrub whilst the farmers sold out to speculators, before accelerating rapidly, reaching 700 kg m^{-2} y^{-1} whilst the area was laid bare during housing construction. With the

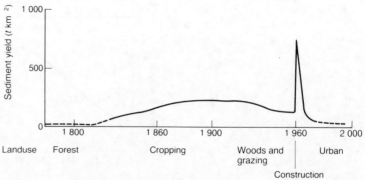

Fig. 1.5   Relationships between sediment yield and changing landuse in the Piedmont region of Maryland (after Wolman, 1967).

completion of urban development, runoff from concrete surfaces is concentrated into gutters and sewers, and soil loss falls to below 0.4 kg m^{-2} y^{-1}.

Erosion and landuse change are very strongly related. Rates of soil loss accelerate quickly to unacceptably high levels whenever the land is misused. Under these conditions, the effects of geomorphological events of moderate and high magnitude in particular are exacerbated. Richter (1980) shows how throughout the history of central Europe erosion has increased when agriculture has extended on to more marginal land and decreased when the area under the plough has contracted. A combination of historical and geomorphological analysis emphasizes that erosion is a natural process, that it can be accelerated if man uses the land unwisely and, therefore, that soil erosion is an integral part of both the natural and cultural environment.

Chapter 2
PROCESSES AND
MECHANICS OF EROSION

Soil erosion is a two-phase process consisting of the detachment of individual particles from the soil mass and their transport by erosive agents such as running water and wind. When sufficient energy is no longer available to transport the particles a third phase, deposition, occurs.

Rainsplash is the most important detaching agent. As a result of raindrops striking a bare soil surface, soil particles may be thrown through the air over distances of several centimetres. Continuous exposure to intense rainstorms considerably weakens the soil. The soil is also broken up by weathering processes, both mechanical, by alternate wetting and drying, freezing and thawing and frost action, and biochemical. Soil is disturbed by tillage operations and by the trampling of people and livestock. Running water and wind are further contributors to the detachment of soil particles. All these processes loosen the soil so that it is easily removed by the agents of transport.

The transporting agents comprise those which act areally and contribute to the removal of a relatively uniform thickness of soil and those which concentrate their action in channels. The first group consists of rainsplash, surface runoff in the form of shallow flows of infinite width, sometimes termed sheet flow but more correctly called overland flow, and wind. The second group covers water flow in small channels, known as rills, which can be obliterated by weathering and ploughing, or in the larger, more permanent features of gullies and rivers. To these agents which act externally, picking up material from and carrying it over the ground surface, should be added transport by mass movements such as soil flows, slides and creep, in which water affects the soil internally, altering its strength.

The severity of erosion depends upon the quantity of material supplied by detachment and the capacity of the eroding agents to transport it. Where the agents have the capacity to transport more material than is supplied by detachment, the erosion is described as *detachment-limited*. Where more material is supplied than can be transported, the erosion is *transport-limited*. The recognition of which factor, detachment or transport, is limiting is important because the success or failure of conservation work relies upon applying remedies to the correct one.

The energy available for erosion takes two forms: potential and kinetic. Potential energy (PE) results from the difference in height of one body with respect to another. It is the product of mass (m), height difference (h) and acceleration due to gravity (g), so that

$$PE = mhg \qquad (2.1)$$

which, in units of kg, m and m s^{-2} respectively, yields a value in joules. The potential energy for erosion is converted into kinetic energy (KE), the energy of motion. This is related to the mass and the velocity (v) of the eroding agent in the expression

$$KE = \tfrac{1}{2}mv^2 \qquad (2.2)$$

which, in units of kg and (m s^{-1})^2, also gives a value in joules. Most of this energy is dissipated in friction with the surface over which the agent moves so that only 3 to 4 per cent of the energy of running water and 0.2 per cent of that of falling raindrops is expended in erosion (Pearce, 1976). An indication of the relative efficiencies of the processes of water erosion can be obtained by applying these figures to calculations of kinetic energy, using equation (2.2), based on typical velocities (Table 2.1). The concentration of running water in rills affords the most powerful erosive agent but raindrops are potentially more erosive than overland flow. Most of the raindrop energy is used in detachment, however, so that the amount available

Table 2.1 Efficiency of forms of water erosion

Form	Mass*	Typical Velocity (ms^{-1})	Kinetic Energy[†]	Energy for Erosion[‡]	Observed Sediment Transport[ς] (g cm^{-1})
Raindrops	R	9	$40.5R$	$0.081R$	20
Overland flow	$0.5R$	0.01	$2.5 \times 10^{-5}R$	$7.5 \times 10^{-7}R$	400
Rill flow	$0.5R$	4[∥]	$4R$	$0.12R$	19 000

* Assumes rainfall of mass R of which 50 per cent contributes to runoff.

† Based on $\tfrac{1}{2}mv^2$.

‡ Assumes that 0.2 per cent of the kinetic energy of raindrops and 3 per cent of the kinetic energy of runoff is utilized in erosion.

ς Totals observed in mid-Bedfordshire on an 11° slope, on sandy soil, over 900 days. Most of the energy of raindrops contributes to detachment rather than transport.

∥ Estimated using the Manning equation of flow velocity for a rill, 0.3 m wide and 0.2 m deep, on a slope of 11°, at bankfull, assuming a roughness coefficient of 0.02.

for transport is less than that from overland flow. This is illustrated by measurements of soil loss in the field in mid-Bedfordshire. Over a 900-day period, on an 11° slope on a sandy soil, transport across a centimetre width of slope amounted to 19 000 g of sediment by rills, 400 g by overland flow and only 20 g by rainsplash (Morgan, 1977).

The processes of water erosion are closely related to the routes taken by water in its passage through the vegetation cover and its movement over the ground surface. Their base thus lies in the hydrological cycle. During a rainstorm, part of the water falls directly on the land, either because there is no vegetation or because it passes through gaps in the plant canopy, a component known as direct throughfall. Part is intercepted by the canopy from where it is either returned to the atmosphere through evaporation or finds its way to the ground by dripping from the leaves, a component termed temporarily intercepted throughfall or leaf drip, or by running down the stem as stemflow. The action of direct throughfall and leaf drip produces rainsplash erosion. The rainfall which reaches the ground may be stored in small depressions or hollows on the surface or it may infiltrate the soil, contributing either to soil moisture storage or, by percolating deeper, to groundwater. When the soil is unable to take in more water the excess will move laterally downslope within the soil as subsurface flow or interflow or it will contribute to runoff on the surface, resulting in erosion by overland flow or by rills and gullies.

The rate at which water passes into the soil is known as the infiltration rate and this exerts a major control over the generation of surface runoff. Water is drawn into the soil by gravity and by capillary forces whereby it is attracted to and held as a thin molecular film around the soil particles. During a rainstorm, the spaces between the soil particles become filled with water and the capillary forces decrease so that the infiltration rate starts high at the beginning of the storm and declines to a level which represents the maximum sustained rate at which water can pass through the soil (Fig. 2.1). This level, the infiltration capacity, corresponds theoretically to the saturated hydraulic conductivity of the soil. In practice, however, it is now believed that it is the actual hydraulic conductivity of the wetted zone which controls infiltration capacity. This is often lower than the saturated hydraulic conductivity because of air entrapped in the soil pores as the wetting front passes downwards through the soil (Slack and Larson, 1981).

Various attempts have been made to describe the change in infiltration rate over time mathematically. One of the most widely used equations is that of Philip (1957):

$$i = A + B \cdot t^{\frac{1}{2}}$$

(2.3)

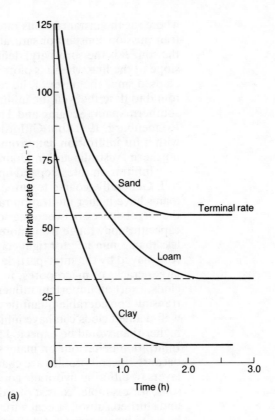

(a)

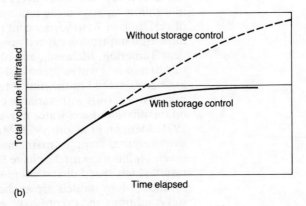

(b)

Fig. 2.1   (a) Typical infiltration rates for various soils (after Withers and Vipond, 1974); (b) Effect of a limiting soil moisture storage on the cumulative infiltration curve (after Knapp, 1978).

where i is the instantaneous rate of infiltration, A is the transmission constant or saturated hydraulic conductivity of the soil, B is the sorptivity, defined by Talsma (1969) as the slope of the line when i is plotted against $t^{\frac{1}{2}}$, and t is the time elapsed since the onset of the rain. This equation has been found to describe well the infiltration behaviour of soils in southern Spain (Scoging and Thornes, 1979; Bork and Rohdenburg, 1981) but Gifford (1976) obtained poorer results with it for infiltration data from semi-arid rangelands in northern Australia and in Utah, USA.

Infiltration rates depend upon the characteristics of the soil. Generally, coarse-textured soils such as sands and sandy loams have higher infiltration rates than clay soils because of the larger spaces between the soil particles. Infiltration capacities may range from more than 200 mm h^{-1} for sands to less than 5 mm h^{-1} for tight clays (Fig. 2.1). In addition to the role played by the inter-particle spacing or micropores, the larger cracks or macropores, found between soil peds and clods, exert an important influence over infiltration. They can transmit considerable quantities of water so that clays with well-defined clods can have infiltration rates that are much higher than would be expected from their texture alone. Infiltration behaviour on many soils is also rather complex because the soil profiles are characterized by two or more layers of differing hydraulic conductivities; most agricultural soils, for example, consist of a disturbed plough layer and an undisturbed subsoil. Local variability in infiltration rates can be quite high because of differences in the structure, compaction, initial moisture content and profile form of the soil and in vegetation density. Field determinations of average infiltration capacity using infiltrometers may have coefficients of variation of 70 to 75 per cent (Thornes, 1979). Eyles (1967) measured infiltration capacity on soils of the Melaka Series near Temerloh, Malaysia, and obtained values ranging from 15 to 420 mm h^{-1} with a mean of 147 mm h^{-1}. Much research has been devoted to the understanding of infiltration in non-uniform soils with variable or intermittent rainfall based on the physics of soil water movement (Childs, 1969; Hillel, 1971; Mein and Larson, 1973; Moore and Eigel, 1981). This work requires complex mathematical analysis and, although several infiltration models have been produced with promising results, high-speed digital computers are often needed for their solution. Many models are applicable to only rather specific soil conditions and do not have general validity.

According to Horton (1945), if rainfall intensity is less than the infiltration capacity of the soil, no surface runoff will occur and the infiltration rate equals the rainfall intensity. If the rainfall intensity exceeds the infiltration capacity, the infiltration rate will equal the infiltration capacity and the excess rainfall will form surface runoff. When plotted cumulatively over time, the volume of water contributing to infiltration follows the pattern shown in Fig. 2.1. As a mechanism for generating runoff, however, this comparison of rainfall intensity and infiltration capacity does not always hold. Studies in Bedfordshire, England (Morgan, 1977) on a sandy soil show that the infiltration capacity is greater than 400 mm h^{-1} and that rainfall intensities rarely exceed 40 mm h^{-1}. Thus no surface runoff would be expected whereas, in fact, the mean annual volume of runoff is about 55 mm from a mean annual rainfall of 550 mm.

The important control for runoff production on these soils is not infiltration capacity but a limiting soil moisture content which, when exceeded, results in a reduction of pore water pressure at the soil surface to zero, allowing ponding of water to take place. This explains why sands which have low levels of capillary storage produce runoff very quickly even though their infiltration capacity is not exceeded by the rainfall intensity. Since hydraulic conductivity is a flux partly controlled by rainfall intensity, increases in intensity can cause conductivity to rise so that, although runoff may have formed rapidly at a relatively low rainfall intensity, higher rainfall intensities do not always produce greater runoff. This mechanism also explains why infiltration rates sometimes increase with rainfall intensity (Nassif and Wilson, 1975). The pattern of cumulative volume of infiltration over time for soils where a limiting soil moisture storage controls the generation of runoff is also shown in Fig. 2.1 (Knapp, 1978).

Once water starts to pond on the surface, it is held in depressions or hollows and runoff will not begin until the storage capacity of these is satisfied. Depression storage is usually treated as a constant value of only a few millimetres but in practice it varies with the roughness of the surface. On agricultural land, depression storage varies seasonally depending upon the type of cultivation which has been carried out and the time since cultivation for the roughness to be reduced by weathering and raindrop impact. Reid (1979) shows that clay soils near Aylesbury, England, have a depression storage capacity of 5 to 7 mm following autumn ploughing but that by the following spring this has been reduced to about 3 mm. Evans (1980) shows that clay soils have 1.6 to 2.3 times more storage volume than sandy clay loams after ploughing but that following drilling and rolling of the seed bed, the difference is reduced to 1.1 times.

2.1 RAINSPLASH EROSION

The action of raindrops on soil particles is most easily understood by considering the momentum of a single raindrop falling on a sloping surface. The downslope component of this momentum is transferred in full to the soil surface but only a small proportion of the component normal to the surface is transferred, the remainder being reflected. The transference of momentum to the soil particles has two effects. First, it provides a consolidating force, compacting the soil, and second, it produces a disruptive force as the water rapidly disperses from and returns to the point of impact in laterally flowing jets. The local velocities in these jets are nearly double those of the raindrop impact (Huang, Bradford and Cushman, 1982) and are sufficient to impart a velocity to some of the soil particles, launching them into the air, entrained within water droplets which are themselves formed by the break-up of the raindrop on contact with the ground (Mutchler and Young 1975). Thus, raindrops are agents of both consolidation and dispersion.

The consolidation effect is best seen in the formation of a surface crust, usually only a few millimetres thick, which results from the clogging of the pores by soil compaction. It has been suggested by Young (1972) that this is associated with the dispersal of fine particles from soil aggregates or clods which are translocated to infil the pores. Studies of crust development under simulated rainfall show that crusts have a dense surface skin or seal, about 0.1 mm thick, with well-oriented clay particles. Beneath this is a layer, 1 to 3 mm thick, where the larger pore spaces are filled by finer washed-in material (Tackett and Pearson, 1965). Hillel (1960) explained crusting by the collapse of the soil aggregates on saturation, but Farres (1978) shows that raindrop impact is the critical process. After a rainstorm, most aggregates on the soil surface have been destroyed but those in the lower layer of the crust remain intact even though completely saturated. A tap of these aggregates, however, causes their instant breakdown. From this evidence, it seems that although saturation reduces the internal strength of the aggregate, it does not disintegrate until struck by raindrops.

The most important effect of a surface crust is to reduce infiltration capacity and thereby promote greater surface runoff. Measurements on a sandy soil in Israel show that crusting reduces the infiltration capacity from 100 mm h^{-1} to 8 mm h^{-1} and on a loess soil from 45 mm h^{-1} to 5 mm h^{-1} (Morin, Benyamini and Michaeli, 1981). The infiltration capacity on sandy soils in Mali ranges from 100 to 200 mm h^{-1}, but where crusting has developed it reduces to 10 mm h^{-1}. Only a few storms are needed to bring about this change; a 50 per cent reduction can occur in one storm (Hoogmoed and Stroosnijder, 1984).

The susceptibility of soils to crusting has been related by De Ploey (1981a) to a consistency index (C_{5-10}). The index is defined as $w_5 - w_{10}$ where w_5 and w_{10} are the water contents as a percentage dry weight at which two sections of a pat of soil placed in a Casagrande cup touch each other over a distance of

10 mm, after 5 and 10 blows respectively. Based on studies of soils in Brabant and Flanders, Belgium, values of the index > 3 denote stable soils and those < 2.5 indicate crust-prone soils. Crustability decreases with increasing contents of clay and organic matter since these provide greater strength to the soil. Thus loams and sandy loams are the most vulnerable to crust formation.

Laboratory studies by Farmer (1973) show that it is the medium and coarse particles that are most easily detached from the soil mass and that clay particles resist detachment. This may be because the raindrop energy has to overcome the adhesive or chemical bonding forces by which the minerals comprising clay particles are linked (Yariv, 1976). One way in which the dispersion of soil particles occurs, in addition to the direct impact of falling raindrops, is by slaking (Bryan, 1969). This is the breakdown of the soil by the compression of air ahead of a wetting front as rainfall starts to infiltrate a dry soil from the surface downwards. More recently, it has been shown that the detachability of a soil by raindrop impact depends upon its shear strength (Cruse and Larson, 1977). This has prompted attempts to understand rainsplash erosion in terms of shear. Detachment of the soil particles is explained by shear failure of the soil, an event which is most likely to occur under saturated conditions when the shear strength of the soil is lowest (Al-Durrah and Bradford, 1982).

Studies of the kinetic energy required to detach one kilogram of sediment by raindrop impact show that minimal energy is needed for particles of 125 μm (Poesen and Savat, 1981) and that particles between 63 and 250 μm are the most vulnerable to detachment (Poesen, 1981). This means that soils with high percentages of particles within this range are the most detachable and that selective removal of these by rainsplash can cause variations in soil texture downslope. Splash erosion on shallow stony loamy soils in the Luxemburg Ardennes has resulted in the soils on the valley sides becoming deficient in clay and silt-size particles and high in gravel and stone content. The colluvial soils at the base of the slopes are enriched by the splashed-out material (Kwaad, 1977). Selective erosion can affect soil aggregates as well as primary particles. Rainfall simulation experiments on clayey soils from Italy show that the splashed-out material is enriched in soil aggregates of 63 to 500 μm in size (Torri and Sfalanga, 1984).

Rain does not always fall on to a dry surface. During a storm it may fall on surface water in the form of puddles or overland flow. Studies by Palmer (1964) show that as the thickness of the surface water layer increases, so does splash erosion. This is believed to be due to the turbulence which impacting raindrops impart to the water. There is, however, a critical water depth beyond which erosion decreases again because all the energy is dissipated in the water and does not affect the soil surface. Laboratory experiments have shown that the critical depth is approximately equal to the diameter of the raindrops (Palmer, 1964) or to one-fifth (Torri and Sfalanga, 1984) or one-third (Mutchler and Young, 1975) of the diameter. These studies were made with a variety of soils covering clays, silt loams, loams and sandy loams. No increase in splash erosion with water depth has been observed, however, on sandy soils (Ghadiri and Payne, 1979; Poesen, 1981).

Experimental and theoretical studies show that the rate of detachment of soil particles by rainsplash varies with the 1.0 power of the instantaneous kinetic energy of the rain (Free, 1960; Quansah, 1981) or with the square of the instantaneous rainfall intensity (Carson and Kirkby, 1972; Meyer, 1981a). The detachment rate (D_r) on bare soil can be expressed by an equation of the form:

$$D_r \propto I^b S^c \qquad (2.4)$$

where I is the rainfall intensity and S is the slope expressed as m m^{-1} or as the sine of the slope angle. Although 2.0 is a convenient value for b, the value may be adjusted to allow for variations in soil texture using the term $b = 2.0 - (0.01 \times \%$ clay) (Meyer, 1981a). Values for c are in the range of 0.2 to 0.3 (Quansah, 1981; Torri and Sfalanga, 1984).

On a sloping surface more particles are thrown downslope than upslope and thus there is a net downslope transport of material. The splash transport per unit width (T_r) can be expressed by the relationship:

$$T_r \propto I^d S^f \qquad (2.5)$$

where $d = 1.0$ (Meyer and Wischmeier, 1969) and $f = 1.0$ (Savat, 1981; Quansah, 1981). There is some evidence to suggest that the value of f decreases on steeper slopes; Mosley (1973) gives a value of 0.8 and Moeyersons and De Ploey (1976) give a value of 0.75 for data where slope angles rise to 20° and 25° respectively.

These relationships for detachment and transport of soil particles by rainsplash ignore the effects of surface water referred to above and the role of wind. Windspeed imparts a horizontal force to the falling raindrops so that they strike the surface at an angle from the vertical. This affects the relative proportions of upslope versus downslope splash as well as increasing the impact velocity of the falling rain (Lyles, Dickerson and Schmeidler, 1974). Moeyersons (1983) shows that where the angle between the falling raindrop and the vertical is 20°, splash transport is reduced to zero for slopes of 17–19° and has a net upslope component on gentler slopes. Where the angle between the falling raindrop and the vertical is 5°, zero splash transport occurs on a slope of 3°.

Since splash erosion acts uniformly over the land surface its effects are seen only where stones or tree roots selectively protect the underlying soil and splash pedestals or soil pillars are formed. Such features frequently indicate the severity of erosion. On sandy soils in Bedfordshire 20 mm high pedestals can form in one year (Morgan, 1977). Splash erosion is most important for detaching the soil particles which are subsequently eroded by running water. However, on the upper parts of hillslopes, particularly on those of convex form, splash transport may be the dominant erosion process. In Calabria, southern Italy, under forest or scattered herb and shrub vegetation, splash transport accounts for 30 to 95 per cent of the total transport of material by water erosion (van Asch, 1983). Studies in Bedfordshire, England, show that splash transport accounts for 15 to 52 per cent of the total transport on land under cereals and grass but only 3 to 10 per cent on bare ground (Morgan, Martin and Noble, 1986). As runoff and soil loss increase, the importance of splash transport declines, although very low contributions of splash to total transport were also measured in Bedfordshire under woodland because of the protective effect of a dense litter layer.

2.2   OVERLAND FLOW

Overland flow occurs on hillsides during a rainstorm when surface depression storage and either, in the case of prolonged rain, soil moisture storage or, with intense rain, the infiltration capacity of the soil are exceeded. The flow is rarely in the form of a sheet of water of uniform depth and more commonly is a mass of anastomosing or braided water courses with no pronounced channels. The flow is broken up by large stones and cobbles and by the vegetation cover, often swirling around tufts of grass and small shrubs.

The hydraulic characteristics of the flow are described by its Reynolds number (Re) and its Froude number (F), defined as follows:

$$Re = \frac{vr}{v} \tag{2.6}$$

$$F = \frac{v}{\sqrt{gr}} \tag{2.7}$$

where r is the hydraulic radius which, for overland flow, is taken as equal to the flow depth and v is the kinematic viscosity of water. The Reynolds number is an index of the turbulence of the flow. The greater the turbulence, the greater is the erosive power generated by the flow. Thus, as has been shown experimentally in the laboratory (D'Souza and Morgan, 1976), soil loss varies with the Reynolds number. At numbers less than 500, laminar flow prevails and at values above 2 000 flow is fully turbulent. Intermediate values are indicative of transitional or disturbed flow, often a result of turbulence being imparted to laminar flow by raindrop impact (Emmett, 1970). When the Froude number is less than 1.0 the flow is described as tranquil or subcritical; values greater than 1.0 denote supercritical or rapid flow which is the more erosive. According to the laboratory studies of Savat (1977), most overland flow is supercritical and Froude numbers can be as high as 15. Field studies of overland flow in Bedfordshire reveal Reynolds numbers less than 75 and Froude numbers less than 0.5 (Morgan, 1980a). Flows with Reynolds numbers less than 40 and Froude numbers less than 0.13 were also observed by Pearce (1976) in the field near Sudbury, Ontario.

The important factor in these hydraulic relationships is the flow velocity. Because of an inherent resistance of the soil, velocity must attain a threshold value before erosion commences (Hjulström, 1935). As can be seen in Fig. 2.2, for grains larger than 0.5 mm in diameter, the critical velocity increases with grain size. A large force is required to move larger particles. For grains smaller than 0.5 mm, the critical velocity increases with decreasing grain size. The finer particles are harder to erode because of the cohesiveness of the clay minerals which comprise them. Once an individual grain is in motion, it is not deposited until velocity falls below the fall velocity threshold. Thus, less force is needed to keep a grain in motion than to entrain it. A soil particle of 0.01 mm requires a flow of 60 cm s^{-1} to detach it but it is not deposited until the flow velocity falls below 0.1 cm s^{-1}. In practice, the actual velocities required to erode soil differ from the values shown in Fig. 2.2 because the latter are derived for surfaces of uniform grain size. With a mixed grain size, the finer particles

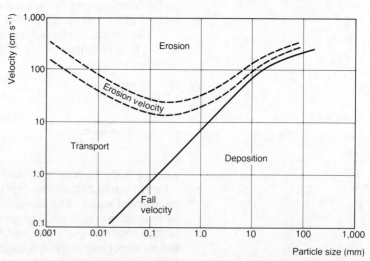

Fig. 2.2   Critical water velocities for erosion, transport and deposition as a function of particle size (after Hjulström, 1935).

are protected by the coarser ones so that they are not removed until velocity is great enough to pick up the larger grains. Counteracting this effect, however, particularly in shallow flows, is the action of rainsplash which may detach soil particles and throw them into the flow. They are then transported until the flow velocity becomes less than the required fall velocity.

The velocity of flow is dependent upon the flow depth or hydraulic radius, the roughness of the surface and the slope (S). This relationship is commonly expressed by the Manning equation:

$$v = \frac{r^{2/3} S^{1/2}}{n} \tag{2.8}$$

where slope is a real number (m m^{-1}), though tan θ or sin θ, where θ is the gradient angle, may be substituted on gentle slopes, and n is the Manning coefficient of roughness. Equation 2.8 assumes that the flow is fully turbulent and moving over a rough surface. Where flow does not satisfy this condition, the exponents in the equation change their values and Savat (1977) recognizes the following variations with Reynolds number:

$$v \propto r^{1.7} \quad S^{0.95} \text{ for } Re = 250 \tag{2.9}$$
$$v \propto r^{0.95} \quad S^{0.7} \quad Re = 500 \tag{2.10}$$
$$v \propto r^{0.5} \quad S^{0.4} \quad Re = 1\,000 \tag{2.11}$$

Using the continuity and Manning's velocity equations, Meyer (1965) shows that

$$v \propto S^{1/3} Qw^{1/3} \tag{2.12}$$

for constant roughness conditions, where Qw is the water discharge or flow rate. Assuming that the detachment D_f and transporting T_f capacities of flow vary respectively with the square and fifth power of velocity:

$$D_f \propto S^{2/3} Qw^{2/3} \tag{2.13}$$
$$T_f \propto S^{5/3} Qw^{5/3} \tag{2.14}$$

(Meyer and Wischmeier, 1969). The last equation compares closely with that derived by Carson and Kirkby (1972) from a consideration of the hydraulics of sediment transport:

$$Qs = 0.008\,5\, Qw^{1.75}\, k^{-1.11}\, (\sin\theta \cos\theta)^{1.625} \tag{2.15}$$

where Qs is the sediment discharge per unit width and k is the particle size of the surface material at which 84 per cent of the grains are finer. Similar equations (2.16 and 2.17 respectively) have been derived by Komura (1976) and Morgan (1980a):

$$Qs = \frac{476\, Ca.Ce\, Qw^{15/8}\, L^{3/8}\, \sin^{3/2}\theta}{d_{50}} \tag{2.16}$$
$$Qs = 0.0061\, Qw^{1.8}\, \sin^{1.13}\theta\, n^{-0.15}\, d_{35}^{-1} \tag{2.17}$$

where Ca is the bare soil area ratio, Ce is an erodibility index, L is slope length and d_{50} and d_{35} are the particle sizes of the surface soil at which 50 and 35 per cent respectively of the grains are finer. All these equations relate to the action of overland flow on its own whereas, in practice, the flow is usually accompanied by rainfall. The interaction with raindrop impact, as already seen, makes the flow more erosive and causes a slight rise in the values of the exponents for discharge and slope. Laboratory experiments by Quansah (1982) with overland flow and rainfall combined gave the relationship:

$$Qs \propto Qw^{2.13} \sin^{2.27} \theta \qquad (2.18)$$

Plots of the relationship between sediment transport by overland flow and the overland flow discharge, as measured in the field, do not always conform with that expected from the expressions given above. Work in Bedfordshire (Jackson, 1984; Morgan, Martin and Noble, 1986) and in southern Italy (van Asch, 1983) shows that sediment transport varies with discharge raised by a power of 0.6 to 0.8. Because of the similarity of this value to that given in equation 2.13, the erosion has been interpreted as being detachment-limited. Intuitively, however, one would expect sediment transport by overland flow to be transport-limited because soil particles are being detached by rainfall so rapidly that they easily satisfy the transport capacity of flows of only a few millimetres depth (Meyer, 1981b). An alternative interpretation of these field data is that the transport process is dominantly one of rolling of the particles over the soil surface as bed load. Equations for bed load show that sediment transport is related to discharge raised by a power that is generally between 0.6 and 1.0 in value. Studies of soil particle transport in shallow unchannelled flows indicate that whilst some suspended load is present, coarser particles and a high proportion of the soil aggregates are moved as bed load. Because of the shallow water depths, bed roughness associated with vegetation and stones causes the hydraulic characteristics of the flow to vary greatly over very short distances. As a result, erosion is often localized and after a rainstorm the surface of a hillside displays a pattern of alternating scours and sediment fans (Moss and Walker, 1978).

It can be seen from the above that the amount of soil loss resulting from erosion by overland flow varies with the velocity and the turbulence of flow. Equally important, however, is the spatial extent of the flow. Horton (1945) describes overland flow as covering two-thirds or more of the hillsides in a drainage basin during the peak period of a storm. The flow results from the intensity of the rainfall being greater than the infiltration capacity of the soil and is distributed over the hillslopes in the following pattern. At the top of a slope is a zone without flow which forms a belt of no erosion. At a critical distance from the crest sufficient water has accumulated on the surface for flow to begin. Moving further downslope, the depth of flow increases with distance from the crest until, at a further critical distance, the flow becomes channelled and breaks up into rills. That overland flow occurs in such a widespread fashion has since been questioned, particularly in well-vegetated areas where such flow occurs infrequently and covers only that 10 to 30 per cent of the area of a drainage basin closest to the stream sources (Kirkby, 1969*a*). Under these conditions its occurrence is more closely related to saturation of the soil and the fact that soil moisture storage capacity is exceeded rather than infiltration capacity. Although, as illustrated by the detailed studies of Dunne and Black (1970) in a small forested catchment in Vermont, the saturated area expands and contracts, being sensitive to heavy rain and snow melt, rarely can erosion by overland flow affect more than a small part of the hillslopes.

Since most of the observations testifying to the power of overland flow relate to semi-arid conditions or to areas with sparse plant cover, it would appear that vegetation is the critical factor. Some form of continuum exists, ranging from well-vegetated areas where overland flow occurs rarely and is mainly of the saturation type, to bare soil where it frequently occurs and is of the Hortonian type. Removal of the plant cover can therefore enhance erosion by overland flow. The change from one type of overland flow to another results from more rain reaching the ground surface, less being intercepted by the vegetation, and decreased infiltration as rainbeat causes a surface crust to develop. Exceptions to this trend occur in areas where high rainfall intensities are recorded. Hortonian overland flow is widespread in the tropical rain forests near Babinda, northern Queensland, where six-minute rainfall intensities of 60 to 100 mm h^{-1} are common, especially in the summer, and the hydraulic conductivity of the soil layer at 200 mm depth is only 13.25 mm h^{-1}. As a result a temporary perched water table develops in the soil soon after the onset of rain, subsurface flow commences and this quickly emerges on the soil surface (Bonell and Gilmour, 1978).

Figure 2.2 shows that the most erodible soil particles by overland flow are in the range of 100 to 300 μm. The sediment carried in overland flow is generally deficient in particles larger than 1.0 mm and enriched in finer material. Thus, over time, areas of erosion on a hillside will become progressively sandier and the areas of deposition will be enriched with clay particles (Alberts, Moldenhauer and Foster, 1980). This effect has been studied for the Kalahari Sands on hillslopes south of Kinshasa, Zaire, but in this case, grain sizes coarser than 214 μm are gradually removed, even those coarser than 1.0 mm, so that the steep slopes are characterized by increasing quantities of fine sands, silts and clays (Savat and Poesen, 1977). A contributory factor to the removal of the coarser material may be the high intensity of the tropical rainfall. Mitchell,

Mostaghimi and Pond (1983) demonstrate in laboratory experiments that erosion is more particle-size selective with low-intensity than with high-intensity rains.

Overland flow, particularly that of the Hortonian type, acts with the detaching power of raindrops to erode soil particles and transfer them downslope. After a heavy rainstorm, the effects of these two processes, together known as interrill erosion, are frequently seen in the deposition of material as fans on footslope areas. Over a longer time period such areas become covered with colluvial material whilst the land upslope is lowered more or less uniformly. Here the effect of interrill erosion can be seen on agricultural land by the turning up of the subsoil during ploughing following thinning of the top soil. Where runoff and soil loss rates are relatively high, overland flow can be the dominant hillslope erosion process, and this appears to be true for many agricultural areas on non-cohesive soils. On loose, freshly-ploughed soils on colluvial deposits on 18–22° slopes in Calabria, Italy, van Asch (1983) found that overland flow accounted for 85 to 95 per cent of the sediment transport. On unvegetated sandy soils in Bedfordshire with an 11° slope, it accounts for 50 to 80 per cent (Morgan, Martin and Noble, 1986).

2.3   SUBSURFACE FLOW

Much attention in recent hydrological research has been paid to the lateral movement of water downslope through the upper layers of the soil. Where this takes place as concentrated flow in tunnels or subsurface pipes its erosive effects through tunnel collapse and gully formation are well known. Less is known about the eroding ability of water moving through the pore spaces in the soil, although it has been suggested that fine particles may be washed out by this process (Swan, 1970; Morgan, 1973b). Field experiments by Burykin (1957) showed that fines could be moved mechanically through the voids in the soil but under the somewhat extreme conditions in which simulated rain was applied to 20–25° slopes at a rate of 2.5 mm min^{-1} for 1 h.

More realistic studies by Roose (1970) in Senegal reveal that soil water flow contributes only about 1 per cent of the total material eroded from a hillside and that this is mainly in the form of colloids and minerals in ionic solution. Subsurface flow is more important, however, than this figure suggests because the concentrations of base minerals in the water are twice those found in surface flow. Essential plant nutrients, particularly those added in fertilizers, can be removed by this process, thereby impoverishing the soil and reducing its resistance to erosion. Even under the more natural conditions of a virgin tropical rain forest site at Pasoh, Negeri Sembilan, Malaysia, where the erosion rates are very low, the material removed as dissolved solids in the subsurface flow amounts to only 15 to 23 per cent of the total sediment transport on 8–14° slopes (Leigh, 1982*a*).

The most important effect of subsurface flow in its unconcentrated form is to bring about the accumulation of moisture in the soil in the foothill and concave parts of the landscape and thereby enhance the likelihood of saturation overland flow (Zaslavsky and Sinai, 1981).

2.4   RILL EROSION

Many soil erosion studies do not distinguish the effects of rill erosion from those of overland flow. Both processes generally affect the same part of a hillslope. Rills are also ephemeral features. Those from one storm are often obliterated before the next storm of sufficient intensity to cause rilling, when the channels may form an entirely fresh network, unrelated to the positions of previous rills. Most rill systems are discontinuous, that is they have no connexion with the main river system. Only occasionally does a master rill develop a permanent course with an outlet to the river.

As outlined earlier, it is widely accepted that rills are initiated at a critical distance downslope where overland flow becomes channelled. Observations in mid-Bedfordshire suggest that this need not always be the case. Here rills develop from a sudden burst of water on to the surface near the bottom of the slope where a small cut is formed which rapidly extends headwards upslope as a channel (Morgan, 1977). Such bursts may well be associated with saturation overland flow rather than flow of the Hortonian type.

The onset of rilling is often associated with the appearance of standing waves in the overland flow but, rather than being the cause of channel cutting, this is most likely to reflect a change in the hydraulic conditions of the flow. Savat (1979) attempted to explain rilling through the exceedance of a threshold condition in the flow expressed by a critical Froude number (F_c) defined by

$$F_c > 1 + 0.003\ 5\ d$$

where d is the median grain size of the soil (μm). Since, in addition, sediment concentrations in rill flow always exceed 20 000 ppm, Boon and Savat (1981) adopted both criteria for predicting whether rills are likely to form. Thus

  if $F \leq F_c$ no rills are expected;
  if $F > F_c$ and ppm $\leq$ 20 000 rills are possible; and
  if $F > F_c$ and ppm $>$ 20 000 rills are definite.

The break-up of shallow overland flow into small channels or micro-rills was examined by Moss, Green and Hutka (1982). They found that, in addition to the main flow path downslope, secondary flow paths developed with a lateral component. Where these converged, the increase in discharge intensified particle movement and small channels or trenches were cut by scouring. Since raindrop impact increases the transport capacity of the flow and, through the detachment of soil particles, increases the sediment concentration, Savat (1979) argued that the interaction of rainfall with the flow would increase the probability of rilling. Quansah (1982), however, found that the particles detached by rain filled in the micro-channels as fast as they could form, so that rilling was inhibited. It appears that at this stage of channel development, two sets of processes compete (Moss, Green and Hutka, 1982) so that either the micro-channels are short-lived because they drain away the overland flow, become laterally isolated and fill in, or the concentration of flow increases its erosive power and the channels deepen and widen and migrate both upslope and downslope. Upslope migration is associated with the development of headcuts on the steep banks at the top end of the channels and its rate is controlled by the cohesiveness of the soil. Downslope extension is controlled by the shear stress exerted by the flow (Savat, 1979). Studies of the hydraulic characteristics of the flow show that the change from overland flow to rill flow passes through four stages: unconcentrated overland flow, overland flow with concentrated flow paths, micro-channels without headcuts and micro-channels with headcuts. The greatest differences exist between the first and second stages suggesting that the flow concentrations within the overland flow should strictly be treated as part of the rill system (Merritt, 1984).

Rill flow can transport large grains so that where it is important the wholesale removal of particles minimizes selective erosion. Meyer, Foster and Nikolov (1975) found that 15 per cent of the particles carried in rills on a 3.5° slope of tilled silt loam were larger than 1 mm in size and that 3 per cent were larger than 5 mm. However, some selectivity can occur because on a 4.5° slope of bare untilled silt loam, 80 per cent of the sediment transported in rills was between 210 μm and 2.0 mm in size. Most of the eroded clay particles was also transported as aggregates within this size range (Alberts, Moldenhauer and Foster, 1980).

As expected from the greater erosive power of concentrated flow, rill erosion may account for the bulk of the sediment removed from a hillside. Studies in the United States on slope plots 4.5 m long show that over 80 per cent of the sediment is transported in rills (Mutchler and Young, 1975). Part of this material is derived from the inter-rill areas and is moved into the rills by overland flow and rainsplash. Foster and Meyer (1975) estimate that up to 87 per cent of the sediment transported by rills may be derived in this way. In their study of rill erosion near Oudenaarde, Belgium, Gabriels, Pauwels and De Boodt (1977) estimate that half of the material removed from the inter-rill areas by overland flow is washed into the rills. Erosion data from the Tien Shan Mountains in central Asiatic USSR show that on slopes of 23° and 30° rill erosion accounts for 51 to 63 per cent of the total water erosion (Mikhailov, 1949).

A major factor determining the importance of rill erosion is the spacing of the rills and the extent of the area affected. At Oudenaarde, rills occur at 8 to 9 m intervals across the hillslope. As a result of an intense storm with hail, an event with a fifty-year return period, near Prešov, Czechoslovakia, on 14 April 1964, 91 ha of land with slopes of 9–18° and loamy soils devoted to oats and spring barley was damaged. About 58 per cent of this was affected by rilling with the channels being spaced on average only 330 mm apart (Midriak, 1965). A cloud burst on 23 May 1958 near Banská Bystrica, Czechoslovakia, nearly destroyed a field of potatoes on a 13–15° slope. About 60 per cent of the area was affected by rills which accounted for 70 per cent of the total sediment eroded (Zachar, 1982). These figures contrast with the situation in mid-Bedfordshire, England, where rills occur at only 300 to 350 m intervals and account for only 20 to 50 per cent of the total erosion (Morgan, Martin and Noble, 1986).

2.5 GULLY EROSION

Gullies are relatively permanent steep-sided water courses which experience ephemeral flows during rainstorms. Compared with stable river channels which have a relatively smooth, concave-upwards long profile, gullies are characterized by a headcut and various steps or knick-points along their course. These rapid changes in slope alternate with sections of very gentle gradient, either straight or slightly convex in long profile. Gullies also have relatively greater depth and smaller width, carry large sediment loads and display very erratic behaviour so that relationships between sediment discharge and runoff are frequently poor (Heede, 1975*a*). Gullies are almost always associated with accelerated erosion and therefore with landscape instability.

At one time it was thought that gullies developed as enlarged rills but studies in the gullies or arroyos of the southwest United States revealed that their initiation is a more complex process. In the first stage small depressions or knicks form on a hillside as a result of localized weakening of the vegetation cover by grazing or by fire. Water concentrates in these depressions and enlarges them until several depressions coalesce and an incipient channel is formed. Erosion is concentrated at the heads of the depressions where near-vertical scarps develop over which supercritical flow occurs. Some soil particles are detached from the scarp itself but most erosion is associated with scouring at the base of the scarp which results in deepening of the channel and undermining of the headwall, leading to collapse and retreat of the scarp upslope (Ologe, 1972). Sediment is also produced further down the gully by streambank erosion. This occurs partly by the scouring action of running water and the sediment it contains and partly by slumping of the banks following saturation during flow. Between flows sediment is made available for erosion by weathering and bank collapse. This sequence of gully formation (Fig. 2.3), described by Leopold, Wolman and Miller (1964) in New Mexico, has also been observed in New Zealand (Blong, 1970) and in the New Forest in England (Tuckfield, 1964).

Not all gullies develop purely by surface erosion, however. Berry and Ruxton (1960), investigating gullies in Hong Kong which formed following clearance of the natural forest cover, found that they could not be attributable to surface flow. Most water was removed from the hillsides by subsurface flow in pipes and when heavy rain provided sufficient flow to flush out the soil in these, the ground surface subsided, exposing the pipe network as gullies. Numerous studies record the formation of gullies by pipe or tunnel collapse. It has been observed in the Sudan (Berry, 1970), on loessial soils in the United States (Buckham and Cockfield, 1950) and in Hungary (Zaborski, 1972), and on sodic soils in the western United States (Heede, 1971). Tunnel erosion has been widely reported in many hilly and rolling areas of Australia where it is associated with duplex soils. These are soils characterized by a sharp increase in clay content between the A and B horizons so that the upper layer, 0.03 to 0.6 m in depth, varies from a loamy sand to a clay loam and the lower layer ranges from a light to heavy clay. Tunnels develop particularly where the clays are of low permeability, sodic and high in exchangeable magnesium (Charman, 1970). According to Downes (1946), overgrazing and removal of the vegetation cover cause crusting of the surface soil, resulting in greater runoff. This passes into the soil through small depressions, cracks and macropores but, on reaching the top of the B horizon, moves along it as subsurface flow. Localized dispersion of the clays in areas of moisture accumulation is followed by piping. Heavy summer rains cause the water in the pipes to break out on to the surface. Eventually, the roof of the pipes collapses and gullying occurs (Floyd, 1974).

Another way in which gullies are initiated is where linear landslides leave deep, steep-sided scars which may be occupied by running water in subsequent storms. This type of gully development has been described in Italy by Vittorini (1972)

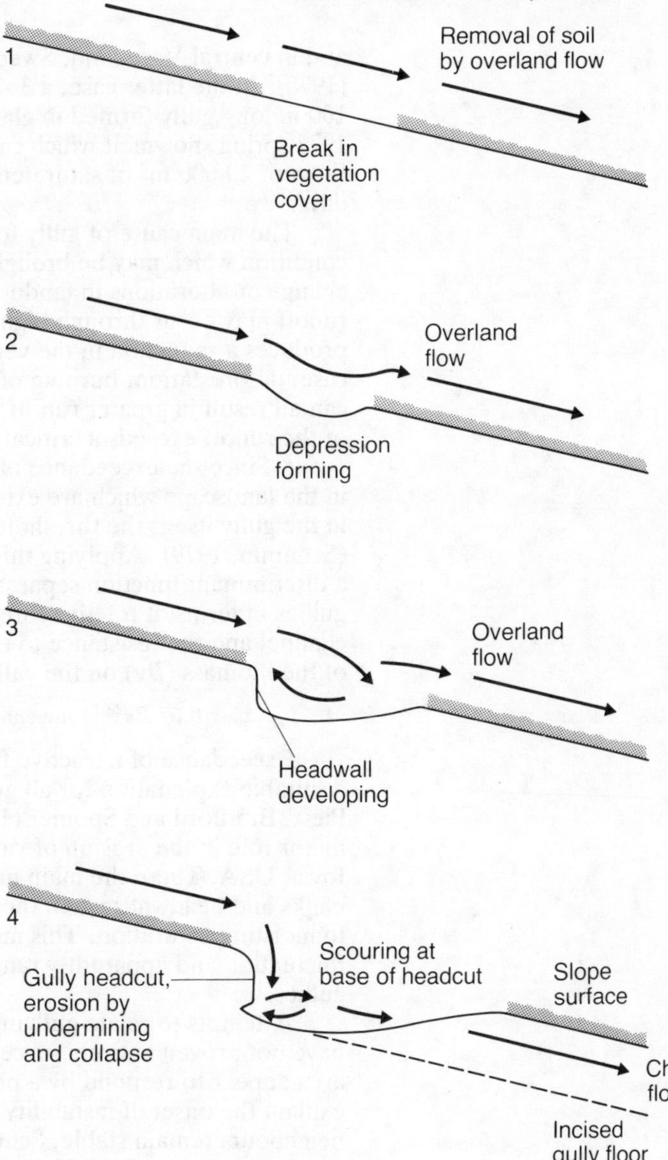

Fig. 2.3 Stages in the surface development of gullies on a hillside.

and in central Värmland, Sweden, by Fredén and Furuholm (1978). In the latter case, a 3–20 m deep, 20–40 m wide and 100 m long gully formed in glaciofluvial deposits following the 1977 spring snowmelt which caused the removal, as a mass flow, of 20 000 m^3 of saturated silt and sand in less than three days.

The main cause of gully formation is too much water, a condition which may be brought about by either climatic change or alterations in landuse. In the first case, increased runoff may occur through higher rainfall or if less rainfall produces a reduction in the vegetation cover. In the second case, deforestation, burning of the vegetation and overgrazing can all result in greater runoff. If the velocity or tractive force of the runoff exceeds a critical or threshold value, gullying will occur. Since the exceedance of the threshold relates to changes in the landscape which are external to the processes operating in the gully itself, the threshold is described as *extrinsic* (Schumm, 1979). Applying this concept, Graf (1979) identifies a discriminant function separating entrenched from stable gullies in terms of tractive force (τ_0) exerted by the flow in the channel and the resistance to erosion afforded by the density of the biomass (Bv) on the valley floor. If

$$\tau_0 \geq 0.07 \, Bv^{2.01} \quad \text{the channels are unstable.}$$

Exceedance of a tractive force threshold does not provide a suitable explanation for all gullying, however. According to Piest, Bradford and Spomer (1975), tractive force plays only a minor role in the erosion of valley head gullies in southwest Iowa, USA. There the main mechanism is the collapse of the banks and headwalls when they become unstable and slip due to moisture saturation. This mechanism explains the fluctuation and apparently random supply of sediment to the gullies.

Attempts to relate gullying to changes in external factors have not proved entirely successful because not all gullies in an area appear to respond by a phase of entrenchment. In order to explain the onset of instability in one gully whilst its neighbours remain stable, Schumm (1979) examined the role of *intrinsic* thresholds which are related to the internal working of the gully. From a review of studies in Wyoming, Colorado, New Mexico and Arizona, a discriminant function was established between stable and unstable conditions in terms of the size of the catchment area, which controls discharge, and the channel slope. When, for a given catchment area, channel slope exceeds a critical value, entrenchment of the channel occurs. Since deposition results in a steepening of the channel, this can trigger the incision; the subsequent scouring lowers the slope, promoting temporary stabilization; this increases the slope again and brings about a new phase of gullying. Thus gullies pass through successive cycles of erosion and deposition.

The interplay of extrinsic and intrinsic thresholds makes

gully erosion an extremely complex process and it is not surprising that it remains poorly understood and that only a qualitative appreciation of the factors influencing it has been obtained. Stocking (1980) shows that the volume of rainfall, antecedent moisture and the height of the headcut are important controls over gullying in Zimbabwe. Zachar (1970) emphasizes the importance of the depth of loose, easily erodible soil. Clearly, the latter may restrict the size of the headcut and this explains why the most spectacular gullies are found on thick sediments.

When designing strategies to control gully erosion it is not possible to treat all gullies in the same way. Indeed, the dangers of so doing are inherent in the failure to take account of whether surface or subsurface erosion is the major cause. Differences between gullies become even more marked when networks rather than individual channels are considered. Three types of network can be recognized, described by De Ploey (1974), based on studies in the Kasserine Basin, Tunisia, as axial, digitate and frontal. The types are related to differences in soils and the effects that these have on the processes of gully formation. *Axial gullying*, which consists of individual gullies with single headcuts that retreat upslope by surface erosion, occurs in gravelly deposits. *Digitate gullying*, where retreat occurs in several headcuts extending in the direction of tributary depressions, is characteristic of clay loams. *Frontal gullying* is associated with piping and is found particularly on loamy sands with columnar structure. This latter type generally starts from river banks where pipes have their outlet and collapse ensues. Since axial and frontal gullies operate along valley lines, they have larger catchment areas and hence more runoff than digitate gullies which are found on hillslopes. They therefore erode faster. Rozhkov (1973) found that in Moldavia SSR, valley-line gullies migrated headwards six times faster than hillslope gullies.

Few studies have been made of the role of gully erosion in sediment transport. Although gullies can remove vast quantities of soil, according to Zachar (1982) gully densities are not usually greater than 10 km km^{-2} and the surface area covered by gullies is rarely more than 15 per cent of the total area. However, where it occurs, gullying can completely destroy the landscape.

2.6 MASS MOVEMENTS

Although mass movement has been widely studied by geologists, geomorphologists and engineers, it is generally neglected in the context of soil erosion. Yet Temple and Rapp (1972) have found that in the western Uluguru Mountains,

Tanzania, landslides and mudflows are the dominant erosion processes. They occur in small numbers every wet season and in large numbers about once every ten years. The quantity of sediment moved from the hillsides into rivers by mass movement is far in excess of that contributed by gullies, rills and overland flow. Further, less than 1 per cent of the slide scars are in areas of woodland, 47 per cent being on cultivated plots and another 47 per cent on land lying fallow. The association of erosion with woodland clearance for agriculture is thus very clear. Further evidence for this is provided by Rogers and Selby (1980) in respect of shallow debris slides on clay and silty clay soils derived from greywackes in the Hapuakohe Range, South Auckland, New Zealand. Clearance of the forest for pasture causes a decline in the shear strength of the soil over the 5- to 10-year period needed for the tree roots to decay. As a result, landslides under pasture are triggered by a storm with a return period of 30 years whereas a storm with a 100-year return period is required to produce slides beneath the forest.

The stability of the soil mass on a hillslope in respect of mass movement can be assessed by a safety factor (F), defined as the ratio between the total shear strength (s) along a given shear surface and the amount of shear stress (τ) developed along this surface. Thus

$$F = \frac{s}{\tau} \tag{2.19}$$

The slope is stable if $F > 1$ and failure occurs if $F \leqslant 1$. For shallow planar slides, F can be defined as (Skempton and Hutchinson, 1969):

$$F = \frac{c' + (\gamma z \cos^2 \theta - u) \tan \phi'}{\gamma z \sin \theta \cos \theta} \tag{2.20}$$

where c' is the effective cohesion of the soil, γ is the unit weight of soil, z is the vertical depth to the failure plane, θ is the slope angle and ϕ' is the effective angle of internal friction of the soil. Applications of this equation to the slides in the Hapuakohe Range show that the value of F is particularly sensitive to changes in c' and z. Thus, control measures should be directed at influencing these (Rogers and Selby, 1980).

Mass movements, in the varied forms of creep, slides, rock falls and mudflows, are given detailed treatment in numerous books (Sharpe, 1938; Leopold, Wolman and Miller, 1964; Zaruba and Mencl, 1969) but, for soil erosion studies, rather than stress the separate forms, it is more helpful to consider them as part of a continuum of flow phenomena, ranging from debris slides, in which the ratio of solid to liquid is high, through mudflows to running water which has a low solid–liquid ratio. The close relationship between mass movement and water erosion is illustrated by the studies of the so-called bottle slides in the Uluguru Mountains (Temple and Rapp, 1972; Lundgren and Rapp, 1974) which develop in areas of large subsurface pipes as a result of the flushing out of a muddy viscous mass of debris and subsequent ground collapse. The scars of these slides are similar to the pear-shaped ravines called lavakas, found in the Malagasy Republic, which, in turn, are not unlike gullies (Tricart, 1972).

2.7   WIND EROSION

The main factor in wind erosion is the velocity of moving air. Because of the roughness imparted by soil, stones, vegetation and other obstacles, windspeeds are lowest near the ground surface. From a height z_0 above the ground surface at which the wind velocity is zero, windspeed increases exponentially with height so that velocity values plot as a straight line on a graph against the logarithmic values of the height (Fig. 2.4). The change in velocity with height is expressed by the relationship (Bagnold, 1941)

$$\bar{v}_z = \frac{2.3}{k} \quad V* \log (z/z_o) \tag{2.21}$$

where $\bar{v}$ is the mean velocity at height z, k is the von Kármán universal constant for turbulent flow and is assumed to equal 0.4 for clear fluids, and $V*$ is the drag or shear velocity. Although the movement of soil particles can be related to a critical wind velocity, most workers use the concept of a critical shear velocity, using it as a surrogate measure for the drag force exerted by the flow. Shear velocity is directly proportional to the rate of increase in wind velocity with the logarithm of height and is therefore the slope of the line in Fig. 2.4(d). Its value can be determined by measuring the windspeed at two heights but, in practice, by assuming $v = o$ at height z_0, it can be obtained by measuring the speed at one height and applying the formula derived from equation 2.21:

$$V* = \frac{k}{2.3} \cdot \frac{v_z}{\log (z/z_o)} \tag{2.22}$$

The entrainment of soil particles by wind is effected by the application of a sufficiently large shear force and by the bombardment of the soil by grains already in motion. Recognizing these two forces, Bagnold (1937) identifies two threshold velocities required to initiate grain movement. The static or fluid threshold applies to the direct action of the wind and the dynamic or impact threshold allows for the bombarding effect of moving particles. Impact threshold velocities are about 80 per cent of the fluid threshold velocities

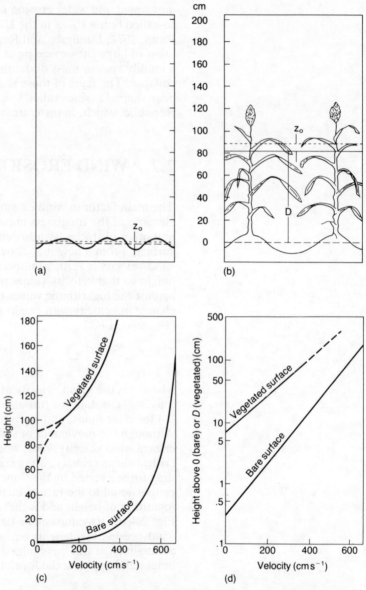

Fig. 2.4 Wind velocity near a soil surface. (a) Zero wind velocity occurs at a height z_0 which lies above the height of the mean aerodynamic surface and below the high points. (b) A crop cover raises the height of the mean aerodynamic surface by a distance D and also increases the value of z_0 so that the plane of zero wind velocity $(D + Z_0)$ occur at a height which is equal to about 70 per cent of the height of the plants. (c) Velocity profiles above a bare surface and a vegetated surface plotted with linear scales. (d) Velocity profiles plotted with a logarithmic scale for height (after Troeh, Hobbs and Donahue, 1980).

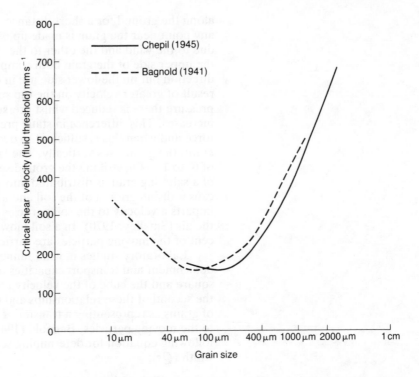

Fig. 2.5 Critical shear velocities of wind for erosion as a
function of particle size (after Savat, 1982).

in value. The critical velocities vary with the grain size of the
material, being least for particles of 0.10 to 0.15 mm in
diameter and increasing with both increasing and decreasing
grain size (Chepil, 1945). The resistance of the larger particles
results from their size and weight. That of the finer particles is
due to their cohesiveness and the protection afforded by
surrounding coarser grains (Fig. 2.5). Compared with water
erosion (Fig. 2.2) the most detachable particles are smaller in
size and the critical velocities are much larger. The reasons for
this are not fully understood but they must relate in part to the
very great difference in the density of the fluids. A sand grain
in the air is about 2 000 times more massive than the
surrounding fluid whereas it is only about 2.6 times more
massive than water (Bagnold, 1979).

The transport of soil and sand particles by wind takes
place in suspension, surface creep and saltation. Suspension
describes the movement of fine particles, usually less than
0.2 mm diameter, high in the air and over long distances.
Surface creep is the rolling of coarse grains along the ground
surface. Saltation is the process of grain movement in a series
of jumps. The movement is explained by considering the
theory of the Bernoulli effect. After a grain has been rolling

along the ground for a short distance, the velocity of the air at
any point near the grain is made up of two components, one
due to the wind and the other to the spinning of the grain. On
the upper side of the grain both components have the same
direction but on the lower side are in opposite directions. As a
result of greater velocity on the top surface of the grain, the
pressure there is reduced whilst pressure at the lower surface
increases. This difference in static pressure produces a lifting
force and when this is sufficient to overcome the weight of the
grain, the grain rises vertically. The fall trajectory has an angle
of 6° to 12°. On striking the ground surface the impact energy
of a saltating grain is distributed into a disruptive part which
causes disintegration of the soil and a dispersive part which
imparts a velocity to the soil particles and launches them into
the air (Smalley, 1970). In a soil blow, between 55 and 72 per
cent of the moving particles are carried in saltation.

Laboratory studies in wind tunnels show that the
detachment and transport capacities of wind vary with the
square and the cube of the velocity respectively. Developing
the second of these relationships and considering the transport
of grains as representing a transfer of momentum from the air
to the moving particles, Bagnold (1941) developed the
following equation for determining sediment discharge per unit
width (Qs):

$$Qs = C(d/D)^{\frac{1}{2}} (\rho/g)\ V_*^3 \qquad (2.23)$$

where C is an experimentally-derived parameter relating to
grain size, d is the average grain diameter of the material, D is
a standard grain diameter of 0.25 mm, ρ is the density of the
air and g is the gravitational constant. A similar equation was
derived by Zingg (1953) from wind-tunnel experiments:

$$Qs = C(d/D)^{\frac{3}{4}}\ \rho V_*^3/g \qquad (2.24)$$

Taking data from studies of dunes in Florida, Texas, Alaska,
Ecuador and Libya, Hsu (1973) successfully predicted sand
transport from the relationship:

$$Qs\ =\ C\left(\frac{V_*}{(gd)^{\frac{1}{2}}}\right)^3 \qquad (2.25)$$

where $\ln C = 4.97\ d - 0.47$ when Qs is in g cm^{-1} s^{-1} and $\ln$
C is the value of C in Naperian logarithms. Chepil (1945)
avoided the need to calculate shear velocities and took account
of erosion only occurring when the windspeed exceeded a
threshold value. He developed a simple relationship:

$$Qs = B(v - v_t)^3 \qquad (2.26)$$

where v is the wind velocity (cm s^{-1}) measured at a height of
1 m and v_t is the threshold velocity for windspeeds measured
at that height, usually taken as 400 cm s^{-1}. Chepil calculated

$B = 52$ but Finkel (1959), in studies of barchans in southern Peru, found that

$$B = \left(\frac{0.174}{\log (z/z_0)}\right)^3 \; C\left(\frac{d\rho^{\frac{1}{2}}}{Dg}\right) \qquad (2.27)$$

where $\log (z/z_0)$ is as previously defined (equation 2.21).

Wind erosion impoverishes the soil and also buries the soil and crops on surrounding land. Although, as already seen, the most erodible particles are 0.10 to 0.15 mm in size, particles between 0.05 and 0.5 mm are generally selectively removed by the wind. Chepil (1946) found that areas of wind-blown deposits are enriched by particles in the 0.30 to 0.42 mm size range. Resistance to wind erosion increases rapidly when primary particles and aggregates larger than 1 mm predominate. If erosion results in armouring of the surface so that more than 60 per cent of the surface material is of this size, the soil is almost totally resistant to wind erosion.

Although an understanding of the mechanics of erosion is vital to the design of a suitable system of erosion control, additional information is necessary for the successful planning of soil conservation works. Account must be taken of the severity of erosion, the frequency at which each process operates and the size of the area affected. Attention to these details requires a study of the factors influencing the soil erosion system.

Chapter 3
FACTORS
INFLUENCING EROSION

The factors controlling the working of the soil erosion system are the erosivity of the eroding agent, the erodibility of the soil, the slope of the land and the nature of the plant cover. In order to understand when and how much erosion is likely to occur, these factors must be examined in detail and the relevant aspects of them identified more precisely. Much of our understanding stems from empirical studies in which a wide range of data on soil loss and presumed controlling variables is collected and the best relationships are sought using statistical techniques, particularly correlation and regression analyses. Since this approach is adopted by numerous researchers working in many different areas of the world, it is not too surprising that the result is a multiplicity of variables being recognized as important but some disagreement as to which are the most significant. In a review of the relationship between erosion and climate, Douglas (1976) lists seven precipitation variables which have been used to explain spatial variations in erosion and a further seven for precipitation and eight describing antecedent conditions used to study temporal variations in erosion at single sites. In trying to simplify such lists, there is the problem of determining which variables merely express the same relationship and which identify truly separate relationships with soil loss. In this chapter, only those variables which are commonly accepted as important are discussed.

3.1   EROSIVITY

3.1.1 Rainfall

Soil loss is closely related to rainfall partly through the detaching power of raindrops striking the soil surface and partly through the contribution of rain to runoff. This applies particularly to erosion by overland flow and rills for which intensity is generally considered to be the most important rainfall characteristic. The effect of rainfall intensity is illustrated by the data for 183 rain events which caused erosion at Zanesville, Ohio, between 1934 and 1942 which show that average soil loss per rain event increases with the intensity of the storm (Table 3.1; Fournier, 1972).

The role of intensity is not always so obvious, however, as indicated by studies of erosion in mid-Bedfordshire. Taking data for the ten most erosive storms between May 1973 and October 1975 (Table 3.2), it can be seen that whilst intense storms, such as the one on 6 July 1973 of 34.9 mm, in which 17.7 mm fell at intensities greater than 10 mm h^{-1}, produce erosion so do storms of long duration and low intensity, like the one of 19 June 1973 when 39.6 mm of rain fell in over 23 h (Morgan, 1977). A similar picture emerges from measurements of erosion made in 1975 in vineyards near Trier, West Germany (Richter and Negendank, 1977) where a storm of 15.6 mm with a maximum intensity of 50.4 mm h^{-1} resulted

Table 3.1 Relationship between rainfall intensity and soil loss

Maximum 5-min Intensity (mm h^{-1})	Number of Falls of rain	Average Erosion per Rainfall (kg m^{-2})
0–25.4	40	0.37
25.5–50.8	61	0.60
50.9–76.2	40	1.18
76.3–101.6	19	1.14
101.7–127.0	13	3.42
127.1–152.4	4	3.63
152.5–177.8	5	3.87
177.9–254.0	1	4.79

Data for Zanesville, Ohio, 1934–42 (after Fournier, 1972).

Table 3.2 Rainfall and soil loss in Bedfordshire

Date	Rainfall (mm)	Intense rain (≥10 mm h^{-1}) (mm)	Rainfall Duration (h)	Soil Loss (g cm^{-1})
6.7.73	34.9	17.7	8.00	70.70
5.5.73	6.7	—	4.16	61.72
21.5.73	7.1	3.9	2.00	55.98
27.8.73	16.8	4.6	6.50	50.90
6.5.73	2.2	1.0	0.33	40.00
8.8.74	17.0	8.8	13.50	36.78
16.7.74	7.6	6.4	13.00	28.66
13.7.74	16.5	9.0	10.50	24.71
19.6.73	39.6	—	23.83	20.38
27.6.73	18.6	2.3	13.83	18.99

Data for bare soil and 11° slope.

in soil loss from a 26° slope of 8 m length of 141 g m^{-1} whilst a storm of 19.8 mm and a maximum intensity of 44.4 mm h^{-1} caused a greater loss of 242 g m^{-1}. Further, a storm of 39 mm spread over two days with a maximum intensity of 25.8 mm h^{-1} produced a loss of 27 g m^{-1} but one of 30.8 mm and 31.2 mm h^{-1} yielded only 17 g m^{-1}. It appears that erosion is related to two types of rain event, the short-lived intense storm where the infiltration capacity of the soil is exceeded and the prolonged storm of low intensity which saturates the soil. In many instances it is difficult to separate the effects of these two types of event in accounting for soil loss.

The response of the soil in terms of erosion to the receipt of rainfall may be determined by previous meteorological conditions. This can again be demonstrated by data for Zanesville, Ohio (Table 3.3; Fournier, 1972). Over the period 9 to 18 June 1940, the first rain fell on dry ground and, in spite of the quantity, little runoff resulted, most of the water soaking into the soil. In the second storm, however, 66 per cent of the rain ran off and soil loss almost trebled. The control in this case is the closeness of the soil to saturation which is dependent on how much rain has fallen in the previous few days. The pattern of low soil loss in the first and high loss in the second of a series of storms is reversed, however, where, between erosive storms, weathering and light rainfall loosen the soil surface. Most of the loose material is removed during the first runoff event leaving little for erosion in subsequent events. This sequence is illustrated by studies in the Alkali Creek watershed, Colorado (Heede, 1975*b*), where a sediment discharge peak of 143 kg s^{-1} with a runoff from snowmelt of 2.21 m^3 s^{-1} was observed in one of the ephemeral gullies on 15 April 1964. This event followed one year without runoff. Next day peak runoff increased to 3.0 m^3 s^{-1} but the sediment discharge fell to 107 kg s^{-1}. Although this type of evidence clearly points to the importance of antecedent events in conditioning erosion, other observations deny its significance. No relationship was obtained between soil loss

Table 3.3 Influence of antecedent rainfall conditions on soil loss

Date	Rainfall (mm)	Runoff (% of rainfall)	Erosion (g m^{-2})
9 June	19.3	25	1.5
10 June	13.7	66	4.0
11 June	23.8	69	8.9
15 June	14.0	65	4.2
17–18 June	13.0	50	4.6

Data for Zanesville, Ohio, June 1940, for five successive rainstorms on a plot of 20 m^2 (after Fournier, 1972).

and antecedent precipitation in mid-Bedfordshire (Morgan, 1977) nor between precipitation, soil loss and soil moisture at the onset of rain in the Trier area (Richter and Negendank, 1977).

The question arises of how much rain is required to induce significant erosion. In Chapter 1 it was noted that whilst the importance of extreme events is emphasised by some observers, most workers agree that most erosion occurs in moderate events exemplified by rainstorms yielding 30 to 60 mm. Similar opinions are evident in attempts to define a critical rainfall intensity for erosion. Hudson (1981a) gives a figure, based on his studies in Zimbabwe, of 25 mm h^{-1}, a value which has also been found appropriate in Tanzania (Rapp, Axelsson, Berry and Murray-Rust, 1972) and in Malaysia (Morgan, 1974). It is too high a value for western Europe, however, where it is only rarely exceeded. Arbitrary thresholds of 10 mm h^{-1} and 6 mm h^{-1} have been used in England (Morgan, 1977) and West Germany (Richter and Negendank, 1977) respectively. Van Asch and Epema (1983) show that an even lower threshold of 2.5 mm h^{-1} may be more appropriate and Bollinne (1977) adopted 1.0 mm h^{-1} for studies of splash erosion in Belgium.

Threshold values vary with the erosion process. The figures quoted above are typical for erosion by overland flow and rills, as indicated by numerous observations. Overland flow occurs in the Kuala Lumpur area of Malaysia with rainfall intensities of 60 to 75 mm h^{-1} (Morgan, 1972). Rill erosion has been reported in Cambridgeshire following a storm of 7.4 mm (Evans and Morgan, 1974) and in Belgium following a month in which 213 mm of rain fell but with totals over 20 mm on only two days (Gabriels, Pauwels and De Boodt, 1977). The return period of overland flow at Kuala Lumpur is 60 days and, whilst insufficient data exist to determine the equivalent return period for eastern England, a rainstorm of 37 mm in Bedfordshire has a recurrence interval of 5 years. That significant erosion can result from only moderate events also applies to landslides. Many of those described by Temple and Rapp (1972) in the Mgeta area of the Uluguru Mountains occurred in a storm of 100.7 mm in three hours on 23 February, 1970, an event with a return period there of only 4.6 years.

As shown in Chapter 1, these rainfall totals and return periods are of a different magnitude from those required to initiate gullying. Instances of fresh gullying have been described in the Appalachian Mountains (Hack and Goodlett, 1960), the Alps (Tricart, 1961), the Kuantan area of Malaysia (Nossin, 1964) and in many parts of eastern Europe (Starkel, 1976) and all relate to events with return periods in excess of 10 years. Although gully erosion and erosion by overland flow are generally associated with meteorological events of different frequencies and magnitudes, the distinction between them is occasionally blurred. This occurs in those areas which, by world standards, regularly experience what may be described as extreme events. Starkel (1972) stresses the importance of regular gully erosion in the Assam Uplands where monthly rainfall may total 2 000 to 5 000 mm and in the Darjeeling Hills where over 50 mm of rain falls on an average of twelve days each year and rainfall intensities are often highest at the end of a rain event. A further problem is that the effects of an extreme event may be long lasting and give rise to high soil losses for a number of years. The length of time required for an area to recover from a severe rainstorm, flooding and gullying has not been fully investigated but in a review of somewhat sparse evidence Thornes (1976) quotes figures up to 50 years.

3.1.2 Rainfall erosivity indices

The most suitable expression of the erosivity of rainfall is an index based on the kinetic energy of the rain. Thus the erosivity of a rainstorm is a function of its intensity and duration, and of the mass, diameter and velocity of the raindrops. To compute erosivity requires an analysis of the drop-size distributions of rain. Laws and Parsons (1943), based on studies of rain in the eastern United States, show that drop-size characteristics vary with the intensity of the rain; for example, the median drop diameter (d_{50}) increases with rainfall intensity (Fig. 3.1). Studies of tropical rainfall (Hudson, 1963) indicate that this relationship holds only for rainfall intensities up to 100 mm h^{-1}. At greater intensities, median drop size decreases with increasing intensity, presumably because greater turbulence makes larger drop sizes unstable. More recent investigations of rainfall in temperate latitudes (Mason and Andrews, 1960; Carter, Greer, Braud and Floyd, 1974) reveal that the relationship between median

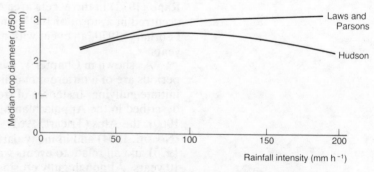

Fig. 3.1 Relationship between median drop diameter and rainfall intensity (after Hudson, 1965).

drop size and intensity is not constant but that both median drop size and drop-size distribution vary for rains of the same intensity but different origins. The drop-size characteristics of convectional and frontal rain are different as are those of rain formed at the warm and cold fronts of a temperate depression.

In spite of the difficulties posed by these variations it is possible to derive a general relationship between kinetic energy and rainfall intensity. Based on the work of Laws and Parsons (1943), Wischmeier and Smith (1958) obtained the equation:

$$KE = 11.87 + 8.73 \log_{10}I \qquad (3.1)$$

where I is the rainfall intensity (mm h^{-1}) and KE is the kinetic energy (J m^{-2} mm^{-1}). For tropical rainfall, Hudson (1965) gives the equation:

$$KE = 29.8 - \frac{127.5}{I} \qquad (3.2)$$

based on measurements of rainfall properties in Zimbabwe. Zanchi and Torri (1980) carried out similar research in Italy and obtained

$$KE = 9.81 + 11.25 \log_{10}I \qquad (3.3)$$

Equations 3.1 and 3.2 show that at intensities greater than 75 mm h^{-1}, the kinetic energy levels off at a value of about 28 J m^{-2} mm^{-1}, whereas the Italian research indicates energy values as high as 34 J m^{-2} mm^{-1} when the intensity is 150 mm h^{-1}. Very high energy values have also been recorded from Nigeria. Kowal and Kassam (1976) report a 20-minute rainstorm at Samaru with a peak intensity of 111 mm h^{-1} and energies ranging from 31.6 to 38.4 J m^{-2} mm^{-1}. A rainstorm at Ibadan with a 7.5-minute intensity of 112 mm h^{-1} produced an energy of 69 J m^{-2} mm^{-1} (Lal, 1981*a*).

To compute the kinetic energy of a storm, a trace of the rainfall from an automatically recording rain gauge is analysed and the storm divided into small time increments of uniform intensity. For each time period, knowing the intensity of the rain, the kinetic energy of rain at that intensity is estimated from one of the above equations and this, multiplied by the amount of rain received, gives the kinetic energy for that time period. The sum of the kinetic energy values for all the time periods gives the total kinetic energy of the storm (Table 3.4).

To be valid as an index of potential erosion, an erosivity index must be significantly correlated with soil loss. Wischmeier and Smith (1958) found that soil loss by splash, overland flow and rill erosion is related to a compound index of kinetic energy and the maximum 30-min rainfall intensity (I_{30}). This index, known as EI_{30}, is open to criticism. First, being based on estimates of kinetic energy using equation (3.1), it is of suspect validity for tropical rains of high intensity. Second, it assumes that erosion occurs even with light intensity rain whereas Hudson (1965) has shown that erosion is almost entirely caused by rain falling at intensities greater than 25 mm h^{-1}. The inclusion of I_{30} in the index is an attempt to correct for overestimating the importance of light intensity rain but it is not entirely successful because the ratio of intense erosive rain to non-erosive rain is not well correlated with I_{30} (Hudson, personal communication). In fact, there is no obvious reason why the maximum 30-min intensity is the most appropriate parameter to choose. Stocking and Ewell (1973*a*) recommend its use only for bare soil conditions. With sparse and dense plant covers they obtain better correlations with soil loss using the maximum 15- and 5-min intensities respectively. In a modification of the EI_{30} index, designed to reduce the likelihood of overestimation for tropical rainfall, Wischmeier and Smith (1978) set maximum values for rainfall intensity of 76.2 mm h^{-1} for the calculation of kinetic energy per unit rain and 63.5 mm h^{-1} for I_{30}. A different approach is suggested from the research of Vuillaume (1969) at Kountkouzout, Niger, where the character of the rain in the first twenty minutes of a storm appears to be the most critical factor. It is during this period that the soil becomes saturated and the most intense rains occur. The latter is unlikely to be the case world-wide, however, particularly in temperate latitudes subjected to prolonged rains of low intensity.

As an alternative erosivity index, Hudson (1965) uses KE > 25 which, to compute for a single storm, means summing the kinetic energy received in those time increments when the rainfall intensity equals 25 mm h^{-1} or greater (Table 3.4). When applied to data from Zimbabwe, a better correlation was obtained between this index and soil loss than between soil loss and EI_{30}. Stocking and Elwell (1973*a*) have reworked Hudson's data and, incorporating more recent information, have suggested that EI_{30} is the better index after all. Since they compute EI_{30} only for storms yielding 12.5 mm of rain and with a maximum 5-min intensity greater than 25 mm h^{-1}, they have removed most of the objections to the original EI_{30} index, however, and produced an index which is philosophically very close to KE > 25. Hudson's index has the advantages of simplicity and less stringent data requirements. Although somewhat limiting for temperate latitudes, it can be modified by using a lower threshold value such as KE > 10 (Morgan, 1977).

By calculating erosivity values for individual storms over a period of 20 to 25 years, mean monthly and mean annual data can be obtained. Unfortunately, the EI_{30} and KE > 25 indices yield vastly different values because of the inclusion of I_{30} in the former. Rapp, Axelsson, Berry and Murray-Rust (1972) quote figures for Morningside Farm in the Morogoro region of Tanzania of 70 000 for the annual value of EI_{30} and 12 000 for KE > 25. The two indices cannot be substituted for each other.

Table 3.4 Calculation of erosivity

Time from Start (min)	Rainfall (mm)	Intensity (mm h^{-1})	Kinetic Energy (J m^{-2} mm^{-1})	Total kinetic Energy (col 2 × col 4) (J m^{-2})
0–14	1.52	6.08	8.83	13.42
15–29	14.22	56.88	27.56	391.90
30–44	26.16	104.64	28.58	747.65
45–59	31.50	126.00	28.79	906.89
60–74	8.38	33.52	26.00	217.88
75–89	0.25	1.00	—	—

Kinetic energy is calculated from equation (3.2).
Erosivity indices
Wischmeier index (EI_{30})

maximum 30-min rainfall   = 26.16 + 31.50
                              = 57.66 mm

maximum 30-min intensity   =   57.66 × 2
                              = 115.32 mm h^{-1}

total kinetic energy   = total of column 5
                              = 2 277.74 J m^{-2}

EI_{30} = 2 277.74 × 115.32
                              = 262 668.98 J m^{-2} . mm h^{-1}

Hudson index (KE > 25)

total kinetic energy for   = total of column 5, lines 2, 3, 4
                              and 5 only

rainfall intensity ⩾ 25 mm h^{-1}
                              = 2 264.32 J m^{-2}

3.1.3 Wind erosivity

The kinetic energy (J m^{-2} s^{-1}) of wind can be calculated from:

$$KE = \frac{\gamma_a \, v^2}{2g} \qquad (3.4)$$

where v is the wind velocity in m s^{-1} and γ_a is the specific weight of air defined in terms of temperature (T) in °C and barometric pressure (P) in kPa by the relationship (Zachar, 1982):

$$\gamma_a = \frac{1.293}{1 + 0.00\,367\,T} \frac{P}{101.3} \qquad (3.5)$$

For $T = 15$ °C and $P = 101.3$ kPa, kinetic energy = 0.0 625 v^2 J m^{-2} s^{-1} which converts to 225 v^2 J m^{-2} h^{-1}. Energy values for windstorms can be obtained by summing the energies for the different windspeeds weighted by their duration.

In practice, kinetic energy is rarely used as a basis for an index of wind erosivity and, instead, a simpler index based only on the velocity and duration of the wind (Skidmore and Woodruff, 1968) has been developed. The erosivity of wind blowing in vector j is obtained from

$$EW_j = \sum_{i=1}^{n} \bar{V}t^3_{ij} \quad f_{ij}, \tag{3.6}$$

where EW_j is the wind erosivity value for vector j, $\bar{V}t$ is the mean velocity of wind in the ith speed group for vector j above a threshold velocity taken as 19 km h^{-1}, and f_i is the duration of the wind for the vector j in the ith speed group. Expanding this equation for total wind erosivity (EW) over all vectors yields:

$$EW = \sum_{j=0}^{15} \sum_{i=1}^{n} \bar{V}t^3_{ij} \quad f_{ij}, \tag{3.7}$$

where vectors $j = 0$ to 15 represent the sixteen principal compass directions beginning with $j = 0 = $ E and working anticlockwise so that $j = 1 = $ ENE and so on.

3.2   ERODIBILITY

Erodibility defines the resistance of the soil to both detachment and transport. Although soil resistance to erosion depends in part on topographic position, slope steepness and the amount of disturbance created by man, for example during tillage, the properties of the soil are the most important determinants. Erodibility varies with soil texture, aggregate stability, shear strength, infiltration capacity and organic and chemical content.

The role of soil texture has been indicated in Chapter 2 where it was shown that large particles are resistant to transport because of the greater force required to entrain them and that fine particles are resistant to detachment because of their cohesiveness. The least resistant particles are silts and fine sands. Thus soils with a high silt content are erodible. Richter and Negendank (1977) show that soils with 40 to 60 per cent silt content are the most erodible. Evans (1980) prefers to examine erodibility in terms of the clay content, indicating that soils with a restricted clay fraction, between 9 and 30 per cent, are most susceptible to erosion.

The use of the clay content as an indicator of erodibility is theoretically more satisfying because the clay particles combine with organic matter to form soil aggregates or clods and it is the stability of these which determines the resistance of the soil. Soils with a high content of base minerals are generally more stable as these contribute to the chemical bonding of the aggregates. Wetting of the soil weakens the aggregates because it lowers their cohesiveness, softens the cements and causes swelling as the water is adsorbed on the clay particles. Rapid wetting can also cause collapse of the aggregates through slaking. In general, aggregate stability depends on the type of clay mineral present. Illite and smectite more readily form aggregates but the more open lattice structure of these minerals and the greater swelling and shrinkage which occurs on wetting and drying render the aggregates less stable than those formed from kaolinite.

In detail, however, the interactions between the moisture content of the soil and the chemical compositions of both the clay particles and the soil water are rather complex. This makes it difficult to predict how clays, particularly those susceptible to swelling, will behave. The identical treatment of different types of clay can have totally different effects (Thornes, 1980). Although most clays lose strength when first wetted because the free water releases the bonds between the particles, some clays, under moist but unsaturated conditions, regain strength over time. This process, known as thixotropic behaviour, occurs because the hydration of clay minerals and the adsorption of free water promote hydrogen bonding (Grissinger and Asmussen, 1963). Strength can also be regained if swelling brings about a reorientation of the soil particles from an alignment parallel to the eroding water to a more random orientation (Grissinger, 1966). The strength of smectitic clays is largely dependent upon the sodium adsorption ratio. As this increases, i.e. the replacement of calcium and magnesium ions by sodium increases, so does water uptake and the likelihood of swelling and aggregate collapse. High salt concentrations in the soil water, however, can partly offset this effect so that aggregate stability is maintained at higher sodium adsorption ratios (Arulanandan, Loganathan and Krone, 1975).

The shear strength of the soil is a measure of its cohesiveness and resistance to shearing forces exerted by gravity, moving fluids and mechanical loads. Its strength is derived from the frictional resistance met by its constituent particles when they are forced to slide over one another or to move out of interlocking positions, the extent to which stresses or forces are absorbed by solid-to-solid contact among the particles, cohesive forces related to chemical bonding of the clay minerals, and surface tension forces within the moisture films in unsaturated soils. These controls over shear strength are only understood qualitatively so that, for practical purposes, shear strength is expressed by an empirical equation:

$$\tau = c + \sigma \tan \phi \qquad\qquad (3.8)$$

where τ is the shear stress required for failure to take place, c is a measure of cohesion, σ is the stress normal to the shear plane (all in units of force per unit area) and ϕ is the angle of internal friction. Both c and ϕ are best regarded as empirical parameters rather than as physical properties of a soil.

Increases in the moisture content of a soil decrease its shear strength and bring about changes in its behaviour. At low moisture contents the soil behaves as a solid and fractures under stress but with increasing moisture content it becomes plastic and yields by flow without fracture. The point of change in behaviour is termed the plastic limit. With further wetting, the soil will reach its liquid limit and start to flow under its own weight. The behaviour of a compressible soil when saturated depends upon whether the water can drain. If drainage cannot take place and the soil is subjected to further loading, pressure will increase in the soil water, the compaction load will not be supported by the particles and the soil will deform, behaving as a plastic material. If drainage can occur, more of the load will be supported and the soil is more likely to remain below the plastic limit and retain a higher shear strength.

Although Chorley (1959) and Eyles (1968a) demonstrated that shear strength affects the broad pattern of landforms with the stronger rocks and soils standing out as higher ground, it has been little used as an indicator of soil erodibility. This is largely because valid data are difficult to obtain since they relate to a surface layer of soil only a few millimetres thick with resistance to shear at near-zero confining stresses and subjected to low velocity impacts, reaching a maximum of 6 to 9 m s^{-1} with raindrops. The mode of failure is usually static, being the result of overcoming the frictional resistance required to initiate motion rather than the dynamic force to maintain one particle sliding over another. As seen in Chapter 2, shear strength is being increasingly used, however, as a basis for understanding the detachability of soil particles by raindrop impact (Cruse and Larson, 1977; Ghadiri and Payne, 1977; Al-Durrah and Bradford, 1982). Since the soils are usually saturated and the process is virtually instantaneous, there is no time for drainage and undrained failure occurs.

Infiltration capacity, the maximum sustained rate at which soil can absorb water, is influenced by pore size, pore stability and the form of the soil profile. Soils with stable aggregates maintain their pore spaces better whilst soils with swelling clays or minerals that are unstable in water tend to have low infiltration capacities. Although estimates of the infiltration capacity can be obtained in the field using infiltrometers (Hills, 1970), it was seen in Chapter 2 that actual capacities during storms are often much less than those indicated by field tests. Infiltration capacities of the Oligocene Tongrian Sands in Belgium are in excess of 200 mm h^{-1} according to field measurements but runoff can occur with rains of only 20 mm h^{-1} (De Ploey, 1977). Similar discrepancies between measured infiltration capacities and rainfall intensities resulting in runoff have been observed on soils of the Lower Greensand in Bedfordshire (Morgan, 1977). Where soil properties vary with profile depth, it is the horizon with the lowest infiltration capacity which is critical. In the case of these sandy soils, the critical horizon is often the surface where a crust of 2 mm thickness may be sufficient to decrease infiltration capacity enough to cause runoff, even though the underlying soil may be dry. A further factor shown in Chapter 2 to influence infiltration capacity is rainfall intensity and there is evidence to suggest that, instead of being a constant value, infiltration capacity increases with rainfall intensity (Nassif and Wilson, 1975; De Ploey, Savat and Moeyersons, 1976). Thus, increasing intensity of rain may not lead to a corresponding increase in runoff and decreasing intensity may even lead to runoff.

The organic and chemical constituents of the soil are important because of their influence on aggregate stability. Soils with less than 2 per cent organic carbon, equivalent to about 3.5 per cent organic content, can be considered erodible (Evans, 1980). Most soils contain less than 15 per cent organic content and many of the sands and sandy loams have less than 2 per cent. Voroney, van Veen and Paul (1981) suggest that soil erodibility decreases linearly with increasing organic content over the range of 0 to 10 per cent. This relationship clearly cannot be extrapolated, however, because some soils with very high organic contents, particularly peats, are highly erodible by both water and wind; also, some soils of very low organic content become very hard and therefore stronger under dry conditions.

Many attempts have been made to devise a simple index of erodibility based either on the properties of the soil as determined in the laboratory or the field, or on the response of the soil to rainfall and wind (Table 3.5). In a review of the indices applied to water erosion, Bryan (1968) favours aggregate stability as the most efficient index. He uses the proportion of water-stable non-primary aggregates larger than 0.5 mm contained in the soil as an indicator of erodibility, the greater the proportion, the more resistant being the soil to erosion. A more commonly used index is the K value which represents the soil loss per unit of EI_{30}, as measured in the field on a standard bare soil plot, 22 m long and of 5° slope. Estimates of the K value may be made if the grain-size distribution, organic content, structure and permeability of the soil are known (Wischmeier, Johnson and Cross, 1971; Fig. 3.2).

Soil erodibility has been satisfactorily described by the K value for many agricultural soils in the USA (Wischmeier and Smith, 1978) and the index has been found appropriate for some ferrallitic and ferruginous soils in West Africa (Roose, 1977). The values need to be determined for soils classified to at least the detail of the Soil Series, the variability at the

Table 3.5 Indices of soil erodibility for water erosion

Static Laboratory Tests

Dispersion ratio	$\dfrac{\%\text{ silt}+\%\text{ clay in undispersed soil}}{\%\text{ silt}+\%\text{ clay after dispersal of the soil in water}}$	Middleton (1930)
Clay ratio	$\dfrac{\%\text{ sand}+\%\text{ silt}}{\%\text{ clay}}$	Bouyoucos (1935)
Surface aggregation ratio	$\dfrac{\text{surface area of particles}>0.05\text{ mm}}{\%\text{ silt}+\%\text{ clay in dispersed soil}-\%\text{ silt}+\%\text{ clay in undispersed soil}}$	André and Anderson (1961)
Erosion ratio	$\dfrac{\text{dispersion ratio}}{\text{colloid content/moisture equivalent ratio}}$	Lugo-Lopez (1969)
Instability index (Is)	$\dfrac{\%\text{ silt}+\%\text{ clay}}{Ag_{air}+Ag_{alc}+Ag_{benz}}$ where Ag is the % aggregates > 0.2 mm after wet sieving for no pretreatment and pretreatment of the soil by alcohol and benzene respectively	Hénin, Monnier and Combeau (1958)
Instability index (*Is*)	$\dfrac{\%\text{ silt}+\%\text{ clay}}{\%\text{ aggregates}>0.2\text{ mm after wet sieving}-0.9\,(\%\text{ coarse sand})}$	Combeau and Monnier (1961)

Static Field Tests

Erodibility index	$\dfrac{1}{\text{mean shearing resistance}\times\text{permeability}}$	Chorley (1959)

Dynamic Laboratory Tests

Simulated rainfall test	comparison of erosion of different soils subjected to a standard storm	Woodburn and Kozachyn (1956)
Water-stable aggregate (WSA) content	% WSA > 0.5 mm after subjecting the soil to rainfall simulation	Bryan (1968)
Water drop test	% aggregates destroyed by a pre-selected number of impacts by a standard raindrop (e.g. 5.5 mm diameter, 0.1 g from a height of 1 m)	Bruce-Okine and Lal (1975)

Table 3.5 (*cont.*)

Dynamic Laboratory Tests

Erosion index	$\dfrac{d\,h}{a}$	Voznesensky and Artsruui (1940)
	where d is an index of dispersion (ratio of % particles > 0.05 mm without dispersion to % particles > 0.05 mm after dispersion of soil by sodium chloride); h is an index of water-retaining capacity (water retention of soil relative to that of 1 g of colloids); and a is an index of aggregation (% aggregates > 0.25 mm after subjecting the soil to a water flow of 100 cm min^{-1} for 1 h)	

Dynamic Field Tests

Erodibility index (K)	soil loss per unit of EI_{30}	Wischmeier and Mannering (1969)

---

higher levels of soil categorization being too great for practical use. Although erodibility generally increases from oxisols through vertisols to alfisols, there is much overlap in K values between these soil orders. Typical values range from 0.01 to 0.22 for oxisols, 0.05 to 0.67 for vertisols and 0.14 to 0.69 for alfisols (El-Swaify, Dangler and Armstrong, 1982).

Where K values have been determined from field measurements of erosion, they are valid. Difficulties arise, however, with attempts to predict the values from the nomograph (Fig. 3.2). Where it is applied to soils with similar characteristics to those in the USA, a close correlation exists between predicted and measured values, as found by Ambar and Wiersum (1980) on soils in west Java, Indonesia. Poorer predictions are obtained where it is necessary to extrapolate the nomograph values. This applies to soils with organic contents above 4 per cent, swelling clays and those where resistance to erosion is a function of aggregate stability rather than primary particle size. Assessments of erodibility of many clay soils based on the destruction of aggregates, for example by the water-drop test, show little correlation with the K values estimated from the nomograph (De Meester and Jungerius, 1978; Bergsma and Valenzuela, 1981). Lindsay and Gumbs (1982) found the K index superior to the drop test, however, for assessing the erodibility of clay and clay loam soils in Trinidad.

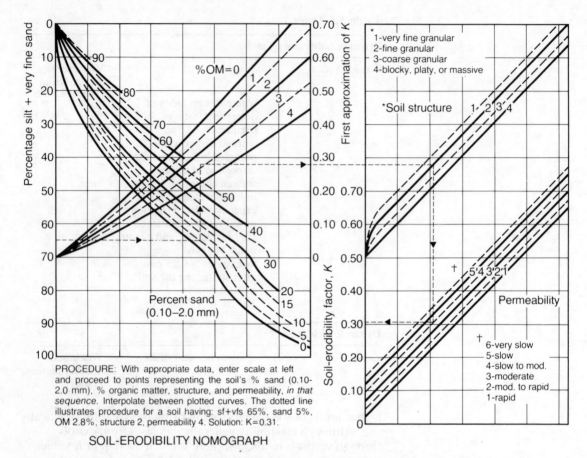

SOIL-ERODIBILITY NOMOGRAPH

PROCEDURE: With appropriate data, enter scale at left and proceed to points representing the soil's % sand (0.10–2.0 mm), % organic matter, structure, and permeability, *in that sequence.* Interpolate between plotted curves. The dotted line illustrates procedure for a soil having: sf+vfs 65%, sand 5%, OM 2.8%, structure 2, permeability 4. Solution: K=0.31.

*-very fine granular
1-very fine granular
2-fine granular
3-coarse granular
4-blocky, platy, or massive

*Soil structure

Permeability

† 6-very slow
5-slow
4-slow to mod.
3-moderate
2-mod. to rapid
1-rapid

Fig. 3.2   Nomograph for computing the *K* value of soil erodibility for use in the Universal Soil-Loss Equation (after Wischmeier, Johnson and Cross, 1971).

The resistance of the soil to wind erosion depends upon dry rather than wet aggregate stability and on the moisture content, wet soil being less erodible than dry soil, but is otherwise related to much the same properties as affect its resistance to water erosion. Chepil (1950), using wind tunnel experiments, has related wind erodibility of soils to various indices of dry aggregate structure but little of the work has been tested in field conditions. Wind tunnels have been used to determine the erodibility in t ha^{-1} h^{-1} of soils in western Siberia and northern Kazakhstan for a range of windspeeds (Dolgilevich, Sofronova and Mayevskaya, 1973). For a velocity of 23 m s^{-1}, values range from 0.06 for a heavy clay solonetz to 2.14 for a loamy chernozem, 8.0 for a sandy chernozem and 21.2 for a sandy dark chestnut soil. Similar studies by Chepil (1960) have been extrapolated to give an index in t ha^{-1} y^{-1} based on climatic data for Garden City, Kansas. Values range from 84 to 126 for non-calcareous silty clay loams, silt loams and loams. They rise to 190 for sandy loams, clays and silty clays, 300 for loamy sand and 356–694 for sands. Both indexes are closely correlated with the percentage of dry stable aggregates larger than 0.84 mm (Table 3.6).

Table 3.6 Assessments of soil erodibility by wind

% dry stable aggregates >0.84 mm	>80	70–80	50–70	20–50	<20
erodibility (t ha^{-1} h^{-1})*	<0.5	0.5–1.5	1.5–5	5–15	>15
erodibility (t ha^{-1} y^{-1})†	<4	4–84	84–166	166–220	>220

* After Dolgilevich, Sofronova and Mayevskaya (1973) for windspeeds of 20–25 m s^{-1}.

† After Chepil (1960) for Garden City, Kansas.

The wind resistance of soils can also be expressed by an index related to cohesion. Shiyatyy, Lavrovskiy and Khmolenko (1972) derive the following index of soil resistance (R):

$$R = 100 - C, \tag{3.9}$$

where C is a measure of actual cohesion based on the clay and sand fractions of the soil, and defined by

$$C = 34.7 + 0.9X_1 - 0.3X_2 - 0.4X_3 \tag{3.10}$$

where X_1 X_2 and X_3 denote the proportions of the soil falling in the textural classes <0.001 mm, 0.05–0.25 mm and >0.25 mm respectively. Higher values of R denote increasing erodibility.

The indexes described above treat soil erodibility as constant over time. They thus ignore changes in organic content, aggregate structure, distribution of soluble and exchangeable ion content, moisture content and surface soil texture, particularly over short time periods. The most significant seasonal variations occur on agricultural land and are associated with tillage operations. Martin and Morgan (1980) observed erodibility to be four times higher in summer than in winter on a bare uncultivated sandy soil in Bedfordshire, England. Under natural conditions, the seasonal activity of burrowing animals is important. Earthworms bring to the surface loose material as casts with low bulk densities and comprising mainly stones and aggregates of low cohesion; the latter are rapidly broken down by splash erosion. Annual rates of cast production range from 0.2 to 5.8 kg m^{-2} on agricultural land (Evans, 1948). Rates of 1.5 kg m^{-2} have been measured in temperate woodland in Luxemburg (Hazelhoff, van Hoof, Imeson and Kwaad, 1981) and

5.0 kg m^{-2} in tropical forest in the Ivory Coast (Roose, 1976). Other animals and their annual rates of production of loose sediment at the soil surface include ants, with 0.4 to 1.0 kg m^{-2} observed in Utah, USA (Thorp, 1949); termites, with 0.12 kg m^{-2} in tropical forest in the Ivory Coast (Roose, 1976); voles and moles, with 1.9 kg m^{-2} in temperate woodland in Luxemburg (Imeson, 1976); and isopods and porcupines with 3 to 70 g m^{-2} on stony land in the Negev Desert, Israel (Yair and Rutin, 1981).

3.3   EFFECT OF SLOPE

Erosion would normally be expected to increase with increases in slope steepness and slope length as a result of respective increases in velocity and volume of surface runoff. Further, whilst on a flat surface raindrops splash soil particles randomly in all directions, on sloping ground more soil is splashed downslope than upslope, the proportion increasing as the slope steepens. The relationship between erosion and slope can be expressed by the equation:

$$Qs \propto \tan^m \theta \; L^n \qquad (3.11)$$

where θ is the gradient angle and L is slope length. Zingg (1940), in a study of data from five experimental stations of the United States Soil Conservation Service found that the relationship had the form:

$$Qs \propto \tan^{1.4} \theta \; L^{0.6} \qquad (3.12)$$

where Qs is expressed per unit area. To express Qs proportional to distance downslope, the value of n must be increased by 1.0. Since the values for the exponents have been confirmed in respect of m by Musgrave (1947) and m and n by Kirby (1969*b*), there is some evidence to suggest that equation (3.12) has general validity. Other studies show, however, that the values are sensitive to the interaction of other factors in the erosion–slope relationship.

Working with data from experimental stations in Zimbabwe, Hudson and Jackson (1959) found that m was close to 2.0 in value, indicating that the effect of slope is stronger under tropical conditions where rainfall is heavier. The effect of soil is illustrated by the laboratory experiments of Gabriels, Pauwels and De Boodt (1975). These authors show that the value of m increases with the grain size of the material, from 0.6 for particles of 0.05 mm to 1.7 for particles of 1.0 mm. The value of m may also be sensitive to slope itself, decreasing with increasing slope steepness. Thus, Horváth and Erödi (1962) found from their laboratory studies that $m = 1.6$ for slopes between 0° and 2.5°, 0.7 for slopes between 3° and

6.5°, and 0.4 for slopes over 6.5°. On still steeper slopes the value may be expected to decrease further as soil-covered slopes give way to rock surfaces and soil supply becomes a limiting factor. Heusch (1970) obtained a value of −3.8 for slopes of 6.5° to 33° in Morocco, attributing the negative exponent to decreasing surface runoff and increasing subsurface flow on the steeper slopes. The exponents vary in value with slope shape. Examining soil loss from 3 m long plots on slopes of average steepness between 2° and 8° under simulated rainfall, D'Souza and Morgan (1976) obtained values for m of 0.5 for convex slopes, 0.4 for straight slopes and 0.14 for concave slopes.

No studies have been made of the influence of slope shape in plan, but Jackson (1984) found from erosion surveys and laboratory experiments that discharge varies with an index of contour curvature (C) to the power of 5.5. If soil loss is assumed to vary with the square of the discharge, the value of m becomes 3.5. Contour curvature is here defined as the proportion of a circle centred on a point on a hillside that lies at a higher altitude than that point. The index ranges from 0 to 1 in value with values < 0.5 indicating diverging slopes, a value of 0.5 a straight slope and values >0.5 converging slopes.

Few studies have examined the effect of varying plant cover and vegetation densities on the exponent values. Quinn, Morgan and Smith (1980) investigated the change in the value of m for soil loss from 1.2 m long plots with slopes of 5° to 30° under simulated rainfall in relation to decreasing grass cover brought about by trampling. They found that $m = 0.7$ for fully grassed straight slopes, rises to 1.9 in the early stages of trampling before falling to 1.1 when only about 25 per cent of the grass cover remains. Lal (1976) obtained a value of $m = 1.1$ for both bare fallow and maize on erosion plots in Nigeria; use of a mulch, however, reduced m to 0.5.

All the values discussed thus far relate to erosion by overland flow. Kirkby (1969b; 1971) notes variations in the values with the process of erosion. Values of n are zero for soil creep and splash erosion, range between 0.3 and 0.7 for erosion by overland flow and rise to between 1.0 and 2.0 if rilling occurs. Values of m are 1.0 for soil creep, range between 1.0 and 2.0 for splash and between 1.3 and 2.0 for overland flow, and may be as high as 3.0 for rivers. It was shown in Chapter 2 that m was about 0.3 and 1.0 in value respectively for detachment and transport of soil particles by rainsplash and about 0.7 and 1.7 respectively for detachment and transport by overland flow. Increases in slope steepness also cause an increase in the intensity of wind erosion on windward slopes and on the crests of knolls. Data presented by Chepil, Siddoway and Armbrust (1964) and Stredňanský (1977) show that $m = 0.4$ for slopes up to 2° and $m = 1.2$ for slopes from about 2–15°.

3.4   EFFECT OF PLANT COVER

The importance of a plant cover in reducing erosion is demonstrated by experiments at the Henderson Research Station in Zimbabwe (Hudson, 1981*a*) where, in the period 1953–56, mean annual soil loss from bare ground was 4.63 kg m^{-2} compared with 0.04 kg m^{-2} from ground with a dense cover of *Digitaria*. The major role of vegetation is in interception of the raindrops so that their kinetic energy is dissipated by the plants rather than imparted to the soil. This role is emphasized by the mosquito gauze experiment of Hudson and Jackson (1959) in which soil loss was compared from two identical bare soil plots. Over one plot was suspended a fine wire gauze which had the effect of breaking the force of the raindrops, absorbing their impact and allowing the water to fall to the ground from a low height as a fine spray. The mean annual soil loss over a ten-year period was 126.6 kg m^{-2} for the open plot and 0.9 kg m^{-2} for the plot covered by gauze.

Although numerous measurements have been made of erosion under different plant covers for comparison with that from bare ground, only a few researchers have examined the relationship between soil loss and changes in the extent of cover. Wischmeier (1975) argued that if the changes in raindrop size because of canopy interception were assumed to be offset by the transfer of some of the water to permanent interception and stemflow, then soil loss would decrease linearly with increasing canopy cover. Elwell (1981) and Shaxson (1981) favour an exponential decrease in soil loss with increasing percentage interception of rainfall energy and, therefore, increasing percentage canopy cover. Such a relationship was suggested by Wischmeier (1975) as applicable to covers in direct contact with the soil surface and has been verified experimentally for crop residues (Laflen and Colvin, 1981; Hussein and Laflen, 1982), stones (van Asch, 1980) and grass cover (Lang and McCaffrey, 1984). Foster (1982) attributes the exponential form of the relationship for covers in proximity to the ground to the ponding of water behind the plant elements which reduces the effectiveness of raindrop impact. Since localized depressions exist on most soil surfaces and these are often filled or partially filled during rainstorms, especially where they lie beneath leaf drips, an exponential relationship could be expected to apply to canopy effects too.

The effectiveness of a plant cover in reducing erosion depends upon the height and continuity of the canopy, the density of the ground cover and the root density. The height of the canopy is important because water drops falling from 7 m may attain over 90 per cent of their terminal velocity. Further, raindrops intercepted by the canopy may coalesce on the leaves to form larger

drops which are more erosive. These effects have been
studied mainly in relation to forest canopies. Chapman (1948)
under pine forest in the USA, Wiersum. Budirijanto and
Rhomdoni (1979) under *Acacia* forest in Indonesia, and
Mosley (1982) under beech forest in New Zealand all show
that whilst interception by the canopy reduces the volume of
rain reaching the ground surface, it does not significantly alter
its kinetic energy which may even be increased compared with
that in open ground. This is because of the greater percentage
of larger drops in the rainfall as a result of the coalescence of
raindrops on the leaves. Similar effects have been observed in
Malaysia under oil palm (Maene and Chong, 1979) where the
rain beneath the canopy is composed predominantly of drops
3.0 to 3.5 mm in diameter. Mosley (1982) found that in a
storm of 51 mm in 36 hours beginning on 8 July 1980, the
amount of material detached by rainsplash under the beech
canopy was 3.1 times that in open ground. Wiersum (1985)
recorded 1.2 times as much detachment under the *Acacia*
canopy as in open ground over 27 rain days with a total rainfall
of 402 mm. This, albeit limited evidence, suggests that
increasing tree canopies will bring about greater rates of
detachment unless, as also observed by Wiersum (1985), the
ground is protected by a litter layer. It seems likely that the
generally observed lower rates of soil loss under forest (Roose,
1971; Dunne, 1979) are a result of decreases in the volume of
runoff brought about by interception of the rainfall at the
canopy and higher rates of infiltration associated with better
aggregated soils and the opening up of macropores in the soil
by root growth.

   Fewer investigations have been made to assess the effects
of lower growing canopies. McGregor and Mutchler (1978)
found that cotton reduced the volume of rain reaching the
ground surface but increased its median volume drop size with
the largest drops being recorded as leaf drips from the
periphery of the plant. Thus, whilst the kinetic energy of the
rain was reduced by 95 per cent under the canopy and 75 per
cent overall, it was locally increased between the rows where
the leaf drips were concentrated. Finney (1984) showed in a
laboratory study that Brussels sprouts, sugar beet and potatoes
reduced the volume of rain at the ground surface and the
energy of the rain both under the canopy and at leaf drips.
Median volume drop sizes of the leaf drip ranged from 4.5 to
6.3 mm compared with the 2.1 mm of the simulated rainstorm.
Detachment rates from leaf drip were 1.7 and 1.3 times those
in open ground for Brussels sprouts and sugar beet at 23 per
cent and 16 per cent canopy cover respectively. These results
indicate that leaf drips, falling continually on saturated soil in
the same spot, can produce more detachment per unit of
rainfall energy than rainfall in open ground. This effect was
not observed, however, from the leaf drip under potatoes.
Increases in detachment rate per unit energy with increasing

canopy cover were recorded by Noble and Morgan (1983) in another laboratory study under Brussels sprouts where the average detachment rate under canopy covers between 10 and 25 per cent was found to be the same as that in open ground. Quinn and Laflen (1983), also in a laboratory experiment, reported that maize reduced the rainfall energy at the ground surface to about 50 per cent of that in open ground and that leaf drips could account for as much as 31 per cent of the total throughfall energy. They did not measure detachment rates. In a field study, however, Morgan (1985a) found that detachment under maize with 88 per cent canopy cover was 14 times greater than that in open ground for a rainfall intensity of 100 mm h^{-1} and 2.4 times greater for an intensity of 50 mm h^{-1}. A similar study under soya bean showed a decrease in detachment rate with increasing canopy cover so that with 90 per cent cover it was 0.2 times that in open ground for a 100 mm h^{-1} rainfall intensity and 0.6 times for a 50 mm h^{-1} intensity.

In addition to intercepting rainfall, a plant cover dissipates the energy of running water and wind, imparts roughness to the flow and thereby reduces its velocity. Since erosion rates vary with either the cube or the fifth power of velocity, the effect on soil loss should be considerable. Detailed observations during laboratory experiments on overland flow through grass cover (De Ploey, 1981b) show that for a given slope angle above about 8°, the erosion under the grass is higher than that from an identical plot without grass until the percentage grass cover reaches a critical value. Beyond this point, the grass has the expected protective effect. Although the grass reduced the mean velocity of flow, eddies developed downstream of the grass blades setting up turbulence and locally high Reynolds and Froude numbers (De Ploey, Savat and Moeyersons, 1976).

The effects of crop cover on windspeed are generally expressed by values of z_0, the height above the ground surface at which the wind velocity is zero. Typical values (cm) are 0.08 for harrowed land, 0.2 for grass, 0.4 for sugar beet and 1.3 for wheat (Voetberg, 1970). Alternately, the effects can be described by a frictional drag coefficient (Cd) exerted by the plant layer and computed from:

$$Cd = \frac{2V*^2}{\bar{v}^2} \tag{3.13}$$

where $\bar{v}$ is the mean wind velocity measured at height z, and z = 1.6 times the average roughness element height. Values generally decrease from about 0.1 in light winds to 0.01 in strong winds for a wide range of crops (Uchijima, 1976; Ripley and Redmann, 1976; Morgan and Finney, 1985). Of greater importance to the likelihood of wind erosion, however, are conditions close to the ground surface. Drag coefficients for the lower few centimetres of the plant layer may be calculated from the relationship:

$$Cd = \frac{2V_*^2}{v_z^2 A_z \, dz}$$ (3.14)

where Cd is the drag coefficient, v is the wind velocity and A is the leaf area per unit volume between height z and the ground surface, and dz is the difference in height between z and the ground surface. Again for a wide range of crops, values for z = 5 cm decrease from about 0.1 with low windspeeds to about 0.001 at high windspeeds. However, when the wind is moderate to strong and consistent over time and the crops are at an early stage of growth, the drag coefficient increases with windspeed (Morgan and Finney, 1985). This is probably due to the waving of the leaves disturbing the surrounding air and creating a wall effect which acts as a barrier to the airflow. The result is that windspeed is reduced close to the ground surface but the air above the crop remains unaffected. This increases the drag velocity of the wind, thereby enhancing the risk of erosion. Increases in the drag coefficient within a crop with windspeed have also been reported for maize by Wright and Brown (1967).

It was shown in Chapter 2 that forest covers generally help to protect the land against mass movements. This is believed to be due to the cohesive effect of the tree roots (Rogers and Selby, 1980). De Ploey (1981*b*), however, believes that trees can sometimes have a triggering effect on landslides through an increase in loading brought about by the weight of the trees and an increase in infiltration which allows more water to penetrate the soil, lowering its shear strength.

Plant covers can play an important role in reducing erosion provided that they extend over a sufficient proportion of the soil surface. Overall, forests are the most effective but a dense growth of grass may be almost as efficient. Agricultural crops vary in their effectiveness depending on their stage of growth and the amount of bare ground exposed to erosion at maturity. For adequate protection at least 70 per cent of the ground surface must be covered (Fournier, 1972; Elwell and Stocking, 1976), but reasonable protection can be achieved with 40 per cent cover (Shaxson, 1981). The effects of a plant cover are clearly not straightforward, however. As the evidence presented above shows, under certain conditions a plant cover can exacerbate erosion. When using plant covers as a basis for erosion control it is vital that these conditions be understood and specified.

Many of the relationships examined in this chapter have been only empirically established and, as is common with empirical studies, there is much disagreement over the precise nature of the equations which express the effect of the various controlling factors on soil loss. Most studies have been concerned with establishing the effects of each factor in isolation and have not attempted to evaluate the significance of interactions between them. As shown in Section 3.3 with respect to slope, these can be important affecting, for example, the value of exponent *m* in the relationship between soil loss and slope steepness. The influence of factor interactions was studied by Quansah (1982) in laboratory experiments of detachment and transport of soil particles by rainsplash and overland flow. Detachment by splash was significantly affected by the interactions of soil type with rainfall intensity and slope steepness with rainfall intensity. The rate at which detachment increased with intensity was thus dependent upon the soil and slope conditions. The transport capacity of combined overland flow and rainsplash was influenced by the interaction of slope steepness with soil type. At a 2° slope the transport capacity was similar for clays, clay loams and sands, but at 4° and 6° the transport capacity was greater for clay and clay loam aggregates than for sand grains. Further separation occurred on an 8° slope where the transport capacity was higher on the clay soils than on the clay loams. These differences in transport capacity were obscured when the effects of slope steepness were averaged over all the soil types. This study is one of many detailed investigations being undertaken world-wide in the field and in the laboratory which are seeking to increase our understanding of erosion processes. Until a sufficient number of these studies has been carried out, the somewhat equivocal evidence of the way in which the soil erosion system operates must provide the foundation for evaluating the risk of excessive soil loss.

Chapter 4
EROSION HAZARD ASSESSMENT

The assessment of erosion hazard is a specialized form of land resource evaluation, the objective of which is to identify those areas of land where the maximum sustained productivity from a given landuse is threatened by excessive soil loss. The assessment aims at dividing a land area into regions, similar in their degree and kind of erosion hazard, as a basis for planning soil conservation work. Since erosion risk is closely related to the plant cover and therefore to the use made of the land, soil erosion surveys often form part of a broader land resources study. In the same way that, depending on their objective, resource studies are undertaken at reconnaissance, semi-detailed and detailed levels, so erosion surveys may be carried out at several scales. In this chapter, generalized and semi-detailed assessments are examined.

4.1   GENERALIZED ASSESSMENTS

Generalized assessments of erosion risk are made at the macro-, often national, scale, and, as befits surveys at this scale (Table 1.2), are based largely on analysing climatic data or make use of measures of the intensity of erosion.

4.1.1 Erosion intensity

Two indexes of erosion intensity were used by Morgan (1974) to assess erosion risk in Peninsular Malaysia. They were drainage density, defined as the length of streams per unit area, and drainage texture, defined as the number of first-order streams per unit area which, being equivalent to the density of source points, is analogous to gully density.

A map of drainage texture was derived as follows from a stratified random sample of third-order drainage basins.

Within each 100×100 km grid square on the 1:63 360
topographical map sheets of the Malaysian Department of
National Mapping, a single 1×1 km square was selected
using random numbers as coordinates. If a third-order basin
did not fall within or across the first square selected, additional
squares up to twelve in number were examined in turn. If no
basin was selected after twelve tries, that 100×100 km square
remained unsampled. This was usually the case in areas of
incoherent drainage patterns and swamp. It was assumed that
the drainage pattern shown on the map sheets commences at
the second order (Eyles, 1966) so that the number of
first-order streams in each sampled basin can be estimated by
multiplying the number of second-order streams by 3.5, which
is the mean bifurcation ratio for Peninsular Malaysia (Eyles,
1968*b*). The average value of drainage texture was
determined, from a sample varying between 9 and 12 basins,
for each of the 132 map sheets. These values were plotted on a
map of Peninsular Malaysia and isolines drawn (Fig. 4.1).

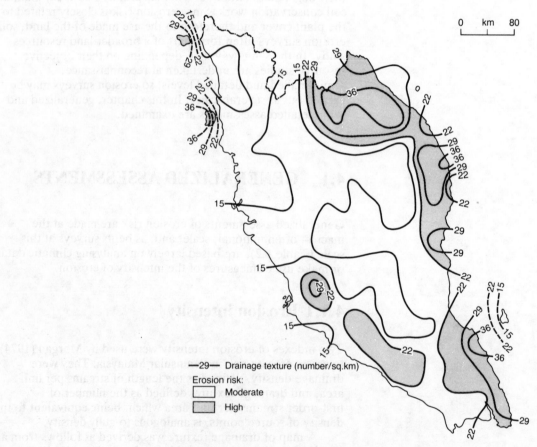

Fig. 4.1 Drainage texture in Peninsular Malaysia.

A similar procedure was adopted for mapping drainage
density (Fig.4.2) but, in this case, use was made of the density
values for 410 fourth-order basins obtained by Eyles (1968*c*).
Average values, based on a sample of four or five basins, were
obtained for each map sheet. For both texture and density, the
number of drainage basins sampled represents about 3 per
cent of their respective basin populations. Based on the work
of Mikhailov (1972) and Iana (1972), arbitrary values of
drainage density of 2 km km^{-2} and 15 km km^{-2} may be
selected to represent moderate and severe erosion risks
respectively. On this basis the whole of Peninsular Malaysia
has a moderate risk of erosion and only in the highlands of the
Trengganu Plateau and the Banjaran Titiwangsa does the risk
become severe. The range of values for drainage density is
low, however, compared to that for drainage texture which
would seem to be the more sensitive parameter to regional
variation. Taking an arbitrary value of 29 for drainage texture
to separate areas of high and moderate erosion risk, high risk

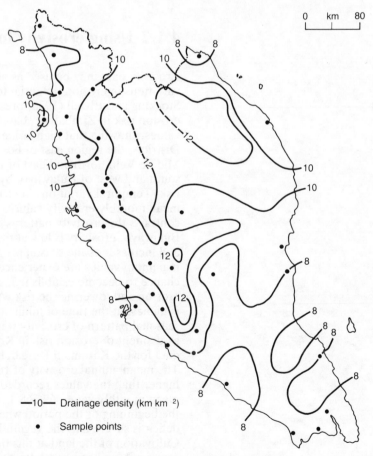

—10— Drainage density (km km^{-2})

•   Sample points

Fig. 4.2   Drainage density in Peninsular Malaysia.

areas are found along the east coast, in western Johor, on Pulau Langkawi and Pulau Pinang and around Kuala Lumpur.

It has been shown elsewhere (Morgan, 1976) that, in Peninsular Malaysia, drainage density and drainage texture are virtually uncorrelated with each other and probably relate to different controlling mechanisms. High values of drainage density are associated with the transport of runoff from regular, moderate rainfalls whereas high values of texture are a response to a more seasonal rainfall regime with rains of greater intensity. Drainage density is perhaps better regarded as an index of runoff rather than erosion.

Where sufficient data are available on sediment yields in rivers they can be used as an alternative to measures of erosion intensity although, as indicated in Chapter 1, they may be unreliable as statements of the rate of erosion on hillslopes. Maps of regional variations in erosion have been prepared from sediment yield information for Yugoslavia (Jovanović and Vukčević, 1958), Romania (Diaconu, 1969) and South Africa (Rooseboom and Annandale, 1981).

4.1.2 Using erosivity indices

Erosivity data may be used as an indicator of regional variations in erosion potential to pinpoint areas of high risk. Stocking and Elwell (1976) present a generalized picture of erosion risk in Zimbabwe, based on mean annual erosivity values, showing that high-risk areas are in the Eastern Districts, the region east of Fort Victoria, and the High and Middle Veld north and east of Harare (Fig. 4.3). The area south and west of Bulawayo, by contrast, has a much lower risk. Temporal variations in erosion risk are revealed by the mean monthly erosivity values. Hudson (1981a; Fig. 4.4) contrasts the erosivity patterns of Bulawayo and Harare. At Bulawayo, erosivity is low at the beginning of the wet season and increases as the season progresses. By the time the maximum values are experienced, the plant cover has had a chance to become established, giving protection against erosion and lowering the risk. At Harare, however, erosivity is highest at the time of minimal vegetation cover. The seasonal pattern of erosivity was also analysed in an assessment of erosion risk in Kenya by Rowntree (1983) taking data for the Katumani Research Station, Machakos District. The mean annual erosivity of 164 352 J mm m^{-2} h^{-1} is much higher than the values recorded in Zimbabwe. The highest mean monthly value, 69 668 J mm m^{-2} h^{-1} occurs in April, the beginning of the period when the potential soil moisture deficit is severe and the vegetation cover poorly established. Cultivation of the land at this time creates a great risk of erosion. May has a much lower erosivity, only

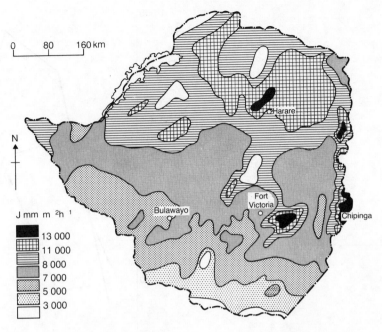

J mm m $^{-2}$h $^{-1}$

	J mm m $^{-2}$h $^{-1}$
■	13 000
▦	11 000
▤	8 000
▒	7 000
░	5 000
□	3 000

Fig. 4.3 Mean annual erosivity in Zimbabwe (after Stocking and Elwell, 1976).

20 961 J mm m^{-2} h^{-1}, and is also a month with a good vegetation cover. Erosivity is very low during the summer with mean monthly values of less than 1 000 but rises again in the short rainy season, reaching 15 306 in November before falling to mean monthly values of about 10 000 during the winter.

Maps of erosivity using a rainfall erosion index, R, defined as mean annual $EI_{30}/100$ when E is in foot-tons per acre and I_{30} is in inches per hour, have been produced for the USA (Wischmeier and Smith, 1978; Fig. 4.5). Values range from about 20 in the arid west to over 500 along the Gulf Coast. These are rather low compared with those occurring in more tropical climates. Values in India range from about 250 in western Rajasthan to over 1 000 along the coasts of Maharashtra and Karnataka and on the southern coast of West Bengal (Central Soil and Water Conservation Research and Training Institute, 1977; Babu, Tejwani, Agarwal and Bhushan, 1978; Fig. 4.6). In contrast, very low values are characteristic of western Europe. Those in France range from 30 in the north and west to 200 in the southern Massif Central and Languedoc (Pihan, 1979; Fig. 4.7). Values in South Africa (Smithen and Schulze, 1982) are lowest in the southwest of Cape Province where they are about 50 to 100 and rise eastwards reaching over 400 in eastern Transvaal and the midlands of Natal (Fig. 4.8).

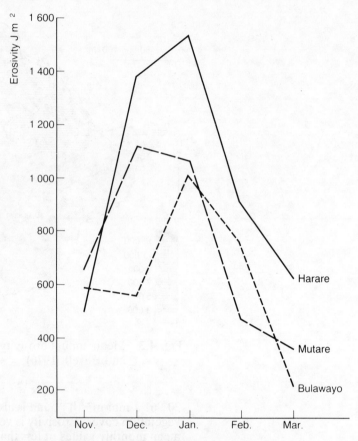

Fig. 4.4   Mean monthly erosivity for three towns in
Zimbabwe (after Hudson, 1965).

In many countries insufficient rainfall records from
autographic gauges are available to calculate erosivity
nationwide. In these cases, an attempt is made, for the
recording stations where erosivity can be determined, to find a
more widely available rainfall parameter which significantly
correlates with erosivity and from which erosivity values may
be predicted using a least-squares regression equation. Roose
(1975a), examining data in the Ivory Coast and Burkina, finds
that mean annual EI_{30} values can be approximated by the
mean annual rainfall totals (mm) multiplied by 50. This
relationship was used to produce a map of R values for west
Africa (Fig. 4.9). Ateshian (1974) built up a map of erosivity
west of the Rocky Mountains based on a power function
relating mean annual erosivity to the 6 h rainfall total with a
two-year return period.

A similar approach was adopted to compile and map data
on mean annual erosivity for Peninsular Malaysia (Morgan,
1974) using, for simplicity, the KE > 25 index. Insufficient

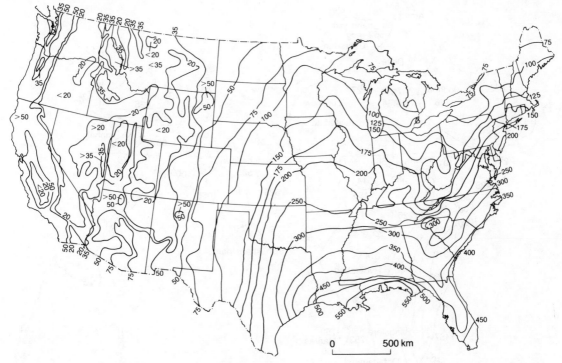

Fig. 4.5 Mean annual values of the rainfall erosion index *R* in the USA (after Wischmeier and Smith, 1978).

information was available to obtain values for this index for more than a few stations. To help overcome this lack of data, the rainfall records for eleven stations of the Malaysian Meteorological Service with autographic rain gauges were examined for 1969 and a relationship sought between mean annual erosivity and a more widely available rainfall parameter. Taking only those days in that year which yielded over 50 mm of rain, the KE > 25 value was calculated for each day. Rainfall intensities were obtained directly from the autographic gauge charts and kinetic energy values were derived using equation (3.2) and the procedure set out in Table 3.4. Based on data for ninety-three days, the following regression equation was obtained:

$$EVd = 16.64Rd - 173.82 \quad \text{with } r = 0.71 \quad (4.1)$$

where *EVd* is daily erosivity (J m^{-2}) and *Rd* is daily rainfall (mm).

Separate equations were derived for the three rainfall regions of the lowlands (Morgan, 1971; Table 4.1). No equation could be obtained for the highlands because of insufficient data. Taking the values of the intercepts in the equations, it can be established that a daily rainfall total of 34 mm is required to register an erosivity value on the KE >

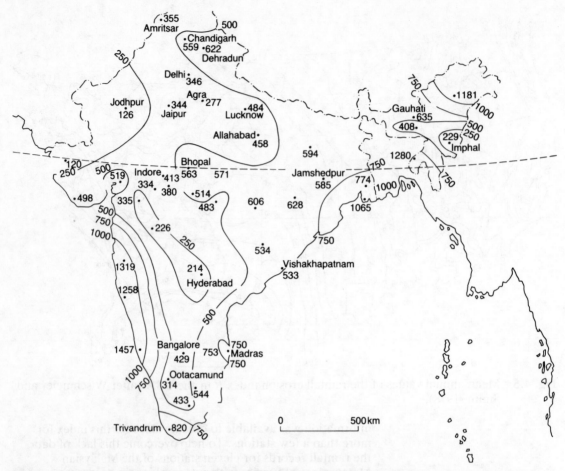

Fig. 4.6 Mean annual values of the rainfall erosion index *R* in India (after Central Soil and Water Conservation Research and Training Institute, 1977).

25 index in all regions. Using the equation appropriate to the location of each place, daily erosivity values were estimated for those days with 34 mm or more of rain, for ten recording stations for the years of 1965, 1966 and 1969. Daily rainfall totals were obtained from the monthly abstracts of the Malaysian Meteorological Service. Thirty values of annual erosivity were calculated by summing the daily values for each station for each year. It was found that these values (*EVa*) could be related to the mean annual rainfall (*P*; mm) by the following equation:

$$EVa = 9.28P - 8\,838.15 \qquad r = 0.81 \qquad (4.2)$$

This equation was used to estimate mean annual erosivity from mean annual rainfall totals, providing the basis for a map of erosivity (Fig. 4.10). The highest erosivity values are found on

Table 4.1   Regression equations for predicting daily erosivity from daily rainfall totals in Peninsular Malaysia

Area	Equation		
Peninsular Malaysia	$EVd = 16.64Rd - 173.82$	$r = 0.71$	$n = 93$
West Coast climate	$EVd = 34.42Rd - 1\,121.97$	$r = 0.71$	$n = 23$
East Coast climate	$EVd = 16.16Rd - 357.17$	$r = 0.77$	$n = 45$
Port Dickson climate	$EVd = 26.06Rd - 553.85$	$r = 0.86$	$n = 16$

Equations from Morgan (1974); climatic types based on Morgan (1971).

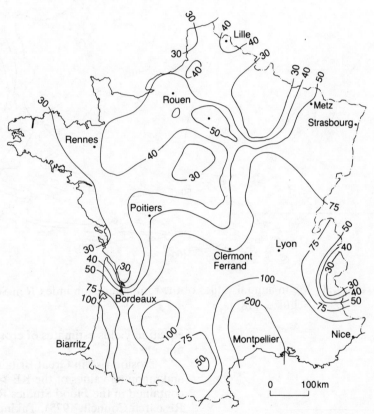

Fig. 4.7   Mean annual values of the rainfall erosion index R in France (after Pihan, 1979).

the eastern side of the country and in a belt between Pulau Pinang and Kuala Lumpur in the west.

It should be emphasized that although this approach to deriving erosivity values is universally valid, the resulting equations are not. Thus, whilst equation (4.2) appears to work well for Peninsular Malaysia, applying it to other countries is less satisfactory. With rainfall totals below 900 mm, the

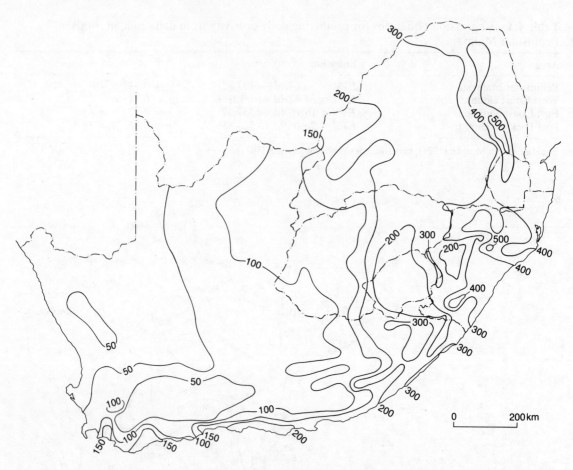

Fig. 4.8 Mean annual values of the rainfall erosion index *R* in South Africa (after Smithen and Schulze, 1982).

equation yields estimates of erosivity which are obviously nonsense.

Erosion risk in Great Britain was assessed by calculating and mapping values of the KE > 10 index using data contained in the Flood Studies Report (Natural Environment Research Council, 1975). Taking the two-day rainfall total with a five-year return period and employing the conversion factors contained in the report, estimates were obtained of the amount of rainfall expected in ten minutes for return periods ranging from twice in one year to once in a hundred years. These rainfall values were then expressed as ten-minute intensity values in mm h^{-1}. The annual frequency of rainfall at 10 mm h^{-1} for ten minutes was also calculated. The kinetic energies of all these intensity values were estimated using equation 3.2. Multiplying the kinetic energy values by their annual frequency of occurrence and integrating over a complete year yields a value for mean annual KE > 10. Mean

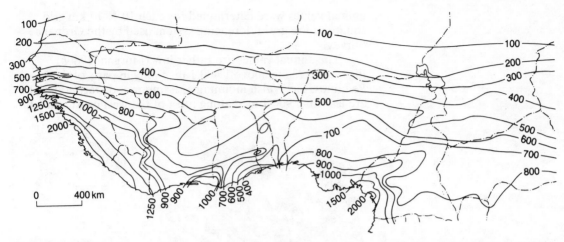

Fig. 4.9   Mean annual values of the rainfall erosion index *R* in west Africa (after Roose, 1977).

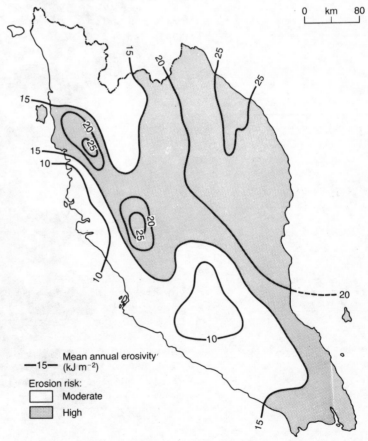

Fig. 4.10   Mean annual rainfall erosivity in Peninsular
Malaysia.

annual values were determined for each 10 × 10 km grid square of the grid referencing system used by the Ordnance Survey.

The annual values are rather low (Morgan, 1980*b*; Fig. 4.11), rising above 1 400 J m^{-2} only in parts of the Pennines, the Welsh mountains, Exmoor and Dartmoor. They are less than 900 J m^{-2} along most of the west coast and fall

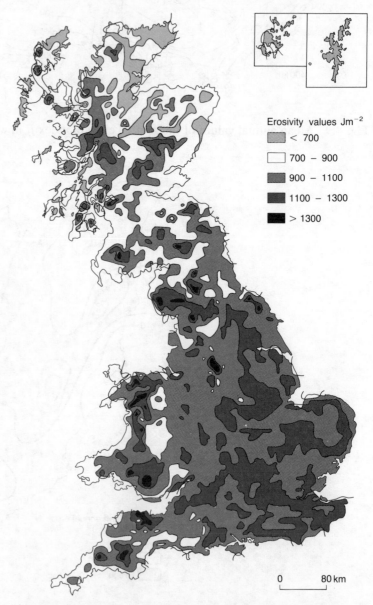

Erosivity values Jm^{-2}

< 700

700 – 900

900 – 1100

1100 – 1300

> 1300

0   80 km

Fig. 4.11   Mean annual rainfall erosivity (KE > 10) in Great Britain (after Morgan, 1980b).

below 700 in the Outer Hebrides, Orkneys, Shetlands and on
the north coast of Scotland. Values over much of eastern and
southern England are around 1 100 to 1 300. Since these are
the main areas devoted to arable farming, it is here that the
greatest risk of agricultural soil erosion occurs.

4.1.3 Rainfall aggressiveness

The most commonly used index, which has been shown to be
significantly correlated with sediment yields in rivers
(Fournier, 1960), is the ratio p^2/P, where p is the highest mean
monthly precipitation and P is the mean annual precipitation.
It is strictly an index of the concentration of precipitation into
a single month and thereby gives a crude measure of the
intensity of the rainfall and, in so far as a high value denotes a
strongly seasonal climatic regime with a dry season during
which the plant cover decays, of erosion protection by
vegetation. Using data from seventy-eight drainage basins,
Fournier (1960) derived the following empirical relationship
between mean annual sediment yield (Qs; g m^{-2}), mean
altitude (H; m) and mean slope of the basin (S):

$$\log Qs = 2.65 \log \frac{p^2}{P} + 0.46 \, (\log H) \, (\tan S) - 1.56 \quad (4.3)$$

This equation has been used by Low (1967) to investigate
regional variations in erosion risk in Peru.

Values of p^2/P were calculated and mapped for Peninsular
Malaysia using rainfall data for 680 recording stations
compiled by the Drainage and Irrigation Department (1970).
From Fig. 4.12 it can be seen that values of p^2/P are highest in
the eastern part of the country and in a belt on the west coast
extending from Pulau Langkawi and Perlis in the north to
Kuala Lumpur in the south. The belt extends eastwards into
the mountain areas in the north but in the middle and south of
the country lies to the west of them in the foothills.

In a study of the relationships between drainage
properties and climate (Morgan, 1976), a significant
correlation was observed between drainage texture and p^2/P
($r = 0.38$; $n = 39$). Both parameters are themselves
significantly correlated with the daily rainfall total with a
ten-year return period ($r = 0.57$; $n = 39$ and $r = 0.80$; $n = 21$
respectively). Because of the similarity between drainage
texture and gully density and the association between high
magnitude rainfall events and extension of the drainage system
by the development of fresh first-order streams, as described
by Nossin (1964) near Kuantan, both p^2/P and drainage
texture may be regarded as indicators of the risk of gully
erosion. In contrast, mean annual erosivity values reflect the
risk of erosion by rainsplash, overland flow and rills (section
3.1.2).

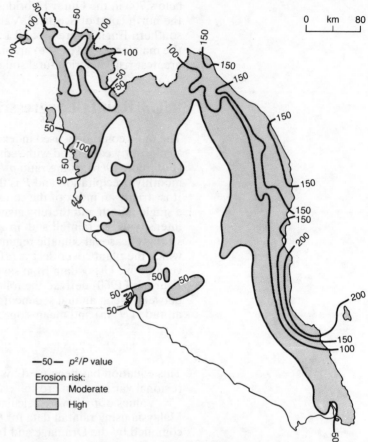

Fig. 4.12   Values of p^2/P in Peninsular Malaysia.

It follows that by superimposing the maps of p^2/P and erosivity, a composite picture of erosion risk over the whole country is obtained (Fig. 4.13). Since there will always be at least a moderate risk of erosion in any tropical environment, the three categories of erosion risk recognized in this reconnaissance survey are designated severe, high and moderate, rather than introduce any category which is described as low.

The areas of severe erosion risk, defined as those where the risk of gully erosion and erosion by overland flow are both high, are found on the eastern side of the country, not only in the mountains of the Banjaran Timor and the Trengganu Plateau but also on the lower land of eastern Pahang and eastern Johor which include the areas occupied by the land settlement schemes of Pahang Tenggara and Johor Tenggara. The severe risk area extends westwards into the Banjaran Titiwangsa and then southwards, swinging to the west of the watershed into the foothills between Kampar and Kuala

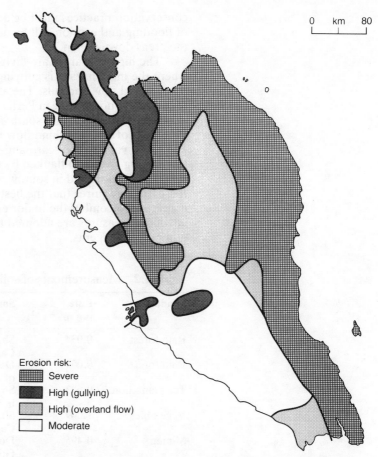

Erosion risk:
- Severe
- High (gullying)
- High (overland flow)
- Moderate

Fig. 4.13 Reconnaissance survey of soil erosion risk in Peninsular Malaysia.

Lumpur. The area from Pulau Pinang eastwards to the southern part of the Banjaran Bintang around Taiping and Kuala Kangsar is also one of severe erosion risk.

Much of the land subject to severe risk is mountainous, steeply sloping and covered with rain forest. The role of the forest cover as a regulator of runoff and therefore a control over flooding has been stressed by Low and Goh (1972). It is therefore doubly important, for flood and erosion control, that this forest be preserved. Soil loss under rain forest is relatively low but increases rapidly when the land is cleared for agriculture (Table 4.2). This is true for the lower, hilly land falling into this category too. Great care is required in managing the development of all the areas with severe erosion risk. Large parts of the land are unsuitable for agriculture and should not be used in this way. It is doubtful whether they should even be exploited for timber. Wherever the land is found suitable for logging or for cultivation, the very best conservation practices must be adopted otherwise the dangers of flooding and erosion will be detrimental both locally and in the areas downstream.

The high-risk areas are divisible into two groups: those where the main hazard is gullying and those where it is erosion by overland flow and rills. The areas of high gully risk are found in the northwest, in Perlis, Kedah and north Perak, and in scattered areas further south around Kelang and Kajang. The areas of high overland flow risk occur in the middle Perak and Kinta valleys, the scarp-and-vale country to the north of the Pahang river and flanked by the Banjaran Titiwangsa and Banjaran Timor, and in southwestern Johor. Development of these areas requires that the best conservation practices are employed to combat the major erosion problem and that adequate measures are adopted to deal with the effects of the other erosive agents.

Table 4.2   Measurements of soil loss in Peninsular Malaysia

Landuse	Rate (kg m^{-2} y^{-1})	Source
Rain forest	0.034	Shallow (1956) from R. Telom in Cameron Highlands.
Rain forest	0.004	Douglas (1972) from headwaters of R. Gombak
Tea plantation	0.673	Shallow (1956) from R. Bertam in Cameron Highlands.
Vegetables	1.009	Shallow (1956) from R. Kial in Cameron Highlands.
Mining	0.495	Douglas (1972) from R. Gombak, north of Kuala Lumpur.
Urban	0.800	Douglas (1972) from R. Anak, Ayer Batu, near Kuala Lumpur.

Note: data from Douglas (1972) have been converted using a bulk density value of 1.0 g cm^{-3}.

The moderate-risk areas consist mainly of the coastal and riverine plains on the western side of the country with their associated hilly terrain. Sound conservation practices are necessary in the hilly areas but the risk on the plains comes more from outside than from any erosion problems generated within them. Where they lie downstream of areas of high and severe erosion risk, they are considerably affected by flooding and sedimentation resulting from poor erosion control in those areas.

An indication of actual rates of erosion can be obtained by using the equations relating mean annual sediment yield to p^2/P derived by Fournier (1960). The following equations are appropriate to Peninsular Malaysia:

$$Qs = 27.12p^2/P - 475.40 \text{ for lowlands} \qquad (4.4)$$
$$Qs = 52.49p^2/P - 513.20 \text{ for highlands} \qquad (4.5)$$

where Qs is in t km^{-2} y^{-1}. These equations predict erosion
rates between 0.88 and 2.23 kg m^{-2} y^{-1} for the lowland areas
with p^2/P values between 50 and 100 respectively, and a rate of
2.11 kg m^{-2} y^{-1} in the highlands with a p^2/P value of 50.
Comparing these predictions with measured rates of 0.495 and
0.80 kg m^{-2} y^{-1} in the lowlands and 0.67 and 1.09 kg m^{-2} y^{-1}
in a part of the highlands where the p^2/P value is less than 50,
it can be seen that they are of the right order of magnitude for
areas affected by man-induced erosion. They are too high,
however, for the rain-forested areas (Table 4.2).

A map of p^2/P values was prepared for Kenya (Rowntree,
1983). The values range from 13 at Lodwar in the north to 123
at Lamu on the coast. Using a value of 50, the same as
adopted above in the study of Peninsular Malaysia, to denote
high erosion risk, three sensitive areas are identified. These
are the coastal belt, the Kitui-Yatta region and the area of the
Aberdare Mountains and Mount Kenya. Two main areas lie in
the category of moderate risk, defined by values between 31
and 50: the lower-lying regions from the Athi-Kapiti plains in
the south through Isiolo to the northern border and the Lake
Basin in the west. The areas of lowest risk with values between
11 and 30 include the low rainfall regions of the east, the Rift
Valley, the Uasin Gishu plateau, the Mau Escarpment and the
Laikipia plateau.

4.1.4 Factorial scoring

A simple scoring system for rating erosion risk has been
devised by Stocking and Elwell (1973*b*) in Zimbabwe. Taking
a 1:1 000 000 base map, the country is divided on a grid system
into units 184 km^2. Each unit is rated on a scale from 1 to 5 in
respect of erosivity, erodibility, slope, ground cover and
human occupation, the latter taking account of the density and
the type of settlement. The scoring is arranged so that 1 is
associated with a low risk of erosion and 5 with a high risk.
The five factor scores are summed to give a total score which is
compared with an arbitrarily chosen classification system to
categorize areas of low, moderate and high erosion risk. The
scores are mapped and areas of similar risk delineated
(Fig. 4.14).

Several problems are associated with this technique. First,
the classification may be sensitive to different scoring systems.
For example, the use of different slope groups may yield
different assessments of the degree of erosion risk. Second,
each factor is treated independently whereas, as shown in
Chapter 3, there is interaction between the factors. Slope
steepness may be much more important in areas of high than

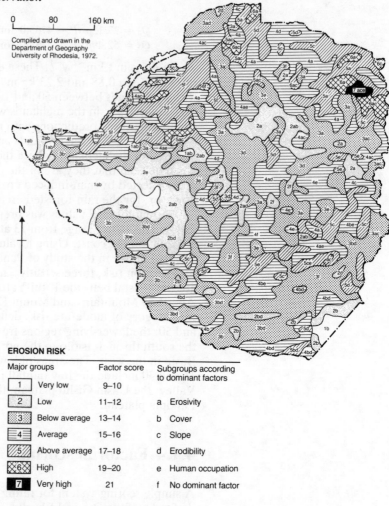

EROSION RISK

Major groups		Factor score	Subgroups according to dominant factors	
1	Very low	9–10		
2	Low	11–12	a	Erosivity
3	Below average	13–14	b	Cover
4	Average	15–16	c	Slope
5	Above average	17–18	d	Erodibility
6	High	19–20	e	Human occupation
7	Very high	21	f	No dominant factor

THE CATEGORIES OF EROSION

Categories		Erosivity (J mm m^{-2} h^{-1})	Cover (mm of rainfall) and basal cover est. (%)	Slope (degrees)	Erodibility	Human occupation*
Low	I	below 5 000	above 1 000 7–10	0–2	ortho-ferralitic regosols	Extensive large scale commercial ranching National Parks or Unreserved
Below average	II	5 000–7 000	800–1 000 5–8	2–4	para-ferralitic	Large scale commercial farms
Average	III	7 000–9 000	600–800 3–6	4–6	fersiallitic	Low density CLs (below 5 p.p.km^2) and SCCF
Above average	IV	9 000–11 000	400–600 1–4	6–8	siallitic vertisols lithosols	Moderately settled CLs (5–30 p.p. km^2)
High	V	above 11 000	below 400 0–2	above 8	non-calcic hydro-morphic sodic	Densely-settled CLs (above 30 p.p. km^2)

(*Notes:* Cover. Erodibility. and Human occupation are only tentative and cannot as yet be expressed on a firm quantitative basis.)
*p.p. km^2 — persons per square kilometre.   CL Communal Lands   SCCF Small Scale Commercial Farms

Fig. 4.14   Erosion survey of Zimbabwe (after Stocking and Elwell, 1973*b*).

in areas of low erosivity. Third, the factors are combined by addition. There is no reason why this should be a more appropriate method of combining them than multiplication. Fourth, each factor is given equal weight. Despite these difficulties, the technique is easy to use and has the advantage that factors which cannot be easily quantified in any other way can be readily included.

Although reconnaissance surveys give a valuable general appreciation of erosion risk, they only indicate potential for erosion. The way in which this potential is turned into real erosion patterns depends upon the influence of factors other than climate on the erosion system. An analysis of soils, slopes and landuse is required and this means carrying out semi-detailed surveys of erosion.

4.2   SEMI-DETAILED ASSESSMENT

4.2.1 Land capability classification

The land capability classification was developed by the United States Soil Conversation Service as a method of assessing the extent to which limitations such as erosion risk, soil depth, wetness and climate hinder the agricultural use that can be made of the land. The United States classification (Klingebiel and Montgomery, 1966) has been adapted for use in many other countries (Hudson, 1981*a*).

The objective of the classification is to regionalize an area of land into units with similar kinds and degrees of limitation. The basic unit is the capability unit. This consists of a group of soil types of sufficiently similar conditions of profile form, slope and degree of erosion as to make them suitable for similar crops and warrant the use of similar conservation measures. The capability units are combined into sub-classes according to the nature of the limiting factor and these, in turn, are grouped into classes based on the degree of limitation. The United States system recognizes eight classes arranged from Class I, characterised by no or very slight risk of damage to the land when used for cultivation, to Class VIII, very rough land which can be safely used only for wildlife, limited recreation and watershed conservation. The first four classes are designated as suitable for arable farming (Table 4.3). Assigning a tract of land to its appropriate class is aided by the use of a flow diagram (Fig. 4.15).

Although the inclusion of many soil properties in the classification may seem to render it useful for landuse planning generally, it must be appreciated that, as befits a classification evolved in the wake of the erosion scare in the United States in the 1930s, its bias is towards soil conservation. This bias is illustrated by the dominance of slope as a factor in determining

Table 4.3   Land capability classes (United States system)

Class	Characteristics and recommended landuse
I	Deep, productive soils easily worked, on nearly level land; not subject to overland flow; no or slight risk of damage when cultivated; use of fertilizers and lime, cover crops, crop rotations required to maintain soil fertility and soil structure.
II	Productive soils on gentle slopes; moderate depth; subject to occasional overland flow; may require drainage; moderate risk of damage when cultivated; use crop rotations, water-control systems or special tillage practices to control erosion.
III	Soils of moderate fertility on moderately steep slopes, subject to more severe erosion; subject to severe risk of damage but can be used for crops provided plant cover is maintained; hay or other sod crops should be grown instead of row crops.
IV	Good soils on steep slopes, subject to severe erosion; very severe risk of damage but may be cultivated occasionally if handled with great care; keep in hay or pasture but a grain crop may be grown once in five or six years.
V	Land is too wet or stony for cultivation but of nearly level slope; subject to only slight erosion if properly managed; should be used for pasture or forestry but grazing should be regulated to prevent plant cover from being destroyed.
VI	Shallow soils on steep slopes; use for grazing and forestry; grazing should be regulated to preserve plant cover; if the plant cover is destroyed, use should be restricted until cover is re-established.
VII	Steep, rough, eroded land with shallow soils; also includes droughty and swampy land; severe risk of damage even when used for pasture or forestry; strict grazing or forest management must be applied.
VIII	Very rough land; not suitable even for woodland or grazing; reserve for wildlife, recreation or watershed conservation.

Classes I–IV denote soils suitable for cultivation.
Classes V–VIII denote soils unsuitable for cultivation.
(Modified from Stallings, 1957).

capability class and by the emphasis given to soil conservation in the recommendations on how each class of land should be treated. Attempts to use the classification in a wider sphere have only drawn attention to its limitations. The classification does not specify the suitability of the land for particular crops;

a separate land suitability classification has been devised to do this (Vink, 1975). The assigning of a capability class is not an indicator of land value which may reflect the scarcity of a certain type of land, nor is it a measure of whether the farmer can make a profit, which is much influenced by the market

LAND CAPABILITY CLASS

	I	II			III		IV	
Permissible slope	0°–1°	0°–1°	1°–2.5°	0°–2.5°	2.5°–4.5°	0°–4.5°	4.5°–7°
Minimum effective depth (Texture here refers to average textures)	1 m of CL or heavier	50 cm of Sal. or heavier	50 cm of SaCl or heavier	50 cm of S or LS 25cm of Sal. or heavier	(a) 50 cm of SaCL (b) 25 cm of CL or heavier	25 cm of any texture	25 cm of SaCl or heavier
Texture of surface soil	CL or heavier	Sal or heavier S, or LS if upper subsoil is Sal or heavier	Sal or heavier	No direct limitations	(a) Sal or heavier (b) CL or heavier	No direct limitations	Sal or heavier
Permeability 5 or 4 to at least–	1 m	50 cm	50 cm	No direct limitations	No direct limitations	No direct limitations	
Not worse than 3 to–		1 m	1 m	1 m or 50 cm if average texture is CL is heavier	1 m		
Physical characteristics of the surface soil– Permissible symbols	Not permitted	t1	t1	t1 and t2	t1 and t2	t1 and t2	t1 and t2
Erosion– Permissible symbols	1	1 and 2	1 and 2	1,2 and 3	1, 2 and 3	1, 2 and 3	1, 2 and 3
Wetness criteria– Permissible symbols	Not permitted	w1	w1	w1	w1	w1 and w2	w1 and w2

S = Sand
Sal = Sandy Loam
LS = Loamy Sand
CL = Clay Loam
SaCL = Sandy Clay Loam

Fig. 4.15 Criteria and flow chart for determining land capability class according to the Classification of the Department of Conservation and Extension, Zimbabwe (after Hudson, 1981*a*).

Fig. 4.15 (*cont.*)

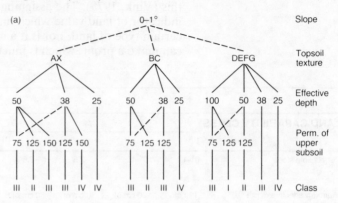

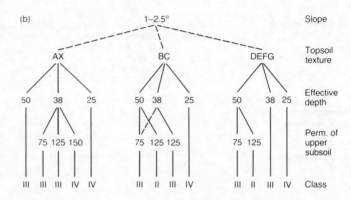

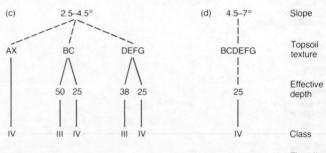

The effective depth is given in cm

prices of the crops grown and the farmer's skill. The stress laid by the classification on arable farming can also be a disadvantage. In Malaysia, where it conflicts with the priorities set for national development, the Economic Planning Unit has modified the system by defining Class I land as that with

Fig. 4.15 (*cont.*)

Effective depth (m)

1	Deep	More than 1.5 m
2	Moderately deep	1 m to 1.5 m
3	Moderately shallow	50 cm to 1 m
4	Shallow	25 cm to 50 cm
5	Very shallow	Less than 25 cm

Texture of surface soil

A	Sand	More than 85% sand
X	Loamy sand	80–85% sand
B	Sandy loam	Less than 20% clay; 50–80% sand
C	Sandy clay loam	20–30% clay; 50–80% sand
D	Clay loam	20–30% clay; less than 50% sand
E	Sandy clay	More than 30% clay; 50–70% sand
F	Clay	30–50% clay; less than 50% sand
G	Heavy clay	More than 50% clay

Permeability	Description	Rate of flow*
	Very slow	Less than 1.25
	Slow	1.25 to 5
	Moderately slow	5 to 20
	Moderate	20 to 65
	Moderately rapid	65 to 125
	Rapid	125 to 250
	Very rapid	over 250

* The rate of flow in mm per hour through saturated undistorted cores under a head of 12.5 mm of water.

Physical characteristics of surface soil

t1	Slightly unfavourable physical conditions. The soil has a tendency to compact and seal at the surface and a good tilth is not easily obtained.
t2	Unfavourable physical conditions. Compaction and sealing of the surface soil are more severe. A hard crust forms when the bare soil is exposed to rain and sun and poor emergence of seedlings can severely reduce the crop. On ploughing, large clods are turned up which are not easily broken.

Erosion

1	No apparent, or slight, erosion.
2	Moderate erosion : moderate loss of topsoil generally and/or some dissection by run-off channels or gullies.
3	Severe erosion, severe loss of topsoil generally and/or marked dissection by run-off channels or gullies.
4	Very severe erosion: complete truncation of the soil profile and exposure of the subsoil (B horizon) and/or deep and intricate dissection by run-off channels or gullies.

Wetness

w1	Wet for relatively short and infrequent periods.
w2	Frequently wet for considerable periods.
w3	Very wet for most of the season.

potential for mineral development (Panton, 1969; Table 4.4). Insufficient attention is given to the recreational use of land. The capability classification implies that land is set aside for recreation only when it is too marginal for arable or pastoral farming but, as shown by studies of footpath deterioration in upland areas (Bayfield, 1973), such land is often marginal for recreational use too. This fact highlights the difficulty of incorporating agricultural and non-agricultural activities in a

Fig. 4.15 (*cont.*)

ADDITIONAL REQUIREMENTS

---

*Factors affecting cultivation

g	Gravelly or stony
b Downgrade Class I to II	Very gravelly or stony
o	Bouldery
s	Very bouldery
v Class VI	Outcrops
r	Extensive outcrops

*Permeability

75 to 500—
otherwise class IV
Not applicable to
basalts or norites

*Erosion

Class: I : 1
II : 1; 2
III : 1; 2; 3

*'t' Factors

Class: II : t1
III : t1; t2
IV : t1; t2

*Wetness

Class: II : w1
III : w1
IV : w2
V : w3

w2 downgrades Class II and III to IVw unless the land is already
Class IV on code, in which case it remains as Class IV.

*Note

Any land not meeting the minimum requirements shown
on this sheet is Class VI.

---

single classification. One approach to this problem is provided by the Canada Landuse Inventory (McCormack, 1971) which employs four separate classifications covering agricultural, forestry, recreation and wildlife.

As a result of these criticisms, the land capability classification has tended, in recent years, to be discredited, often unfairly, as many of the criticisms arise from attempts to use the classification for purposes for which it was not intended. The value of land capability assessment lies in identifying the risks attached to cultivating the land and in indicating the soil conservation measures which are required. Improvements to the classification rest on making the conservation recommendations more specific, as is the case with the treatment-oriented scheme developed in Taiwan and

Table 4.4   Land capability classes recognized by the
Economic Planning Unit, Malaysia

Class	Description
I	Land with a high potential for mineral development.
II	Land with a high potential for agricultural development with a wide range of crops.
III	Land with a moderate potential for agricultural development with a restricted range of crops; best used for crops with a wide range of soil tolerance.
IV	Land with potential for productive forest development; best suited to commercial timber exploitation.
V	Land with little or no mineral, agricultural or forest development potential; suitable for development as protective reserves for conservation, water catchment, game, recreation, or similar purpose.

After Panton (1969).

tested in hilly land in Jamaica by Sheng (1972*a*; Table 4.5;
Fig. 4.16).

Information contained in land capability surveys can be
combined with that on erosivity to give a more detailed
assessment of erosion risk. The susceptibility of soils to water
and wind erosion is one factor considered in the description of
the management characteristics of the capability sub-classes
mapped by the Soil Survey of England and Wales (1979). It is
also considered in the descriptions of the Soil Associations
contained in the legend to the 1:250,000 Soil Map of England
and Wales (Soil Survey, 1983). This information can be
combined with that on rainfall erosivity (Fig. 4.11) and wind
velocity to produce a map showing areas vulnerable to soil
erosion (Morgan, 1985*b*; Figure 4.17). A threshold value of
1 100 J m^{-2} for mean annual KE >10 is selected to denote a
high risk of water erosion. Values of 900–1 100 J m^{-2} and less
than 900 J m^{-2} indicate moderate and no risk respectively. It
is assumed that the whole country is likely to experience wind
speeds greater than the threshold level for erosion at least
once a year. The following areas are recognized as having an
erosion risk: (1) the Vale of York, parts of Nottinghamshire
and north Norfolk where sandy and coarse loamy soils are
prone to both water and wind erosion when used for arable
farming; (2) much of the Midlands, the Welsh Marches,
particularly Shropshire and Herefordshire, a belt extending
from Berkshire northeastwards into Bedfordshire,
Cambridgeshire and Suffolk, parts of south Devon, south
Somerset, Dorset, Isle of Wight, east Hampshire and the

Table 4.5   Treatment-oriented land capability classification

Group	Class	Characteristics and recommended treatments
Suitable for tillage	C_1	Up to 7° slope; soil depth normally over 10 cm; contour cultivation; strip cropping; broadbase terraces.
	C_2	Slopes 7°–15°; soil depth over 20 cm; bench terracing (construction by bulldozers); use of four-wheel tractors.
	C_3	Slopes 15–20°; soil depth over 20 cm; bench terracing on deep soil (construction by small machines); silt-pits on shallower soils; use of small tractors or walking tractors.
	C_4	Slopes 20–25°; soil depth over 50 cm; bench terracing and farming operations by hand labour.
	P	Slopes 0–25°; soil depth too shallow for cultivation; use for improved pasture on rotational grazing system; zero grazing where land is wet.
	FT	Slopes 25–30°; soil depth over 50 cm; use for tree crops with bench terracing; inter-terraced areas in permanent grass; use contour planting; diversion ditches; mulching.
	F	Slopes over 30° or over 25° where soil is too shallow for tree crops; maintain as forest land.
Wetland, liable to flood; also stony land	P	Slopes 0–25°; use as pasture.
	F	Slopes over 25°; use as forest.
Gullied land	F	Maintain as forest land.

After Sheng (1972*a*).
The scheme is most suitable for hilly lands in the tropics.

Slope / Soil Depth	1. Gentle sloping <7°	2. Moderate sloping 7°–15°	3. Strongly sloping 15°–20°	4. Very strongly sloping 20°–25°	5. Steep 25°–30°	6. Very steep >30°
Deep (D) >36 in. (>90 cm)	C_1	C_2	C_3	C_4	FT	F
Moderately deep (MD) 20–36 in. (50–90 cm.)	C_1	C_2	C_3	C_4 / P	FT / F	F
Shallow (S) 8–20 in. (20–50 cm.)	C_1	C_2 / P	C_3 / P	P	F	F
Very shallow (VS) <8 in. (<20 cm.)	C_1 / P	P	P	P	F	F

Fig. 4.16   Chart for determining land capability class according to the treatment-orientated scheme of Sheng (1972*a*; Table 4.5).

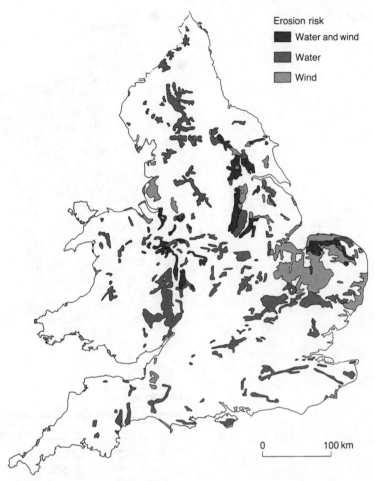

Erosion risk
■ Water and wind
■ Water
■ Wind

0   100 km

Fig. 4.17   Areas susceptible to agricultural soil erosion in
England and Wales (after Morgan, 1985*b*).

North and South Downs where water erosion can occur on
sandy, sandy loam, loamy and silty soils used for arable; (3)
areas of sandy and sandy loam soils in north Norfolk, east
Suffolk, parts of Lincolnshire, Yorkshire and Nottinghamshire
and areas of lowland peat soils in the Fens, western Lancashire
and Somerset which are prone to wind erosion when under
arable; (4) extensive areas of the Pennines, Welsh Mountains,
and smaller areas in the Lake District, Exmoor and Dartmoor
where upland blanket peats are highly vulnerable to water,
especially gully, erosion; and (5) areas of coastal sands which
are subject to wind erosion. The inclusion of land capability in
the assessment procedure means that the map indicates areas
with a risk of erosion when the land is used in accordance with
its capability rating.

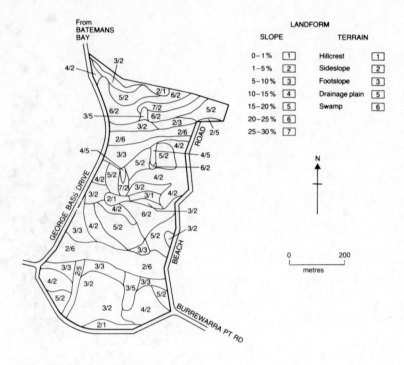

LANDFORM

PHYSICAL CRITERIA AND URBAN LANDUSE

Slope class	Terrain component	Potential hazards related to topographic location and slope and which will affect urban landuse	Suitable urban landuse
0–5%	Drainage plain	Flooding, seasonally high water-tables, high shrink-swell soils, high erosion hazard.	Drainage reserves/stormwater disposal.
	Floodplain	Flooding, seasonally high water-tables, high shrink-swell soils, saline soils, gravelly soils.	Open space areas, playing fields.
	Hillcrests Sideslopes Footslopes	Shallow soils, stony/gravelly soils. Overland flow, poor surface drainage and profile drainage. Impedence in lower terrain positions, deep soils. Others—swelling soils, erodible soils, dispersible soils.	Residential; all types of recreation; large-scale industrial, commercial and institutional development.
5–10%	Hillcrests Sideslopes Footslopes	Shallow soils. Overland flow Deep soils, poor drainage. Others—swelling soils, erodible soils, dispersible soils.	Residential subdivisions, detached housing, medium-density housing/unit complexes, modular industrial, active recreational pursuits.
10–15%	Sideslopes	Overland flow. Geological constraints—possibility of mass movement. Swelling soils. Erodible soils.	Residential subdivisions, detached housing, medium-density housing/unit complexes, modular industrial, passive recreational.
15–20%	Sideslopes	Overland flow. Geologic constraints—possibility of mass movement Swelling soils. Erodible soils.	Residential subdivisions, detached housing, medium-density housing/unit complexes, modular industrial, passive recreational.
20–25%	Sideslopes	Geologic constraints. Mass movement. High to very high erosion hazard.	Residential subdivision, passive recreational.
25–30%	Sideslopes	Geologic constraints. Possible mass movement. High to very high erosion hazard.	Upper limit for selective residential use, low-density housing on lots greater than 1 ha, passive recreation.
>30%	Sideslopes	Geologic constraints. Mass movement. Severe erosion hazard.	Recommend against any disturbance for urban development.

Fig. 4.18 Urban capability classification for soil erosion control (after Hannam and Hicks, 1980).

Fig. 4.18 (*cont.*)

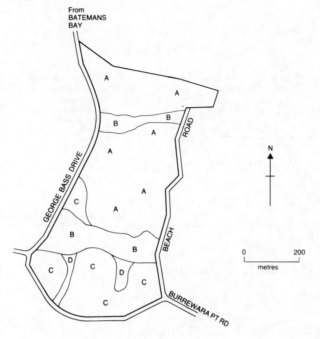

SOILS

SUMMARY OF PROPERTIES OF SOILS

Map Unit	Dominant soils	Lithology and physiography	Erosion hazard	Limitations
A	Shallow gravelly soils	Metasediments: cherts, phyllites, etc., with quartz veination. Ridges, sideslopes and some footslopes.	High	Impeded soil drainage, shallow soil depth, high stone and gravel contents.
B	Swamp alluvial soils	Metasediments: cherts, phyllites, etc., with quartz veination. Alluvial parent materials, swamp and drainage plains.	Very high to extreme	Seasonally high water-tables, poor to impeded soil drainage.
C	Yellow duplex soils	Metasediments: cherts, phyllites, etc., Crests, sideslopes and some footslopes.	High to very high	Low to moderate shrink-swell potential, poor soil drainage.
D	Drainage plain alluvial soils	Metasediments: cherts, phyllites, etc. Alluvial/colluvial parent materials and surface materials.	Very high	Seasonally high water-tables, poor to impeded soil drainage.

A system of land capability classification has been devised by the Soil Conservation Service of New South Wales for the planning of urban landuse with particular reference to erosion control (Hannam and Hicks, 1980). An example of its application to a small area at Guerilla Bay on the south coast of New South Wales is presented in Figure 4.18. A map of landform regions is produced by combining information on slope, divided into seven classes, and topographic position, here called terrain, divided into six classes. The potential hazards related to urban landuse are tabulated for each region. This information is combined with data on soils, paying attention to erosion hazard and limitations to urban

Fig. 4.18 (*cont.*)

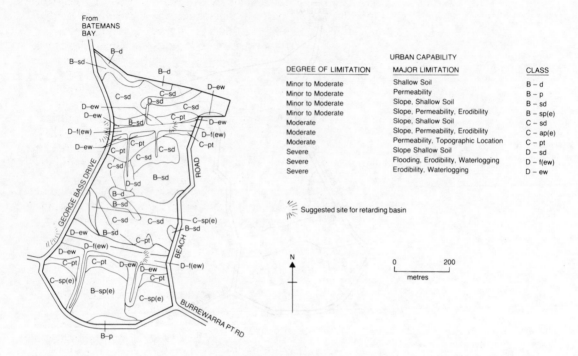

DEGREE OF LIMITATION	MAJOR LIMITATION	CLASS
	URBAN CAPABILITY	
Minor to Moderate	Shallow Soil	B – d
Minor to Moderate	Permeability	B – p
Minor to Moderate	Slope, Shallow Soil	B – sd
Minor to Moderate	Slope, Permeability, Erodibility	B – sp(e)
Moderate	Slope, Shallow Soil	C – sd
Moderate	Slope, Permeability, Erodibility	C – ap(e)
Moderate	Permeability, Topographic Location	C – pt
Severe	Slope Shallow Soil	D – sd
Severe	Flooding, Erodibility, Waterlogging	D – f(ew)
Severe	Erodibility, Waterlogging	D – ew

Suggested site for retarding basin

N

0   200

metres

URBAN CAPABILITY

Definitions of the classes used in urban capability assessment are:

Class A — Areas with little or no physical limitations to urban development.

Class B — Areas with minor to moderate physical limitations to urban development. These limitations may influence design and impose certain management requirements on development to ensure a stable land surface is maintained both during and after development.

Class C — Areas with moderate physical limitations to urban development. These limitations can be overcome by careful design and by adoption of site management techniques to ensure the maintenance of a stable land surface.

Class D — Areas with severe physical limitations to urban development which will be difficult to overcome, requiring detailed site investigation and engineering design.

Class E — Areas where no form of urban development is recommended because of very severe physical limitations, to such development, that are very difficult to overcome.

development, to produce a map showing urban capability using five classes. A suitable form of landuse is then determined for each area consistent with its capability class, physical limitations and the degree of disturbance it can sustain without causing excessive erosion and sedimentation.

4.2.2   Land systems classification

Land systems analysis is used to compile information on the physical environment for the purpose of resource evaluation.

The land is classified into areal units, termed land systems, which are made up of smaller units, land facets, arranged in a clearly recurring pattern. Since land facets are defined by their uniformity of landform, especially slope, soils and plant community, land systems comprise an assemblage of landform, soil and vegetation types. Land systems classification has been described and discussed in many texts (Cooke and Doornkamp, 1974; Young, 1976) as a method of integrated resource survey, a role which lies beyond the scope of this book. What is important here, considering that many of the factors examined in land systems analysis are relevant to the soil erosion system, is its value for erosion risk evaluation. The extent to which land systems conform to discrete units of kind and degree of erosion hazard was examine by Higginson (1973) in the Hunter Valley, New South Wales. He carried out an erosion survey of the area from aerial photographs, using a classification recognizing seven grades of erosion severity, and analysed the distribution of erosion classes falling within each land system. Far from each system being distinct, he found that the land systems could be combined into four groups. It would seem, therefore, that the relationship between erosion risk and land systems is poor and that the land systems classification provides only a generalized assessment. To a large extent this is expected because, by their make-up, land systems are likely to comprise areas of markedly different erosion risk. A similar study at the land facet level might prove more fruitful.

4.2.3 Soil erosion survey

The first types of erosion survey were essentially static in concept and consisted of mapping, often from aerial photographs, the rills, gullies and blow-outs occurring in the area (Jones and Keech, 1966; Vink, 1968). Erosion hazard was estimated by calculating simple indices such as gully density. No attempt was made to map the factors that influence erosion and which could therefore provide the basis for predicting change. The approach to analysing change was the sequential survey in which mapping was carried out at regular intervals, using photography of different dates. In this way changes in gully density could be examined in relation to changing agricultural practices and increasing population pressure (Keech, 1969). More recently, the need for a dynamic approach in which both the erosion features and the factors influencing them are mapped and relationships sought has become apparent.

Because of the similarity of content in the studies of soil erosion and fluvial geomorphology, it seems logical to seek a method for a dynamic approach to erosion survey in the various systems of geomorphological mapping. A geomorphological map shows the form of the land surface, the properties of the soils and rocks beneath the surface, and the kind and magnitude of the geomorphological processes at work. Not surprisingly, most mapping systems are too complex for applied use and special-purpose geomorphological maps have to be produced for specific tasks (Demek, 1971). In the ITC System of Geomorphological Survey (Verstappen and van Zuidam, 1968) three maps are produced: a general geomorphological map, a morpho-conservation map, and a hydrological map. The morpho-conservation map is intended for erosion evaluation and has been so used in southern Italy (van Genderen, 1970; Rao, 1975). On the map are shown slope steepness, slope shape, present landuse, areas of rill and gully erosion and areas of mass movement.

A geomorphological mapping system for soil erosion survey has been derived from the ITC System and the work of Gerlach and Niemirowski (1968) by Williams and Morgan (1976). The aim is to portray information on the distribution and type of erosion, erosivity, runoff, slope length, slope steepness, slope curvature in profile and plan, relief, soil type and landuse. As much detail as possible is shown on a single map but, to avoid clutter, overlays can be used and are recommended for erosivity, soils and slope steepness. The legend (Fig. 4.19) is designed for use with colour: blue for water features, including river terraces; brown for relief features such as contours and crest lines; red for accelerated erosion by water or wind; yellow for aeolian features; green for plant covers; and black for man-made features, including badly located and ill-designed conservation structures.

Although much information is obtained from aerial photographs, this needs to be checked and supplemented by additional data collected in the field. The severity of erosion can be rated by a simple scoring system taking account of the exposure of tree roots, crusting of the soil surface, formation of splash pedestals, the size of rills and gullies, and the type and structure of the plant cover (Table 4.6). Observations are made using quadrat sampling over areas of 1 m^2 for ground cover, crusting and depth of ground lowering, 10 m^2 for shrub cover, and 100 m^2 for tree cover and the density of rills and gullies.

In interpreting the results of field survey, it is important to place the data in its time perspective. This is clearly indicated by the results of a survey of rangelands in northern Mexico (Table 4.7). In the study area the land divides into four main units: high, rocky mountains; dissected lower sierra; flatter piedmont slops or *mediano*; and the alkali flats or *bajío*. Grazing is on a rotational basis, utilizing the bajío in the summer, the sierra in the winter, and the mediano in the autumn and spring. At the time of survey in late August 1976, a surprisingly poor correlation was obtained between erosion

SYMBOL	FEATURE	COLOUR
∿	Perennial water course	blue
⌐⌐⌐⌐	Seasonal water course	blue
– – –	Crest line	brown
⌒	Contour line	brown
⋁⋁⋁⋁⋁⋁⋁	Major escarpment	brown
◡◡◡◡◡	Convex slope break	brown
××××	Concave slope break	brown
—╫—╫—	Waterfall	blue
—┤├—	Rapids	blue
— — —	Edge of flood plain	blue
▾▾▾▾▾	Edge of river terrace	blue
— ⸱— ⸱—	Back of river terrace	blue
ᐞ ᐞ ᐞ ᐞ	Swamp or marsh	blue
≡≡≡⫐	Active gully	red
≡≡≡⫐	Stable gully	blue
↘↘↘↘	Active rills	red
≡ ≡ ≡	Sheetwash/rainsplash (inter-rill erosion)	red
—↓—	River bank erosion	red
⌢⌢⌢⌢⌢	Landslide or slump scar	red
⸦ɛ ɛ ɛ	Landslide or slump tongue	red
⸜⸜⸜⸜⸜	Small slides, slips	red
⧄⧄⧄⧄	Colluvial or alluvial fans	brown
░░░	Sedimentation	brown
∼⸱∼⸱∼	Landuse boundary (landuse denoted by letter e.g. R – rubber; F – forest; P – grazing land; L – arable land.)	green
———	Roads and tracks	black
—+—+—	Railway	black
⊥⸱⊥⸱⊥⸱⊥	Cutting	black
▾▾▾▾	Embankment	black
▪⸱▪⸱▪⸱▪	Buildings	black
⌒⌒	Terrace	black
═══	Waterway	black

SLOPES

☐	0°–1°
▦	2°–3°
▨	4°–8°
▮	9°–14°
■	15°–19°
▦	over 19°

Fig. 4.19 Legend for mapping soil erosion.

severity and the proportion of bare ground. But, on the sierra and mediano pastures, a good correlation was found between erosion severity and the percentage of the ground covered by grass and trees. The bajío, however, had a better grass cover than would be expected from its erosion coding. This reflects not only the erodibility of the bajío but also that it had

Table 4.6 Coding system for soil erosion appraisal in the field

Code	Indicators
0	No exposure of tree roots; no surface crusting; no splash pedestals; over 70% plant cover (ground and canopy).
$\frac{1}{2}$	Slight exposure of tree roots; slight crusting of surface; no splash pedestals; soil level slightly higher on upslope or windward sides of plants and boulders; 30–70% plant cover.
1	Exposure of tree roots, formation of splash pedestals, soil mounds protected by vegetation, all to depths of 1–10 mm; slight surface crusting; 30–70% plant cover.
2	Tree root exposure, splash pedestals and soil mounds to depths of 1–5 cm; crusting of surface; 30–70% plant cover.
3	Tree root exposure, splash pedestals and soil mounds to depths of 5–10 cm; 2–5 mm thickness of surface crust; grass muddied by wash and turned downslope; splays of coarse material due to wash or wind; less than 30% plant cover.
4	Tree root exposure, splash pedestals and soil mounds to depths of 5–10 cm; splays of coarse material; rills up to 8 cm deep; bare soil.
5	Gullies; rills over 8 cm deep; blow-outs and dunes; bare soil.

remained ungrazed for the previous nine months, giving time for the grass to recover. The most severe erosion was observed on land recently grazed, with poor grass cover and no trees. That this is a direct result of greater runoff following a reduction in the vegetation cover, exposing the surface to livestock trampling and rain beat, is indicated by the greater compaction and crusting found in these areas which causes a lowering of the infiltration rate. With a change in rangeland condition from excellent pasture to bare soil, infiltrometer tests

Table 4.7 Field survey of rangelands in northern Mexico

Region	Transect	Grass	% Plant Cover			Grass+ trees	%Bare ground	Erosion code
			Forbs	Shrubs	Trees			
Sierra	1	22	4	8	13	35	65	0.31
	2	18	3	6	11	29	74	0.75
	3	25	2	14	1	26	63	1.00
	4	18	4	9	0	18	69	4.12
Mediano	5	28	3	5	0	28	70	1.33
	6	19	5	6	0	19	67	1.83
Bajío	7	48	0	0	0	48	52	1.66
	8	53	0	0	0	53	47	0.66

% Plant cover and % bare ground do not always total 100 because the same area of land may be covered by grass and a tree canopy.
% Bare ground includes rocky and stony surfaces and bare soil.
Erosion code is based on Table 4.6.
Data are averages of 8 sample sites on each transect on the sierra, 6 on the mediano and 3 on the bajío.
Transects are aligned across the slope on the contour and arranged from high (1) to low (8) ground.
Field survey was carried out in late August 1976 by the author, Sr L. Carlos Fierro and Sr J. Jabalera Ramos.

show that the amount of water which can infiltrate the soil from a dry state is reduced over 60 min from 280 mm to 110 mm on the sierra and from 360 mm to 105 mm on the mediano, and over 150 min from 267 mm to 130 mm on the mediano and from 150 mm to 73 mm on the bajıo (Josué Martinez and González, 1971; Sánchez Muñoz and Valdés Reyna, 1975).

4.2.4 Semi-detailed erosion survey in central Pahang, Peninsular Malaysia

Procedure

The objectives of semi-detailed erosion surveys are to identify the extent and type of soil erosion taking place in an area and to assess the relative importance of the various factors influencing soil loss. The mapping system of Williams and Morgan (1976) was adopted. In order to cover as large an area as rapidly as possible, most information was obtained by the interpretation of aerial photographs. Since most erosion features can be seen in direct stereoscopic image, the use of aerial photography can considerably reduce the cost per unit area of the survey compared with ground survey techniques. An indication of the extent of the reduction can be gauged from studies made of the costs of soil surveys. With only 15 per cent of the time spent on aerial photograph interpretation (Young, 1973), the saving on survey effort is over 50 per cent (Bie and Beckett, 1971).

Aerial photograph interpretation must be supported by fieldwork which allows the recognition of features on the photographs to be checked on the ground and the reproducibility of the interpretation to be assessed. A further and equally important aspect of fieldwork is to obtain data which cannot be derived from the photographs, particularly on soils and slopes.

The integration of aerial photograph interpretation and fieldwork is essential. For a semi-detailed survey the following procedure is recommended:

1   lay out the photographs or use satellite images, if available, as a photomosaic and draw boundaries between areas having distinctive photographic tones and patterns and which are therefore presumed to represent the boundaries between the major landform regions;
2   carry out stereoscopic examination of the photographs, plotting as much detail of the erosion features and related factors as possible;
3   carry out fieldwork to check this and obtain additional information;

4   carry out a second stereoscopic examination, finalizing the details to be mapped in the light of the fieldwork;
5   fair-draw the maps;
6   analyse and interpret the data;
7   assess or predict erosion risk; and
8   write report.

Although, as stated above, most erosion features are visible in direct stereoscopic image and are therefore identifiable by their form, shape and size, and their association with other features, the interpreter also makes use of tone, texture, shadow and pattern. The main erosion features mapped in this semi-detailed survey are: areas of rainsplash erosion and erosion by overland flow, rills, gullies and river-bank erosion. Areas of soil wash by overland flow and splash erosion are recognized on black-and-white panchromatic photography as light grey tones, frequently in association with the top and middle slope segments. These light tones result from exposure of the subsoil, following removal of the top soil, and contrast with the darker tones of uneroded soils where the top soil with its organic content remains. Occasionally, where the parent rock and subsoil are dark in colour, this relationship between photographic tone and erosion is reversed (Bergsma, 1974).

The tonal patterns associated with splash and wash erosion are non-directional. Where the tones follow a linear pattern, especially with a downslope orientation, they are interpreted as rills. Under high magnification, a slight definition of depth to the rills may be apparent. Frequently rills show as an anastomosing pattern of light linearly arranged tones.

According to Brice (1966), a gully has steep sides, a steeply sloping or vertical headwall, a width greater than 0.3 m and a depth over 0.6 m. Gullies are thus distinguishable on aerial photographs from rills by a clear definition of depth and from rivers by a channel with greater depth than width. Depending upon the quality and scale of the photography, and the degree of magnification used, width and depth measurements may be possible. Active gullies, usually carrying flow intermittently, have steep, unvegetated banks, sometimes with evidence of slumping. Stable gullies have partially or even fully vegetated banks.

River-bank erosion is characterized by the absence of vegetation, sometimes the presence of slumping, light tones and an association with the outside of bends. Additional features which may be recognizable on aerial photographs are landslides, earth flows and areas of sedimentation.

Study area

The study area lies in the centre of Peninsular Malaysia, west of the River Pahang, between Jerantut in the north and

Temerloh in the south. The rocks consist of alternating shales
and sandstones of the Kerdau Series, Triassic in age, and these
have been moulded into smooth, steep-sided hills which rise
abruptly from narrow valley floors. The local relief is low, only
100 to 120 m, but the dominantly convex slopes steepen
rapidly from their crests to a maximum angle of 21°. At their
lower end, a sharp break in slope angle occurs below which a
piedmont slope grades gently into the valley floor (Fig. 4.20).
There is a catenary sequence of soils with the Melaka Series
occupying the hillslopes, the Durian Series on the lower slopes
and the Batu Anam Series on the valley floors (Eyles, 1967).
The mean annual rainfall is 2 052 mm and there is no dry
season. The return period of a daily rainfall of 50 mm is 118
days and a daily total with a ten-year return period is 186 mm.
The hillslopes are covered in a mosaic of tropical rain forest,
rubber plantations and secondary forest in various stages of
growth. The valley floors are either used for wet rice
cultivation or left as swamp.

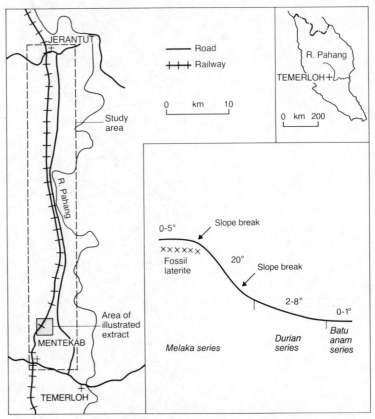

Fig. 4.20   Location of the semi-detailed erosion survey,
central Pahang, and detail of a typical slope profile in
the area (after Eyles, 1967).

Erosion map

A soil erosion map of the area was produced from panchromatic aerial photography, flown in1966 and with a nominal scale of 1:25 000, using a Wild ST4 Mirror Stereoscope with 3 × magnification and a Zeiss Interpretoscope with up to 15 × magnification. No satellite imagery was available so the photographs were used to form the photomosaic for the first stage of the work. The stereoscopic examination of the photographs proceeded as follows using the legend shown in Fig. 4.19 for plotting the information:

1   the study area was delimited on the photographs;
2   the stream pattern was plotted, separating permanent drainage lines from intermittent streams and dry valleys;

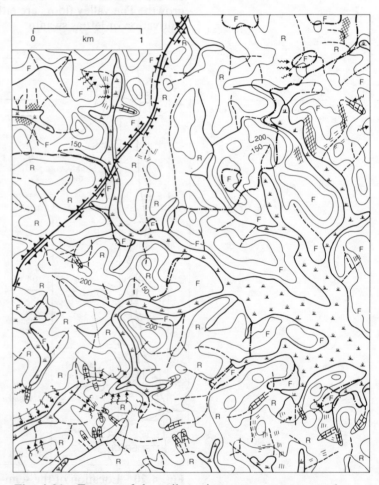

Fig. 4.21   Extract of the soil erosion survey map, central Pahang. Contour interval 50 ft.

3   the crest pattern was plotted;
4   erosion features were identified and plotted, e.g. areas
     eroded by rainsplash and overland flow, rills, gullies,
     mass movements, river-bank erosion;
5   areas of sedimentation were identified and plotted;
6   man-made features were shown, e.g. settlements and
     communications; areas affected by erosion due to runoff
     from badly located roads, poorly maintained terraces or
     inadequate waterways were marked;
7   areas where high runoff from adjacent uplands or
     convergence of surface flows is probable were identified
     and marked; and
8   the main landuse types were plotted.

The contour and drainage patterns shown on the
1:63 360 scale topographical map sheets covering the area
were redrawn at 1:25 000 scale to provide a base on which to
copy the information contained on the photographic plots. The
whole was then fair-drawn at a scale of 1:10 000. An extract of
the erosion map is shown in Fig. 4.21. It should be emphasized
that the clarity of the erosion maps depends upon the use of
colour and that reproduction in black and white, as here, can
result in a somewhat cluttered effect.

Slope map

Although information on slope length and slope shape can be
obtained from the erosion map and slope steepness can be
calculated for specific localities from the contour data, there is
insufficient room to show the spatial pattern of slope steepness
on the same map. A map of slope classes, based on steepness,
is therefore produced separately as an overlay (Fig. 4.22).

It is possible, though tedious, to produce the slope map
from aerial photographs, using photogrammetric techniques,
or to build up a map from field measurements. The latter are
more appropriate for a detailed erosion survey over a small
area. A reasonably accurate map, sufficient for the purpose of a
semi-detailed survey, can be obtained relatively easily and
rapidly from topographic maps using the method devised by
Olofin (1972). Taking the 1 × 1 km grid squares shown on the
maps as a base, each square is divided into 0.14 × 0.14 km
squares and, for these units, the maximum slope is estimated
from the distance apart of the contours. The slope estimates
are assigned to slope steepness classes according to the system
developed by Olofin (1974) for use in Malaysia for planning
purposes. In this system, slope classes are based on
morphological and theoretical ideas, relating slope angle and
geomorphological processes, and on relationships between
slope angle, limits to cultivation and the use of machinery.
Detailed field checks by Olofin (1972) show that there is a
very strong correlation between slope angles estimated by this
method and those measured in the field with an Abney level.

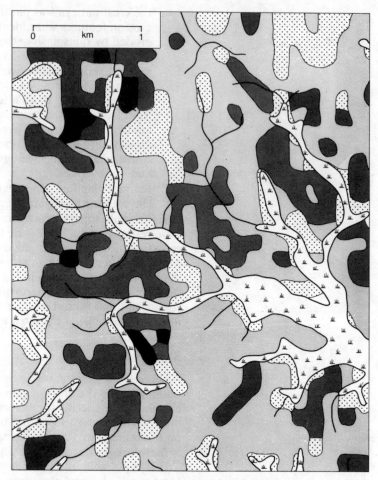

Fig. 4.22 Extract of the slope map, central Pahang.
(key to shading in Figure 4.19).

Fieldwork

The supporting field survey is designed to collect sufficient
information to build up a realistic picture of the study area.
Because of the impossibility of surveying the whole area in the
field in a reasonable period of time, the survey is based on
observations made at sample sites. The selection of these sites
is critical. It must be made without bias, if their
representativeness is to be assured, a condition which is
essential if the results of the survey are to be extrapolated over
the whole area.

The first step is to delimit drainage basins of the
third-order using the erosion map as a base. Third-order basins
are chosen because they are of a size which confines them to
similar lithological and relief conditions. The drainage basins

are given numbers and, using random number tables, a selection is made for field study.

The next stage is to select sample slope profiles within the drainage basins. A simple selection scheme is described by Young (1972). Each sample basin is treated separately and, using either a topographical map or aerial photographs, the divide and main drainage lines are plotted. The mid-slope line, which lies half-way between the divide and the drainage lines, is then drawn. Points along this line are selected either at random or at regular intervals and lines drawn from each point, along the steepest part of the slope, at right angles to the contours, to the divide and the drainage line. In practice, it is not always possible to survey all the transects selected because of inaccessibility. Where a transect cannot be surveyed, an alternative transect along a parallel line in close proximity may be substituted or it is omitted from the sampling scheme. In some cases, it is only possible to survey part of the transect.

Many observations on each transect are made at points and the selection of these is either at regular intervals or based on free survey, at the discretion of the surveyor. Normally, three points are used on each transect, located on the upper convexity, the mid-slope and the lower concavity.

The question of the representativeness of and the accuracy obtained from the sampling design is best approached at the point or site level. For each parameter being recorded, the required sample size can be determined which will result in a value for the sample mean which is within plus or minus a value (d) of the true mean, for a specified probability level (p). A preliminary sample of between ten and thirty observations is taken and the best estimate of the standard deviation ($\hat{s}$) from the mean is calculated from

$$\hat{s} = \sqrt{\frac{\Sigma(x - \bar{x})^2}{(n - 1)}} \qquad (4.6)$$

where x is the value of any observation, $\bar{x}$ is the arithmetic mean of the series of observations and n is the number of observations in the preliminary sample. The sample size (N) for given values of d and p is obtained from

$$N = \frac{(\hat{s}t_{p,\ n-1})^2}{d} \qquad (4.7)$$

where t is the value of Student's 't', obtained from tables, for probability level (p) and a preliminary sample size of n observations and $n - 1$ degrees of freedom. Reynolds (1975) has applied equation (4.7) to a study of soil properties and finds that to measure soil depth, pH, texture and organic content to an accuracy yielding a sample mean which differs from the true mean by the respective values of $\pm$ 5 cm, 0.1 units, 1 per cent and 5 per cent, at the 95 per cent probability level, requires a sampling density of 10 observations per

1 000 m^2. Clearly, standard soil survey procedures are less rigorous. Burrough, Beckett and Jarvis (1971) recommend a standard of five observations per cm^2 on the map. For a map at a scale of 1:20 000, 1 cm^2 = 40 000 m^2, which, according to the standard, requires 1 observation per 8 000 m^2. Generally, sampling density has to be adjusted to the time available for fieldwork.

Each slope transect is surveyed, beginning at either the divide or drainage line. Slope angles are measured to the nearest 1° with an Abney level, along successive sight lines, normally 10 m in length. Where the sight line is crossed by a marked break in slope, a shorter length is used, stopping the sight line at the slope break.

At the three selected sites on each transect, soil samples are taken with a 75 mm bore auger at 300 to 450 mm depth. In

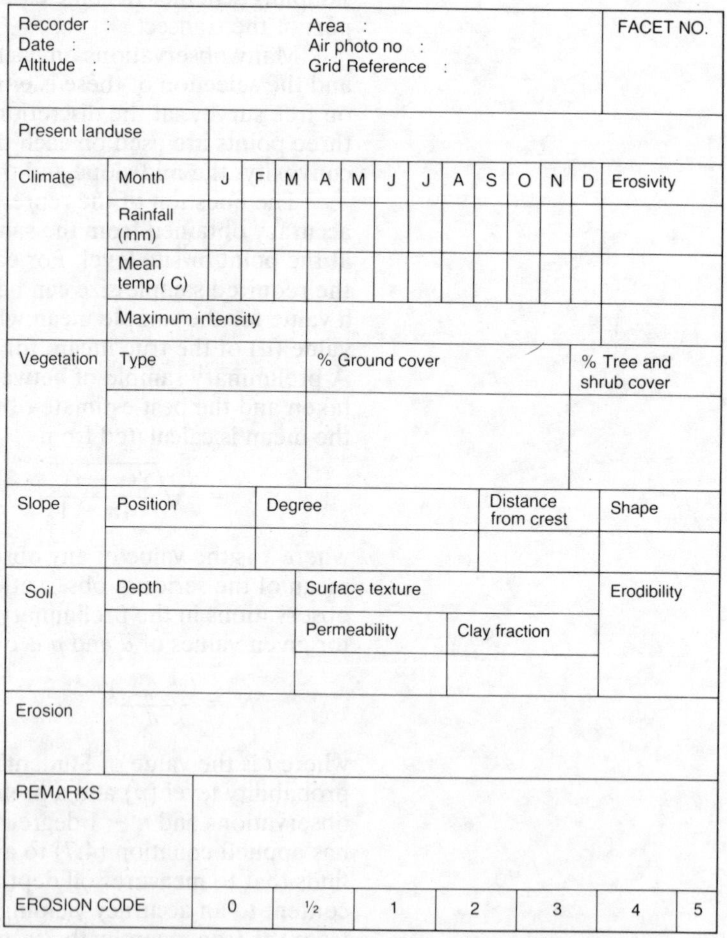

Recorder : Date : Altitude :						Area : Air photo no : Grid Reference :							FACET NO.	
Present landuse														
Climate	Month	J	F	M	A	M	J	J	A	S	O	N	D	Erosivity
	Rainfall (mm)													
	Mean temp (C)													
	Maximum intensity													
Vegetation	Type			% Ground cover							% Tree and shrub cover			
Slope	Position		Degree					Distance from crest			Shape			
Soil	Depth		Surface texture								Erodibility			
			Permeability			Clay fraction								
Erosion														
REMARKS														
EROSION CODE		0	½		1		2		3		4		5	

Fig. 4.23 Pro forma for recording soil erosion in the field (devised by Baker, personal communication).

cultivated areas this depth is usually sufficient to avoid disturbance of the top soil by terracing. The samples are removed to the laboratory for analysis of grain-size distribution, organic content and aggregate stability. Field tests may be made of infiltration capacity and shear strength using a cylindrical infiltrometer and a portable shear vane respectively (Eyles, 1968*a*). Records of the plant cover, such as species, percentage ground cover, decaying vegetal matter and surface litter, are made within 1×1 m quadrats, centred on the sample points. Larger, 10×10 m quadrats are used to record bush and tree species and to analyse the structure of the plant association, particularly the number of layers involved and the extent of the canopy. Within the larger quadrat, an assessment is made of the state of erosion using a simple scoring system similar to that given in Table 4.6.

So that no items are forgotten, a standard booking procedure is adopted. A recording sheet or pro forma (Fig. 4.23) is prepared, listing all the information required, and in the field an entry is made against each item even if only to denote its absence or that, for certain reasons, no observation was made.

Because detailed field studies of the type described above were carried out by Eyles (1967; 1968*c*), no supporting field survey was conducted in this instance. Two reconnaissance visits were made to the area for checking purposes.

Soil properties

The soils have an inherently low erodibility. The top soils of the Melaka, Durian and Batu Anam Series have clay contents of 60 to 70 per cent (Ng, 1969), far higher than the upper limit associated with erodible soils (Evans, 1980). The soils are therefore cohesive and resistant to detachment. Measurements of shear strength, at a depth of 0.3 m, and infiltration capacity made in the field (Eyles, 1970; Table 4.8) show that soils of the Melaka Series are highly resistant to erosion. Their high shear strength means that they are not subject to slumping and the high infiltration capacity means that surface runoff is extremely rare. Soils of the Durian and Batu Anam Series are

Table 4.8 Properties of soils near Kerdau, Pahang, Peninsular Malaysia

Soil Series	Shear Strength ($kN\ m^{-2}$)	Infiltration Capacity ($mm\ h^{-1}$)	Number of Samples
Melaka	284.07	146.8	15
Durian	106.87	43.4	6
Batu Anam	143.42	12.2	5

After Eyles (1970)

more susceptible to erosion. Rainfall intensities in excess of the infiltration capacity, and therefore surface runoff, are likely to occur as frequently as every 100 days on the Durian Series and every month on the Batu Anam Series.

Analysis

A study of the erosion map (Fig. 4.21) reveals a close relationship between the severity of erosion and landuse. All the areas of accelerated erosion are confined to land cleared of the rain forest vegetation. Much eroded land has been temporarily abandoned and, at the time of the survey, was reverting to secondary forest.

Within these cleared areas, the location and type of erosion is determined by the interaction of slope form and soils. The summit areas are resistant to erosion, being covered by soils of the Melaka Series. Erosion is here limited to rainsplash because overland flow and slumping rarely occur. The eroded areas are below the altitude of 45 m and are therefore concentrated almost entirely on the Durian Series. The slope forms with their rapidly steepening convexity and lengths between 30 and 100 m are typical of erodible areas (Evans, 1980). Where the slopes are straight in plan, erosion is by rainsplash, overland flow and rills. Where the slopes are concave in plan and there is moisture convergence towards the base of the slopes, gullies are found. Thus, gullying is restricted to the headwater areas and rill erosion to the valley sides. Occasionally, as in the area shown in the northeast of the extract, this erosion sequence in an individual drainage basin is completed downstream by deposition of sediment. Such a sequence emphasizes the importance of conservation in the headwaters for protection of the land downstream.

An index of soil erosion density was devised based on the product of the number and length of gullies per unit area. Data were collected from the erosion map for forty-two third-order drainage basins on: erosion density; drainage density, used as an index of runoff; relief; average maximum slope on the hillside above and contributing to the head of each first-order stream; average slope length between the head of each first-order stream and the divide; percentage area of the basin under tree crops, secondary forest and rain forest; relief ratio, defined as the difference in altitude between the highest and lowest points in the basin divided by the maximum basin length; and, as an index of basin shape, the lemniscate ratio, which relates maximum basin length (L) to basin area (A) in the form $L^2/4A$. Significant correlations exist between the soil erosion density index and drainage density ($r = 0.62$) and relief ($r = 0.33$). The best-fit regression equation, explaining 45 per cent of the variation in erosion density, is:

$$SED = 1.55Dd - 5.16K - 1.09 \qquad (4.8)$$

where *SED* is soil erosion density (km km^{-2}), *Dd* is drainage density (km km^{-2}) and *K* is the lemniscate ratio. This equation and the above correlations imply that to reduce erosion requires a decrease in runoff and modifications to the form of the catchment effectively to lower the relief and make it more pear-shaped and less square or circular.

This empirical analysis and the predictions of sediment yield based on p^2/P (section 4.1.3) enable erosion risk to be assessed at a drainage basin scale. A semi-detailed erosion survey also permits the risk to be assessed at a hillslope scale. A simple way of carrying out this assessment is to predict soil loss using the following equation (Kirkby, 1976):

$$Qs = 0.017Qw^2 \tan \theta \qquad (4.9)$$

where Qs is annual sediment yield (kg m^{-2}), Qw is annual runoff (m^3 m^{-2}) and θ is slope angle. The annual runoff can be estimated from the mean annual rainfall using typical rainfall–runoff ratios of 0.25 for rain forest, 0.35 for rubber and 0.75 for urban areas (Low and Goh, 1972). For a rainfall total of 2 052 mm, these give respective runoff totals of 513, 718 and 1 539 mm. These values convert to 0.513, 0.718 and 1.539 m^3 m^{-2}. Predicted sediment yields for four slope angles are given in Table 4.9. If it is assumed that the objective of soil conservation is to maintain soil loss at a rate equal to the rate of soil formation and that this rate is roughly equal to the erosion rate under natural vegetation, then, based on measurements by Douglas (1967a) in rain forest areas, a value of 2.0 g m^{-2} y^{-1} represents an acceptable sediment yield. Putting this value into equation (4.9) and predicting θ for the above runoff totals yields the maximum permissible slope angles at which acceptable sediment yields can be maintained. These are 3° for urban landuse, 13° for rubber and 24° for rain forest (Table 4.9). For rubber, conditions of mature trees and good ground cover are assumed.

Table 4.9 Predicted sediments yields near Kerdau, Pahang, Peninsular Malaysia

Landuse	Annual runoff (m^3 m^{-2})	Annual sediment yield (g m^{-2})				Maximum permissible slope*
		5°	10°	15°	20°	
Forest	0.513	0.39	0.79	1.20	1.63	24°
Rubber	0.718	0.77	1.55	2.35	3.19	13°
Urban	1.539	3.52	7.10	10.70	14.66	3°

* Based on acceptable sediment yield of 2.0 g m^{-2}.

Implications

In the light of the analysis of erosion risk, the following procedure for planning landuse and soil conservation strategies is recommended.

1   Using the slope map (Fig. 4.22) as a base, mark on an overlay the areas of land up to 14° and above 14° slope. This division represents a first shot at separating the land of lower slope, where the erosion risk from tree crop cultivation is acceptable, from that of steeper slope, where it is not.

2   Remove from the 0–14° slope area all the valley floors, including the freshwater swamps, as these are too wet for tree crops.

3   Mark the drainage system on the overlay and, using the Strahler system of stream ordering (Gregory and Walling, 1973), delimit the third-order drainage basins.

4   Remove from the 0–14° slope area all the headwater areas in square or circular third-order basins as having too great a risk of gully erosion to permit cultivation.

5   Add to the 0–14° slope area, all straight valley sideslopes between 15° and 19°, where tree crop cultivation is permissible

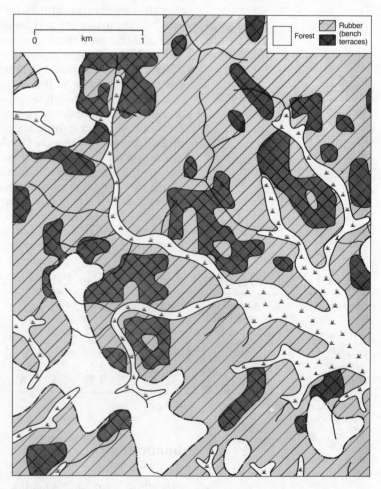

Fig. 4.24 Proposed landuse, central Pahang.

if the relief of the land can be effectively reduced. It should be noted here that the legal upper slope limit for cultivation in Malaysia is 18.5°.

6   Three main landuse regions are now shown on the overlay, namely swampy valley floors, areas suitable for tree crops, and areas to be maintained under rain forest. Conservation measures can be designed for each region (Fig. 4.24).

The areas assigned to rain forest must be kept under dense vegetation to minimize erosion. They comprise steeply sloping land and areas of gentler slope with flow convergence on the more erodible soils of the Durian Series. It may be possible to carry out well-managed logging operations using selective felling on land up to 24° slope but these should be undertaken only with the best erosion control. The natural erosion rate on land steeper than 24° is higher than the acceptable target value and this land should be protected as a watershed conservation measure. Attempts should be made to control erosion in the gullies shown on the erosion map by planting ground covers and shrubs and placing temporary dams across the channels.

In the areas devoted to tree crops it is essential that a dense ground cover is maintained using ground creepers if necessary. In addition, bench terracing should be installed on slopes between 13° and 19° to reduce the relief available for surface runoff development by shortening slope length. Normally, bench terracing is recommended in tropical areas on slopes above 7° (Sheng, 1972*a*). In order to give maximum protection against erosion and enable a reasonably continuous network of terraces to be laid out, it is advisable to bench terrace all land between 9° and 19° slope. The terraces should be graded to natural depressions on the hillsides which drain downslope to the rivers and freshwater swamps.

Few conservation measures are necessary on the valley floors although stream banks liable to erosion should be stabilized. The adoption of the measures recommended in the other areas will prevent the valley floors from being subjected to excessive sedimentation.

4.2.5 Summary

The maps produced in soil erosion surveys can be used in several ways. First, they depict the location and nature of erosion and distinguish between natural and accelerated erosion. Spatial variations in erosion intensity can be examined relative to the topographical, ecological and cultural information shown on the maps. Second, they not only indicate the location of an erosion problem but also enable the significance of that location in an erosion sequence to be appreciated. Often, complete sequences from erosion to deposition can be discerned in downslope, downstream or downwind directions. An understanding of such sequences is essential for predicting the broader, regional effects of changes in landuse or the installation of conservation works. Third, length, area and height measurements can be made from the maps. These, together with the knowledge of relief which the maps provide, are essential information for designing such conservation measures as terraces, grass waterways and contour bunds. Fourth, the maps contain much of the material required for assessing land capability. Thus, through erosion survey, investigations of the severity of erosion, land capability and conservation treatment can be better linked, aiding the soil conservationist in the delineation of areas suitable for arable farming, grazing and non-agricultural activities.

In addition to these four uses, the maps provide the foundation for estimating erosion risk and determining the chief factors influencing soil loss. To a limited extent these objectives can be achieved by employing simple indices such as gully density or a factorial scoring system similar to the one described earlier. More valuable, however, is to incorporate the data contained on the maps in models of the soil erosion system.

Chapter 5
MODELLING
SOIL EROSION

The techniques described in the last chapter enable the risk of soil erosion to be assessed. Before planning conservation work it is helpful if this assessment can be transformed into a statement of how fast soil is being eroded. Estimates of the rate of soil loss may then be compared with what is considered acceptable. In addition, it is useful if the effects on erosion rates of different conservation strategies can be determined. What is required, therefore, is a method of predicting soil loss under a wide range of conditions.

Most of the models used in soil erosion studies are of the empirical grey-box type (Table 5.1). They are based on defining the most important factors and, through the use of observation, measurement, experiment and statistical techniques, relating them to soil loss. In recent years it has been realized that this approach is less than satisfactory in meeting another important objective in formulating models, that of increasing our understanding of how the erosion system functions and responds to changes in the controlling factors. Significant advances have been made in our knowledge of the mechanics of erosion and the interrelationships between erosion processes. It is now appreciated that the hillslope erosion system may be broken down into rill and interrill erosion and that this requires two separate considerations of soil erodibility. Interrill erosion can be divided into that by rainsplash and that by overland flow. Each erosion process also requires separate analysis for the detachment and transport phases. Against this background, greater emphasis is being placed at present on developing white-box and physically-based models. Along with this goes a switch from using statistical techniques to employing mathematical ones frequently requiring the solution of partial-differential equations.

Before selecting an approach to modelling, the objective must be specified, whether prediction or explanation. This chapter is concerned only with predictive models since these are the most useful for practical applications. Different objectives exist for these, however, and this has implications

Table 5.1 Types of models

Type	Description
PHYSICAL	Scaled-down hardware models usually built in the laboratory; need to assume dynamic similitude between model and real world.
ANALOGUE	Use of mechanical or electrical systems analogous to system under investigation, e.g. flow of electricity used to simulate flow of water.
DIGITAL	Based on use of digital computers to process vast quantities of data.
(*a*) Physically-based	Based on mathematical equations to describe the processes involved in the model, taking account of the laws of conservation of mass and energy.
(*b*) Stochastic	Based on generating synthetic sequences of data from the statistical characteristics of existing sample data, useful for generating input sequences to physically-based and empirical models where data only available for short period of observation.
(*c*) Empirical	Based on identifying statistically significant relationships between assumed important variables where a reasonable data base exists. Three types of analysis are recognized. *black-box:* where only main inputs and outputs are studied; *grey-box:* where some detail of how the system works is known; *white-box:* where all details of how the system operates are known.

After Gregory and Walling (1973).

for how well the model must perform. *Screening models* are simple in concept and designed to identify problem areas. Usually it is sufficient if predictions are of the right order of magnitude. *Assessment models* need to predict with greater accuracy because they are used for evaluating the severity of erosion under different management systems and may be intended as design tools for the selection of conservation practices to control erosion. For this type of application, predictions of erosion are required for periods of 20 to 30 years either on an annual basis or as an annual average over the time span. The value of being able to predict the effects of a single storm is much less than is the case when, for example, assessing the effects of using a pesticide which may create a problem for only a few days following application.

Unfortunately, our understanding of erosion processes is greatest over very short time periods of only a few minutes. Whilst it may be feasible to apply this understanding to slightly longer periods, continuous extrapolation is not possible. A single event or storm is probably the upper limit to which relationships established for instantaneous conditions can be applied. Thus longer-term modelling can only be achieved by the summation of predictions for individual storms. The alternative is to develop models empirically using data collected on an annual or mean annual basis.

The scale of operation must also be considered. The detailed requirements for modelling erosion over a large drainage basin differ from those demanded by models of soil loss from a short length of hillslope or at the point of impact of a single raindrop. Scale influences the number of factors which need to be incorporated in the model, which ones can be held constant and (Table 1.2) which can be

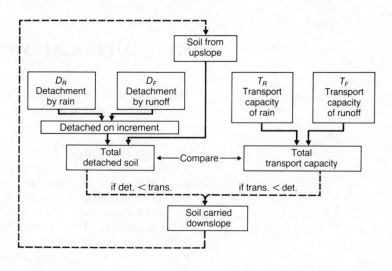

$D_R = k_1 A I^2$

$D_F = k_2 A S^{2/3} Q_w^{2/3}$

$T_R = k_3 S I$

$T_F = k_4 S^{5/3} Q_w^{5/3}$

Where A = area, I = rainfall intensity,

S = ground slope (sin θ),

Q_w = runoff

Fig. 5.1 Flow chart for the model of the processes of soil erosion by water (after Meyer and Wischmeier, 1969).

designated primary factors around which the model must be constructed.

Ideally, a predictive technique should satisfy the conflicting requirements of reliability, universal applicability, easy usage with a minimum of data, comprehensiveness in terms of the factors included, and the ability to take account of changes in landuse and conservation practice. It should also be tested with operating values close to zero and infinity to see whether it gives plausible results for extreme conditions. For practical purposes, however, the requirement to do so may be less important than its ability to perform well over a range of commonly experienced conditions. If a model is restricted in its application in this way, the limits of that range need to be specified. Because of the complexity of the soil erosion system, with its numerous interacting factors, the most promising approach for developing a predictive procedure lies in formulating a conceptual model of the erosion process such as the scheme presented in Fig. 5.1.

5.1   EMPIRICAL MODELS

The simplest model is a black-box type relating sediment loss to either rainfall or runoff. A typical relationship is:

$$Qs = aQw^{b.} \tag{5.1}$$

where Qs is sediment discharge and Qw is water discharge. Jovanović and Vukčević (1958), using data for sixteen gauging stations in Yugoslavia, established that $b = 2.25$ whilst, according to Leopold, Wolman and Miller (1964), b ranges in value from 2.0 to 3.0. The value of a is an index of erosion severity. Thus, in the Yugoslav example, $a > 0.000\ 7$ denotes excessive soil loss and $a < 0.000\ 3$ indicates a low erosion rate. Parsons, Apmann and Decker (1964) noted a fall in the value of b from 1.46 to 0.86 for the Buffalo River, New York, following channel stabilization. Since the latter study is based on sediment concentration (ppm) rather than sediment discharge (kg s^{-1}), these values should be increased by 1.0 to compare with the Yugoslav work. It is not always possible to establish the values with confidence. The relationship between sediment and water discharge may vary with the volume of runoff and therefore change seasonally. During a single storm the value of b often differs on the rise of a flood wave from that on the recession (Gregory and Walling, 1973). The main disadvantage of this type of model, however, is that it gives no indication of why erosion takes place.

Greater understanding of the causes of erosion is

achieved by grey-box models. These, as seen in Chapter 2, frequently culminate in expressing the relationship between sediment loss and a large number of variables with a regression equation. One example is equation (4.3) of Fournier (1960) relating mean annual sediment yield to rainfall, altitude and slope. Another is the following equation derived by Walling (1974*a*) which explains 96 per cent of the variation in suspended sediment yields (kg) of single storm runoff events for a small catchment near Exeter in terms of storm duration (*DUR;* h), peak runoff (*Qw;* 1 s^{-1}), peak surface runoff, defined as runoff less base flow (*Qq;* 1 s^{-1}), total surface runoff (*QQ;* mm), flow level preceding the hydrograph rise (*Qap;* 1 s^{-1}), and the day of the year (*DY*) evaluated as sine (radians) 2 π D/365, where D is the day of the year numbered from 1 January:

$$\begin{aligned} \log Qs = {} & -1.140\ 2 - 0.052\ 4 DUR - 0.776\ 4 \log_{10} Qw \\ & + 1.373\ 5 \log_{10} Qq + 0.989\ 2 \log_{10} QQ \\ & - 0.496\ 1 \log_{10} Qap + 0.269\ 3\ DY. \end{aligned} \quad (5.2)$$

Many of the variables included in this type of model are themselves intercorrelated and it is often difficult to identify the most important ones. Thus, although, as in this case, the equation may have a highly explanatory and, therefore, predictive value in a statistical sense, it has a low explanatory value conceptually. Walling (1974*a*) suggests using a principal components analysis to reduce the number of variables by identifying the redundant ones. This technique was employed successfully by Douglas (1968) in a study of suspended sediment yields of rivers in northern Queensland. Ten possible controlling factors were reduced to four basic factors: wetness, drainage basin morphology, lithology and terrain roughness. He derived the following equation to explain 82 per cent of the variation in annual suspended sediment yield (*SS;* m^3 km^{-2}):

$$\log SS = -8.73 + 3.81 \log_{10} QwA - 1.54 \log_{10} \text{R/L} \quad (5.3)$$
$$+ 4.82 \log_{10} DD,$$

where *QwA* is mean annual runoff (mm), R/L is the relief/length ratio of the drainage basin (ft mi^{-1}) and DD is drainage density (ft mi^{-2}).

A further problem of these empirical models is that the equations cannot be extrapolated beyond the data range with confidence, either to more extreme events or to other areas. Although equation (4.3) is often assumed to have general validity, its limitations were recognized by Fournier (1960) who also produced four other regression equations relating sediment yield to the p^2/P index for specific conditions of relief and climate (Fig. 5.2). Probably the nearest approach to an equation with world-wide applicability is that developed by Douglas (1967*b*) relating

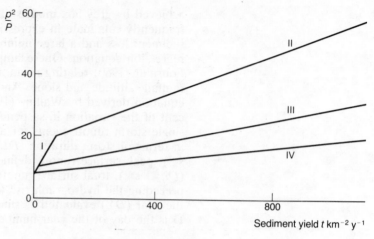

I   Low relief (mean valley floor gradient < 1:100), $p^2/P \leq 20$

   Sediment yield = $6.14 \dfrac{p^2}{P} - 49.78$

II   Low relief (mean valley floor gradient < 1:100), $p^2/P > 20$

   Sediment yield = $27.12 \dfrac{p^2}{P} - 475.40$

III   High relief (mean valley floor gradient ≥ 1:100), $P > 600$ mm

   Sediment yield = $52.49 \dfrac{p^2}{P} - 513.20$

IV   High relief (mean valley floor gradient ≥ 1:100), $200 \leq P \leq 600$ mm

   Sediment yield = $91.78 \dfrac{p^2}{P} - 737.62$

Method is inapplicable to areas where $P < 200$ mm

Fig. 5.2   Relationship between mean annual suspended sediment yield of rivers and rainfall aggressiveness (after Fournier, 1960).

mean annual suspended sediment yield (m³ km⁻²) to effective precipitation (PE):

$$Qs = \frac{1.631(0.039\,37PE)^{2.3}}{1 + 0.007(0.039\,37PE)^{3.3}} \qquad (5.4)$$

The numerator in this equation represents the direct erosive effect of rainfall whilst the denominator attempts to take account of the protective effect of the plant cover.

5.1.1 Universal Soil-Loss Equation

All the predictive equations discussed so far refer to drainage basins and do not provide a suitable technique for assessing soil loss from smaller areas such as hillslopes and fields. The first attempt to develop a soil loss equation for hillslopes was that of Zingg (1940) who related erosion to slope steepness and slope length (equation 3.12). Further developments led to the addition of a climatic factor based on the maximum 30-min rainfall total with a two-year return period (Musgrave, 1947), a crop factor, to take account of the protection-effectiveness of different crops (Smith, 1958), a conservation factor and a soil erodibility factor. Changing the climatic factor to the rainfall erosivity index (*R*) ultimately yielded the Universal Soil-Loss Equation (Wischmeier and Smith, 1962):

$$E = R.K.L.S.C.P., \qquad (5.5)$$

where *E* is mean annual soil loss (t ac^{-1} y^{-1}). The derivation of the factors in the equation is as follows.

R.   This is the rainfall erosivity index which is equal to the mean annual erosivity value (section 4.1.2) divided by 100:

$$R = \frac{EI_{30}}{100} \qquad (5.6)$$

K.   This is the soil erodibility index (section 3.2) defined as mean annual soil loss per unit of erosivity for a standard condition of bare soil, no conservation practice, 5° slope of 22 m length.

LS.   The factors of slope length (*L*) and slope steepness (*S*) are combined in a single index. A value of 1.0 applies to the standard 5° slope, 22 m long. The appropriate value can be obtained from nomographs (Hudson, 1981*a*) or from the equation:

$$LS = \frac{\sqrt{L}}{22.13} \quad (0.065 + 0.045S + 0.0065S^2) \quad (5.7)$$

where *L* is in m and *S* in per cent.

C.   This is the crop factor. It represents the ratio of soil loss under a given crop to that from bare soil. Since soil loss varies with erosivity and the morphology of the plant cover (section 3.4), it is necessary to take account of changes in these during the year in arriving at an annual value. The year is divided into periods corresponding to different stages of crop growth. For annuals, these are: (i) fallow – turn-ploughing to seeding; (ii) seedbed – seeding to one month thereafter; (iii) establishment – 1 to 2 months after seeding; (iv) growing period – from establishment to harvest; and (v) residue or stubble. For the last period, three options are considered: leaving the residue in the field without seeding an off-season crop; leaving the residue and seeding an off-season crop; and removing the residue and leaving the ground bare. For a given crop, separate ratio values are obtained for each period from tables (Wischmeier and Smith, 1978) summarizing data collected over many years by the United States Soil Conservation Service at their experimental stations. The values vary not only with the crop but also, for a single crop, with yield, plant density and the nature of the previous crop. The individual values for each period are weighted according to the percentage of the mean annual erosivity falling in that period and summed to give the annual value for *C*.

P.   This is the conservation practice factor. Values are obtained from tables of the ratio of soil loss where contouring and contour strip-cropping are practised to that where they are not. With no conservation measures, the value of *P* is 1.0. Where terracing is adopted, the value for strip-cropping is used for the *P* factor, and the *LS* index is adjusted for the slope length which represents the horizontal spacing between the terraces.

As the example in Table 5.2 shows, the equation is

Table 5.2   Prediction of soil loss using the Universal Soil-loss Equation

Calculation of mean annual soil loss on a 100 m long slope of 7° on soils of the Rengam Series under maize cultivation with contour bunds, near Kuala Lumpur.

Basic equation

Soil loss = $R \times K \times LS \times C \times P$

Estimating *R* (rainfall erosion index).

Method 1:	Mean annual precipitation (*P*) From Roose (1975a), mean	=	2 695 mm
	annual value of *R* .	=	$P \times 0.5$
	Rainfall erosion index (*R*) in US units	=	$2\ 695 \times 0.5$
		=	1 347.5
Method 2:	From Morgan (1974), mean annual erosivity	=	$9.28\ P - 8\ 838$
	(KE > 25)	=	$(9.28 \times 2\ 695) - 8\ 838$
		=	$16\ 171.6$ J m^{-2}
	Convert to Nm	=	$16\ 171.6$ N m m^{-2}
	Convert to kgf m	=	$16\ 171.6 \times 0.102$
		=	$1\ 649.5$ kgf m m^{-2}
	Multiply by I_{30} (use 75 mm h^{-1}; maximum value recommended by Wischmeier and Smith (1978)	=	$1\ 649.5 \times 75$
		=	$123\ 712.5$ kgf m m$^{-2} \times$ mm h^{-1}
	Convert to rainfall erosion index (*R*) in US units	=	$\dfrac{123\ 712.5}{173.6}$
		=	712.6
Method 3:	From Foster, Lane, Nowlin, Laflen and Young (1981), mean annual EI_{30}	=	$0.276\ P \times I_{30}$ kgf m m$^{-2} \times$ mm h^{-1}
		=	$0.276 \times 2\ 695 \times 75$
		=	$55\ 786.5$ kgf m m$^{-2} \times$ mm h^{-1}
	Convert to rainfall erosion index (*R*) in US units	=	$\dfrac{55\ 786.5}{173.6}$
		=	321.4

Best estimate: discard result from Method 3 which is rather low; take average value of results from Methods 1 and 2   =   1 030

Table 5.2 (*cont.*)

Estimating K (soil erodibility index)

From Whitmore and Burnham (1969), the soils have 43% clay, 8% silt, 9% fine sand and 40% coarse sand; organic content about 3%.
Using the nomograph (Fig. 3.2), gives a first approximation
K value   =   <u>0.05</u>

Estimating LS (slope factor)

For slope length (L) and slope steepness (S) in m and per cent respectively,

$$LS = \frac{\sqrt{L}}{22} \quad (0.065 + 0.045S + 0.006\ 5\ S^2)$$

For $L = 100$ m and $S = 12\%$ (approximation of 7°)

$$LS = \frac{\sqrt{100}}{22} \quad (0.065 + 0.045 \times 12 + 0.006\ 5 \times 12^2)$$

$$= 2.13 \times 1.54$$

$$LS = \underline{3.28}$$

Estimating C (crop practice factor)

According to Roose (1975*a*), the C value for maize ranges between 0.4 and 0.9, depending upon the cover.

During the three-month period from seeding to harvest, the cover varies from 9 to 45 per cent in first month, to 55 to 93 per cent in second month, and 45 to 57 per cent in third month.

Therefore, assume C values of 0.9, 0.4 and 0.7 for the three respective months.

Maize can be planted at any time of the year in Malaysia but assume planting after the April rains, allowing growth, ripening and harvesting in June and July which are the driest months. Land is under dense secondary growth prior to planting ($C = 0.001$) and allowed to revert to the same after harvest (assume $C = 0.1$).

Of the mean annual precipitation, 32 per cent falls between January and April inclusive, 10 per cent in May, 6 per cent in June, 7 per cent in July, and 45 per cent between August and December. Assuming that erosivity is directly related to precipitation amount, these values can be used to describe the distribution of erosivity during the year.

From these data, the following table is constructed.

MONTHS	C VALUE	ADJUSTMENT FACTOR (% R VALUE)	WEIGHTED C VALUE (col 2 × col 3)
January – April	0.001	0.32	0.000 32
May	0.9	0.10	0.09
June	0.4	0.06	0.024
July	0.7	0.07	0.049
August – December	0.1	0.45	0.045
		Total	0.208 32

C factor for the year = <u>0.028</u>

Estimating P (conservation practice factor)

From Roose (1975*a*), P value for contour bunds = <u>0.3</u>

Soil loss estimation

Mean annual soil loss	$= 1\ 030 \times 0.05 \times 3.3 \times 0.208 \times 0.3$
(t ac^{-1} y^{-1})	$= 10.6$
Convert to kg m^{-2} y^{-1}	$= \dfrac{10.6}{4.46}$
Mean annual soil loss	$= 2.38$ kg m^{-2}

normally used to predict soil loss. Since it was derived from and tested on data from experimental stations in the United States which, when combined, represent over 10 000 years of records, it is widely accepted as reliable. It has become the standard technique of soil conservation workers (FAO, 1965; Hudson, 1981a). The equation can be rearranged so that, if an acceptable value of E is chosen, the slope length (L) required to reduce soil loss to that value can be calculated. In this way, appropriate terrace spacings can be determined. Alternatively, the C value may be predicted and the tables searched to find the most suitable cropping practice which will give that value.

Although the equation is described as universal, its data base, though extensive, is restricted to the United States east of the Rocky Mountains. The base is further restricted to slopes where cultivation is permissible, normally 0 to 7°, and to soils with a low content of montmorillonite. Several attempts have been made to apply the equation more widely. Hudson (1961) has modified if for Zimbabwe and Roose (1975a) has investigated its applicability to the Ivory Coast and, in so doing, has concentrated on defining values for the C factor for crops which are not grown in the United States.

In addition to these practical limitations, there are theoretical problems with the equation. There is considerable interdependence between the variables and some are counted twice. For instance, rainfall influences the R and C factors and terracing the L and P factors. Other interactions between factors, such as the greater significance of slope steepness in areas of intense rainfall (section 3.3), are ignored. The rainfall erosion index is based on studies of drop-size distributions of rains which, as seen in section 3.1.2, may have limited applicability. One important factor to which soil loss is closely related, namely runoff, is omitted. To overcome this, Foster, Meyer and Onstad (1973) have suggested replacing the R factor with an energy term, W, which is a function of rainfall and runoff energy, defined as:

$$W = 0.5R + 15Qq_p{}^{1/3.} \tag{5.8}$$

where R is the rainfall erosivity factor, Q is storm runoff (in) and q_p is storm peak runoff rate (in h^{-1}).

The Universal Soil-Loss Equation was developed as a design tool for conservation planning but because of its simplicity, attempts have been made to use it as a research technique. Applying the equation to purposes for which it was not intended, however, cannot be recommended (Wischmeier, 1978). Since it was designed for interrill and rill erosion, it should not be used to estimate sediment yield from drainage basins or to predict gully or stream-bank erosion. Care should be taken in using it to estimate the contribution of hillslope erosion to basin sediment yield because it does not incorporate a sediment delivery ratio. Since the equation was developed to estimate long-term mean annual soil loss, it cannot be used to predict erosion from an individual storm. If applied in this way, it provides an estimate of the average soil loss expected from such a storm and this may be quite different from the actual soil loss. The equation should not be applied to conditions for which the factor values have not been determined and therefore need to be estimated by extrapolation.

5.1.2 Stehlík method

A method was developed by Stehlík (1975) for predicting the annual rate of soil erosion in Czechoslovakia. It uses the equation:

$$X = D.G.P.S.L.O \tag{5.9}$$

where X is the mean annual soil loss (mm y^{-1}). The other factors in the equation are derived as shown in Table 5.3. The results of this calculation are most sensitive to changes in slope steepness whereas those from the Universal Soil-Loss Equation are most sensitive to changes in the value of the C factor. In absolute terms, however, changes in slope steepness and slope length affect the predictions of both equations about equally. At a lower level of sensitivity, the Stehlík equation gives more importance to changes in the rainfall factor and less importance to changes in soil erodibility. An example of its use is presented in Table 5.4.

5.1.3 The Morgan, Morgan and Finney method

Morgan, Morgan and Finney (1984) developed a model to predict annual soil loss from field-sized areas on hillslopes which, whilst endeavouring to retain the simplicity of the Universal Soil-Loss Equation, encompasses some of the recent advances in understanding of erosion processes. The model was compiled by bringing together the results of research by geomorphologists and agricultural engineers.

The model separates the soil erosion process into a water phase and a sediment phase (Fig. 5.3). It requires fifteen input parameters (Table 5.5) and six operating functions (Table 5.6).

The sediment phase is a simplification of the scheme described by Meyer and Wischmeier (1969; Fig. 5.1). It considers soil erosion to result from the detachment of soil

Table 5.3 The Stehlík method for estimating soil loss

Basic equation

Mean annual soil loss = $D.G.P.S.L.O.$

D.   This is the climatic factor and is expressed in terms of the precipitation falling at intensities (mm min^{-1}) equal to or greater than $\sqrt{5t}$ where t is the duration of the rainfall (min). Values in Czechoslovakia range from 0.26 in the lowlands to 0.82 in the mountains. From data presented in Zachar (1982), its value may be estimated from mean annual precipitation (R) using the equation:

$$D = 0.001\ 4\ R - 0.38$$

G.   This is the petrological factor and assesses the rock type according to the permeability of its weathered debris.

Permeability of rock	Granulation of weathered debris	G
Low	Fine	1.5–1.3
Slight	Sandy loam	1.3–1.1
Moderate	Loamy sand	1.1–0.9
High	Coarse sand to stony	0.9–0.7

P.   This expresses the erodibility of the soil based on the percentage of particles smaller than 0.1 mm in size and the organic content.

Type of soil	Content of clay (<0.01 mm) [%]	Content of humus		
		<2%	2–3%	>3%
Sandy	<10	1.4	1.1	1.0
Loamy sand to sandy loam	10–30	1.5	1.25	1.75
Loamy	30–45	1.25	1.0	0.8
Clay/loam	45–60	1.4	1.15	0.9
Clay	>60	1.5	1.25	1.0

S.   This expresses slope steepness according to the relationship:

$$S = 0.24 + 0.106\ s + 0.0028\ s^2$$

where s is the slope in per cent.

Slope gradient [%]	5	7	9	12	15	20	30	40	50
Slope factor, S	0.35	0.65	1.0	1.45	2.0	3.0	5.35	8.61	12.02

L.   This is the slope length factor.

Slope length [m]	20	50	100	150	200	250	>300
Slope length factor, L	1.0	1.6	2.5	3.2	3.8	4.3	5.0

O.   This is the vegetation factor and is dependent upon the percentage cover.

Percentage cover	100	95	90	80	70	60	50	40	20	0
Vegetation factor, O	0.2	0.25	0.3	0.4	1.0	1.22	2.0	2.5	3.2	4.0

Source: Zachar (1982).

particles by raindrop impact and the transport of those particles by overland flow. The processes of splash transport and detachment by runoff are ignored. Thus the sediment phase comprises two predictive equations, one for the rate of splash detachment and one for the transport capacity of

Table 5.4 Prediction of soil loss using the Stehlík equation

Calculation of mean annual soil loss on a 100 m long slope of 7° on soils of the Rengam Series under maize cultivation with contour bunds, near Kuala Lumpur (compare with Table 5.2).

Estimating D

Mean annual precipitation (R)	= 2 695 mm
From Table 5.3, D	= 0.001 4 R − 0.38
	= 0.001 4 × 2 695) − 0.38
	= 3.39

Estimating G

Rengam Series is developed from underlying granitic rocks which weather into material rich in clays and sands and low in silts; this results in a loamy texture.

From Table 5.3, assume G = 1.1

Estimating P

From the textural characteristics given in Table 5.2, the soil is a sandy clay; assume that content <0.01 mm equals all the clay and half of the silt, i.e. 43% + 4% = 49%; organic content = 3%.

From Table 5.3, P = 1.15

Estimating S

From Table 5.3, for slope of 12%, S = 1.45

Estimating L

Assume contour bunds at 20 m spacing,
from Table 5.3, L = 1.0

Estimating O

For the conditions described in Table 5.2 and taking values of O from Table 5.3,

MONTHS	% COVER (average estimate)	O VALUE	WEIGHTED O VALUE (col 1 × col 3)
January – April	100	0.2	0.8
May	20	3.2	3.2
June	80	0.4	0.4
July	50	2.0	2.0
August – December	80	0.4	2.0
			8.4

Average weighted value = 8.4/12 = 0.7
O = 0.7

Mean annual soil loss	= 3.39 × 1.1 × 1.15 × 1.45 × 1.0 × 0.7
	= 4.35 mm y^{-1}

Convert to kg m^{-2} y^{-1} assuming bulk density for soil of 1.4 Mg m^{-3}

Mean annual soil loss	= 4.35 × 1.4
	= 6.09 kg m^{-2}

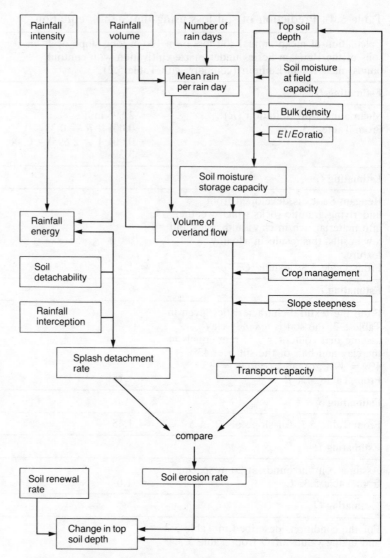

Fig. 5.3   Flow chart for the Morgan, Morgan and Finney
method of predicting soil loss.

overland flow. The inputs to these equations of rainfall
energy and runoff volume respectively are obtained from the
water phase.

The basic input parameter to the water phase is the
annual rainfall (R). Rainfall energy (E) is determined by
calculating the energy for a typical intensity of erosive rains,
using equation 3.1, and multiplying the energy term by the
annual rainfall amount. Guide values for rainfall intensity
are 11.0 mm h^{-1} for temperate climates, 25 mm h^{-1} for
tropical climates and 30 mm h^{-1} for strongly seasonal

Table 5.5 Input parameters to the Morgan, Morgan and Finney method of predicting soil loss

MS	Soil moisture content at field capacity or $\frac{1}{3}$ bar tension (% w/w).
BD	Bulk density of the top soil layer (Mg m^{-3}).
RD	Top soil rooting depth (m) defined as the depth of soil from the surface to an impermeable or stony layer; to the base of the A horizon; to the dominant root base; or to 1.0 m, whichever is the shallowest. Reasonable values are 0.05 for grass and cereal crops and 0.1 for trees and tree crops.
SD	Total soil depth (m) defined as the depth of soil from the surface to bedrock.
K	Soil detachability index (g J^{-1}) defined as the weight of soil detached from the soil mass per unit of rainfall energy.
W	Rate of increase in soil depth by weathering at the rock–soil interface (mm y^{-1}).
V	Rate of increase of the top soil rooting layer (mm y^{-1}) as a result of crop management practices and the natural breakdown of vegetative matter into humus.
S	Steepness of the ground slope expressed as the slope angle.
R	Annual rainfall (mm).
R_n	Number of rain days in the year.
I	Typical value for intensity of erosive rain (mm h^{-1}).
A	Percentage rainfall contributing to permanent interception and stemflow.
E_t/E_0	Ratio of actual (E_t) to potential (E_o) evapotranspiration.
C	Crop cover management factor. Combines *C* and *P* factors of the Universal Soil-Loss Equation to give ratio of soil loss under a given management to that from bare ground with downslope tillage, other conditions being equal.
N	Number of years for which the model is to operate.

climates such as the Mediterranean type. Where local information is available on typical intensities of erosive rain, it should be used in preference.

The annual volume of overland flow is predicted from the annual rainfall using an equation presented by Carson and Kirkby (1972). This assumes that runoff occurs when the daily rainfall total exceeds a critical value which represents the soil moisture storage capacity (R_c) of the soil–landuse combination, and that daily rainfall amounts approximate an exponential frequency distribution. The value of R_c is determined following Withers and Vipond (1974) from soil parameters and is adjusted for the effects of evapotranspiration using the procedure adopted by Kirkby

Table 5.6 Operating functions for the Morgan, Morgan and Finney method of predicting soil loss

Water phase

$$E = R\,(11.9 + 8.7\,\log_{10}I)$$
$$Q = R\exp(-R_c/R_o)$$

where

$$R_c = 1\,000\ MS.BD.RD(E_t/E_o)^{0.5}$$
$$R_o = R/R_n$$

Sediment phase

$$F = K\,(E\,e^{-aA})^b \cdot 10^{-3}$$
$$G = C\,Q_d\sin S \cdot 10^{-3}$$

E = kinetic energy of rainfall (J m^{-2}).
Q = volume of overland flow (mm).
F = rate of splash detachment (kg m^{-2}).
G = transport capacity of overland flow (kg m^{-2}).
Values of exponents: $a = 0.05$; $b = 1.0$; $d = 2.0$

(1976). Typical values for the soil parameters are given in Table 5.7 and those for the E_t/E_o ratio in Table 5.8.

The sediment phase is divided into the components of detachment by rainsplash and transport by runoff. Detachment is modelled as a function of rainfall energy using the well-established power relationship with a value of 1.0 for exponent b (Meyer, 1981a) and interpreting the intercept term k as an index of soil detachability (Quansah, 1981; Table 5.7). The relationship is modified to allow for the effects of rainfall interception of the crop, assuming that rainfall energy reduces exponentially with increasing interception with a value of 0.05 for exponent a (Laflen and Colvin, 1981). Typical values for interception are given in Table 5.8.

The transport capacity of overland flow is determined from an equation developed by Kirkby (1976) and depends on the volume of overland flow, the slope steepness and the effect of crop cover. The relationship between transport

Table 5.7 Typical values for soil parameters used in the Morgan, Morgan and Finney method of predicting soil loss

Soil	MS	BD	K
Clay	0.45	1.1	0.02
Clay loam	0.40	1.3	0.4
Silty clay	0.30	–	–
Sandy loam	0.28	1.2	0.3
Silt loam	0.25	1.3	–
Loam	0.20	1.3	–
Fine sand	0.15	1.4	0.2
Sand	0.08	1.5	0.7

Sources: *MS* – Brady (1974), Withers and Vipond (1974); *BD* – Hall (1945), Brady (1974); *K* – Quansah (1981).

capacity and the sine of the slope angle is similar to that derived theoretically in equation 2.17 (Morgan, 1980*a*). The value of 2.0 for the runoff exponent is close to the 1.7 power found in most sediment transport equations and has field support with annual data in the studies of Mou and Xiong (1980). The *C* factor values of the Universal Soil-Loss Equation (Table 5.8) provide a convenient expression of the crop cover managment factor.

The effects of soil conservation practices can be allowed for within the separate phases of the model. For example, the introduction of agronomic measures to control erosion

Table 5.8 Typical values for plant parameters used in the Morgan, Morgan and Finney method of predicting soil loss

	$A(\%)$	E_t/E_o	C
Wet rice		1.35	0.1–0.2
Wheat	43	0.59–0.61	0.1–0.2 (winter sown) 0.2–0.4 (spring sown)
Maize	25	0.67–0.70	0.2
Barley	30	0.56–0.60	0.1–0.2
Millet/sorghum		0.62	0.4–0.9
Cassava/yam			0.2–0.8
Potato	12	0.70–0.80	0.2–0.3
Beans	20–25	0.62–0.69	0.2–0.4
Groundnut	25	0.50–0.87	0.2–0.8
Cabbage/Brussels sprouts	17	0.45–0.70	
Banana		0.70–0.77	
Tea		0.85–1.00	0.1–0.3
Coffee		0.50–1.00	0.1–0.3
Cocoa		1.00	0.1–0.3
Sugar cane		0.68–0.80	
Sugar beet	12–22	0.73–0.75	0.2–0.3
Rubber	20–30	0.90	0.2
Oil palm	30	1.20	0.1–0.3
Cotton		0.63–0.69	0.3–0.7
Cultivated grass		0.85–0.87	0.004–0.01
Prairie/savanna grass	25–40	0.80–0.95	0.01–0.10
Forest/woodland	25–35 (coniferous & tropical) 15–25 (temperate broad-leaved)	0.90–1.00	0.001–0.002 (with undergrowth) 0.001–0.004 (no undergrowth)
Bare soil	0	0.05	1.00

Sources: summarized in Morgan, Morgan and Finney (1982).

Note: *C* values should be adjusted by the following ratios if mechanical soil conservation measures are practised:
contouring: multiply by 0.6
contour strip-cropping: multiply by 0.35
terracing: multiply by 0.15

will bring about changes in evapotranspiration, interception and crop management which will affect respectively the volume of runoff, the rate of detachment and the transport capacity.

The model compares the predictions of detachment by rainsplash and the transport capacity of the runoff and assigns the lower of the two values as the annual rate of soil loss, thereby denoting whether detachment or transport is the limiting factor.

The predictions obtained by the model are most sensitive to changes in annual rainfall and soil parameters when erosion is transport-limited and to changes in rainfall interception and annual rainfall when erosion is detachment-limited. Thus, good information on rainfall and soils is required for successful prediction (Morgan, Morgan and Finney, 1984). An example of the use of the model is presented in Table 5.9. Like the Universal Soil-Loss Equation, the model cannot be used for predicting sediment yield from drainage basins or soil loss from individual storms.

5.1.4 River basin models

The development and application of river basin models for runoff and sediment production in detail is beyond the scope of this book. However, some reference to them is necessary because they generally include a hillslope component. Indeed, the major challenge of developing a river basin model is finding a satisfactory way of linking the upland or hillslope phase with the lowland or channel phase (Bennett, 1974). Many river basin models have a deterministic structure and make use of mathematical relationships to describe the relevant hydrological and erosion processes. They are therefore a mixture of physically-based and empirical approaches.

The closest approach to a white-box model for sediment production in the Stanford Sediment Model (Negev, 1967) which is an addition to the Stanford Watershed Model used to predict runoff. The model is best illustrated as a flow chart (Fig. 5.4). Rainfall, overland flow and channel flow comprise the inputs to the model and outputs consist of sediment removed from the hillslopes by overland flow and sediment derived from rill, gully and channel erosion. The operation of the model is based on several functions, each of which describes a process in the erosion system and is expressed by an equation. Although the model applies to a drainage basin, separate models of the section covering erosion by overland flow have been developed (David and Beer, 1975).

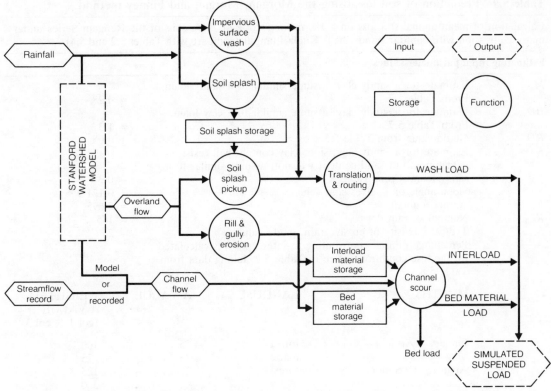

Fig. 5.4   Flow chart for the Stanford Sediment Model (after Gregory and Walling, 1973).

The work on the Stanford model has evolved into a river Basin Model for Water and Sediment Resource Assessment (Fleming, 1983). It consists of a runoff component, an erosion component and a routing component. The erosion component is used to compute the amount of sediment entering the river system from the hillslopes. It takes account of erosion as two processes, detachment and transport, and allows for selective erosion by particle size. The runoff component provides estimates of the volume of overland flow, used as input to the erosion component, and the total flow contributing to the river channels. It has the ability to deal with snow accumulation and melt. The routing component models the movement of water and sediment through the river channel system. Like many models of its type, it needs to be calibrated using recorded data on runoff and sediment yield. After calibration it can be used to predict future runoff and sediment production and the effects of changes in a catchment, such as in landuse. It can also be applied to neighbouring ungauged catchments of similar characteristics. With calibration, successful predictions of daily runoff can

Table 5.9 Prediction of soil loss using the Morgan, Morgan and Finney method

Calculation of mean annual soil loss on a 100 m long slope of 7° on soils of the Rengam Series under maize cultivation with contour bunds, near Kuala Lumpur (compare with Tables 5.2 and 5.4).

Estimating input parameter values

MS	Estimate for a sandy clay; assume similar to a sandy loam. From Table 5.7	= 0.28
BD	Estimate for a sandy clay; assume similar to a clay loam. From Table 5.7	= 1.3
RD	Guide value from Table 5.5	= 0.05
K	Estimate for a sandy clay; since clay content will resist detachment but sand content will not, assume similar to a sandy loam. From Table 5.7	= 0.3
S	Slope angle of 7° gives sine value	= 0.121 9
R	Annual rainfall	= 2 695
R_n	Number of rain days	= 185
I	Typical intensity of erosive rain; guide value	= 25
A	Percentage rainfall contributing to interception is calculated for landuse conditions given in Table 5.2, taking data from Table 5.8	

MONTHS	LANDUSE	A VALUE	WEIGHTED A VALUE (col 1 × col 3)
January – April	forest	25	100
May – July	maize	25	75
August – December	forest	25	125
			300

	Average weighted A value = 300/12		= 25
E_t/E_o	Calculation of time-weighted average value, taking data from Table 5.8		

MONTHS	LANDUSE	E_t/E_o VALUE	WEIGHTED E_t/E_o VALUE
January – April	forest	0.90	3.6
May – July	maize	0.70	2.1
August – December	forest	0.90	4.5
			10.2

	Average weighted E_t/E_o value = 10.2/12		= 0.85
C	Calculation of time-weighted average value, taking data from Table 5.8		

MONTHS	LANDUSE	C VALUE	WEIGHTED C VALUE
January – April	forest	0.001	0.004
May – July	maize	0.2	0.6
August – Dcember	forest regrowth	0.1	0.5
			1.104
	Average weighted C value = 1.104/12		= 0.09

Estimating rainfall energy (E)

From Table 5.6

$$E = 2\ 695\ (11.9 + 8.7 \log_{10} 25)$$
$$= 64\ 847\ \text{J m}^{-2}$$

Table 5.9 (*cont.*)

Estimating volume of overland flow (Q)

From Table 5.6

$$R_c = 1\,000 \times 0.28 \times 1.3 \times 0.05 \times 0.85^{0.5}$$
$$= 16.78 \text{ mm}$$
$$R_n = 2\,695/185$$
$$= 14.57$$
$$Q = 2\,695 \cdot e^{-16.78/14.57}$$
$$= 851.9 \text{ mm}$$

Estimating rate of detachment (F)

From Table 5.6

$$F = 0.3 \times (64\,847 \times e^{-0.05 \times 25})\, 1.0 \times 10^{-3}$$
$$= 5.57 \text{ kg m}^{-2}$$

Estimating transport capacity of overland flow (G)

From Table 5.6

$$G = 0.09 \times 851.9^2 \times 0.1219 \times 10^{-3}$$
$$= 7.96 \text{ kg m}^{-2}$$

Mean annual soil loss equals the lower of the values R and G
$$= 5.57 \text{ kg m}^{-2}$$

be obtained (Fleming and Fattorelli, 1984), provided sufficient detail is available on daily rainfall and seasonal changes in catchment conditions (Fleming and Fattorelli, 1981). Since annual runoff and sediment yield are determined by summation of daily predictions, an extensive file of input data needs to be compiled and a large number of daily simulations completed to obtain mean annual values.

5.1.5 Wind Erosion Prediction Equation

A similar technique to the Universal Soil-Loss Equation has been developed for predicting wind erosion (Woodruff and Siddoway, 1965) taking account of soil erodibility (I), wind energy, expressed by a climatic factor (C), surface roughness (K), length of open wind blow (L) and the vegetation cover (V). The equation is:

$$WE = f(I, C, K, L, V) \tag{5.10}$$

where WE is the annual wind erosion (t ha^{-1}), I is expressed in t ha^{-1} y^{-1}, L is in m, V is the quantity of vegetative cover expressed as small grain equivalent in kg ha^{-1} and C and K are dimensionless. The equation allows for interactions between the factors and so it cannot be solved by multiplying the values of the various factors together. Factor relationships are rather complex and predictions can only be obtained by using complicated nomographs or specially developed equations in a set sequence (Table 5.10).

Table 5.10   Prediction of wind erosion

Basic equation

$$WE = f(I, C, K, L, V)$$

Estimating *I* (soil erodibility index)

Values represent the potential annual soil loss (t ha^{-1}) for a level bare dry field near Garden City, Kansas. They have been determined from wind tunnel studies (section 3.2; Table 3.6) and may be estimated by knowing the percentage of dry stable aggregates larger than 0.84 mm in the soil. The values are adjusted by a term *Is* to take account of the steepness of the windward slope (Woodruff and Siddoway, 1965).

Estimating *C* (climatic index)

The index takes account of wind erosion as a function of wind velocity and soil moisture content. The former is expressed by the mean annual wind velocity (v; m s^{-1}) measured at a height of 9 m and the latter by the Thornthwaite *P-E* index. The index is then expressed as a percentage of its value of 2.9 for Garden City, Kansas. Thus:

$$C = \frac{v^3}{(P - E)^2}$$

where

$$P-E = 115 \sum_{i=1}^{12} \left(\frac{P}{T-10}\right)^{10/9}$$

where *P* is the mean precipitation for month *i* (in) and *T* is the mean temperature for month *i* (°F); a minimum value of 18.4 is adopted for *T*−10.

Estimating *K* (ridge roughness index)

The roughness of ridges produced by tillage and planting equipment is expressed by a roughness factor (*R*) calculated from

$$R = \frac{H^2}{I}$$

where *H* is the ridge height (mm) and *I* is the distance between the ridges. Values of *K* are expressed by

$$
\begin{aligned}
K &= 1 & R < 2.27 \\
K &= 1.125 - 0.153 \ln R & 2.27 \le R < 89 \\
K &= 0.336 \exp(0.003\,24\,R) & R \ge 89
\end{aligned}
$$

Estimating *L* (length of open wind blow)

The value of *l* is calculated as a function of field length (l; m), field width (w; m), field orientation expressed as the clockwise angle between field length and north (ϕ; rad), and wind direction clockwise from north (α; rad):

$$L = \frac{lw}{l\left[\cos(\frac{\pi}{2} + \alpha - \phi)\right] + w\left[\sin(\frac{\pi}{2} + \alpha - \phi)\right]}$$

Table 5.10 *(cont.)*

Estimating *V* (vegetation cover index)

The vegetation cover index depends on standing live biomass, standing dead residue and flattened crop residue. The original work on the effects of vegetation was carried out for flattened wheat straw and so all weights of living or dead vegetative matter need to be converted into flattened wheat straw equivalents defined as 254 mm tall stalks lying flat on the soil in rows perpendicular to the wind direction with 254 mm row spacing and stalks oriented perpendicular to the wind direction. Values of *V* for various crops are given in Woodruff and Siddoway (1965) and for perennial rangeland grasses in Lyles and Allison (1980). For a wide range of crops, an estimate of the flattened wheat straw or small grain equivalent weight of residue (*SGe;* kg ha^{-1}) can be obtained from:

$$SGe = 0.162 \, Rw/d + 8.708 \, (Rw/d\gamma)^{\frac{1}{2}} - 271$$

where *Rw* is the weight of the standing residue of the crop (kg ha^{-1}), *d* is the average stalk diameter (cm) and γ is the average specific weight of the stalks (Mg m^{-3}) (Lyles and Allison, 1981).

Applying the equation

Step 1:	E1	=	$I \cdot Is$
Step 2:	E2	=	$E1 \cdot K$
Step 3:	E3	=	$E2 \cdot C$
Step 4:	E4	=	$(F^{0.348\,4} + E3^{0.348\,4} - E2^{0.348\,4})^{2.87}$
	where *F*	=	$E2 \, [1 - 0.121\,8 \, (L/Lo)^{-0.382\,9} \, \exp (-3.33 \, L/Lo)]$
	Lo	=	$1.56 \times 10^{6} \, (E2)^{-1.26} \, \exp (-0.001\,56 \, E2)$
Step 5:	E5	=	$g \, E4^{h}$
	where *g*	=	$952.5^{(1-h)}$
	h	=	$\dfrac{1}{0.053\,7 + 0.943\,6 \, \exp (-0.000\,112 \, V)}$
Step 6:	WE	=	E5

5.2   PHYSICALLY-BASED MODELS

Physically-based models incorporate the laws of conservation of mass and energy. Most of them use a particular differential equation known as the continuity equation which is a statement of the conservation of matter as it moves through space over time. The equation can be applied to soil erosion on a small segment of a hillslope as follows. There is an input of material to the segment as a result of detachment of soil particles on the segment itself and an influx of sediment from the slope above. There is an output of material through the processes of transport by rainsplash and runoff. If the transporting processes have the capacity to remove all the material supplied, there is a net loss of soil to the segment. If the transport capacity is insufficient, there is a net gain of soil. Thus, for the slope segment:

$$\text{input} - \text{output} = \text{loss or gain of matter.} \qquad (5.11)$$

This approach, illustrated by a flow chart (Fig. 5.1), has been employed by Meyer and Wischmeier (1969) in a mathematical model designed to simulate soil erosion as a dynamic process. The operation of the model uses four equations to describe the separate processes of soil detachment by rainfall, soil detachment by runoff, transport capacity of rainfall and transport capacity of runoff. Using these equations and applying the model to consecutive downslope segments in turn, sediment can be routed and the pattern of erosion evaluated along a complete slope profile.

Because of its simplicity, the model has significant limitations. Steady-state conditions are assumed for rainfall intensity, infiltration rate and runoff rate. No other erosion processes and no weathering are allowed for. The soil is assumed bare of plant cover and no account is taken of tillage practices. Surface depression storage is ignored. There is no removal of material from the base of the slope and the altitudes of the highest and lowest points of the slope remain fixed through time. All these limitations are, of course, recognized by the authors.

Equation 5.11 can be applied to the continuity of mass for sediment transport downslope in the form:

$$dQs/dx = Di + Dr \qquad (5.12)$$

where Qs is the sediment load per unit width per unit time, x is the distance downslope, Di is the delivery rate of particles detached by interrill erosion to rill flow and Dr is the rate of detachment or deposition by rill flow. This relationship does not consider interaction between detachment and sediment load; this can be allowed for, however, by adopting the equation proposed by Foster and Meyer (1972):

$$(Dr/Dc) + (Qs/Tc) = 1 \qquad (5.13)$$

where Dc and Tc are the detachment and transport capacities respectively of the rill flow. This implies that if a flow is carrying less material than it has the capacity to transport, it will detach more particles to fill this capacity. Alternatively, if the sediment load is greater than the transport capacity, deposition will occur. The rate of deposition (Dp) is determined by

$$Dp = a(Tc - Qs) \qquad (5.14)$$

where a, a first-order reaction coefficient, $= \epsilon\, Vs/Qw$ in which Vs is the particle fall velocity, Qw is the rate of runoff per unit width and $\epsilon = 0.5$ for overland flow and 1.0 for channel flow. These equations provide the physical basis of a method of estimating sediment yield from field-sized areas which, together with elements of the Universal Soil-Loss Equation, forms the erosion component of the CREAMS model.

CREAMS is a field-scale model, developed in the USA, for assessing the chemicals, runoff and erosion arising from various agricultural management systems. It was designed as a state-of-the-art model to evaluate non-point source pollution and to investigate quantitatively the environmental consequences of different agricultural practices (Knisel, 1980). The model consists of three components: hydrology, erosion and chemistry. The hydrology component is used to estimate runoff volume and peak runoff rate, infiltration, evapotranspiration, soil water content and percolation on a daily basis. The erosion component provides an estimate of erosion and sediment yield including the particle-size distribution of the eroded material at the edge of a field, also on a daily basis. The chemistry component includes elements for plant nutrients and pesticides and gives estimates of storm loads and average concentrations of adsorbed and dissolved chemicals in the runoff, sediment and percolated water.

The erosion component has elements for overland flow, defined here as including interrill and rill erosion; channel flow, as in a terrace channel or grass waterway; and deposition of sediment where water is impounded, as at a fence line, road culvert or tile-outlet terrace. The overland flow element operates by estimating detachment by interrill and rill flow and comparing the quantity of detached particles with the sediment transport capacity of the rill flow to determine the rates of erosion and deposition. Interrill detachment rate (Di, g m^{-2} s^{-1}) is estimated from:

$$Di = 4.57(EI) \, (\sin \theta + 0.014) \, KCP \, (Qp/Qw) \qquad (5.15)$$

where EI is the storm EI_{30} value (mJ m^{-2} × mm h^{-1}), θ is the slope angle, Qp is peak runoff rate (m s^{-1}), Qw is runoff volume (m^3 m^{-2}) and K, C and P are factors from the Universal Soil-Loss Equation. The K value has units of g per EI_{30} as defined here and can be obtained by multiplying K values in American units by 131.7. The P factor is used only for contouring because strip-cropping and deposition in terrace channels are taken account of directly in the model. The rill detachment rate (Df; g m^{-2} s^{-1}) is estimated from:

$$Df = 6.86 \times 10^6 \, m \, Qw \, Qp^{\frac{1}{2}} \, (x/22.1)^{m-1} \sin^2 \theta \, KCP \, (Qp/Qw)$$
$$(5.16)$$

where m is the slope length exponent from the Universal Soil-Loss Equation and equals 0.5 for straight slopes; and x is slope length (m). Transport capacity (Tc; in units of mass time^{-1} width^{-1}) is calculated from a modification of the Yalin (1963) equation:

$$Tc = 0.635 \, \delta \, V_* \, Sg \, \rho_w \, d \, [1 - (1/\sigma) \log (1 + \sigma)] \quad (5.17)$$

where $\sigma = A\delta$

$$A = 2.45 \, Sg^{-0.4} \, Y_c^{0.5}$$
$$\delta = 0 \qquad\qquad Y < Y_c$$
$$\delta = (Y/Y_c) - 1 \qquad Y \geq Y_c$$
$$Y = \frac{V_*{}^2}{(Sg - 1) \, gd}$$
$$V_* = (\tau/\rho_w)^{\frac{1}{2}}$$
$$\tau = \gamma \, h \, S \, (n_b/n_c)^{0.9}$$
$$h = [Q_w \, n_b/S^{\frac{1}{2}}]^{0.6}$$

With this notation, V_* is the shear velocity, g the acceleration of gravity, R the hydraulic radius, S the friction slope, Sg the particle specific gravity, d the particle diameter, Y_c the critical lift force obtained by extrapolation of the Shields' diagram, ρ_w the mass density of the fluid, τ the shear stress acting on the soil, γ the weight density of water, h the flow depth for a bare smooth soil, n_b the value of Manning's n for bare soil, n_c the value of Manning's n for rough or vegetated surfaces, and Qw the discharge rate per unit width. Full details of these equations and those for using the channel and impoundment elements are contained in Foster, Lane, Nowlin, Laflen and Young (1981).

The CREAMS model can be operated without the need to calibrate it against observed data (Knisel, 1980) to provide a reasonable representation of the hydrological and erosion system and give a qualitative appraisal of the effects of different management strategies. It is not then a predictive model in absolute quantity (Knisel and Svetlosanov, 1982). For use as a predictive tool, calibration with locally available data is desirable. CREAMS is a daily simulation model and estimates of longer-term erosion rates are obtained by summation of the daily predictions. The erosion component can be operated in two ways: on its own using observed data for rainfall and runoff or in relation to the hydrology component, using the latter to predict values for EI_{30}, runoff volume and runoff peak from observed rainfall. Since the hydrology component uses a runoff predictor which estimates the median rather than actual response to a rainfall event, predictions of actual storm erosion cannot be obtained when the erosion component is operated in this way. When applied in this form to a hillside in Bedfordshire, England, the CREAMS model predicted erosion on ten occasions between May 1973 and July 1979 compared with 113 recorded events. Since five of the

Table 5.11 Comparison of observed mean annual runoff and soil loss in Bedfordshire with values predicted by the CREAMS model

Site	Runoff ($l\ m^{-1}$)		Soil loss ($kg\ m^{-2}$)	
	Observed	Predicted	Observed	Predicted
Silsoe, bare sandy soil, 11° slope, 2 plots	64.6		3.28	
	70.4	152.7	4.44	4.76
Silsoe, grass, sandy soil, 7° and 11° slope, 2 plots	18.6		0.15	
	14.4	43.6	0.31	0.04
Maulden, woodland, sandy loam soil, 16° slope	4.8	1.1	0.001	0.002
Woburn, oats, wheat, beans rotation, sandy loam soil, 7° slope	10.9	9.8	0.06	0.09
Ashwell, wheat, chalky soil, 10° slope	4.7	5.1	0.07	0.09
Pulloxhill, barley, clayey soil, 10° slope	1.1	0.6	0.07	0.10
Meppershall, wheat, barley rotation, clayey soil, 10° slope	5.6	4.2	0.05	0.27

predicted events were for days when no erosion occurred, it was concluded that the model could not be relied upon to predict erosion on the right days and certainly not to the right amount (Morgan, Morgan and Finney, 1985). Mean annual predictions of soil loss for several sites in Bedfordshire, however, were extremely good (Table 5.11). When the erosion component was used with observed values for rainfall and runoff, reasonable predictions of soil loss were obtained for 31 storms with a significant correlation ($r = 0.87$; $p < 0.001$) between the predicted and observed values (Morgan, 1980c).

Although CREAMS is only one of many hillslope models with a partial physical base, it is the most widely tested. Trials with the erosion component have been carried out in the USA (Foster and Lane, 1981), UK (Morgan, Morgan and Finney, 1985), Czechoslovakia (Holý, Svetlosanov, Handová, Kos, Váska and Vrána, 1982) and Lithuania, USSR (Kairiukstis and Golubev, 1982). Other slope erosion models are being developed for a range of spatial and temporal scales (Kirkby, 1971; Ahnert, 1976).

Physically-based modelling must be seen as the ultimate objective of research into soil erosion models. At present, the work is in its infancy. Many of the models are simplistic, few have been tested against observed data or have immediate practical value. When perfected, however, such models will provide a more comprehensive and widely applicable technique than empirical models for assessing the relative importance of the various factors of the soil erosion system. They will strengthen the basis on which strategies for conserving soil are designed.

5.3   MODEL VALIDATION

The success of any model must be judged by how well it meets its objectives or requirements. With a predictive model this means deciding on the time and space scale for which predictions are required and the level of accuracy. The failure of the Universal Soil-Loss Equation and, under some circumstances, the erosion component of the CREAMS model to predict storm erosion does not make them bad models since, as emphasized above, they were not designed to make this kind of prediction. If they successfully meet their objective of evaluating mean annual soil loss, they must be classed as satisfactory models. Also, in one of the examples given above of using the erosion component of the CREAMS model to predict storm soil loss, its failure was attributed to poor quality input data rather than to deficiencies in the model itself. Thus in making a judgement on the utility of a model, it is necessary to distinguish between failures due to misuse, those related to inadequate input data and those associated with the structure of the model or its operating functions. In the latter case, failure may result from poor conceptualization of the problem, omission of important factors or inaccurate representation of a particular element in the model by the operating function or equation employed. The solution is to modify or in some instances completely rethink the model.

The accuracy of model predictions is usually tested by comparing predicted with measured values and assessing the closeness of fit by correlation coefficients or an error statistic. In addition, a least-squares regression line can be fitted to the data and tested against the ideal conditions of the slope of the line being equal to 1.0 and the intercept value being zero. These types of tests, however, assume that a given level of error is equally important over the full range of values whereas for many purposes higher levels may be acceptable at very low values of soil loss. A predicted value for mean annual soil loss of 0.02 kg m^{-2} may be acceptable in relation to a recorded value of 0.002 kg m^{-2} for evaluating erosion-control strategies since neither value indicates an erosion problem. However, a predicted value of 20 kg m^{-2} against a recorded value of 2 kg m^{-2} would not be acceptable, since it would give a misleading impression of the severity of the problem. Both predictions may be unsatisfactory when modelling pollution. Use of a least-squares regression line assumes that there will be some error in the predicted value but not in the observed value or, if there is error in the latter it is very small in comparison with that expected in the predicted value. This assumption is certainly questionable and it may be preferable to recognize this and use a reduced major axis line instead (Kermack and Haldane, 1950; Till, 1973).

A simpler assessment of goodness of fit is to calculate the ratio of the predicted to observed value and see if it lies within a range predetermined as acceptable, for example, between 0.5 and 2.0. For some purposes, such as comparing the effectiveness of different conservation strategies, it may be enough for the models to predict realistic percentage differences in erosion between the strategies without giving absolute values.

Surprisingly little information is available on the utility of the models described in this chapter. The Universal Soil-Loss Equation will predict mean annual soil loss to within ± 0.5 kg m^{-2} 84 per cent of the time when applied to agricultural land in the USA (Wischmeier and Smith, 1978). No similar assessment exists on its applicability to other conditions. The Morgan, Morgan and Finney model was evaluated against criteria which viewed the prediction as successful if (1) the annual predicted and observed values were both less than 0.1 kg m^{-2}, both therefore indicating that there is no erosion problem, or otherwise (2) the ratio of the predicted to observed value was between 0.5 and 2.0. The model successfully predicted annual soil loss for 47 out of 67 sites in twelve countries, a 70 per cent success rate. When considering only those sites, 31 in all, where data on soil properties were based on field measurements, the success rate rose to 90 per cent (Morgan, Morgan and Finney, 1984).

When selecting a model, care needs to be taken to avoid its misuse, extrapolating it to conditions beyond those of the data base from which it was derived and being attracted to sophisticated schemes for which data input is difficult to obtain or which have not been properly validated. Despite the comments made above on the desirability of physically-based models, the present state of model development is such that a simple empirical model is often more successful in predicting soil erosion than a complex physically-based one which is difficult to operate and has been only partially evaluated. Often it is helpful to apply several models and see if a consensus exists in the predicted value. Since the success of all predictive techniques depends on how closely the estimated rates of erosion compare with those measured in the field, the development of models is necessarily tied up with data collection on rates of soil loss. Data are needed not only to test the performance of models but also, especially in the case of empirical models, to formulate them.

Chapter 6
MEASUREMENT OF SOIL EROSION

Data on soil erosion and its controlling factors can be collected in the field or, for simulated conditions, in the laboratory. Whether field or laboratory experiments are used depends on the objective. For realistic data on soil loss, field measurements are the most reliable, but because conditions vary in both time and space, it is often difficult to determine the chief causes of erosion or to understand the processes at work. The mechanics of erosion are best studied in the laboratory where the effects of many factors can be controlled. Because of the artificiality of laboratory experiments, however, some confirmation of their results in the field is desirable.

Attempts have been made to distinguish in concept between measurement and experiment (De Ploey and Gabriels, 1980). Measurements are used to collect information on rates of soil erosion whilst experiments are designed to lead to explanation. Since experiments generally also involve measurement, it is difficult in practice to separate the two.

Experiments are usually carried out to assess the influence of one or more factors on the rate of erosion. In a simple experiment to study the effect of slope steepness, it is assumed and, as far as possible, built into the experimental design that all the other factors likely to influence erosion can be held constant. The study is carried out by repeating an experiment for different slope steepnesses. A decision is necessary on the range of steepnesses, the specific steepnesses within the range and whether these should reflect some regular progression, e.g. $2°, 4°, 6° \ldots n°$, rising in intervals of $2°$ or $5°48', 11°36', 17°30' \ldots n°$, rising in intervals of 0.1 sine values. The range can be selected to cover the most common slope steepnesses or extended to include extreme conditions. A decision is also needed on what levels to set for the factors being held constant, e.g. slope length set at 5 m or 50 m.

Measurements are subject to error. Since no single measurement of soil loss can be considered as the absolutely correct value, it is virtually impossible to quantify errors.

However, they can be assessed in respect of variability. This requires replicating the experiment several times to determine the mean value of soil loss, for example for a given slope steepness in the above experiment, and the coefficient of variation of the data. This is frequently rather high. In a review of field and laboratory studies of soil erosion by rainsplash and overland flow, Luk (1981) finds typical values of 13 to 40 per cent for the coefficient of variation. Extreme values of soil loss, expressed by three standard deviations from the mean, therefore range from ±39 to ±120 per cent. To achieve a measurement of soil loss to an accuracy of ±10 per cent with 95 per cent confidence for three different Canadian soils required 6, 25 and 29 replications of the experiment. A decision therefore needs to be made between carrying out between 5 and 10 replications and accepting data with a coefficient of variation of generally between 20 and 30 per cent or completing 30 or more replications to obtain a more accurate assessment of erosion. Generally, the variability in field measurement is higher than that in laboratory studies (Luk and Morgan, 1981). Roels and Jonker (1985) found coefficients of variation of 20 to 68 per cent in measurement of interrill erosion using unbounded runoff plots.

Systematic errors can be built into an experiment, for example, by starting a laboratory study on slope steepness effects with the work on the gentlest slope, carrying out the rest of the study in the sequence of increasing slope steepness and following the same procedure for all the replications. In this way, the soil loss measured at a particular slope steepness can be influenced consistently by the amount of erosion which has taken place on the next lowest slope steepness in the sequence. Remaking of the soil surface between the separate runs of the experiment may not entirely eliminate this effect. Strictly, the order of the runs should be randomized but there is often a need to balance randomization with expediency and conduct some runs in sequence where it is very time-consuming to keep switching operating conditions. For instance, in a study of slope steepness effects involving simulated rainfall of several intensities, it is expedient to complete all the runs at one intensity before proceeding to the next because of the problems encountered in continually altering the operation of the simulator. It must be appreciated, however, that failure to randomize an experiment may limit the use that can be made of statistical techniques in processing the data. Certain techniques, such as two-way analysis of variance, assume randomness in the data.

Many experiments are designed to investigate the effects of more than one factor and therefore require a randomized factorial study. An example is a study of detachment of soil particles by rainsplash which might be conducted with four soil types, five slope steepnesses, four rainfall intensities and four replications, giving 320 separate runs. Although in theory no limits exist on the number of factors that may be incorporated in such an experiment, in practice it is usually limited by the amount of time and money available (De Ploey and Gabriels, 1980).

Experiments should be set up in such a way that they can be easily understood and repeated by other workers. Errors may then arise due to different operators (Luk and Morgan, 1981) or to the use of slightly different equipment, for example, different rainfall simulators (Bryan and De Ploey, 1983). Unfortunately, so few studies exist on these sources of error that their importance cannot be properly quantified at present.

A problem faced in many experiments is how much data to collect. For instance, if the objective of a study is to measure the total soil loss over a period of time, this can be achieved by collecting in bulk all the soil washed or blown from an area or by collecting the soil at regular shorter time intervals so as to obtain a total by summation of the loss in these time periods but also to learn about the pattern of loss over time. Restricting the measurement system to its bare essentials is usually cheaper and the data are generally easier to interpret. However, potentially useful information on whether most of the soil is eroded early or late in a storm is lost. This type of conflict is more apparent where the data are collected automatically, for example, by using an autographic rain gauge to measure daily rainfall. A decision then needs to be made on whether or not to analyse the shorter-period data.

There are no easy solutions to the problems of experimental design. Guidelines are to set up a study with clearly conceived objectives, define what needs to be measured and with what level of accuracy, and keep the experimental design simple. This often means relying on one's experience and initiative (De Ploey and Gabriels, 1980). This is also necessary in respect of the choice of techniques and equipment. In much soil erosion and conservation work, equipment has been built by individual researchers and is not commercially available. Thus it needs to be constructed anew and in some cases modified; sometimes entirely novel equipment needs to be designed and built. The result of this is that there is a multiplicity of methods and equipment in use for erosion measurement and little standardization. The techniques described in this chapter are restricted to those in most common use.

6.1   FIELD EXPERIMENTS

Field experiments may be classified into two groups: those carried out at permanent research or experimental stations and those designed to assess erosion at a number of sample sites over a large area.

Work at experimental stations is based on bounded runoff plots of known area, slope steepness, slope length and soil type from which both runoff and soil loss are monitored. The number of plots depends upon the purpose of the experiment but usually allows for at least two replications. Thus, to assess the rate of erosion under two crop types would require a minimum of four plots. The introduction of a soil variable would increase the number to eight, if two soil types were involved. The plot layout is designed to give a random pattern with respect to variables not directly related to the investigation (Fig. 6.1). The most common uses of runoff plots are to compare the effects of different crops or management practices and to determine rates of runoff and soil loss on major soil types in different climatic regions.

The standard plot is 22 m long and 1.8 m wide although other plot sizes are sometimes used. The plot edges are made of sheet metal, wood or any material which is stable, does not leak and is not liable to rust. The edges should extend 150–200 mm above the soil surface. At the downslope end is positioned a collecting trough or gutter, covered with a lid to prevent the direct entry of rainfall, from which sediment and runoff are channelled into collecting tanks. For large plots or where runoff volumes are very high, the overflow from a first collecting tank is passed through a divisor which splits the flow into equal parts and passes one part, as a sample, into a second collecting tank (Plates 1 and 2). Examples are the Geib multislot divisor (Plate 3) which samples one-fifth of the overflow and the Coshocton wheel which samples one-hundredth. On some plots, prior to passing into the first collecting tank, the runoff is channelled through a flume, normally an H-flume, where the discharge is automatically monitored. This flume is chosen because it is non-silting and is unlikely to become blocked with debris. Rainfall is measured with both standard and autographic gauges adjacent to the plots. A flocculating agent is added to the mixture of water and sediment collected in each tank. The soil settles to the bottom of the tank, and the clear water is then drawn off and measured. The volume of soil remaining in the tank is determined and a sample of known volume is taken for drying and weighing. The sample weight multiplied by the total volume gives the total weight of soil in the tank. If all the soil has been collected in the tank, this gives the total soil loss from the

EXPERIMENTAL PLOT LAYOUT

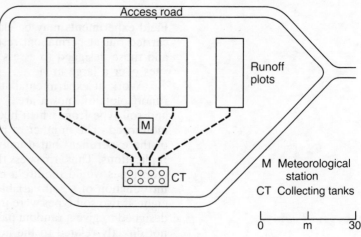

DETAIL OF COLLECTING APPARATUS

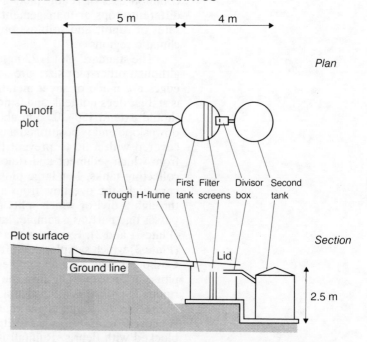

Fig. 6.1 Typical layout of runoff plots at a soil erosion and
conservation research station (after Hudson, 1965).

plot. For tanks below a divisor, the weight of soil in the
tank needs to be adjusted in accordance with the proportion
of the total runoff and sediment passing into the tank. Thus
for the layout shown in Fig. 6.1, the total soil loss from the
plot is the weight of soil in the first tank plus five times the

Plate 1   Apparatus for collecting runoff and sediment at base of erosion plots, Era Valley, near Firenze, Italy.

weight of soil in the second tank if a Geib multislot divisor is used. Full details of the equipment, manufacturing instructions for the divisors and operation of runoff plots are found in Agricultural Handbook No. 224 of the United States Department of Agriculture (1979).

Although the bounded runoff plot gives probably the most reliable data on soil loss per unit area, there are several sources of error involved with its use (Hudson, 1957). These include silting of the collecting trough and pipes leading to the tanks, inadequate covering of the troughs against rainfall, and the maintenance of a constant level between the soil surface and the sill or lip of the trough. Other problems are that runoff may collect along the boundaries of the plot and form rills which would not otherwise develop, and that the plot itself is a partially closed system, being cut off from the input of sediment and water from upslope.

An alternative method of measuring sediment loss and runoff has been developed by Gerlach (1966) using simple metal gutters, 0.5 m long and 0.1 m broad, closed at the sides and fitted with a movable lid (Fig. 6.2). An outlet pipe runs from the base of the gutter to a collecting bottle. In a typical layout, two or three gutters are placed side-by-side across the slope and groups of gutters are installed at different slope lengths, arranged *en echelon* in plan to ensure a clear run to each gutter from the slope crest (Gerlach, 1967; Morgan, 1977). Because no plot boundaries are used, edge effects are avoided. It is normal to express soil loss per unit width but if an areal assessment is required, it is necessary to assume a catchment area equal to the width of

Plate 2   Flume, depth recorder and sediment tanks on an
erosion plot, Hangchat, near Lampang, Thailand.

the gutter times the length of the slope. A further
assumption is that any loss of water and sediment from this
area during its passage downslope is balanced by inputs from
adjacent areas. This assumption is reasonable if the slope is
straight in plan. On slopes curved in plan, the catchment
area must be accurately surveyed in the field. This
disadvantage is offset by the flexibility of monitoring soil
loss at different slope lengths and steepnesses which the

Plate 3   Geib multislot divisor.

method provides. The gutters have been used, for example, to study soil loss along crest lines where the latter fall in altitude on spur-ends (Yair, 1972). The method also allows the measurement of erosion within an open system.

Because of their cheapness and simplicity, Gerlach troughs can be employed for sample measurements of soil loss at a large number of selected sites over a large area. They are thus suitable for erosion studies on a watershed scale. Small bounded plots of 4 m^2 and 8 m^2 have been similarly used by Soons and Rainer (1968) in New Zealand and Kellman (1969) in the Philippines respectively. With very small plots, however, it is not possible to study all the relevant processes. Plots of only 1 m^2 in size will allow investigations into infiltration and the effects of rainsplash but are too short for studies of overland flow. Field studies of soil erodibility in Bedfordshire using small plots showed that erodibility increased with increasing fine sand content in the soils. This reflected the selectivity of fine sands to detachment by rainsplash. The results did not accord with erodibility assessments at the hillslope scale which incorporated runoff effects (Rickson, 1985). Plots must be at least 10 m long for studies of rill erosion. Much larger plots are required for evaluating farming practices such as strip cropping and terracing. Although there is little uniformity on the size of plot for these types of experiment they are generally in the range of 6 to 13 m wide and 15 to 32 m long.

Investigations of sediment production must be carried out on hillslopes and in rivers if a full picture of erosion over a large watershed is to be obtained. In many cases, the amount of sediment leaving a drainage basin is less than that removed from the steeper sections of the hillsides. This points to deposition of material at the base of the hillslopes and on flood plains. Where more sediment leaves a basin than is contributed to the rivers from the hillslopes, the balance is derived from erosion of the river banks.

The selection of measurement sites to establish the pattern of sediment movement poses a problem of sampling. One approach is to divide a large watershed into sub-basins and set up recording stations on the rivers at the mouth of each. Discharge is measured automatically using weirs and water depth recorders. Suspended sediment concentrations are determined from water samples taken at set times with buckets or specially designed sediment samplers, or they are monitored continuously by recording the turbidity of the water (Gregory and Walling, 1973). Within each sub-basin, slope profiles are chosen at regular intervals or at random along the mid-slope line which lies half-way between the main river and the divide. Gerlach troughs are installed either randomly or in set positions on the profiles. A typical layout is shown in Fig. 6.2.

The standard runoff plot, described above, provides information on water erosion by rainsplash, overland flow and rills combined. Attempts to assess the relative contributions of each are based on separate measurements of splash erosion and rill erosion with the balance being attributed to overland flow. Splash erosion has been measured in the field by means of splash boards (Ellison, 1944; Kwaad, 1977) or small funnels or bottles (Sreenivas, Johnston and Hill, 1947; Bollinne, 1975; Gorchichko, 1977; Fig. 6.3). These are inserted in the soil to protrude 1 to 2 mm above the ground surface, thereby eliminating the entry of overland flow, and the material splashed into them is collected and weighed. An alternative approach is the field splash cup (Morgan, 1978; Fig. 6.3) where a block of soil is isolated by enclosing it in a central cylinder and the material splashed out is collected in a surrounding catching tray. A third approach involves the monitoring of painted stones (Kirkby and Kirkby, 1974) or radioactive tracers (Coutts, Kandil, Nowland and Tinsley, 1968; De Ploey, 1969) as they are splashed over a hillside. To be satisfactory, the method chosen must isolate the splash process from the effects of overland flow and provide data on the total amount of material detached from the soil surface and its direction of splash. The latter is needed at

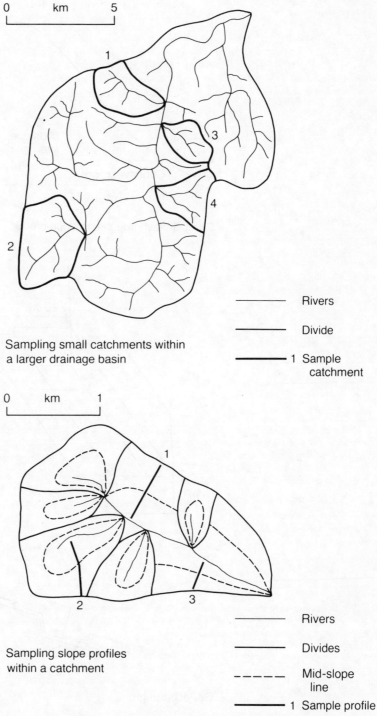

0   km   5

1

3

4

2

Sampling small catchments within
a larger drainage basin

——— Rivers

——— Divide

—■— 1 Sample
        catchment

0   km   1

1

2   3

Sampling slope profiles
within a catchment

——— Rivers

——— Divides

----- Mid-slope
        line

—— 1 Sample profile

Fig. 6.2 Sampling scheme and equipment for measuring soil
loss from hillslopes.

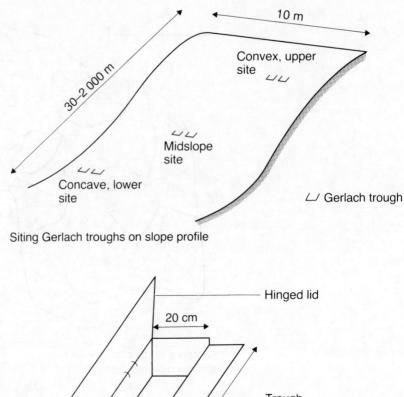

Siting Gerlach troughs on slope profile

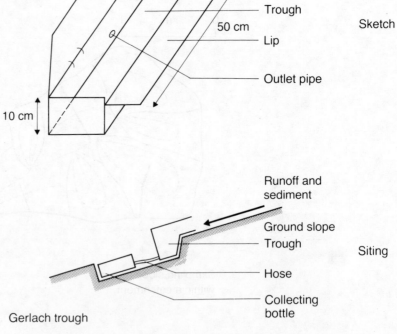

Fig. 6.2 (*cont.*)

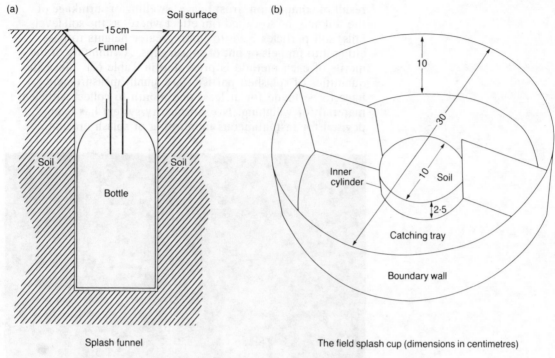

(a) Splash funnel

(b) The field splash cup (dimensions in centimetres)

Fig. 6.3 Methods of measuring splash erosion in the field (after (a) Bollinne, 1975; (b) Morgan, 1978).

Table 6.1 Merits of devices used for measuring splash erosion in the field (after Morgan, 1981*b*)

Method	Measurement constraints				Measurement requirements		
	Isolation of splash	Rim effect	Rainfall interference	Environ-mental acceptibility	Total splash	Direction of splash	Height/distance of splash
Splash boards	−	0	−	+	+	+	−
Bottles/funnels	−	−	+	+	+	−	−*
Marked stones†	−	0	+	+	+	+	+
Tracers	−	0	+	−§	+	+	+
Field splash cups	+	0	0	+	+	+	−

+ points favouring technique, 0 points of no strong influence, − points against technique.

* Gorchichko's device (1977) provides data on the height of the splashed particles.

† Not feasible for soil particles.

§ Radioactive tracers.

least in upslope and downslope directions to determine net transport downslope. The method should not interfere with the rainfall close to the ground and should not be affected by relative changes in the height of the device with respect to the level of the soil surface. Height changes occur as a result of compaction, frost heave, swelling or shrinkage of the soil and the so-called rim effect where, as the soil level falls, soil particles have to jump greater heights to pass either into funnels or out of splash cups. A summary of the merits of each method is presented in Table 6.1. Since the quantities of splashed particles are small, measurements have to be made for at least one month to collect sufficient material for weighing. No satisfactory system has been devised for instantaneous monitoring of splash erosion.

Plate 4   Bagnold sand catcher.

The simplest method of assessing rill erosion is to establish a series of transects, 20 to 100 m long, across the slope and positioned one above another. The cross-sectional area of the rills is determined along two transects. The average of the two areas multiplied by the distance between the transects gives the volume of material removed. By knowing the bulk density of the soil, the volume is converted into the weight of soil loss and this, in turn, is related to an area defined by the length and distance apart of the transects (Bučko, 1975). Since this method ignores the contribution of interrill erosion to the sediment carried in the rills and also depends upon being able to identify distinctly the edge of the rills, it is likely to underestimate rill erosion by 10 to 30 per cent (Zachar, 1982).

The techniques for measuring wind erosion are less well established than those for monitoring water erosion. Various types of traps are used to catch sand moving in a band of unit width. Horizontal traps consist of troughs set in the ground level with the surface and parallel with the direction of the wind. The trap is sometimes divided into compartments so that rolling and saltating sand particles fall into different compartments according to their length of hop. Alternatively, several traps of different lengths may be used. The horizontal traps have the advantage of minimum interference with the wind but a considerable length is required to collect a representative sample. Studies by Borsy (1972) in maize fields on sand dunes near Hajdúböszörmény in the Duna-Tisza interfluve region of Hungary show that in a storm of 2h 30 min, with a wind velocity of 8–10 m s^{-1}, the amount of sand collected in 10 cm wide horizontal traps varied from 218 g for 1 cm length, to 370 g for 50 cm length and 570 g for 1 m length. Vertical traps consist of a series of boxes placed one above the other so as to catch all the

Plate 5   Silsoe College sand trap.

particles moving at different heights. Many traps are unsatisfactory aerodynamically, however, because it is difficult to supply a sufficiently large exhaust to permit the free flow of air. The build-up of back pressure causes resistance to the wind which is deflected from the traps. By careful adjustment of the ratios between the sizes of the inlet, outlet and collecting basin, a satisfactory trap can be produced. Examples are those designed by Horikawa and Shen (1960), the Bagnold catcher (Plate 4) and the Silsoe College trap (Plate 5). The latter, mounted on a pole and attached to a wind vane, can swing into the direction of the

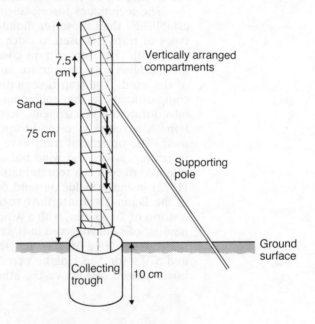

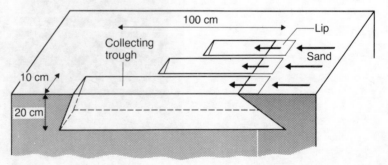

Fig. 6.4 Sand traps.

wind whereas a problem with both horizontal and vertical traps (Fig. 6.4) is that they cannot be easily reoriented as the wind direction changes. In order to collect sand from all directions, De Ploey (1977), at the Kalmthout Dune Station, near Antwerp, uses a circular collector consisting of a 60 cm high pile of 16 cm diameter cake tins.

6.2   LABORATORY EXPERIMENTS

The key questions arising with laboratory studies concern the scale of the experiment, the greater influence of boundary effects and the extent to which field conditions are simulated. It is not usually possible to construct a scaled-down version of field conditions, for example by using a small plot to represent a large hillslope, because scale-equivalence cannot be maintained in the other factors. Raindrop size and soil particle size cannot be reduced without affecting their basic properties or behaviour. It is therefore preferable to treat laboratory experiments as representative of a true-to-scale field simulation. Even so, many factors cannot be properly simulated and, unless the laboratory facilities are very large, nor can processes such as rill erosion and the saltation of soil particles by wind.

Many laboratory studies centre around the use of a rainfall simulator which is designed to produce a storm of known energy and drop-size characteristics which can be repeated on demand. The most important design requirements of the simulator are that it should reproduce the drop-size distribution, drop velocity at impact and intensity of natural rainfall with a uniform spatial distribution and that these conditions should be repeatable. The need to reproduce energy of natural rainfall for the intensity being simulated is generally regarded as less important (Bubenzer, 1979).

Many simulators are available but none accurately recreate all the properties of natural rain (Hall, 1970). There is insufficient height in a laboratory for water drops to achieve terminal velocity during fall so their kinetic energy is low. To overcome this, water is released from low heights under pressure. This results in too high an intensity and, because the increase in pressure produces small drop sizes, unrealistic drop-size distributions. The intensity can be brought down by reducing the frequency of rain striking the target area, either by oscillating the spray over the target or by intermittently shielding the target from the spray. Rainfall simulators are classified according to the drop-formers used. These range from hanging yard (Ellison, 1947) to tubing tips. either hypodermic needles or capillary tubes (De Ploey,

Savat and Moeyersons, 1976), and nozzles (Morin, Goldberg and Seginer, 1967). Meyer (1979) describes the various approaches to attaining the desired rainfall characteristics in simulators. The design, manufacture, assembly and operation of an effective simulator based on an osillating spray nozzle is presented by Meyer and Harmon (1979). Reviews of a large number of simulators produced by different researchers are made by Bubenzer (1979) and Hudson (1981*a*).

Studies of splash erosion are made in the laboratory by filling containers with soil, weighing them dry, subjecting them to a simulated rainstorm of preselected intensity and duration and measuring the weight loss from the containers on drying. In this way different soils can be compared for their detachability. The standard container is the splash cup first used by Ellison (1944), a brass cylinder 77 mm in diameter and 50 mm deep with a wire mesh base. A thin layer of cotton wool or sponge rubber is placed in the bottom of the cup which is then filled with the soil, oven dried to a constant weight and weighed. The soil in the cup is brought to saturation prior to rainfall simulation.

Where several soils are being compared it is important to treat them all the same. Moldenhauer (1965) recommends collecting them from the field under uniform moisture conditions, achieved by flooding the surrounding area with 100 mm of water and covering it with polythene sheet for 48 h before taking the sample; this gives a condition close to field capacity. The use of disturbed samples is justified for studies of soil erosion on agricultural land because the soil is disturbed anyway by tillage. When the samples are brought back to the laboratory they should be dried to a constant weight and split into 200 g portions. These are poured into the splash cups uniformly, reversing the direction of pouring regularly so that all the large aggregates do not accumulate at one end. Differences in the moisture content and surface distribution of stones and aggregates are the main reasons for the high level of variability in measurements of splash erosion in laboratory experiments (Luk, 1981). Although the soils are free draining, their condition does not represent the field situation because they are uncompacted and not subject to suction. Attempts to simulate soil suction on such a small scale have generally not been successful and it is difficult to achieve repeatable compaction. Fortunately, a soil in a loose saturated state is at its most erodible so laboratory experiments reproduce the worst conditions likely to result in erosion. Further processing of the soil, for example passing it through 4 mm or finer sieves to remove stones or break up aggregates, may reduce the variability in the splash measurements but can produce misleading results compared with small plot studies in the field (Rickson, 1985).

Where the target is in the form of a small soil plot, the rainfall simulator may be supplemented by a device to supply a known quantity of runoff at the top of the plot, instead of relying solely on runoff resulting from the rainfall. This facility is helpful for studies of the hydraulics of overland flow during rain (Savat, 1977). The set up at the Experimental Geomorphology Laboratory, University of Leuven, consists of an aluminium and plexiglass flume, 4 m long and 0.4 m wide, which is fed by water at its upper end through a cylinder with ten openings. The discharge is controlled by a tap through which water is pumped to the cylinder from a container; a constant water level is maintained in the container (Savat, 1975). The set-up at Silsoe College comprises a wooden soil tray, 1.0 m long, 0.8 m wide and 0.3 m deep, with a wire-mesh base. A layer of foam rubber is placed over the mesh to allow infiltration and the tray is then filled with the test soil. Upslope of the tray is a 0.2 m long wooden approach slope to which runoff is supplied as overflow from a tank. The discharge is controlled and can be varied by the rate of inflow of water to the tank. The approach slope is covered with a thin layer of sandy soil mixed with an adhesive to allow soil roughness effects to be imparted to the flow before it reaches the test soil. Both the Silsoe and Leuven flumes can be adjusted to different slope steepnesses.

The main problem arising with these small flumes is

Plate 6   Rainfall simulator based on design of Meyer and Harmon (1979)

that edge effects are difficult to eliminate. They can be reduced, however, by collecting the runoff and sediment washing off a narrow strip down the centre of the plot instead of collecting for the whole of the plot width. The short length of the flumes makes it difficult to simulate rill erosion although the supply of runoff at the top of the slope can be adjusted to simulate the effect of different slope lengths. Sediment can also be added to the runoff upslope of the test soil.

Almost all the basic studies on wind erosion have been carried out in the laboratory in wind tunnels: wind is supplied by a fan which either sucks or blows air through the tunnel. The tunnel is shaped so that air enters through a honeycomb shield, serving as a flow straightener, into a convergence zone, where flow is constricted, passes through the test section, and leaves through a divergence zone, in which flow is diffused. A mesh screen at the outlet traps most of the sand particles whilst allowing the air to blow through without a build-up of back pressure. Realistic wind profiles are produced only in the test section and the value of the tunnel depends on the length of this. Small tunnels, such as the one described by De Ploey and Gabriels (1980) with a test section only 1.5 m long, do not permit a satisfactory sand flow to be attained. At least a 15 m long section is required for this though Bagnold (1937) was able to simulate sand flow in a 10 m long tunnel by feeding a stream of sand into its mouth.

The principles of wind tunnel design are described by Pope and Harper (1966). Most of the tunnels used for soil erosion research are of the open-circuit type where air is drawn in from outside. These are cheaper than closed-circuit tunnels and afford easier control over the air flow in the test section because there is less upstream contact between the air and the boundary walls and therefore less turbulence. In a close-circuit tunnel (Fig. 6.5), the fan is located in a loft

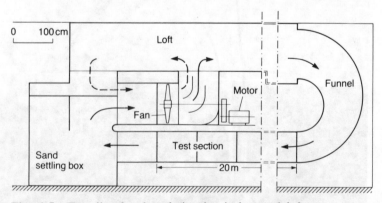

Fig. 6.5 Details of a closed-circuit wind tunnel (after Knottnerus, 1979).

above the test section and dry centrally-heated air is forced
downwards and into the test section through a funnel where
unwanted turbulence is likely to be induced. Closed-circuit
tunnels are less noisy and give good control over air
humidity. The latter is important because it influences the
critical wind velocity for particle movement. Studies with an
erodible sandy soil in the Netherlands show that the critical
velocity, as measured at 10 m height, is 8 m s^{-1} when the
relative humidity of the air is 50 per cent, but 13 m s^{-1}
when the humidity is 70 per cent (Knottnerus, 1979). Soil
trays are placed in the floor of the tunnel in the test section
and these can be removed for weighing. Thus the amount of
erosion can be determined by weight loss. Wind tunnels
have been used to simulate the effects of soil roughness,
especially that related to stones (Logie, 1982), and low-
growing plants (Knottnerus, 1976) at full scale but have also
been applied, using the principles of engineering similitude
(Woodruff, Fryrear and Lyles, 1963), to evaluating the
effectiveness of shelterbelts in scaled-down experiments
(Woodruff and Zingg, 1953; 1955).

6.3   COMPOSITE EXPERIMENTS

In recent years greater use has been made of field experiments
combined with rainfall simulation. They have now virtually
replaced the natural runoff plot as the major research tool in
the USA (Moldenhauer and Foster 1981). The
combination has the advantages of field conditions for soils,
slope and plant cover, all of which cannot be easily
reproduced in the laboratory, with the benefits of using a
repeatable storm. Reliance on natural rainfall means that
field experiments are long-term because the rains with the
intensities of most interest have return periods of once or
twice a year. Even when they recur, they are not true
replicates because the surface vegetation, surface roughness
and soil moisture conditions are likely to be different.

For studies with small plots, the rainfall simulators used
in the laboratory can be transferred directly to the field. The
rainfall simulator of Meyer and Harmon (1979) can be used
in this way for plots 1 m^2 in size (Plate 6) and a large
number of other portable simulators of this type have been
produced throughout the world. Larger simulators can be built
by joining together modules of the smaller ones. Thus
modules of a simulator built on the same lines as that of
Meyer and Harmon (Bazzoffi, Torri and Zanchi, 1980) have
been combined to form a field simulator capable of covering
a standard field runoff plot (Zanchi, Bazzoffi, D'Egidio and
Nistri, 1981, Plate 7). Alternatively, large-area simulators

Plate 7   Field rainfall simulator designed by the Istituto
Sperimentale per lo Studio e la Difesa del Suolo,
Firenze, Italy.

can be purpose-designed and built. The best example is the
rotating-boom simulator (Swanson, 1965; Plate 8) in which
nozzles are mounted on a series of spray booms positioned
radially from a central stem. The nozzles spray water from a
height of 3 m and the booms rotate at four revolutions per
minute to give a uniform distribution of rain over a circular
area large enough to accumulate two plots, 10.5 m by 4.3 m.

Plate 8   Rotating-boom rainfall simulator.

Less use has been made of field wind tunnels partly because, as noted above, small ones, which would be the most portable, are of limited value. Since experimental field plots are not used in wind erosion research, there is little demand for large permanently-sited tunnels. However, some large wind tunnels have been developed for field use (Zingg, 1951: Chepil, Woodruff and Zingg, 1955, Fryrear, 1984; Bocharov, 1984).

Chapter 7
STRATEGIES FOR
EROSION CONTROL

The aim of soil conservation is to obtain the maximum sustained level of production from a given area of land whilst maintaining soil loss below a threshold level which, theoretically, permits the natural rate of soil formation to keep pace with the rate of soil erosion. In addition, there may be a need to reduce erosion to control the loss of nutrients from agricultural land to prevent pollution of water bodies; to decrease rates of sedimentation in reservoirs, rivers, canals, ditches and harbours; and to limit crop damage by wind and by burial beneath water- and wind-transported sediments. In the longer term, erosion must be controlled to prevent land deteriorating in quality until it has to be abandoned and cannot be reclaimed, thereby limiting options for future landuse. Since erosion is a natural process it cannot be prevented, but it can be reduced to an acceptable rate. A decision on what that rate is must match the requirements for sustained agricultural production with those of minimizing the environmental impacts of erosion.

7.1   SOIL LOSS TOLERANCE

The maximum acceptable rate of erosion is known as the soil loss tolerance. Unfortunately, deciding the tolerance level theoretically as that at which the rates of soil loss and soil formation balance is not possible in practice. It is difficult to recognize when this balanced state exists and, although rates of soil loss can be measured (see Chapter 6), rates of soil formation are so slow that they cannot be easily determined. According to Buol, Hole and McCracken (1973), rates of soil formation throughout the world range from 0.01 to 7.7 mm y^{-1}. The fastest rates are clearly exceptional, however, because the average is about 0.1 mm y^{-1} (Zachar, 1982). Kirkby (1980) suggests rates of about 0.1 mm y^{-1} for the northeast USA and the UK,

0.2 mm y^{-1} for the loess soils of the Great Plains a
0.02 mm y^{-1} for the arid southwest USA. Evans (1981,
considers 0.1 mm y^{-1} as a realistic rate for the UK. Dunne,
Dietrich and Brunengo (1978) have estimated rates in Kenya
to range from 0.01 to 0.02 mm y^{-1} in the humid areas but to
fall below 0.01 mm y^{-1} in the semi-arid areas. If it is
assumed that all the soils in Iceland have formed in the last
10 000 years, the average thicknesses of silt loam profiles at
the present time would indicate rates of formation of 0.05 to
0.15 mm y^{-1} (Jóhannesson, 1960). Where deposition of
wind-blown material has added to contemporary soils, higher
rates of formation have been measured. In eastern Iceland
soil formed at rates of 0.12 mm y^{-1} between 1850 BC and
750BC; between AD 1362 and 1845, the rate was
0.27 mm y^{-1}; from AD 1875 to 1950, the rate increased to
1.11 mm y^{-1} (Thórarinsson, 1958).

A soil formation rate of 0.1 mm y^{-1} is equivalent to
0.1 kg m^{-2} y^{-1}, assuming a bulk density for the soil of
1.0 Mg m^{-3}. Such a rate, based largely on estimates of the
rates of rock weathering, may be a rather crude indicator for
the development of an agriculturally-productive soil. Bennett
(1939) and Hall, Daniels and Foss (1979) suggest that in soils
of medium to moderately-coarse texture on well-managed crop
land the annual rates of formation of the A horizon exceed
1.12 kg m^{-2}. This is because the subsoil can be improved by
incorporating it with the top soil during tillage and by the
addition of fertilizers and organic matter. It is against this
background that values for soil loss tolerance are set using the
criteria of maintaining an adequate rooting depth and avoiding
significant reductions in yield if the surface layer of soil is
removed by erosion (McCormack and Young, 1981). Thus, in
practice, the soil loss tolerance value is defined as that at which
soil fertility can be maintained over 20 to 25 years. A mean
annual soil loss of 1.1 kg m^{-2} is generally accepted as the
maximum permissible but values as low as 0.2 to 0.5 kg m^{-2}
are recommended for particularly sensitive areas where soils
are thin or highly erodible (Hudson, 1981*a*). Although these
figures represent targets which should always be aimed at, they
may be unrealistic for areas where erosion rates are naturally
high, as in mountainous terrain with high rainfall. Under these
conditions a target of 2.5 kg m^{-2} is more reasonable. Where
soils are deeper than 2 m, the subsoils capable of improvement
and reductions in crop yield are unlikely to be brought about
by erosion over the next 50 years or more, some scientists
favour increasing the soil loss tolerance to 1.5 or even
2.0 kg m^{-2} y^{-1} (Schertz, 1983). All of these soil loss rates apply
to field size units and they should be modified to take account
of the greater likelihood of deposition of sediment within
rather than loss from larger areas. Target values of 0.2 kg m^{-2}
and 2.5 kg m^{-2} have been suggested for areas larger than
10 km^2 and smaller than 1 ha respectively (Morgan 1980*d*).

These recommendations on soil loss tolerance are based solely on agricultural considerations. Much lower rates of less than 0.1 kg m^{-2} y^{-1} may be required to control pollution (Moldenhauer and Onstad, 1975) and those to minimize crop damage by water and wind will be between 0.01 and 0.1 kg m^{-2} y^{-1} depending upon the crop. Also there is concern that the generally recommended value of 1.1 kg m^{-2} y^{-1} is too high and that whilst this may maintain a productive A horizon over a 25- or even 50-year period, the overall soil depth will still be reduced. Over a 100- to 200-year period the surface material may become closer to a gravel than a farming soil (Kirkby, 1980). Current values for soil loss tolerance are thus highly dubious. A better guideline is likely to be an assessment of the rate of natural erosion in the area. Assuming that the environment is reasonably stable under natural conditions, this rate will be close to that of the rate of new soil formation by weathering. This guideline would lead to tolerance values of 0.1 to 0.2 kg m^{-2} y^{-1}, i.e. an order of magnitude lower than the current recommendations. In some areas the rates of natural erosion may be even lower at 0.01 to 0.02 kg m^{-2} y^{-1}.

7.2   APPROACHES TO SOIL CONSERVATION

From the discussion (Chapter 2) of the mechanics of the detachment and transport of soil particles by rainsplash, runoff and wind, it follows that the strategies for soil conservation must be based on covering the soil to protect it from raindrop impact; increasing the infiltration capacity of the soil to reduce runoff; improving the aggregate stability of the soil; and increasing surface roughness to reduce the velocity of runoff and wind. The purpose and use of various conservation techniques can be described under the widely-accepted headings of agronomic measures, soil management and mechanical methods (Stallings, 1957; Schwab, Frevert, Edminster and Barnes, 1966; Troeh, Hobbs and Donahue, 1980a). Agronomic or biological measures utilize the role of vegetation in helping to minimize erosion. Soil management is concerned with ways of preparing the soil to promote dense vegetative growth and improve its structure so that it is more resistant to erosion. Mechanical or physical methods depend upon manipulating the surface topography, for example, by installing terraces or shelterbelts, to control the flow of water and air. In a rather general way, mechanical methods can be viewed as an attempt to control the energy available for erosion, soil management as a means of increasing the resistance to erosion, and agronomic measures as a way of affording protection to the soil (Fig. 1.1).

Agronomic measures combined with good soil management can influence both the detachment and transport phases of the erosion process whereas mechanical methods are effective in controlling the transport phase but do little to prevent soil detachment (Table 7.1).

Table 7.1 Effect of various soil conservation practices on the detachment and transport phases of erosion (after Voetberg, 1970; Morgan, 1980*d*).

Practice	Control over					
	Rainsplash		**Runoff**		**Wind**	
	D	**T**	**D**	**T**	**D**	**T**
Agronomic measures						
Covering soil surface	*	*	*	*	*	*
Increasing surface roughness	–	–	*	*	*	*
Increasing surface depression storage	+	+	*	*	–	–
Increasing infiltration	–	–	+	*	–	–
Soil management						
Fertilizers, manures	+	+	+	*	+	*
Subsoiling, drainage	–	–	+	*	–	–
Mechanical measures						
Contouring, ridging	–	+	+	*	+	*
Terraces	–	+	+	*	–	–
Shelterbelts	–	–	–	–	*	*
Waterways	–	–	–	*	–	–

– no control; + moderate control; * strong control
D = Detachment, T = Transport.

When deciding what conservation measures to employ, preference is always given to agronomic treatments. These are less expensive and deal directly with reducing raindrop impact, increasing infiltration, reducing runoff volume and decreasing wind and water velocities. It is also easier to fit them into an existing farming system. Mechanical measures are largely ineffective on their own because they cannot prevent the detachment of soil particles. Their main role is in supplementing agronomic measures, being used to control the flow of any excess water and wind that arise. Many mechanical works are costly to install and maintain. Some, such as terraces, create difficulties for farmers. Unless the soils are deep, terrace construction exposes the less fertile subsoils and may therefore result in lower crop yields. On irregular slopes, terraces are varied in width, making for inefficient use of farm machinery, and only where slopes are straight in plan can this problem be overcome by parallel terrace layouts (Kohnke and Bertrand, 1959). Also, there is always a risk in severe storms with return periods of twenty years or more of terrace failure. When this occurs, the sudden release of the water ponded up on the hillside can do more damage than if no terraces had been constructed. For all these reasons, terracing is often unpopular with farmers.

7.3   THE ASSESSMENT SEQUENCE

Soil conservation schemes must be well designed if they are to reduce erosion effectively and not fail. Their ultimate success depends on how well the nature of the erosion problem has been identified and on the suitability of the conservation measures selected to deal with the problem and relate to the agricultural or landuse system so that farmers and others are willing to implement them. These features of an erosion-control strategy are just as important as the ability of the engineer to design the conservation structures required. Correct identification of the major areas of erosion and therefore the main sources of sediment is essential. Too often expensive conservation work has been carried out on areas of land which were thought to be important sediment sources but in fact were not (Perrens and Trustrum, 1984).

Soil conservation design most logically follows a sequence of events (Fig. 7.1) beginning with a thorough assessment of erosion risk using the techniques described in Chapter 4. This must be followed in turn by a sound landuse plan based on using the land for what it is best suited under present or proposed economic and social conditions, land tenure arrangements and production technology. The use must also be compatible with the maintenance of environmental stability. By adopting the land capability classification as the methodology for landuse planning, the distinction will be made between areas where erosion is likely to occur when the land is used in accordance with its capability and that which will arise from misuse of the land. Clearance of the land and its use for agriculture will increase the rate of erosion on most soils, even where the land is deemed suitable for farming. In this case, however, the erosion can be reduced to a tolerable level by suitable conservation practices. Where land is used for farming but is not suitable for that purpose, it will be expensive and difficult, if not impossible, to control the erosion. The land is likely to become so degraded that eventually it will have to be abandoned. The risk of permanent abandonment is greater in the semi-arid areas than in the humid areas (Perrens and Trustrum, 1984). Much money can be spent on sizeable conservation works in an attempt to reclaim land where soil degradation has become virtually irreversible. The low productivity of the land means that the investment can never be repaid and its justification is highly questionable.

Once the most appropriate landuse has been determined, soil conservation is a matter of good management of the land. This means that the erosion-control measures proposed must be relevant to the farming system. What is feasible on a 100 to 200 ha farm with a high level of mechanization in the Mid-West of the USA is unlikely to be applicable to a smallholding in the tropics of less than 0.5 ha (Perrens and Trustrum, 1984). The

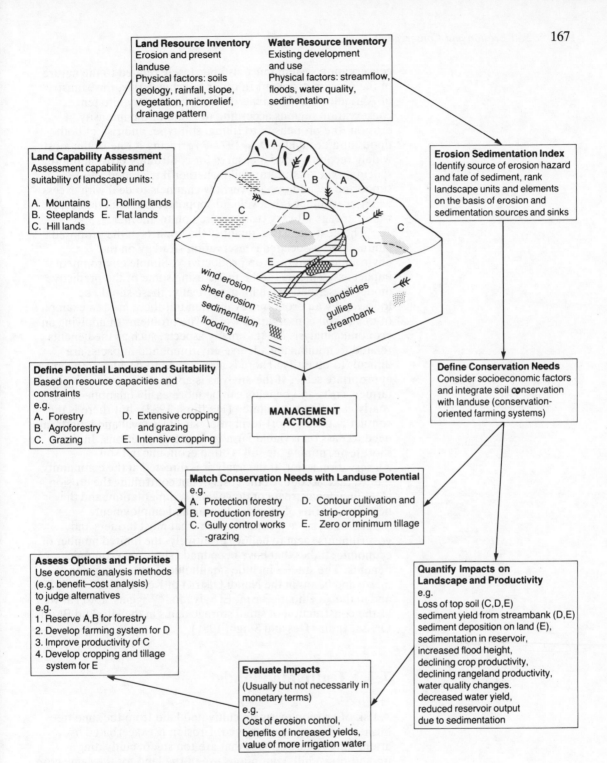

Land Resource Inventory
Erosion and present
landuse
Physical factors: soils
geology, rainfall, slope,
vegetation, microrelief,
drainage pattern

Water Resource Inventory
Existing development
and use
Physical factors: streamflow,
floods, water quality,
sedimentation

Land Capability Assessment
Assessment capability and
suitability of landscape units:

A. Mountains   D. Rolling lands
B. Steeplands E. Flat lands
C. Hill lands

Erosion Sedimentation Index
Identify source of erosion hazard
and fate of sediment, rank
landscape units and elements
on the basis of erosion and
sedimentation sources and sinks

wind erosion
sheet erosion
sedimentation
flooding

landslides
gullies
streambank

Define Potential Landuse and Suitability
Based on resource capacities and
constraints
e.g.
A. Forestry   D. Extensive cropping
B. Agroforestry   and grazing
C. Grazing   E. Intensive cropping

**MANAGEMENT
ACTIONS**

Define Conservation Needs
Consider socioeconomic factors
and integrate soil conservation
with landuse (conservation-
oriented farming systems)

Match Conservation Needs with Landuse Potential
e.g.
A. Protection forestry   D. Contour cultivation and
B. Production forestry   strip-cropping
C. Gully control works   E. Zero or minimum tillage
  -grazing

Assess Options and Priorities
Use economic analysis methods
(e.g. benefit–cost analysis)
to judge alternatives
e.g.
1. Reserve A,B for forestry
2. Develop farming system for D
3. Improve productivity of C
4. Develop cropping and tillage
   system for E

**Quantify Impacts on
Landscape and Productivity**
e.g.
Loss of top soil (C,D,E)
sediment yield from streambank (D,E)
sediment deposition on land (E),
sedimentation in reservoir,
increased flood height,
declining crop productivity,
declining rangeland productivity,
water quality changes.
decreased water yield,
reduced reservoir output
due to sedimentation

Evaluate Impacts
(Usually but not necessarily in
monetary terms)
e.g.
Cost of erosion control,
benefits of increased yields,
value of more irrigation water

*A, B, C, D, E refer to landscape units shown in the diagram.

Fig. 7.1   Sequence of events in planning a soil conservation
strategy (after Perrens and Trustrum, 1984).

conservation system must also be closely related to the nature of the erosion problem. In order to achieve this, the Ministry of Agriculture in India has divided the country into ten conservation regions according to climate, the intensity of erosion, the propensity to rilling, soil type, and risk of both floods and droughts (Das, 1977). Terracing is one of the most widely recommended measures for controlling erosion but the spacing, type of structure and whether it is graded and supported by additional overflow channels to deal with excess water or whether it is level and supported by small tanks for water storage all vary from one region to another.

The next stage is to quantify the impacts of the proposed landuse and associated conservation strategy on the environment and on crop productivity. Simple environmental impact assessments can be made using some of the predictive models described in Chapter 5. Ideally, these should be followed by an economic evaluation but there are few examples of this in soil conservation work. The problems of applying an economic analysis are that many aspects, such as the benefits related to minimizing adverse environmental impacts, are difficult to quantify. There is also a need to decide on the most appropriate scale. If the analysis is applied to an individual farmer, costs and benefits can be more easily quantified and yearly cash flows calculated (Hedfors, 1983), but there is the conflict between short-term interests of survival and long-term need to pass on a viable farm to future generations. In the short term, mining the soil is often economic but soil conservation is not. If the analysis is directed at the community it must take account of the costs of not controlling the erosion, including downstream or downwind sedimentation, and the benefits in terms of crop production and employment. Surprisingly, since it conflicts with what most farmers and governments seem to believe intuitively, the limited number of economic studies that have been made show net economic benefits. The studies include smallholder farmers growing maize and beans in the Nandi District of Kenya (Hedfors, 1983) and in the Acelhuate Basin, El Salvador (Wiggins, 1981) as well as the construction of small storage dams in the Hirakud Basin, Orissa, India (Das and Singh, 1981).

7.3.1 Cultivated lands

A risk of erosion exists on cultivated land from the time trees, bushes and grass are removed. Erosion is exacerbated by attempting to farm slopes that are too steep, cultivating up-and-down hill, continuous use of the land for the same crop without fallow or rotation, inadequate use of fertilizers and organic manures, compaction of the soil through the use of heavy machinery and pulverization of the soil when trying to create a seed-bed. Erosion control is dependent upon good management which implies establishing sufficient crop cover and selecting appropriate tillage practices. Thus soil conservation relies strongly on agronomic methods combined with sound soil management whilst mechanical measures play only a supporting role (Fig. 7.2).

Conservation strategies are aimed at establishing and maintaining good ground cover. The feasibility of this is determined by what crops are being grown and how quickly, under the local climatic and soil condition, they attain 40 to 50 per cent canopy cover. From the results of the studies discussed in Chapter 3, it is clear that the crops which are least effective in protecting the soil are those in rows, tall tree crops and low-growing crops with large leaves. Continuous production of cereals, rubber, oil palm, grape vines, maize, sugar beet, broccoli and Brussels sprouts can produce moderate to serious erosion problems. Rapid growth of crops is important, particularly in those parts of the world where erosion risk is high at and immediately after planting, for example where the first rains of a wet season are highly erosive. With timely planting of sorghum early in the rainy season followed by a crop of good yield, 40 per cent canopy cover can be obtained by about 20 July in the Indore area of India. With late planting and a poor yield, a 40 per cent cover is not attained until 30 September, thereby extending the period of erosion risk throughout the summer monsoon (Shaxson, 1981). Aina, Lal and Taylor (1977) found that the time to establish 50 per cent canopy cover from the date of

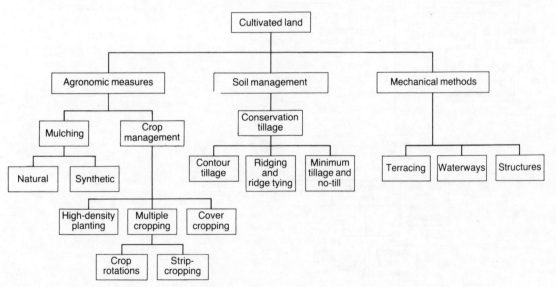

Fig. 7.2 Soil conservation strategies for cultivated land (after El-Swaify, Dangler and Armstrong, 1982).

planting varied from 38 days for soya beans to 46 days for
pigeon peas and 63 days for cassava. Soil loss under these
crops was proportional to the time needed for the canopy
cover to develop. Thus quick-growing crops may be viewed as
soil-conserving crops. Unfortunately, the crops which present
erosion problems are also those of considerable value either
for industrial purposes or as food crops upon which the
survival of the world's population depends. The challenge is to
develop soil conservation strategies that will allow these crops
to be grown on a sustained basis.

7.3.2 Pasture lands

These comprise areas of improved pasture where grasses and
legumes suited to the local soil and climatic conditions are
planted and managed by regular applications of lime,

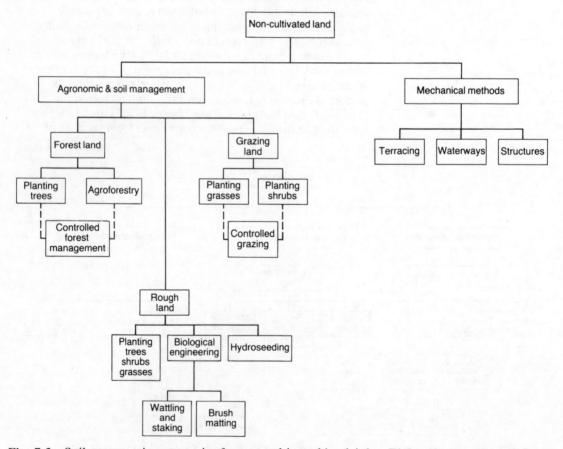

Fig. 7.3   Soil conservation strategies for non-cultivated land (after El-Swaify, Dangler and
Armstrong, 1982).

fertilizers and organic manures, as well as areas of rangeland composed of native grasses and shrubs. Since grass provides a dense cover, close to the soil surface, it is a good protector of the land against erosion. Erosion problems arise only when this cover is removed through overgrazing, although they can be exacerbated by drought and excessive burning. Erosion control depends largely on the use of agronomic measures (Fig. 7.3). These are directed at determining and maintaining suitable stocking rates, although this can be difficult if not impossible in areas where people attach cultural and social value to the size of their herds (Hudson, 1981*b*), and at planting erosion-resistant grasses and shrubs. The latter are characterized by vigorous growth, tolerance to drought and poor soils, palatability to livestock and resistance to the physical effects of trampling. Specialized measures designed to increase the resistance of the soil may be required around field gates, watering points and salt boxes.

7.3.3 Forest lands

Forests provide excellent protection of the soil against erosion. They maintain high rates of evapotranspiration, interception and infiltration and therefore generate only small quantities of runoff. Low runoff rates and the protective role of the litter layer on the surface of the soil produce low erosion rates. Increases in erosion occur where the land is permanently or, in the case of shifting cultivation, temporarily cleared for agriculture. Whilst the forest cover remains largely intact, the most important erosion problems are associated with cropping of the trees for firewood; destruction of the trees and surrounding shrub and ground cover by grazing; and logging operations.

An estimated 40 per cent of the world's population use wood as the primary fuel. In the rural areas of Tanzania and Thailand, consumption ranges from 1 to 2 tonnes per capita each year (Brown, 1981). In Sudan, Colombia, Ethiopia, Nigeria and Indonesia, fuel wood accounts for 80 per cent or more of annual timber removals. This rate of removal can lead to large-scale deforestation, followed by the washing and blowing away of the soil. Afforestation schemes which include rapid-growing tree species that can be cropped for firewood are an important feature of erosion-control strategies (Fig. 7.3).

Livestock grazing is frequently detrimental to the survival of forests. The animals trample and compact the soil, injure roots close to the surface and browse on tree seedlings. At the time of settlement during the years AD 875 to 930 about 40 000 km^2 of Iceland or 39 per cent of its land surface was covered with vegetation, mainly low-growing birch forest with a luxuriant undergrowth of forbs and grasses (Thorsteinsson, Ólafsson and van Dyne, 1971). The productivity of the ground vegetation in these forests is about 70 per cent higher than the average for other grazing areas in the country (Thorsteinsson, 1980*a*) so they provide the best grazing lands. Overgrazing and stripping of the bark from the trees has prevented the regeneration of the forest, much of which has also been cut for fuel. As a result the area under forest has been reduced by 95 per cent and trees now cover only 1 per cent of the total area of the country (Sveinbjörnsson, 1979; Sigurbjörnsson, 1980).

Logging causes limited disturbance because erosion is confined to the area of land where the trees have been removed. With good management, the vegetation cover regenerates quickly so that high erosion rates are restricted to the first and sometimes the second and third years after felling. The level of disturbance is related to the method of clearance. Studies of three practices in Nigeria (Lal, 1981*b*) showed that more erosion followed mechanical clearance using crawler tractors with tree-pusher and root-rake attachments than manual clearance using chain saws. Least erosion followed manual clearance with machete and axe. Erosion immediately after clearance is generally associated with surface runoff. Another effect of forest removal, however, is the gradual loss of shear strength of the soil following the decay of the root mat (O'Loughlin, 1974; O'Loughlin and Watson, 1979). This induces a risk of landslides which is greatest about five years after clearance (Bishop and Stevens, 1964) although some researchers suggest a slower deterioration with maximum slide hazard only being reached fifteen years after logging (Rice and Krammes, 1970).

The main erosion problems in logged areas are associated with skid trails and roads which are frequently areas of bare compacted soil. Also the cut and fill slopes on roadsides are often steeper than the angle of repose of the soil and are subject to landslides. As reported by Swanson and Dyrness (1975), who measured 230 Mg m^{-2} on a roadside in western Oregon, USA, annual erosion rates from logging roads are very high. Roads, tracks and paths can be major contributors to total sediment yield. They contribute between 15 and 35 per cent in catchments devoted to agriculture in the Aberdare Mountains, Kenya (Dunne, 1979) but in a forested area where the sediment yield on the surrounding land is much lower, their contribution will be greater. Skid trails in an area of logged rain forest in northern Queensland, Australia, occupy 18 to 21 per cent of the area and 70 per cent of this is bare ground (Gilmour, 1977). By implication, these will also be major contributors to sediment yield. A third source of sediment, widely reported from afforestation schemes in Wales (Newson, 1980; Robinson and Blyth, 1982; Murgatroyd and Ternan, 1983), occurs where the land has to be drained by surface ditches and the banks of these erode as the channels adjust from their relatively deep and narrow form when cut to a shallower, wide one. In addition, the increased runoff from the ditches causes bank erosion in the rivers immediately downstream.

In recent years much attention has been given to promoting agroforestry whereby crops and livestock are combined with the planting of trees (Lundgren and Nair, 1985). The trees can provide one or more of the local requirements for timber, fuel, fruits, nuts or fodder. They also provide shelter for crops, which may increase their yield, and shade for livestock (Wenner, 1981).

7.3.4 Rough lands

Areas of rough ground remaining in their natural habitats because they are too marginal for other forms of landuse include hilly and mountainous terrain with shallow stony soils and steep slopes, alpine grasslands, arctic tundras and sand dunes. Since they are often areas of spectacular scenery, they attract recreational use. Their marginality, however, means that they are sensitive to any disturbance, and their ability to withstand recreational impacts is low. The main problems of land degradation are associated with footpaths (Coleman, 1981), tracks created by horses and motor cycles (Weaver and Dale, 1978) and off-road vehicles (Iverson, 1980), and very intensive use as in car parks and on camp sites. Overuse of paths and tracks results in a reduction in overall vegetation cover, modifications to species composition because some resist trampling better than others, compaction of the soil and changes in soil moisture. The latter may increase in dry soils following compaction but decrease in wet areas.

Approaches to controlling erosion range from exclusion of people, appropriate in areas of special scientific interest or in nature reserves, to use of erosion-resistant plant species, supported where necessary by artificially strengthening or reinforcing footpaths. Although few plants can withstand prolonged and heavy pressure from walkers and horses, studies of footpath erosion in the English Lake District show that grasses, including *Nardus stricta*, *Agrostis* spp. and *Festuca* supp., resist trampling much better than *Calluna* heathland (Coleman, 1981), *Poa pratensis* and *Festuca idahoensis* grassland was found to suffer less from the effects of hikers, motor cyclists and horse riders than a *Pinus albicaulis* forest with shrubby understorey of *Vaccinium scoparium* in the northern Rocky Mountains, Montana, USA (Weaver and Dale, 1978). One way of comparing the vulnerability of different habitats to trampling is to apply wear by walking and determine the number of passes they can withstand before the plant cover is reduced from about 100 to 50 per cent. Sand dune pasture can withstand between 1 100 and 1 800 passes, alpine plant communities less than 60 and arctic tundra only about 8 passes (Liddle, 1973). Trampling of a grass cover on a clay soil with a moisture content close to field capacity resulted in runoff rising rapidly between 0 and 50 passes, then levelling off before rising again between 700 and 900 passes. The rate of soil loss, however, increased linearly with increasing number of passes. Since patches of bare ground did not appear until 250 passes and even after 900 passes between 25 and 50 per cent cover remained, the results imply that the critical period when increased runoff and erosion are initiated occurs before any decrease in the vegetation cover is seen (Quinn, Morgan and Smith, 1980).

7.3.5 Urban areas

Urban development follows a sequence of events which begins with the clearance of the natural vegetation or agricultural landuse, moves into a period of construction when the land is stripped to bare soil, and finishes with the creation of the built-up area with impervious surfaces of streets, pavements, roofs, gutters and sewers (Wolman, 1967). The construction phase is characterized by intensive erosion for a short period, often with gully formation and a large sediment yield to the rivers. The final phase results in a decrease in infiltration and an increase in runoff which can cause bank erosion in the rivers downstream of the urban area. These effects have been reported world-wide, for example in Maryland, USA (Wolman, 1967; Yorke and Davis, 1971), near Exeter (Walling, 1974*b*) and near Harlow (Hollis, 1974) in the UK, on the coast of New South Wales, Australia (Hannam, 1979), around Kuala Lumpur, Malaysia (Douglas, 1978; Leigh, 1982*b*) and in Singapore (Gupta, 1982). An additional problem, not dealt with in these studies, is the stability of roadside slopes (Ramaswamy, Aziz and Narayanan, 1981).

The construction phase results in higher volumes of peak runoff, shorter times to peak flow, higher and more frequent flood flows and rapid increases in erosion by overland flow, rills and gullies, producing high sediment concentrations. Residential development, often on a speculative basis, has been going on in the Anak Ayer Batu catchment in Kuala Lumpur since the mid-1960s. By 1970 the river was choked with sediment, the channel was therefore shallower but erosion had widened and steepened it so that it could evacuate the more frequent flood flows. Flooding and deposition of sand on the flood plain regularly covered the sports field and roads on the University of Malaya campus. Suspended sediment concentrations ranged from 4 to 81 230 mg l^{-1} (Douglas, 1978). By 1977 the situation had changed little with sediment concentrations ranging from 3.7 to 15 343 mg l^{-1} (Leigh, 1982*b*). These rapid increases in erosion compared with sediment concentrations of 7 to 1 080 mg l^{-1} in rain forest areas have occurred with only 10 per cent of the catchment in bare or semi-bare condition; about 40 per cent is still in secondary scrub forest or *belukar*. One area of 6.3 ha cleared in 1970 for housing development was abandoned by 1977 when gullies were up to 10 m deep and extending rapidly headwards (Leigh, 1982*b*). Similar sediment concentrations with peaks between 15 000 and 49 000 mg l^{-1} have been recorded on the new campus of the University of Singapore on the Kent Ridge and at the old campus at Bukit Timah (Gupta, 1982).

Strategies for erosion control in urban areas depend on scheduling developments to retain as much plant cover as possible, but since this is generally feasible to only a limited extent, a much greater reliance is placed on mechanical methods than is the case with other types of landuse. Erosion control in the final phase when urban development is complete requires rapid establishment of plant cover and permanent use of purpose-designed waterways and embankment-stabilizing structures (Fig. 7.4).

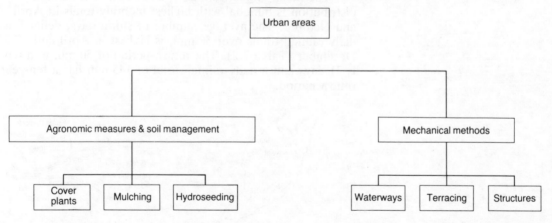

Fig. 7.4   Soil conservation strategies for urban areas (after El-Swaify, Dangler and Armstrong, 1982).

7.4   FARM PLANNING

Farm planning comprises dividing a farm holding into areas of arable, pasture, tree plantations, homestead, roads, water supply, drainage and soil conservation structures and locating each so as to obtain the best use of the land. The planning has to consider the ground conditions such as the type and erodibility of the soil; occurrence of rock outcrops and steepness of slope; present erosion; and suitability of the land for arable, livestock and trees (Wenner, 1981). An example is described here for a small catchment on the University of Malaya campus near Kuala Lumpur.

The catchment occupies an area of 0.09 km² in the north of the campus. The bedrock consists of alternating sandstones and shales of the Kenny Hill Formation, interlensing in irregular sequence. The soil pattern is complex, reflecting the geology. Soils derived from the sandstones have about 35 per cent clay and those on the shales over 40 per cent clay. The catchment has a relative relief of 61 m and slopes of a two-phase form (Fig. 7.5). The upper convexo-concave phase has maximum slopes of 19° to 25° and the lower phase comprises rectilinear segments of 30° to 48°. Sharp breaks, across which the slope angles differ by 10° or more, mark the boundary between the two phases and also the junction between the lower phase and a narrow flood plain. The catchment is drained by a second-order stream fed by three first-order gullies (Fig. 7.6).

The mean annual rainfall is 2 695 mm. The rainfall distribution is bimodal with highest monthly totals in April and October. The average number of storm days, defined as daily rainfall totals over 50 mm, is highest in April and December (Table 7.2). The return period of 50 mm in a day is 31 days and a daily rainfall total of 145 mm has a ten-year return period.

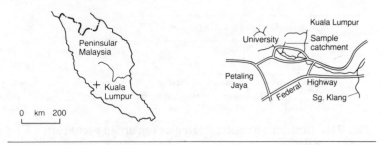

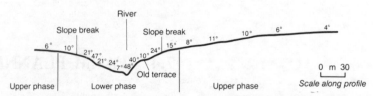

Fig. 7.5   Location of the detailed erosion survey, University of Malaya, Kuala Lumpur, and detail of a typical slope profile (after Morgan, 1972).

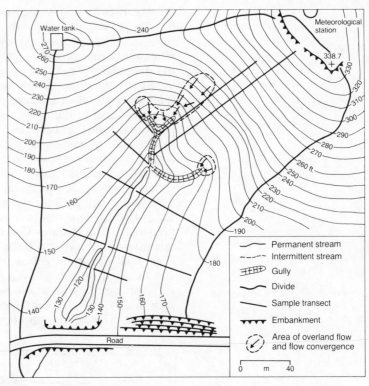

Fig. 7.6   Soil erosion map, study catchment, University of Malaya. Contour interval 10 ft.

Table 7.2 Rainfall data for the University of Malaya

	J	F	M	A	M	J	J
Mean monthly total (mm)	185	119	233	328	272	152	185
Mean days/month with over 50 mm	0.8	0.3	1.0	1.3	1.0	0.7	1.0

	A	S	O	N	D
Mean monthly total (mm)	198	178	307	277	262
Mean days/month with over 50 mm	1.0	0.6	0.9	0.7	1.3

Data from the Department of Geography, University of Malaya, Meteorological Station, 1963–69.

At the time of survey in 1969 and 1970, the eastern part of the catchment formed part of the field area of the Faculty of Agriculture and was planted with oil palm up to a height of 60 m and with rubber above that altitude. As a conservation measure the slopes had been cut with 1 m wide bench terraces and a leguminous cover crop grown on the inter-terrace areas. The western part was occupied by the

Science Faculty and was covered with reverted rubber and *belukar* or secondary growth.

A detailed erosion survey was carried out using aerial photograph interpretation supported by fieldwork following the procedures described in section 4.2.4. Slopes were measured along ten sample transects (Fig. 7.6) and soil samples were taken at three points on each transect corresponding to the convex segment on the upper slope phase, the junction between the upper and lower slope phases and the mid-slope segment of the lower slope phase (Fig. 7.5). Because some sites had to be abandoned through difficulty of access, soils were sampled at 24 sites only, giving a density of observations of 1 per 3 750 m². A slope map was compiled from the field measurements and a 1:1 584 scale plan, contoured at 10-ft (3.048-m) intervals, prepared by the Estates Office, University of Malaya. On this map are shown the slope breaks greater than 10° (Fig. 7.7). The main gullies, the areas of flow convergence and the land subject to overland flow are shown in Fig. 7.6.

The soils belong to the Serdang Series. Soil properties vary locally with lithology, slope steepness and distance from the crest. The relationship between clay content and

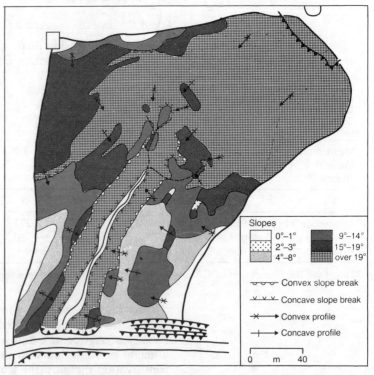

Fig. 7.7 Slope map, study catchment, University of Malaya.

lithology has been outlined above. Silt content is higher on the steeper slopes and there is a significant correlation between silt content and slope angle ($r = 0.71$; $n = 24$). This implies that an increase in steepness promotes the selective erosion of the finer particles. Silt/clay ratios increase with distance from the crest, ranging from 0.64 on the upper phase, to 0.80 at the boundary between the upper and lower slope phases, and 1.33 on the lower phase (Table 7.3).

The silt/clay ratio may be used as an index of weathering (van Wambeke, 1962). A low ratio denotes a well-weathered soil, the development of which requires relatively stable conditions with minimal erosion. High ratios are associated with erodible areas where the continual removal of the soil allows insufficient time for a high degree of weathering to occur. Since the silt/clay ratio reflects the rate at which erosion is taking place, it can also be used as an index of erodibility. In fact, for this catchment, there is a significant correlation ($r = 0.95$; $n = 24$) between the silt/clay ratio and estimates of the K-value of erodibility determined from the nomograph (Fig. 3.2) of Wischmeier, Johnson and Cross (1971). Soil properties also change with depth, the clay content decreasing to 25 per cent in the subsoil and 20 per cent in the weathered bedrock. The silt/clay ratio increases with depth at first, reaching a maximum value at about 45 cm, before decreasing with greater depth (Fig. 7.8).

Table 7.3 Soil properties in a small catchment, University of Malaya

Site	Clay %	Silt %	Silt/clay Ratio	K value (*)
Lower slope phase (top soil)	35	47	1.33	0.17
Phase boundary (top soil)	33	26	0.80	0.14
Upper slope phase (top soil)	36	23	0.64	0.13
Upper slope phase (sub soil)	25	25	1.00	0.25
Upper slope phase (weathered bedrock)	20	42	2.10	0.31

(*) based on Figure 3.2.

The catchment was observed regularly in the field between September 1969 and April 1970 to monitor the frequency of overland flow and gully erosion. Observations were made at 09.00 h local time every Monday, Wednesday

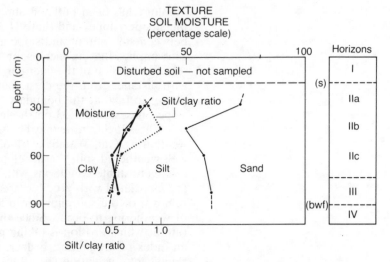

TEXTURE
SOIL MOISTURE
(percentage scale)

The horizons are: I—loose soil disturbed by terracing; IIa—relatively well-weathered subsoil (35% clay, 40% silt): material is sticky, may be squeezed with difficulty; IIb—sandy-clay loam (25% clay, 25% silt); IIc—loam (22% clay, 36% silt); III—weathered bedrock retaining textural lines of parent material (42% silt, 20% clay), easily broken with hammer; IV—sandstone bedrock. s—subsoil junction, abrupt; bwf—basal weathering front, abrupt and smooth

Fig. 7.8   Characteristics of a soil profile, study catchment, University of Malaya.

and Friday, and at other times during or immediately following heavy rain. Precipitation recordings were made at the Meteorological Station of the University of Malaya, sited on the divide in the northeast of the catchment. Although many occurrences of flow over the hillsides and in gullies were missed by not installing automatic monitoring equipment, sufficient data were obtained to provide an indication of the frequency and magnitude of rainfall events which cause erosion.

Overland flow was observed on three occasions, 16 October 1969, 30 and 31 March 1970, following the receipt of 16 mm or more of rain within an hour. It was never observed over the whole catchment but was restricted to those slopes adjacent to and above the gully heads. The flow was seen to converge downslope towards the gullies, pouring over their lips and down their backwalls before continuing downstream within the confines of the gully channels. On 16 October 1969, overland flow occurred for a distance of 60 m upslope of the gullies. Because of the dense vegetation cover, the overland flow did not cause erosion.

Channel flow in the gullies was observed on 18 occasions but only one event, that of 16 October 1969, when

73 mm of rain fell in an hour, resulted in erosion. Following this storm, it was found that scouring had locally increased the depths of the gullies by 0.30 to 0.45 m and that, in one place, bank collapse had reduced the width of the gully by 2 m. Although nine occurrences of over 25 mm of rain in an hour were recorded in the study period, including one with an hourly total of 54 mm, no further erosion took place. It is concluded elsewhere (Morgan, 1972) that a rainfall total in excess of 60 mm h^{-1}, or possibly even 75 mm h^{-1}, is required to contribute sufficient overland flow to the gullies to cause erosion. These events have a return period of about 60 days in this catchment.

The mean annual erosivity, estimated from the mean annual rainfall, using equation 4.2, is 16 171 J m^{-2}; the p^2/P value is 39. These figures are indicative of a high erosion risk by overland flow and a moderate risk of gully erosion (section 4.1.2). This is in line with the process studies which reveal that most gully erosion results from the concentration of overland flow. The clay contents and K-values of the top soil imply that erodibility is relatively low. Once the top soil is broken through, as in the gully channels, the subsoil is highly erodible. The least erodible soils are found on the upper slope phase and erodibility increases rapidly downslope of the phase boundary. The most erodible area is clearly the valley head where slopes of comparable steepness to those of the lower phase occur in an area of flow convergence.

The catchment can be divided into three areas according to the degree of erosion risk, namely the valley head, the lower valley side slopes and the upper valley side slopes. Greatest risk exists in the valley head where overland flow and gully erosion are already taking place. Any decrease in plant cover will aggravate the erosive condition and the area should be classed as a conservation zone and maintained with a dense vegetation cover. The valley side slopes of the lower phase have a potential erosion risk and should not therefore be cultivated. The valley side slopes of the upper phase possess stable soils with relatively low erodibility and gentle slope angles. The main risk is from erosion by rainsplash and this can be counteracted by maintaining a dense ground cover if the area is to be cultivated.

A landuse plan was simulated by applying the following procedure based on that adopted in semi-detailed erosion surveys. First, the objective was set to devote as much land as possible to tree crops without causing unacceptable erosion risk. Second, a mean annual sediment yield of 2.0 g m^{-2} was selected as the maximum acceptable. Third, the maximum permissible slope angles at which this level of sediment yield can be maintained were determined using equation (4.9). Annual runoff values were estimated for the annual rainfall of 2 695 mm, using the rainfall–runoff ratios quoted in section 4.2.4. The results of this analysis show that rubber can be grown with the use of ground covers on slopes up to 7° and that the maximum acceptable sediment yield is exceeded under rainforest on slopes over 14°. It is recommended therefore that any extension of the rubber-growing area on to steeper land using bench terracing should not incorporate all land up to the legal cultivable limit of 18.5° but should be restricted to slopes of 7° to 14°.

Clearly, this simulated plan envisages a considerably different landuse pattern from that existing at the time of survey and implies that some of the land in the catchment is being misused. It should also be noted that the maximum permissible slope angles are much lower than those prescribed for central Pahang (section 4.2.4) because of the higher rainfall.

Next, those factors which affect the implementation and likely success of any conservation strategy must be considered. One approach to assessing the feasibility of a particular scheme is to pose a series of questions of which the following may serve as examples.

1   Does the size of the net farm area constitute a viable economic holding? The net farm area is that part of the holding devoted to activities yielding an income either as revenue or in kind. Thus, on a rubber estate it would include the land planted with rubber trees but exclude land kept under forest and that taken up with access roads, waterways and buildings.

2   Is the net farm area sufficiently continuous that it provides a logical working unit? Where the area comprises several parts, is each part large enough to form a suitable working unit? Where a landuse proposal results in small disconnected units these must either be combined by farming the intervening areas which would not otherwise be cultivated or, where the erosion risk is too great to permit this, be taken out of cultivation.

3   Is there easy access to each part of the net farm area so that any necessary machinery can be brought in and produce removed?

4   Where terraces and waterways are planned, is the terraced area large enough for an efficient terrace and water-disposal system to be installed?

5   How well do the proposed conservation measures fit in with existing agricultural practices? If new measures are recommended, what evidence is there that these are economically and socially acceptable? What is the effect of the measures on crop yield?

6   Is the system legal? The main constraints here are to ensure that laws specifying upper slope limits to cultivation are adhered to and that no runoff is channelled on to another person's land which would not flow there naturally.

In the light of factors such as these, modifications are frequently necessary to the original proposals in order to design a strategy which stands a good chance of being successfully adopted.

Taking account of the erosion risk assessment and the maximum permissible slopes for different types of landuse, landuse allocation is straightforward. All land on the upper slope phase of the valley sides up to 14° slope may be safely used for tree crops. Land between 7° and 14° slope should be bench-terraced. The rest of the catchment should remain under or be allowed to revert to a forest cover.

No special treatment of the hillslopes under forest is required but a dense cover must be maintained. Because erosion is naturally high on slopes as low as 15°, the forest should not be worked commercially for timber. This recommendation applies particularly to the valley head which is the most erodible area. Erosion control measures are required in the gullies but because the area has no commercial value, high-cost permanent structures are not justified. Reliance must be placed on the protection afforded by the forest cover on the adjacent hillslopes supplemented by temporary dams.

The areas where tree crops may be safely grown occur on the upper valley sides in the east and west of the catchment and on the divide in the north (Fig. 7.9). The latter area suffers from poor access and will not be considered further. It is important that in the tree-crop growing areas a dense ground cover is provided to minimize the impact of raindrops and water drops falling from the canopy on the soil surface. Land clearance should be undertaken in June and July when erosivity is relatively low and ground creepers planted immediately so that they become established during August and September before the erosive rains in October. The most suitable creepers are *Pueraria phaseoloides, Calopogonium mucunoides* and *Centrosema pubescens* (Williams and Joseph, 1970). The ground cover must be maintained throughout the life of the trees.

Bench terracing must be constructed on land over 7° and on land of gentler slope where this is necessary to obtain a continuous terrace system. Construction should be carried out in late June or early July following land clearance. A modified bench-terrace system system for tree crops should be adopted and the land between the terraces planted immediately with a ground creeper. Benches about 2 m wide are sufficient for tree crops. Using the spacing formula for bench terraces in Sheng (1972*b*) gives vertical interval spacings of 0.405 m on a 10° slope and 0.228 m on a 6° slope, corresponding to distances along the slope of 2.3 m and 2.18 m respectively. The wider spacing required on the steeper slopes reflects that fewer terraces are permissible in

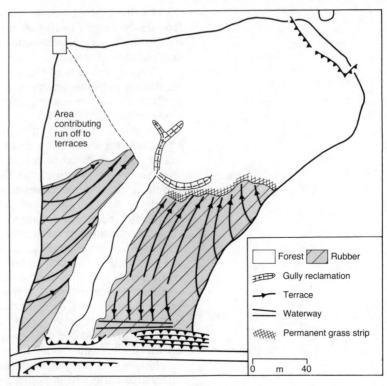

Fig. 7.9 Conservation scheme, study catchment, University of Malaya.

areas of greater erosion risk. These spacings are unsuitable for rubber cultivation, however, as the trees need to be placed about 9 m apart in one direction and 2.5 m in the other. The cheapest way of arriving at this spacing is to build the terraces 9 m apart and plant the trees at intervals of 2.5 m on each terrace.

The terraces should be located so that marked convex breaks of slope can be incorporated in the riser and concave breaks in the shelf. This avoids the problem of having sharp changes in slope, which are localities of higher erosion risk, often requiring extra protection, on land between the terraces. The terraces should be graded to a slope of 1:250 (Hudson, 1981*a*) and their length kept below 100 m (Sheng, 1972*b*). On the western side of the catchment, the terraces can begin at the divide and be graded northeastwards. On the eastern side it is convenient to use a slight spur in the middle of the terraced area and grade the terraces both north and south of it (Fig. 7.9).

The accompanying waterway network is relatively simple. Only one area, in the west, could contribute runoff to the cultivated area and, because of its small size and the apparent lack of overland flow in that part of the catchment, it can be ignored. No diversion channels are therefore required. The terraces draining northwards can be allowed to empty into the forested areas without the need for a waterway, but a grass strip should be maintained between the end of the terraces and the forest to reduce the velocity of any runoff and filter out the sediment. A grass waterway is required for the terraces draining southwards on the eastern side of the catchment to intercept the runoff and prevent it cascading down the embankment above the road.

Two changes are proposed to the existing landuse. The valley head, at present given over to rubber as part of the Faculty of Agriculture field area, should be taken out of cultivation and allowed to revert to secondary forest. The land in the west of the catchment which is currently under secondary growth is suitable for tree crops and could be cleared and planted with rubber.

The conservation scheme is feasible only if the catchment is considered as part of a larger area. The hectarage of the two areas where rubber is the proposed landuse is too small to comprise a viable economic unit even for a smallholder. Individually, however, the areas are large enough for working units within a larger holding. For the proposals to be realistic, the areas assigned to rubber would need to be extended, along with their associated terrace systems, across the divides on to similar land in the neighbouring catchments. Such extension is possible and, at the time of survey, had already taken place across the eastern divide within the Faculty of Agriculture field area. Access by tappers to the rubber areas is possible from the main road by climbing the divide and walking from there along the terraces. There is no reason to suppose that the recommended conservation practices are unacceptable to farmers because they are the standard measures employed in rubber-growing areas throughout the country. The proposals comply with legal requirements.

Chapter 8
CROP AND VEGETATION MANAGEMENT

Agronomic measures for soil conservation are based on the role of the plant cover in reducing erosion (section 3.4). Because of differences in their density and morphology, plants differ in their effectiveness in protecting the soil from erosion. This can be shown by studying erosion rates measured from small plots in the field under different plant covers (FAO, 1965; Kellman, 1969; Roose, 1971; Temple, 1972a). Generally, row crops are the least effective and give rise to the more serious erosion problems (section 7.3.1). This is because of the high percentage of bare ground, particularly in the early stages of crop growth, and the need to prepare a seed bed. In designing a conservation strategy based on agronomic measures, row crops must be combined with protection-effective crops in a logical cropping pattern.

8.1   ROTATION

The simplest way to combine different crops is to grow them consecutively in rotation. The frequency with which row crops are grown depends upon the severity of erosion. Where erosion rates are low, they may be grown every other year, but in very erodible areas, they may be permissible only once in five or even seven years. A high rate of soil loss under the row crop is acceptable because it is counteracted by low rates under the other crops so that, averaged over a six- or seven-year period, the annual erosion rate remains low.

Suitable crops for use in rotations are legumes and grasses. These provide good ground cover, help to maintain or even improve the organic status of the soil, thereby contributing to soil fertility, and enable a more stable aggregate structure to develop in the soil. These effects are often sufficiently long-lasting as to reduce erosion and increase yield during the first year of row-crop cultivation, but they rarely extend into the second year. For this reason, two continuous years of planting with a row crop should be avoided. Hudson (1981*a*) shows that a rotation of tobacco–grass–grass–tobacco–grass–grass is more effective in Zimbabwe than one of two consecutive years of tobacco followed by four years of grass. The respective mean annual soil loss rates are 1.2 and 1.5 kg m^{-2}. The same effect is illustrated more dramatically by Kellman (1969) for shifting cultivation in the Philippines where, during the cropping period, soil loss from land under rice averages 0.38 g m^{-2} day^{-1} on a new clearing but rises to 14.91 g m^{-2} day^{-1} on a clearing in its twelfth year of cultivation.

8.1.1 Shifting cultivation

Shifting cultivation is a traditional method of reducing soil erosion in the tropics by rotating the location of the fields. An area of forest is cleared by slash-and-burn, the soil loosened by hand hoeing and a crop planted. Where two crops a year can be obtained, a second crop is grown after the harvest of the first, otherwise the land is left as a weed fallow. The same area may be cropped for a second year before being allowed to revert to scrub and secondary forest. The typical crops grown are cassava, maize, upland rice and yam. The residual effect of the forest on the organic content and aggregate stability of the soil generally lasts for the first year of farming so that the soil loss remains low. The clearance of an area of secondary forest, the growing and harvesting of a crop of upland rice and reversion of the land to bush fallow on a shallow loamy soil on a 25° slope in Sarawak, Malaysia, produced 3.3 g m^{-2} of soil loss for the year compared with 3.8 g m^{-2} under forest in the year prior to clearance (Hatch, personal communication). As already indicated, however, erosion rates rise rapidly if the land continues to be cropped in subsequent years. The practice of shifting cultivation will maintain soil fertility and reduce soil erosion to acceptable levels provided the associated conditions of low crop yields and low ratio of population to land area remain socially and economically desirable. The critical factor in the system is the length of the fallow period. This is traditionally between 7 and 20 years in West Africa (Okigbo, 1977) and should be between 10 and 50 years in northern Thailand (Hurni, 1981). Increases in the density of population and the desire of people to raise their standard of living by changing from subsistence to cash cropping are causing greater pressure on the land, resulting in a reduction and sometimes the elimination of the fallow period. Serious erosion problems are being created and alternative farming practices to the shifting cultivation system are required to solve them.

8.1.2 Row-crop cultivation

Particular problems are associated with maize which, when grown as a row crop with conventional tillage and clean weeding, results in an annual soil loss on 2–5° slopes of between 1 and 12 kg m^{-2} taking data from the USA (FAO, 1965), Zimbabwe (Hudson, 1981*a*), Senegal (Charreau, 1972) and Malaysia (Sulaiman, Maene and Mokhtaruddin, 1981). These rates are well above most soil loss tolerance levels. Where maize is grown in a more traditional manner with cultivation being restricted to ploughing and with no weeding, it presents fewer difficulties. At the Abbo Ager Research Station, Wallo Province, Ethiopia, the soil loss on a 9° slope was 1.5 kg m^{-2} under maize in 1983 when the rainfall was 1 180 mm, compared with 5.6 kg m^{-2} in 1982 when the land was cropped to *ajja* (Emmer wheat) followed by beans and the rainfall was 1 480 mm. The higher erosion in 1982 was attributed to the double cropping which required a second ploughing and cultivation of the soil (Hurni, 1983; 1984). The maize yield at about 0.18 kg m^{-2} is rather low compared with yields regularly above 0.47 kg m^{-2} achieved in the USA. There is an urgent need to find a way of increasing the yield without increasing the erosion.

When considering the use of crop rotation, attention must be paid to the order in which the crops are grown, which affects both the degree of erosion control and the yield. Lal (1976) found that in 1973, two crops of maize grown on a 6° slope near Ibadan, Nigeria, resulted in a soil loss of 0.72 kg m^{-2} whereas a crop of maize followed by one of cowpeas with no tillage produced a loss of only 0.02 kg m^{-2}. Growing cowpeas followed by maize but with tillage gave a soil loss of 0.62 kg m^{-2}. Although it is difficult to isolate the effects of zero tillage, it seems probable that a maize–cowpeas sequence produces less erosion than cowpeas–maize because maize is a soil-depleting crop and when grown second is planted into an already partially-exhausted soil. Also, soil loss is greater under maize than cowpea (Lal, 1977*a*; Rao, 1981; Sulaiman, Maene and Mokhtaruddin, 1981) and the difference between the two crops is likely to be enhanced when maize rather than cowpea is the second crop. Crop yields at Ibadan in 1974 were 0.49 kg m^{-2} for maize and 0.43 kg m^{-2} for cowpea in the maize–cowpea sequence but 0.50 kg m^{-2} for cowpea and only 0.21 kg m^{-2} for maize in the cowpea–maize sequence. Thus it is always preferable to grow maize as the first crop in the rotation. A suitable four-year rotation for the

Ibadan area is maize–cowpeas; pigeon peas–sorghum; maize interplanted with cassava; and fallow crop (Okigbo and Lal, 1977).

Soya beans are often recommended as an alternative to cowpeas because of their apparent ability to reduce soil loss arising from a rather high rainfall interception. At 90 per cent canopy cover, soya bean intercepts 58 per cent of the rainfall, compared with 40 per cent for maize interplanted with cassava and only 28 per cent for cassava on its own. Respective annual soil losses are 0.40, 0.69 and 1.10 kg m^{-2} in the Ibadan area (Aina, Lal and Taylor, 1979). Despite soya bean being a legume, studies in the Mid-West of the USA indicate that it can result in as much if not more erosion than maize. Morgan (1985*a*) found that soya bean and maize intercepted comparable amounts of rainfall throughout their growing period. The *C*-factor values are similar for the two crops when they are grown in an identical management system (Wischmeier and Smith, 1978). The average annual soil loss on a 4° slope with a silt loam soil over seven years was 0.70 kg m^{-2} for continuous maize, 0.65 kg m^{-2} for maize following soya beans and 0.96 kg m^{-2} for soya beans following maize. Surprisingly, the main reason for the increased erosion when soya beans rather than maize are grown as the second crop in the rotation is that higher soil loss occurs under the beans in the stage of growth between 75 per cent canopy cover and harvest. This is the stage when both crops would be expected to afford good protection to the soil (Laflen and Moldenhauer, 1979).

In addition to controlling erosion, the inclusion of grasses and legumes in a rotation can increase yields of the main crop. Yields of maize greater than 0.50 kg m^{-2} were obtained at Ibadan following a year with the land under *Centrosema pubescens, Setaria splendida* or *Stylosanthes gracilis* (Okigbo and Lal, 1977). Unless the fallow crops can be used for grazing or fodder, however, they have no immediate value to the farmer. Thus, crop rotations with grasses or legumes are rarely practised in the main cereal-growing areas of the world and are unlikely to be acceptable anywhere if their inclusion gives no income to the farmer. Under these conditions, an alternative approach to erosion control is required.

8.1.3 Grazing land management

Rotation is commonly practised on grazing land, moving the stock from one pasture to another in turn, to give time for the grass to recover. Generally, grasslands should not be exploited to more than 40 to 50 per cent of their annual production (Fournier, 1972) and should be allowed to regenerate sufficiently to provide a 70 per cent ground cover at the times of erosion risk. Grazing land has to be very carefully managed. Whilst overgrazing can lead to deterioration of the rangeland and the onset of erosion, undergrazing can result in the loss of nutritious grasses, many of which regenerate more rapidly when grazed. An increase in the numbers of sheep and a decrease in the length of the growing season from 240 to 210 days between 1944 and 1968 created pressure on the better pastures of the Peak District in the UK, leading to a breakdown of the turf mat and soil erosion. A fall in sheep numbers in 1969 combined with a slightly longer growing season allowed vegetation to colonize the bare soil patches. The overgrazing resulted in a change in sward type from *Agrostis-Festuca* to *Nardetum* (Evans, 1977) and therefore in a lowering of the sheep-carrying capacity. This change in vegetation type and also that from heather to grassland has been observed generally in the UK following overgrazing of the upland pastures (Fenton, 1937).

Although erosion rates are high from burnt-over land, controlled burning is essential for the removal of undesirable plant species. Uncontrolled burning can prevent plants from re-establishing and, by increasing the extent of bare ground, result in serious erosion. Imeson (1971) attributes soil erosion on the North Yorkshire Moors to burning of the heather every two or three years. This frequency of burn compares with a six-year period necessary for *Calluna* to develop from seed to a height of 30 to 40 cm and provide a complete canopy to the ground surface. The greatest risk of erosion is on peaty soils where ground-lowering rates up to 45 mm y^{-1} have been measured following a burn. Shallow, intermittent gullies, from a few decimetres to 4 m deep, cross the *Calluna* moorland. Where the vegetation cover is poor, these have been found to increase in width at rates of 17 to 80 mm y^{-1}. Clearly, burning must be practised on a rotational basis and only carried out with a frequency which will permit plants to regrow and maintain soil loss, when averaged over six or seven years, at an acceptably low level. Prescribed burning modifies the density, stature and composition of brush stands but only kills a few species outright. Most brush species sprout vigorously after fire to the detriment of grass. Fire can be used to topkill and open up mature stands of brush and to make a seed bed for the establishment of grasses. Once the brush resprouts, however, it has a competitive advantage over the young grass and needs to be controlled by herbicides until the grass is strong enough to carry fire. After this stage has been reached, burning can be used periodically to control brush (Hibbert, Davis and Brown, 1975).

A critical factor in a rotational grazing system is the

quality of the poorest rangeland. On the rangelands of northern Mexico, the recommended stocking rates to maintain the pasture in 'good' condition, a state defined locally as having at least 50 per cent desirable grasses in the vegetation cover, are one animal per 20 ha in the mountains, one animal per 14 ha on the mediano, and one animal per 14 ha on the sierra and bajío (González, 1971). With the rotational pattern described in section 4.2.3 in operation, any upgrading of the mediano pastures will strain the capacity of the other pastures in the system. Similar strains are being experienced on the hill pastures in Wales where farmers, having improved the grasses of the lower slopes and valleys, have increased stocking densities, resulting in greater numbers of sheep being put to graze on the unimproved upland pastures during the summer. Overgrazing of these pastures may be one cause of soil erosion in the Clwyd Range (Baker, Morgan, Brown, Hawkes and Ratcliffe, 1979). The traditional sheep-grazing system in Iceland relies on cultivated pastures close to the farm which are grazed in the spring and autumn and on communal upland pastures which are grazed in the summer whilst two crops of hay are cut from the cultivated lands. Today the farmers are reducing the time that sheep spend in the uplands with the result that only one crop of hay is obtained and winter feed has to be imported (Pálsson and Stefánsson, 1968). With increasing sheep numbers, the pressure on the summer grazings has been intensified rather than reduced and overgrazing is causing erosion. The loss of upland pastures is important because, whilst the productivity of the lowland pastures is greater, giving a biomass of 835 kg DM ha^{-1} y^{-1} compared with 666 kg DM ha^{-1} y^{-1} for the uplands (Thorsteinsson, 1980a), it has been found that lambs grazed on the cultivated pastures in summer have only similar and sometimes lower rates of growth compared with those grazed in the uplands (Guðmunsson, 1980). The availability of summer pasture is now the limiting factor in sheep production (Thorsteinsson, Ólafsson and van Dyne, 1971). Avoiding overgrazing and erosion in the uplands through the adoption of appropriate stocking rates is therefore vital.

There is no universal formula for determining stocking rates, and the carrying capacity of pastures is usually imprecisely defined. The determination is more difficult in regions with high variability in rainfall from year to year so that overgrazing is almost inevitable when several years of drought follow in succession.

The sheep-grazing capacity of the pastures in Iceland has been assessed by mapping the vegetation of the country from aerial photography and a supporting field survey and classifying it into 94 different types (Steindórsson, 1980).

The average annual production of dry matter has been determined for each type (Thorsteinsson, 1980a), Based on this work, a knowledge of the palatability of the plant species of each type to sheep and limiting the annual removal to 50 per cent of the annual growth of the palatable species, the carrying capacity can be calculated (Thorsteinsson, 1980b; 1980c). The required level of grazing intensity is reached when about 10 to 15 per cent of the annual growth of woody species is removed. A different approach is used to estimate the carrying capacity of pastures in Ireland based on the way grass growth on different soil types responds to controlled inputs of fertilizer (Lee and Diamond, 1972). Although these surveys take account of productivity and the potential for erosion, they cannot indicate the actual carrying capacity at a given moment: this depends upon local soil and vegetation conditions and on variations in climate. Regular inspection and judgement of the quality of the pastures are thus needed to determine when stock should be moved from one area to another in the rotation system.

8.1.4 Forest management

The principles of rotation can be applied to other forms of landuse. The timber resources of forests are often exploited commercially by patch-cutting, also termed clear felling, on a rotational basis. Erosion rates are highest in the years immediately following logging operations but decline in subsequent years either with natural vegetation regrowth or replanting so that averaged over twelve years or more they may be little different from those of undisturbed land. Leaf (1970) shows that in Fool Creek, Colorado, in the Rocky Mountains, soil loss averaged 22.4 g m^{-2} y^{-1} whilst logging and road construction were in progress in the 1950s but, since 1958, a year after operations ceased, has averaged only 9.86 g m^{-2} y^{-1}. The latter figure compares with soil loss of 4.81 g m^{-2} $^{-1}$ from uncut forest land. Further north in western Oregon, annual sediment yield from the Deer Creek catchment averaged 97 g m^{-2} for the period 1959 to 1965. Roads were constructed in late 1965 for the patch-cutting of 25 per cent of the catchment in late 1966. The sediment yield in 1966 increased by 150 per cent but the increase in 1967 was only 40 per cent above the pre-cutting average. Sediment production in subsequent years was similar to the pre-cutting average until 1972 when it was 170 per cent above because of several mass failures along roadsides in the patch-cut area. The 1973 sediment yield was again similar to the pre-cutting average. Thus, provided the erosion on roadside embankments can be controlled, an area can recover quickly from the effects of a small amount of patch-cutting. Clearance of much larger areas can create longer-term problems, however. In the neighbouring Needle Branch watershed, pre-cutting sediment yield averaged 53 g m^{-2} y^{-1}. Following similar treatment but patch-cutting 82 per cent of the catchment in 1966, sediment yield was 50 per cent above the pre-cutting average in 1966, 260 per cent above in 1967 and did not return to the pre-cutting levels until 1973. The average annual sediment yield for 1966 to 1973 was 146 g m^{-2} (Beschta, 1978). Forest fires represent an additional hazard once an area has been cut because, as shown by observations following wild fire in Pine Creek, Boise National Forest, central Idaho, the erosion directly attributable to burning is greater in cut than in uncut areas (Megahan and Molitor, 1975). Replanting needs to take place quickly after clear felling before the loss of top soil and plant nutrients through erosion reduces the quality of the land. If planting is delayed, it is desirable to establish ground cover using some of the cover crops referred to in section 8.2.

Although with careful management and limiting clearance to small areas at a time patch-cutting may be an acceptable management technique, in very erodible areas, soil loss may be too severe during logging to permit its use. In mountainous areas of Peninsular Malaysia, slides and gullies develop rapidly when the forest is cleared (Berry, 1956; Burgess, 1971) and increased erosion and runoff may result in problems of sedimentation and flooding downstream. In these areas, selective felling, whereby only the mature trees are removed and the other trees remain to provide a plant cover, is better conservation practice. Rich (1972) has observed that selective felling does not significantly increase runoff compared with undisturbed forest areas. Since, in his study area of Arizona, annual precipitation averages less than 800 mm, he recommends managing the Ponderosa pine forests by clear cutting in order to increase water yield.

In recent years, as the problem of erosion in recreational areas has become recognized, interest has focused on whether rotational practices can be adapted to people. Although there is a reluctance to treat people in the same way as livestock, it appears to be increasingly necessary in heavily used areas to fence off sections of land and to close certain footpaths and access routes so that the vegetation cover has a chance to regenerate. In many upland areas, where grazing, forestry and recreation are complementary but sometimes competing activities, the prospect of applying a common conservation measure is extremely attractive.

8.2   COVER CROPS

Cover crops are grown as a conservation measure either during the off-season or as ground protection under trees. In the United States they are grown as winter annuals and, after harvest, are ploughed in to form a green manure. Typical crops used are rye, oats, hairy vetch, sweet clover and lucerne in the north, and Austrian winter peas, crimson clover, crotalaria and lespedeza in the south. The sowing broadcast of winter rye at a rate of 120–130 kg ha^{-1} as early as possible in the autumn is practised to control wind erosion successfully on the sandy soils of the northern Netherlands where sugar beet, potatoes and maize are grown. Mid-September sowing is possible for sugar beet and potatoes but sowing with the maize is delayed until after the harvest in October. Early sowing is essential because a good crop cover must be obtained by the end of December since the climate is too cold for growth in February and March, the period when the soil surface is dry and strong winds with low humidity are most common. The crop is spray-killed with paraquat at a suitable time in the spring, usually before drilling the sugar beet or before emergence of potatoes and maize. Wind tunnel studies have shown that winter rye sown at the recommended density can prevent blowing of the soil with windspeeds up to 21 m s^{-1} as measured at a height of 10 m (Knottnerus, 1976). Plot experiments at the Santa Ana Fields near Huancayo in the Central Highlands of Peru for the 1975–76 season showed that the growing of potatoes followed by *Lupinus mutabilis* as a cover crop, later buried as a green manure, reduced the soil loss for the year to 0.22 kg m^{-2} compared with a loss of 0.47 kg m^{-2} for potato followed by a fallow with the natural vegetation being allowed to regrow (Felipe-Morales, Meyer, Alegre and Vittorelli, 1979). The planting of sunn crotalaria in September following the wheat harvest and turning it in as a green manure the next spring decreases soil erosion in western Shanxi by about 50 per cent compared with leaving the land fallow in the off-season (Cheng, 1984).

Ground covers are grown under tree crops to protect the soil from the impact of water drops falling from the canopy. They are particularly important with tall crops such as rubber where the height of fall is sufficient to cause the drops to approach their terminal velocity (section 3.4). The most common crops used in tropical areas are *Pueraria phaseoloides*, *Calopogonium mucunoides* and *Centrosema pubescens*. Although these covers have the advantages of rapid growth and retaining nutrients in the soil which would otherwise be removed by leaching, these are sometimes offset by problems. First, there is a risk that a satisfactory cover will not be attained. This is because, as the main crop becomes established, ground conditions change from strong, open sunshine to shade, causing some plants to die out. Second, the cost of growing cover crops may outweigh the benefits an individual farmer receives. Most covers give no income and this restricts their use on smallholdings where farmers do not have sufficient cash reserves to wait for the tree crop to mature. Research is required to find suitable cover crops, particularly varieties of beans and peas, which the smallholder can grow. Third, ground covers compete for the available moisture and, in dry areas, may adversely affect the growth of the main crop. Studies in rubber plantations in eastern Java show that cover crops may reduce the soil moisture by up to 50 per cent during the dry season compared with clean-weeding (Williams and Joseph, 1970). An alternative conservation measure is required in these circumstances.

8.3   STRIP-CROPPING

With strip-cropping, row crops and protection-effective crops are grown in alternating strips aligned on the contour or perpendicular to the wind. Erosion is largely limited to the row-crop strips and soil removed from these is trapped in the next strip downslope or downwind which is generally planted with a leguminous or grass crop. Strip-cropping is best suited to well-drained soils because the reduction in runoff velocity, if combined with a low rate of infiltration on a poorly drained soil, can result in waterlogging and standing water.

When used to protect land against water erosion, strip-cropping is not normally required on slopes less than 3° and, on its own, is insufficient to conserve soil on slopes over 8.5°. Strip widths vary with the degree of erosion hazard but are generally between 15 and 45 m. Where possible, crop rotation is applied to the strips but, on steeper slopes or on very erodible soils, it may be necessary to retain some strips in permanent vegetation. These buffer strips are usually 2 to 4 m wide and are placed at 10 to 20 m intervals. The selection of strip widths and the design of strip layouts are based on practical experience. Guidelines for widths are given in Table 8.1 (FAO, 1965; Cooke and Doornkamp. 1974). Figure 8.1 shows some sample layouts for schemes involving crop rotation and the use of buffer strips (Schwab, Frevert, Edminster and Barnes 1966; Troeh, Hobbs and Donahue, 1980).

The main disadvantage of strip-cropping is the need to farm small areas. This limits the kind of machinery that can be operated and, therefore, the technique is not compatible

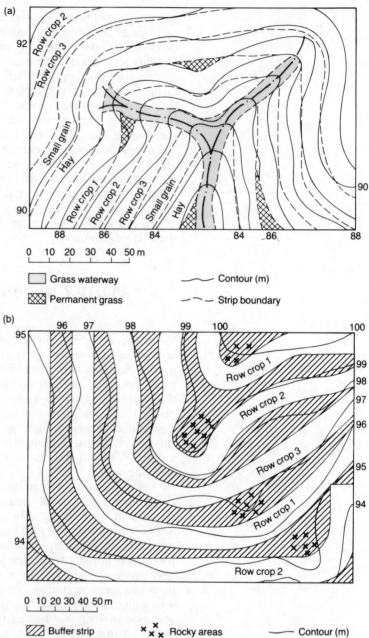

Fig. 8.1 Contour strip-cropping designs for (a) a five-year crop rotation and (b) the use of buffer strips. The contour lines are in metres above an arbitrary datum. Note the use of a grass waterway to evacuate excess runoff from the strip-cropped area and the inclusion of rocky areas which cannot be farmed within the buffer strips (after Troeh, Hobbs and Donahue, 1980).

Table 8.1 Recommended strip widths for strip-cropping (after FAO, 1965; Cooke and Doornkamp, 1974).

Water erosion (soils with fairly high water intake)	
2–5 per cent slope	30 m
6–9 per cent	25 m
10–14 per cent	20 m
15–20 per cent	15 m

Wind erosion (strips perpendicular to wind direction)	
Sandy soil	6 m
Loamy sand	7 m
Sandy loam	30 m
Loam	75 m
Silt loam	85 m
Clay loam	105 m

with highly mechanized agricultural systems. Although this is a less relevant consideration on smallholdings, the difficulty here is that much land is taken up with less valuable protection-effective crops. Where grass is grown, it cannot be used for pasture until after harvest unless the row-crop areas are fenced to keep out the stock. Insect infestation and weed control are additional problems associated with strip cropping.

8.4   MULTIPLE CROPPING

The aim of multiple cropping is to increase the production from the land whilst providing protection of the soil from erosion. The method involves either sequential cropping, growing two or more crops a year in sequence, or intercropping, growing two or more crops on the same piece of land at the same time. Many schemes involve a mixture of the two. Multiple cropping has been traditionally practised in the West Indies in the kitchen gardens which, averaging 0.2 ha in size, provide the subsistence component of fruits and vegetables for many families in the rural areas. Those in Grenada are dominated visually by fruit trees with banana the most ubiquitous but also including coconut, cocoa, mango and breadfruit. About two-thirds of the tilled land in the garden are devoted to vegetables, especially root crops such as sweet potatoes and yams. Pigeon peas, groundnuts, dasheen, okra, pepper and tomatoes are also grown. Although the garden has a confused appearance (Fig. 8.2), the organization of the cropped land is systematic and the better farmers carry out regular weeding, selective application of fertilizers and irrigation (Brierley, 1976).

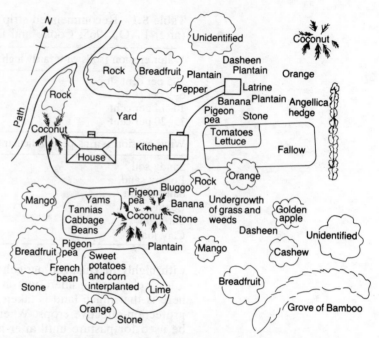

Fig. 8.2 Landuse in a kitchen garden, near Concord, St John's, Grenada, showing an example of multiple cropping (after Brierley, 1976).

The intercropping of maize with cassava was found in Nigeria to offer the advantages of a two-storey canopy, giving a higher interception capacity than either maize or cassava alone (section 8.1). On a 6° slope, mixed maize–cassava reduced annual soil loss to 8.6 kg m^{-2} compared with 12.5 kg m^{-2} for cassava as a monoculture (Lal, 1977a). Both values, however, are well above most soil loss tolerance levels. Hurni (1984) examined the effects on erosion of multiple cropping of maize with haricot beans at the Gununo Research Station, Sidamo Province, and maize, sorghum, beans and peas at the Harar Research Station, Harar Province, Ethiopia. Although multiple cropping led to reduced soil loss in both cases compared with monocultures, in neither instance was the erosion below the soil loss tolerance level which was set at 1.0 kg m^{-2} y^{-1}. Thus the method generally needs to be combined with other practices.

8.5   HIGH-DENSITY PLANTING

High-density planting is used to try to obtain the same effect for a monoculture that multiple cropping achieves with two or more crops. Again the technique may need to be supplemented by other practices. Hudson (1981*a*) showed in Zimbabwe that increasing the planting density of maize from 2.5 to 3.7 plants per square metre and using a trash mulch at the higher density reduced the annual soil loss from 1.23 to 0.07 kg m^{-2}. In general, increasing maize yield from 0.1 to 0.5 kg m^{-2} will reduce annual erosion rates from 5.0 to 1.0 kg m^{-2}. Mannering and Johnson (1969) found that by growing soya beans in narrow rows of 510 mm spacing instead of 1 020 mm spacing increased infiltration by 24 per cent and reduced soil loss by 35 per cent. Adams, Richardson and Burnett (1978) applied the same reduction in spacing to grain sorghum and obtained 39 per cent less runoff and a complete canopy cover 35 days after emergence instead of 63 days. Although soil loss was not measured, it is implicit that a reduction in erosion would also occur. Adoption of the closer row spacing can reduce wind erosion under grain sorghum by between 29 and 55 per cent (Skidmore, Nossaman and Woodruff, 1966).

8.6   MULCHING

Mulching is the covering of the soil with crop residues such as straw, maize stalks, palm fronds or standing stubble. The cover protects the soil from raindrop impact and reduces the velocity of runoff and wind. From the conservation viewpoint, a mulch simulates the effect of a plant cover. It is most useful as an alternative to cover crops in dry areas where insufficient rain prevents the establishment of a ground cover before the onset of heavy rain or strong winds, or where a cover crop competes for moisture with the main crop.

In semi-humid tropical areas, the side effects of a mulch in the forms of lower soil temperatures and increased soil moisture are beneficial and may increase the yields of coffee, banana and cocoa. Elsewhere the effects of mulching can be detrimental. In cool climates, the reduction in soil temperature shortens the growing season whilst in wet areas, higher soil moisture may induce gleying and anaerobic conditions. Other problems with mulching are that the mulch competes with the main crop for nitrogen as it decomposes, special equipment is required to plant crops beneath a mulch and, with normal usage, weed growth is encouraged.

The effectiveness of mulching in reducing erosion is demonstrated by the field experiments of Borst and Woodburn (1942) who found that, on a silt–loam soil on a 7° slope, annual soil loss was 2.46 kg m^{-2} from uncultivated, bare land but only 0.11 kg m^{-2} on land covered with a straw mulch applied at 0.5 kg m^{-2}. Similar results have been obtained in laboratory studies for the same soil, slope and mulch conditions by Lattanzi, Meyer and Baumgardner (1974). These authors quote soil loss rates under simulated rainfall of 1.87 kg m^{-2} h^{-1} with no mulch and 0.31 kg m^{-2} h^{-1} with the mulch. Applying a mulch of lalang grass (*Imperata cylindrica*) at a rate of 0.3 kg m^{-2} to maize grown on a sandy loam soil on a 4° slope on the Experimental Farm of the Universiti Pertanian Malaysia, near Serdang, Selangor, reduced the soil loss over the period from October 1978 to July 1979 to 0.05 kg m^{-2} compared with 0.75 kg m^{-2} recorded for maize grown without a mulch and 1.95 kg m^{-2} for bare soil (Mokhtaruddin and Maene, 1979). Using pruned fronds to cover harvesting paths in an oil palm plantation in Johor, Malaysia, reduced annual soil loss to 0.42 kg m^{-2} from 1.49 kg m^{-2} recorded on unprotected paths (Maene, Thong, Ong and Mokhtaruddin, 1979). Lal (1976) found that covering an alfisol on a 6° slope with 0.6 kg m^{-2} of straw mulch resulted in an annual soil loss of 0.02 kg m^{-2}, a considerable reduction compared with 2.33 recorded for bare soil. A mulch of 0.11 kg m^{-2} of standing wheat stubble residue or 0.22 kg m^{-2} of flattened wheat straw will reduce annual wind erosion rates to a tolerable level of 0.02 kg m^{-2}. To achieve the same effect with sorghum stubble requires a mulch of 0.67 kg m^{-2} (Chepil and Woodruff, 1963).

There is considerable experimental evidence (Wischmeier, 1973; Lal, 1977*b*; Foster and Meyer, 1975; Laflen and Colvin, 1981) to show that the rate of soil loss decreases exponentially with the increase in the percentage area covered by a mulch. The mulch factor (*MF*), defined as the ratio of soil loss with a mulch to that without, is related to the percentage residue or mulch cover (*RC*) by the expression (Laflen and Colvin, 1981)

$$MF = e^{-a.RC} \tag{8.1}$$

where *a* ranges in value from 0.03 to 0.07 and a value of 0.05 is recommended as being generally applicable. Hussein and Laflen (1982) found that the exponential relationship applied only to rill erosion and that the rate of interrill erosion decreased linearly with increasing residue cover. Since for most soils the contribution of interrill erosion to total soil loss is quite small for slope lengths in excess of 25 m and for all but very low percentage residue covers, equation 8.1 can be used to obtain mulch factor values which, when multiplied by the *C*-factor values, allow the effects of mulching to be included in the Universal Soil-Loss Equation (section 5.1.1). Singer and Blackard (1978) in a study of the effects of oat straw, oak leaves and redwood litter as mulches found that soil loss did not begin to decrease until a 50 per cent cover was reached, after which it declined rapidly with increasing cover. This relationship, the reverse of that described by equation 8.1, was obtained with a plot 0.37 m² in size and so may have validity only for very small areas.

A mulch should cover 70 to 75 per cent of the soil surface. With straw, an application rate of 0.5 kg m⁻² is sufficient to achieve this. A lesser covering does not adequately protect the soil whilst a greater covering suppresses plant growth. Denser mulches are sometimes used under tree crops, once these have reached maturity, and, in these cases, they may successfully control weeds. An estimate of the required application rate to control erosion can be made for a preselected set of conditions using the Manning equation for flow velocity (equation 2.8) and the relationship between Manning's *n* and mulch rate for maize straw determined by Foster, Johnson and Moldenhauer (1982):

$$n_{\mathrm{m}} = 0.071 \, M^{1.12} \qquad \text{interrill erosion} \qquad (8.2)$$
$$n_{\mathrm{m}} = 0.105 \, M^{0.84} \qquad \text{rill erosion} \qquad (8.3)$$

where n_{m} is the value of *n* due to the mulch and *M* is the mulch rate (kg m⁻²) (Table 8.2). No similar procedure exists for determining mulch rates to control wind erosion, but the effectiveness of standing crop residues depends upon the number of stalks per unit area and their size. From wind tunnel studies, Lyles and Allison (1976) obtained the relationship:

$$\frac{V^*}{V_{*\mathrm{t}}} = 1.638 + 17.044 \, \frac{N \, A_{\mathrm{s}}}{A_{\mathrm{t}}} - 0.177 \, \frac{L_{\mathrm{y}}}{L_{\mathrm{x}}} + (1.0236)^c - 1 \qquad (8.4)$$

where V^* is the drag velocity for a given open wind velocity, $V_{*\mathrm{t}}$ is the critical drag velocity for the soil, N/A_{t} is the number of stubble stalks per cm⁻², A_{s} is the average projected area of a single stalk facing the wind (cm²), L_{y} is the distance between the stalks in a line perpendicular to the wind (cm), L_{x} is the distance between the stalks in a line in the same direction as the wind (cm) and *C* is the percentage of dry soil aggregates larger than 1 cm in diameter. This relationship needs to be confirmed for field conditions.

Controlling erosion with a mulch poses special problems for the arable farmer because tillage tools become clogged with the residue, weed control and pest control are more difficult, planting under the residue is not always successful and crop yields, especially in humid and semi-humid areas, are sometimes lower. Mulching on its own is not always an appropriate technique but where it is combined with conservation tillage, many of these problems can be overcome, and it has tremendous potential as a method of erosion control.

Table 8.2   Estimating the required density of a maize stalk mulch to control water erosion

---

Estimation is made for the following conditions:

Sandy soil, desired maximum flow velocity	$= 0.75$ m s^{-1}
Flow depth in small channels	$= 100$ mm
Slope	$= 5°$

Estimating required value for total Manning's n

From the Manning equation (equation 2.8)

$$n = \frac{r^{0.67} s^{0.5}}{v}$$

For simplicity, assume the hydraulic radius (r) is approximated by the depth of flow and that slope (s) can be represented by the tangent of the slope angle. Thus

$$n = \frac{0.1^{0.67}\ 0.087\ 5^{0.5}}{0.75}$$

$$n = 0.084\ 3$$

Estimating required value for Manning's n due to mulch (n_m)

According to Foster, Johnson and Moldenhauer (1982)

$$n_m = (n^{3/2} - n_s^{3/2})^{2/3}$$

Taking a value of Manning's n due to the soil (n_s) = 0.02 gives

$$n_m = (0.084\ 3^{3/2} - 0.02^{3/2})^{2/3}$$

$$n_m = 0.076\ 7$$

Estimating required mulch application rate (M)

Rearranging equation 8.3 gives

$$M = \left(\frac{n_m}{0.105}\right)^{1.06}$$

$$M = \left(\frac{0.076\ 7}{0.105}\right)^{1.06}$$

$$M = \underline{0.72 \text{ kg m}^{-2}}$$

Theoretically this procedure can be used to determine application rates for other mulches but in practice the relationships between M and n_m have not been established. Equation 8.3 cannot therefore be used for wheat straw, soya bean residue, palm fronds or other mulch materials.

8.7   REVEGETATION

Vegetation plays the major role in the process of erosion control on gullied areas, landslides, sand dunes, road embankments, construction sites and mine spoils. Rapid revegetation is also necessary for replanting forest in areas cleared by patch-cutting and for covering land cleared of forest in favour of agriculture. The first-listed cases represent marginal environments for plant growth where the risk of vegetation failing to re-establish is high. The second-listed cases are less marginal and the objective must be to minimize damage during clearance and to establish cover quickly before the environment has time to deteriorate.

When developing a plan for revegetating an area, a soil test should be carried out to establish pH, nutrient levels, moisture status, salinity levels and the presence of toxic ions, all of which will influence the range of species which will grow. Climatic conditions should also be studied, including the frequency of drought and waterlogging. Topographic influences on the local climate are important, for example, differences in temperature and moisture between sunny and shady slopes, and frost hollows. Topography also determines the location of dry and wet sites through its effects on movement of water through the soil. Plant species should be selected for their properties of rapid growth, toughness in respect of diseases and pests, ability to compete with less desirable species and adaptability to the local soil and climatic conditions. Wherever possible, native species of plant should be chosen. A study of neighbouring sites often gives a good indication of what species are most likely to survive and thrive. The use of introduced or exotic species should not be ruled out, however, especially where the local environment has deteriorated beyond that of adjacent sites or where numbers of local species are limited. The revegetation plan should allow for plant succession which will take place naturally. In many cases, the objective is to establish pioneer species which will give immediate cover and improve the soil, permitting native species to come in and take over as the pioneer plants decline. Generally, a mix of plant species is required because it is impossible to predict the success of any one species in marginal environments where the vegetation is going to receive little or no maintenance. A monoculture is also more susceptible to disease. Thus a greater management input in terms of fertilizers and weed, pest and disease control is needed where land is being replanted with stands of trees or being prepared for improved pasture, arable or tree crops. The species mix should include grasses, forbs and woody species, both bushes and trees, except where specific requirements make such a mix undesirable, as with certain types of gully reclamation.

The most common way of planting grasses and forbs is by broadcast seeding. On small areas this can be carried out by hand but over large areas, aerial seeding is used. Hydroseeding is the application of the seed in a water slurry, usually along with fertilizer and sometimes with a mulching material. Woody species are planted either by spot seeding or as cuttings. Grasses, forbs and woody plants may all be established by transplanting. This provides a quick method of obtaining ground cover but it needs to be undertaken when there is adequate moisture in the soil. The limited availability of water is a frequent cause of transplant failure (Gray and Leiser, 1982).

8.7.1 Restoration of gullied lands

Revegetation is used in gully erosion control as a method of increasing infiltration and reducing surface runoff. The area around the gullies should be treated with grasses, legumes, shrubs and trees or combinations thereof, aided in the early stages by mulching if necessary. Research carried out at the Suide Soil and Water Conservation Experimental Station of the Huang He Conservancy Commission shows that afforestation can reduce runoff in the gullied loess areas by 65 to 80 per cent and soil loss by 75 to 90 per cent. Growing grass will reduce runoff by 50 to 60 per cent and soil loss by 60 to 80 per cent (Gong and Jiang, 1977). By

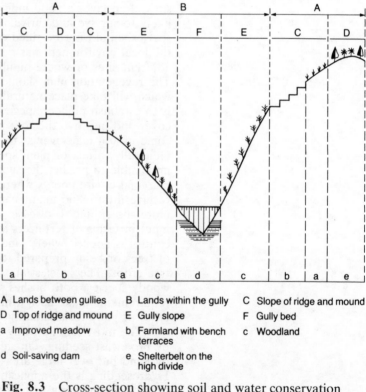

A Lands between gullies	B Lands within the gully	C Slope of ridge and mound
D Top of ridge and mound	E Gully slope	F Gully bed
a Improved meadow	b Farmland with bench terraces	c Woodland
d Soil-saving dam	e Shelterbelt on the high divide	

Fig. 8.3 Cross-section showing soil and water conservation measures adopted in the gullied loess area of China (after Jiang, Qi and Tan, 1981).

planting trees and herbs on the steep slopes of the gully sides and raising crops on bench terraces on the gentler slopes of the divides (Fig. 8.3), the land can be stabilized and sediment prevented from entering the gullies. By supporting these measures with mechanical control techniques of check dams and reservoirs along the gully beds, the volume of sediment entering the Huang He from gullies in the Wuding Valley has been reduced by 44 per cent over the period 1971 to 1978 (Jiang, Qi and Tan, 1981). The main types of trees and herbs used are *Caragana* sp., locust, poplar, Chinese pine, jujube, pear, apple, alfalfa, sweet clover and *Astragalus* sp.

Treatments to control gully erosion in the loessial hills of Mississippi (Miller, Woodburn and Turner, 1962) showed that using a mixed plant cover was always more successful. The greatest reductions in runoff were obtained with a treatment combining trees, grass and mulch but almost as good reductions were observed using trees and mulch alone. Trees and mulch used separately were rarely effective and no success was obtained by planting kudzu vine.

In these two case studies of gully erosion control, the main objective was to increase infiltration. Achieving this will help reduce gullying when surface processes are involved but where the gullies are being fed by subsurface pipes or tunnels, it is necessary to produce a uniform pattern of infiltration as well. Since trees and grasses have different root densities and their root networks extend to different depths, their mixture may result in more infiltration under the trees which may, in turn, feed water into a pipe system. Even if the pipe network has been previously broken up by subsurface ripping, concentrations of water in the soil may encourage pipes to reform. This is more likely to occur if tree species with long tap roots are planted. Thus, the best vegetative treatment for tunnelled areas is to establish a dense, uniform grass cover. Where conditions are too marginal for grass to grow, shrubs and trees will have to be used but species with a good system of lateral rather than vertical roots should be chosen.

8.7.2 Restoration of landslide scars

Tree planting is recommended as a method of stabilizing slopes prone to mass movement. Although the addition of trees to a hillside may sometimes induce sliding because of the increase in weight (De Ploey, 1981*b*), this effect is generally offset by an increase in cohesion associated with the binding of the soil within the root network and by the tensile strength of the roots themselves. Living tree roots can contribute up to 20 kPa to the soil shear strength

(O'Loughlin and Watson, 1979). It is believed that the lateral roots contribute most to binding because of their greater density whereas the vertical roots add most of the tensile strength (Gray and Leiser, 1982). Deep-rooted species are preferred for stabilizing the slope and increasing its resistance to sliding. Bishop and Stevens (1964) show that large trees can increase the shearing stress required for sliding by 2.5 kPa which is why, as seen in section 7.3.3, their removal can promote landslides.

Closing off an area, particularly from livestock but also from wild animals, will allow vegetation to colonize landslide scars naturally. The rate of recovery is slow, however. Herbs come in first followed by grasses but only about four years after the slide do perennial grasses dominate the cover and shrubs start to appear. After seven years the cover on scars in the Mgeta Valley, Tanzania, was only 25 per cent (Lundgren, 1978). Recovery of soil slip scars in the Wairarapa hill country, New Zealand, takes twenty years but even then the productivity of the pasture is only 80 per cent of that on uneroded land. Despite recolonization, the quality of the land deteriorates (Trustrum, Thomas and Lambert, 1984). Tree planting was attempted on the slide scars in the Mgeta Valley but the species used, *Acacia mearnsii*, *Cupressus lusitanica* and *Eucalyptus maidenni*, proved unsuitable. All the *Cupressus lusitanica* seedlings died and the survival of the others is threatened by gully erosion (Lundgren, 1978). This example emphasizes the need for careful selection of species in relation to the environmental conditions.

8.7.3 Afforestation

Tree planting is recognized as a suitable method of reducing runoff and erosion, especially if applied to headwater catchments as a means of regulating floods. Many countries now have afforestation programmes aimed at arresting erosion. Those in India, Malagasy Republic, Philippines, Bolivia, Jamaica, Trinidad and Tobago and Mexico are briefly described by El-Swaify, Dangler and Armstrong (1982). Most schemes involve closing of the land to other uses.

In the Vasad and Kota areas of Gujarat, India, closing of gullied lands to grazing allowed the establishment first of a good grass cover of desirable species (Tejwani, Srinivasan and Mistry, 1961) and then an increase in tree numbers through natural colonization. Afforestation trials were also successfully implemented, with bamboo, teak, sissoo and eucalyptus as the most promising species (Tejwani, 1981). Afforestation has been applied to the Taihang Mountains where, prior to the rise of the Qing Dynasty in the sixteenth century, the area was densely forested. By 1949, however, only 2 per cent remained under trees but this has now been increased to 10 per cent. Trees are planted along with bushes and grasses and the treated areas are closed to grazing and fuel gathering (Yu, 1984). Around Baisongling Mountain, the forested area has increased from 8.5 per cent in 1970 to 90 per cent today with *Pinus bungeana* a particularly successful species. Peak flood flows have been reduced and flow from springs has increased (Zhao, B. L., 1984). The importance of using a mixture of species is illustrated by the experience in west Liaoning where it was found that when Chinese pines were planted in stands they exhibited damage by insects and constituted a fire hazard. A mixed forest of Chinese pines and oaks, however, formed a stable community (Zhao, R. H., 1984).

The principal species in the forest plantations in Kenya, *Cupressus lusitanica, Pinus patula, Pinus radiata* and *Eucalyptus saligna*, are selected because of their rapid growth rather than their value in soil and water conservation (Konuche, 1983). Although the pines are generally satisfactory, the cypress results in a bare forest floor liable to erosion by overland flow unless the stands are pruned and thinned. The role of eucalypts is unclear because of evidence that when planted in wet areas they result in a reduction of water supply in springs and rivers (Gosh, Kaul and Subba-Rao, 1978) yet when grown in drier areas they do not consume large quantities of water (Konuche, 1983). Since eucalypts develop their root systems rapidly and promote infiltration and subsurface drainage, they may induce mass movements when planted on steep slopes with shallow soils. This is because of the impedance to subsurface water movement at the soil–rock interface and the reduction in the shear strength of the soil as the moisture content increases to saturation. This mechanism has been invoked as a cause of landslides in the forested areas of the Serra do Mar, Brazil (De Ploey and Cruz, 1979).

8.7.4 Restoration for pasture

Revegetation of lands for pasture is the major activity of Landgraeðsla Ríkisins, the State Soil Conservation Service of Iceland. Work is concentrated on restoration of bare moving sands and gravels using aerial seeding. The land is first fenced to keep out livestock and *Elymus arenarius* is planted on the moving dunes. This thrives well in drifting sand and collects and fixes its own dunes. Once the sand has been stabilized, the *Elymus* dies out and *Festuca rubra, Poa pratensis* and *Phleum pratensis* are seeded. Fertilizer is applied aerially each year for the next two to four years by which time a reasonable vegetation cover has been obtained. The next step depends on whether the land is upland rough grazing or is lowland to be used for cultivated pastures and hay production. In the first case, the land remains fenced but no further work is carried out. In the absence of further fertilizer application, the seeded grasses die out and there is a period about seven to ten years after the start of reclamation when the vegetation cover becomes poor. Sufficient stability and organic matter have been achieved, however, to allow native vegetation to colonize. The land remains protected for thirty years. In the second case, the land continues to be fertilized and the grass is cut annually for hay. Reseeding sometimes becomes necessary again if the grass suffers from winter kill. At present the reclamation relies on imported seeds because the local climate is too severe to provide a reservoir of locally available seed. Experiments are in progress on the use of *Lupinus nootkatensis* which seems well adapted to Icelandic conditions and provides a good ground cover as well as a supply of seed (Arnalds, 1980).

8.7.5 Other restoration problems

The main plants used in stabilizing sand dunes in coastal areas of Europe and the USA are marram grass (*Ammophila arenaria*) and American beach grass (*Ammophila breviligulata*). These have strong extensive root networks in both lateral and vertical directions which enable them to bind the sand whilst the grass acts as a sediment trap (Hesp, 1979). They thrive well in an environment of moving sand and low nutrient availability. Grasses should be planted as 10–15 cm wide culms rather than seeded because of the risk of the seeds being blown away and the young plants being damaged by sand blasting. Once stabilization of the dunes has occurred, they can be planted with shrubs and trees. Scots pine, Corsican pine and Lodgepole pine were successfully used in the stabilization of Culbin Sands near Nairn, Scotland. Similar approaches are used to stabilize desert dunes whereby the establishment of pioneer plants binds the sand and leads to an improvement in soil conditions. Within eight years of establishing the fast-growing *Tamarix aphylla* on sands near the Al Hasa oasis in Saudi Arabia, the depth of the organic horizon had increased from zero to 10 mm and the calcium carbonate content decreased from 30 per cent to 15 per cent (Stevens, 1974).

Closing the land and replanting with trees, shrubs and grasses is also adopted to renovate areas eroded through recreational use. Examples are the Tarn Hows project in the English Lake District (Barrow, Brotherton and Maurice, 1973) and the reclamation of gullies in the Box Hill area of the North Downs in southeast England (Streeter, 1977). In addition to ensuring that the species used for replanting are compatible with the physical environment, plant selection may be influenced by aesthetic considerations so as to enhance landscape quality and by the need to create varied and interesting wildlife habitats.

The greatest opportunities for combining nature conservation with soil conservation occur on mining spoils, construction sites and road embankments. Rapid establishment of a grass or legume cover is essential and this is commonly accomplished by hydroseeding a seed and fertilizer mix. Where immediate erosion reduction is necessary, mulches should be used to provide protection of the soil and prevent the seeds from being washed away. Straw mulch was found to reduce erosion to acceptable levels on roadside slopes in western Oregon (Dyrness, 1975) and in the Ivory Coast (Roose, 1975*b*). Alternatively, natural turf may be planted over the slope as is standard practice in the urban areas of Singapore (Ramaswamy, Aziz and Narayanan, 1981). Prior to seeding, the slopes should be covered with 100 mm of top soil and a seed bed prepared. Once the slope has been stabilized, ornamental trees and shrubs may be planted or the land can be left to be colonized by native vegetation.

8.8   AGROFORESTRY

Trees can be incorporated within a farming system by planting them on land which is not suitable for crop production, along river banks, on terraces and contour bunds, on areas being revegetated to control erosion, as windbreaks and shade trees and as ornamentals around the homestead (Wenner, 1981; Lundgren and Nair, 1985). Trees help to preserve the fertility and structure of the soil and prevent its erosion. They are attractive to the farmer where they provide additional needs, especially fuel, fodder and fruits.

The shifting cultivation system of farming can be modified by the planting of fast-growing trees which will yield firewood or fodder during the fallow period instead of allowing the forest to regenerate naturally. Using this *taungya* method, farmers in southeast Nigeria have been able to reduce the fallow period to seven years instead of fifteen (Roche, 1974). Alternatively, fodder–fuel plantations can be established, as in parts of Gujarat, India (Tejwani,

1981), or the trees can be intercropped with food crops on contour bunds (Getahun, 1983).

The most important tree species used in agroforestry are *Leucaena leucocephala* which is a quick-growing fodder tree but also provides timber for fuel and pulpwood; *Prosopis juliflora* and *Prosopis chilensis* which are drought-resistant and provide wood for fuel and poles; *Acacia albida* which is well-adapted to sandy soils and produces good fodder, *Acacia nilotica* and *Sesbania grandiflora*.

Agroforestry is being encouraged by the forestry departments of several developing countries and is strongly recommended in others. As a result of clearance of the forest for firewood and the reduction of the forest area through overgrazing, soil erosion is a serious problem in Nepal. Fodder is scarce and, faced with long walks to collect fuel, farmers are burning the dung previously applied to the land as fertilizer (Eckholm, 1976). Yet the planting of trees along contour bunds and on river banks is traditional practice as is the maintenance of forests around shrines and springs (Nepali, 1981). Also, Nepal contains at least 100 different species of fodder trees of which *Alnus nepalensis* regenerates rapidly and naturally in eroded areas. It has been calculated that if each farmer maintained thirty fodder trees and if 10 per cent of the farm area was turned into a fodder tree orchard, Nepal would have 10 to 20 per cent more fodder production within ten to fifteen years and the ability to support livestock on a sustained basis (Pandey, 1981).

Chapter 9
SOIL MANAGEMENT

The aims of sound soil management are to maintain the fertility and structure of the soil. Highly fertile soils result in high crop yields, good plant cover and, therefore, in conditions which minimize the erosive effects of raindrops, runoff and wind. These soils have a stable, usually granular, structure which does not break down under cultivation, and a high infiltration capacity. Soil fertility can thus be seen as the key to soil conservation.

9.1 ORGANIC CONTENT

One way of achieving and maintaining a fertile soil is to apply organic matter. This improves the cohesiveness of the soil, increases its water retention capacity and promotes a stable aggregate structure.

Organic material may be added as green manures, straw or as a manure which has already undergone a high degree of fermentation. The effectiveness of these three kinds of material varies with the isohumic factor, which is the quantity of humus produced per unit of organic matter (Table 9.1; Kolenbrander, 1974). Green manures, which are normally leguminous crops ploughed in, have a high rate of fermentation and yield a rapid increase in soil stability. The increase is short-lived, however, because of a low isohumic factor. Straw decomposes less rapidly and so takes longer to affect soil stability but has a higher isohumic factor. Previously fermented manures require still longer to influence soil stability but their effect is longer lasting because these have a still higher isohumic factor (Fournier, 1972).

As seen in section 3.2, soils with less than 2 per cent organic content are generally erodible. To increase the resistance of an erodible soil by building up organic matter is a lengthy process, however, because organic content must

Table 9.1 Farmyard manure equivalents of some organic materials (after Kolenbrander, 1974)

Material	Isohumic factor	FYM equivalent
Plant foliage	0.20	0.25
Green manures	0.25	0.35
Cereal straw	0.30	0.45
Roots of crops	0.35	0.55
Farmyard manure	0.50	1.00
Deciduous tree litter	0.60	1.40
Coniferous tree litter	0.65	1.60
Peat moss	0.85	2.50

be raised by 1 to 2 per cent before any effect on stability is observed. Also, the quantity of material needed to bring about such an increase can pose problems in terms of supply. Ploughing in maize residue at 0.5 to 1.0 kg m^{-2} was found in Nigeria to increase the organic carbon content of the soil in absolute terms by only 0.004 to 0.017 per cent whilst application of farmyard manure at 1 kg m^{-2} was sufficient only to maintain the existing level of organic content and did not increase it (Jones, 1971). A three-year grass ley, however, was equivalent to an annual application of farmyard manure at 1.2 kg m^{-2}. This pattern of the effects of different organic materials is supported by numerous field experiments world-wide which show that the addition of straw, green manures and farmyard manure lessens the rate of decrease in structural stability of the soil under arable farming compared with no return of crop residues but that grass leys are the only effective way of building up the organic content. One reason for this is that the stability of the larger soil aggregates depends on the density of the roots and hyphae and this is increased by pasture and decreased by arable cropping (Tisdall and Oades, 1982). Thus with the trend in many parts of the world towards larger mechanized arable farms where there is no demand for grass, clover or alfalfa, the addition of organic matter becomes uneconomic.

In a review of trends in the organic content of arable soils, Newbould (1982) refers to studies in Sweden which show a fall in the organic carbon content of soils from 3.5 to 2.5 per cent over sixty years of cereal production except where straw residue was returned to the soil and nitrogen added regularly. In the Great Plains of Canada the organic content has been reduced from 1.7 per cent in 1900 to 0.9 per cent today under continuous cereal cropping until 1935 and alternating cereals and fallow since. On the silty clay loams at Rothamsted Experimental Station, Harpenden, England, however, organic carbon contents have remained virtually unchanged in trials started in 1852 on unmanured and chemically-fertilized plots and have increased slightly on plots treated annually with 3.5 kg m^{-2} of farmyard manure. In contrast, on the sandy loam soils of the Woburn Experimental Farm, Bedfordshire, England, organic carbon contents have fallen from 1.5 to 0.76 per cent over 100 years and rotational cropping has not halted this decline. The use of three-year leys in a five-year rotation with the addition of farmyard manure to the first arable crop every five years was the only treatment to bring about an increase in organic carbon, from 1.02 to 1.44 per cent (Johnston, 1982).

The value of organic matter is enhanced by the presence of base minerals in the soil as these combine with the organic materials to form by chemical bonding the compounds of clay and humus which make up the soil aggregates. The base minerals are thus retained in the soil rather than removed by leaching or subsurface flow. Where these minerals, which provide the essential nutrients for plant growth, are absent, they should be added to the soil as fertilizer in the amounts normally recommended for the crop being grown. The addition of 13.5 g m^{-2} of P_2O_5 with the sowing of winter crops neutralizes the lack of phosphorus in the eroded carbonate chernozem soils of the northern Caucasus, USSR, and encourages sufficient crop growth to minimize wind erosion, particularly in the most vulnerable month of February following the structural breakdown of the soil through temperature changes and effects of snow cover during the winter (Tregubov, 1981).

Mineral fertilizers on their own have no long-term effect on the state of humus in the soil and they need organic support to bring about an improvement in aggregate structure. Moreover, the continual use of mineral fertilizers without organic manures may lead to structural deterioration of the soil and increased erodibility. Lime should also be applied to the soil as this reduces acidity and, by encouraging the growth of legumes, may ensure the success of their use in erosion control.

9.2   TILLAGE PRACTICES

When managed so as to maintain their fertility, most soils retain their stability and are not adversely affected by standard tillage operations. Indeed, tillage is an essential management technique: it provides a suitable seed bed for plant growth and helps to control weeds. The effect of wheeled traffic and tillage implements on a soil depends upon its shear strength, the nature of the confining stresses and the direction in which the force is applied. The main effect of driving a tractor across a field is to apply force from above and compact the soil. This may result in an increase in shear strength through an increase in bulk density and in the number of clods larger than 30 mm in diameter, but these effects are often more than offset by decreased infiltration and increased runoff so that wheelings are frequently zones of concentrated erosion. The pattern of compaction depends upon tyre pressure, the width of the wheels and the speed of the tractor, the latter controlling the contact time between the wheel and the soil. Compaction generally extends to the depth of the previous tillage, up to 300 mm for deep ploughing, 180 mm for normal ploughing and 60 mm with zero tillage (Pidgeon and Soane, 1978).

The tillage tools pulled by the tractor are designed to apply an upward force to cut and loosen the compacted soil, sometimes to invert it and mix it, and to smooth and shape its surface. When the moisture content of the soil is below the plastic limit (section 3.2), the soil fails by cracking with the soil aggregates sliding over each other but remaining unbroken. The soil ahead of the loosening tool moves forwards and upwards over the entire working depth. A distinct shear plane is formed from the base of the tool which is crescentic in shape in the case of tines but is modified where the tool turns and inverts the soil as with a ploughshare. Soil loosening is effective where the confining stresses resisting upward movement are less than those resisting sideways movement of the soil. Vertical confining stress is obviously zero at the surface and increases with depth until, at a critical depth, it equals the lateral confining stresses and crescentic failure ceases to occur. Below this depth the soil moves only forwards and sideways, no distinct shear plane is formed and lateral failure occurs with a risk of compaction (Godwin and Spoor, 1977).

9.2.1 Conventional tillage

Over the years a reasonably standard or conventional system of tillage, involving ploughing, secondary cultivation with one or more disc harrowings, and planting, has been found suitable for a wide range of soils. Ploughing is carried out with the mouldboard plough although, on stony land or with soils which do not fall cleanly off mouldboards, the disc plough is often used. Ploughs invert the plough furrow and lift and move all the soil in the plough layer usually to a depth of 100 to 200 mm. Secondary cultivation to form the seed bed and remove weeds is carried out by either disc or tine cultivators. With disc cultivators the soil is broken up by the passage of saucer-shaped metal discs mounted on axles. The most common tine cultivator is the chisel type which consists of a series of metal blades mounted on a frame. The blades vary in width from narrow, 50 mm, to wide, 75 mm, but may be up to 300 mm wide. Another tine cultivator is the sweep or blade type which has V-shaped blades between 0.5 and 2 m wide. Ploughing produces a rough cloddy surface with local variations in height of 120 to 160 mm. Secondary cultivation reduces the roughness to 30 to 40 mm whilst drilling and rolling decrease it still further (Evans, 1980). Roughness is also reduced over time by raindrop impact and water and wind erosion. Soil loss (*SL*) by water erosion decreases with increasing roughness (*R*) according to the relationship (Cogo, Moldenhauer and Foster, 1984)

$$SL \propto e^{-0.5R} \qquad\qquad (9.1)$$

which means that small increases in roughness from a virtually smooth surface can have substantial effects on reducing erosion but much larger increases will be needed to have the same effect with an already rough surface. This explains why tillage can often be successfully used to roughen the surface to control wind erosion in an emergency (Woodruff, Chepil and Lynch, 1957). Usually a chisel is used to produce ridges and furrows across the path of the prevailing wind.

9.2.2 Conservation tillage for problem soils

Conventional tillage causes problems on dusty, fine sandy soils, particularly when dry; on very heavy, sticky soils; and on structureless soils, especially those with a high sodium content.

In the first case, conventional tillage practice tends to produce a large number of failure planes, pulverize the soil near the surface and create a compacted layer at plough depth which reduces infiltration and results in increased runoff. The soil is then readily eroded by water and, on drying into a fine dust, also by wind. Thus whilst tillage can improve the coarse structures on heavy soils, it can destroy the structure of non-cohesive soils. To overcome these effects, tillage operations are restricted either by cutting down on their number by carrying out as many operations as possible in one pass, as with mulch tillage and minimum tillage, or by concentrating them only on the rows where the plant grows and leaving the inter-row areas untilled, as with strip-zone tillage (Schwab, Frevert, Edminster and Barnes, 1966; Table 9.2).

Table 9.2 Tillage practices used for soil conservation

Practice	Description
Conventional	Standard practice of ploughing with disc or mouldboard plough, one or more disc harrowings, a spike-tooth harrowing, and surface planting.
Strip or zone tillage	Preparation of seed bed by conditioning the soil along narrow strips in and adjacent to the seed rows, leaving the intervening soil areas untilled: e.g. plough–plant; wheel-track planting; listing.
Mulch tillage	Practice that leaves a large percentage of residual material (leaves, stalks, crowns, roots) on or near the surface as a protective mulch.
Minimum tillage	Preparation of seed bed with minimal disturbance. Use of chemicals to kill existing vegetation, followed by tillage to open only a narrow seedband to receive the seed. Weed control by herbicides.

After Schwab, Frevert, Edminster and Barnes (1966).

Numerous studies have been undertaken in recent years to examine the effects of different types of conservation tillage on soil erosion rates, soil conditions and crop yields. The results show that the success of the systems is highly soil specific and also dependant upon how well weeds, pests and diseases have been controlled. Generally the better-drained, coarse and medium-textured soils with low organic content respond best and the systems are not successful on poorly drained soils with high organic contents or on heavy soils where use of the mouldboard plough is essential.

The practice of no tillage, whereby drilling takes place directly into the stubble of the previous crop and weeds are controlled by herbicides, has been found to increase the percentage of water stable aggregates in the soil compared with tine or disc cultivation and ploughing (Aina, 1979; Douglas and Goss, 1982). The plough–plant system was used for maize cultivation on research plots of the University of Science and Technology, Kumasi, Ghana, and reduced soil loss from 23 storms totalling 452 mm of rain to 0.02 kg m^{-2} compared with 0.09 kg m^{-2} with a plough–harrow–plant sequence and a surprisingly high 0.14 kg m^{-2} with traditional tillage using a hoe and cutlass (Baffoe-Bonnie and Quansah, 1975). The plough–plant system caused the least soil compaction, conserved the most soil moisture and reduced losses of organic matter, nitrogen, phosphorus and potassium (Quansah and Baffoe-Bonnie, 1981). Plough–plant systems have not become popular, however, because of problems of weed control and the slower speed of planting which is reduced to the time taken to prepare the seed bed.

Difficulties with weed control, operating with large amounts of residue and, in many cases, lower yields have prevented the widespread take-up of stubble-mulch tillage. Nevertheless, this system can be used successfully to control wind erosion and conserve moisture in drier wheat-growing areas. Chepil and Woodruff (1963) carried out wind tunnel tests in Nebraska and found that stubble mulching resulted in a soil loss of 0.18 kg m^{-2} compared with 2.4 kg m^{-2} on land which had been clean-tilled with a mouldboard plough. Average annual soil loss over eight years was 0.20 kg m^{-2} on stubble-mulched land compared with 0.65 kg m^{-2} on conventionally tilled land (Fenster and McCalla, 1970).

The practices of no tillage and minimum tillage reduced erosion rates under maize (Bonsu and Obeng, 1979) and millet (Bonsu, 1981) in Ghana to levels comparable with those achieved by multiple cropping but generally not to the levels obtained with surface mulching. Also, no tillage was not always effective in the first year of its operation because of the low percentage of crop residues on the surface. No tillage reduced annual soil loss under maize with two crops per year near Ibadan, Nigeria, to 0.007 kg m^{-2} compared with 0.56 kg m^{-2} for hoe and cutlass, 0.83 kg m^{-2} with a mouldboard plough and 0.91 kg m^{-2} for a mouldboard plough followed by harrowing (Osuji, Babalola and Aboaba, 1980). No tillage, however, was less effective in rainfall simulator tests on a Russell silt loam in the mid-west of the USA when subjected to a two-hour storm of 64 mm h[1]; the resulting soil loss was 3.3 kg m^{-2}. Comparable losses were 2.1 kg m^{-2} from land ploughed with a mouldboard in the autumn and disced in the spring, 1.8 kg m^{-2} from land chiselled in the autumn and disced in the spring, and 1.2 kg m^{-2} from land cultivated in the spring only with a sweep (Cogo, Moldenhauer and Foster, 1984). Minimum tillage using one disc cultivation prior to planting led to an increase in runoff over that from conventional tillage on a silty clay soil under continuous wheat production near Pisa, Italy. This was because the minimum tilled plots retained moisture and this in turn reduced the cracking which plays a major role in promoting infiltration of water in these soils. Despite the higher runoff, annual soil loss was lower under minimum tillage at 0.16 kg m^{-2} compared with 0.41 kg m^{-2} from conventional tillage (Chisci and Zanchi, 1981). In studies aimed at controlling wind erosion, the use of no tillage and herbicides resulted in less weed growth, higher soil moisture storage and higher grain yields than conventional tillage during six-year periods at North Platte (Wicks and Smika, 1973) and Sidney (Fenster and Wicks, 1977), Nebraska.

Farmers are generally reluctant to take up tillage practices which leave large amounts of residue on the surface and so, despite the large research effort being directed at no and minimum tillage, they are not widely adopted. A more attractive practice is chiselling instead of ploughing with a mouldboard in the autumn to produce a rough surface but retain residue cover followed by disc cultivation in the spring to smooth the seed bed and cover the residue. This form of conservation tillage can reduce soil loss by an order of magnitude over that recorded with conventional tillage (Siemens and Oschwald, 1978; Johnson and Moldenhauer, 1979) and it is now widely practised in the Corn Belt of the USA. A similar system can be used to control erosion during replanting of pineapple plantations. It involves slashing the old pines and placing the residues in the furrows. A chisel is then used to rip the ridges and the new pineapples are planted along the rip line. This method reduced soil loss on a very erodible soil in Eastern Cape Province, South Africa, to 0.05 kg m^{-2} y^{-1} compared with 3 kg m^{-2} y^{-1} with conventional methods (McPhee, Hartmann and Kieck, 1983). The chisel–disc treatment is effective because whilst, as shown earlier, soil loss decreases with both increasing roughness and increasing residue cover, tillage increases roughness but reduces the surface residue. The treatment thus represents a good compromise between managing residue and roughness effects.

Since conservation tillage does not break up the soil surface, there is concern that in the long term it may lead to a less porous surface with a resulting increase in runoff and erosion. Soane and Pidgeon (1975) found that chisel ploughing produced a less porous surface than the mouldboard plough on a loamy soil in Scotland and, as noted above, Chisci and Zanchi (1981) found that no tillage led to an increase in runoff. Some researchers, however, believe that these effects are short-lived and that after using conservation tillage with a chisel plough for three or four years the porosity of the top 150 mm of soil is the same as that of a mouldboard-ploughed soil. After seven years, the porosities of the top 300 mm of soil are similar. These effects were observed on a silty clay loam (Voorhees and Lindstrom, 1984). Kemper and Derpsch (1981) suggest that no tillage can be effective in restoring the porosity of oxisols and alfisols where it has been reduced by the development of a plough pan but that it will take ten to twelve years.

9.2.3 Alternatives to conservation tillage

An alternative approach to conservation tillage is to attempt, through careful timing of operations in relation to soil conditions, to use tillage to produce an erosion-resistant surface. Several farmers on sandy soils in the Midlands counties of England have adopted the Glassford system of ploughing and pressing the soil to produce a cloddy surface to control wind erosion on land devoted to sugar beet. When the soil is moist but not wet, a chisel is used to break up the crust and produce ridges and furrows. The land in the furrows is then rolled either in the same operation, by modifying the chisel plough to incorporate a roll press, or as soon as possible in a second operation before the soil dries out. This tillage is preferably carried out in January and the resulting surface of hills and valleys remains stable throughout the spring blowing period even after it has been broken up by drilling. This is generally carried out transverse to the press ridges. The Glassford system can thus be practised with standard farm equipment. Since the stability of soil clods to raindrop impact and slumping on wetting depends upon the soil conditions at the time of clod formation and these have a much greater effect than subsequent changes in soil moisture and the influence of weathering, it may be feasible to devise a similar tillage system to produce a surface which is resistant to water erosion (Stuttard, 1984). Some attempts have already been made to do this but they rely on specially designed conservation ploughs for imprinting the soil surface with complex geometric patterns (Dixon and Simanton, 1980).

Heavy sticky soils with a moisture content above the plastic limit will fail compressively during tillage, produce few or no fissures and become smeared (Spoor and Godwin, 1979). The type of clay mineral in the soil will determine its behaviour under these conditions (Spoor, Leeds-Harrison and Godwin, 1982). Unconfined swelling is likely to take place with smectitic or micaceous clays and this may cause either the disappearance of aggregates or the formation of new but less stable ones. If drainage cannot occur and the failure is undrained, an already smeared soil may become puddled or even turn into a slurry. Reductions in runoff and therefore erosion on heavy soils are best achieved by increasing the rate of subsurface water movement by drainage. Erodible soils with more than 20 per cent clay content will benefit from the installation of mole drains and from the break-up of compacted layers at depth by subsoiling.

Deep tillage using a crawler tractor to pull two chisels through the ground to open up furrows about 100 mm wide and 500 to 700 mm deep is also recommended practice to break up subsurface pipes and tunnels (Colclough, 1965; Crouch, 1978). This treatment aids the establishment of grasses, forbs and legumes and is therefore carried out prior to reseeding the land for pasture. Control of tunnel erosion is dependent upon the success of the revegetation because the effects of ripping decline after three to five years (Aldon, 1976).

Conservation tillage has not proved appropriate to the management of the highly plastic, sticky, calcareous black clay soils of the tropics and subtropics. These vertisols have a high percentage of smectitic clays which undergo pronounced shrinkage when dry, resulting in deep cracks which close only after prolonged wetting. Drainage is a problem when these soils are wet because the infiltration rate is very low; even rains of light intensity cause runoff and erosion. On the Indian vertisols, in order to obtain a good crop cover to protect the soil from erosion in the rainy season, sowing has to be carried out in the dry soil in advance of the rains. There is then a problem of preparing a good seed bed in the hard soil and any reduction in tillage is likely to reduce crop yield. Attempts to use stubble mulching to reduce water erosion on the vertisols devoted to continuous wheat production in Australia show that these soils may not respond well to reduced tillage. Stubble mulching failed to increase the aggregate stability of the soil compared with conventional tillage (Marston and Hird, 1978) and did not reduce erosion to an acceptable level (Marston and Perrens, 1981). Alternative approaches to erosion control using mechanical methods are required.

9.3   SOIL STABILIZERS

Improvements in soil structure can be achieved by applying soil conditioners, which may consist of organic by-products, polyvalent salts and various synthetic polymers. Polyvalent salts such as gypsum bring about flocculation of the clay particles while organic by-products and synthetic polymers bind the soil particles into aggregates.

Gypsum has been used successfully to improve the structure of sodic soils in southeast Australia (Davidson and Quirk, 1961; Rosewell, 1970). Sodic soils are highly erodible because the excess of sodium results in the dispersal of the clay minerals on contact with water with consequent structural deterioration. Such soils appear to be particularly susceptible to tunnel erosion. The most effective treatment is therefore to apply gypsum as this supplies a cation to replace the sodium. A good drainage system must also be provided to assist with washing out the sodium from the soil. This treatment is extremely expensive to employ over large areas, however, and, unless accompanied by ripping to break up the tunnels and the sowing of grass, gives only temporary relief. Gypsum has also been used to reduce surface crusting and runoff on red-brown earths in the wheat-growing region of South Australia where the soils are unstable because of high contents of exchangeable magnesium (Grierson, 1978) and on grey and brown clays in the Gwydir Valley, near Moree, New South Wales, also a wheat-growing area, where the structural instability is due to exchangeable sodium (So, Tayler, Yates and McGarity, 1978).

Temporary stability, lasting from two weeks to six months, can be obtained on most soils by using soil stabilizers or soil conditioners. These oil- or rubber-based compounds, normally applied with water as a spray, are poly-functional polymers which develop chemical bonds with the minerals in the soil. They are too expensive for general agricultural use but, where the cost is warranted, are helpful on special sites like sand dunes, road cuttings or embankments and stream banks, to provide a short period of stability between the times of seeding and establishment of a plant cover. Soil conditioners fall into two groups, those that render the soil hydrophobic and therefore decrease infiltration and increase runoff, and those that make the soil hydrophyllic, increase infiltration and decrease runoff (De Vleeschauwer, Lal and De Boodt, 1979). The hydrophobic conditioners have been more widely tested. Those based on bitumen are generally effective in controlling water erosion for only a few storms and are therefore not always suitable for soil conservation purposes. They can, however, be employed to increase water yield; for example, to supply farm ponds (Laing, 1978). Asphalt and latex emulsions will also seal the surface and increase runoff, but they are effective in stabilizing the soil and preventing crusting and erosion at least until the seal is broken. When applied to agricultural soils, for example, subsequent discing to a depth of 200 mm may partially destroy the seal and promote aggregate destruction (Gabriels and De Boodt, 1978). This problem can be alleviated to some extent by incorporating the emulsion in the top 100 to 200 mm of the soil (Gabriels, Maene, Lenvain and De Boodt, 1977). The critical factor in this case is the size of aggregates which are produced: if they are too small, infiltration rates remain low. For effective infiltration with hydrophobic conditioners, the aggregates should be at least 2 mm in size and ideally larger than 5 mm (Pla, 1977).

Experiments with polyacrylamide conditioners which are hydrophyllic show that high infiltration rates can be obtained regardless of aggregate size but these emulsions are more expensive to use. Polyurea polymers contain a mixture of hydrophyllic ethylene oxide and hydrophobic propylene oxide in proportions determined according to the degree of hydrophylicity or hydrophobicity required. They have been used successfully to stabilize sand dunes at Oulled Dhifallah, Tunisia, where they provided a resistant skin, 5 mm thick, to the soil which was resistant to water erosion. It was also found that *Acacia cyanophylla* plants, used in the revegetation programme, had a higher survival rate and made faster growth on the soil-stabilized areas (De Kesel and De Vleeschauwer, 1981).

Numerous materials have been tested for use in soil stabilization. They include animal slurries (Mazurak, Chesnin and Tiarks, 1975; Mitchell and Gunther, 1976), factory waste lime, sewage sludge (Astill, 1981), ferric and calcium sulphate (Chisci, Lorenzi and Piccolo, 1978), a mixture of natural rubber latex and mineral oil (Soong, 1979), industrial date and sugar beet waste (Hardan and Al-Ani, 1978) and rice husk ash (Subrahmanyam, Lee and Lee, 1981). Most are too expensive for agricultural use except with high-value crops such as vegetables or, like the slurries and sludges, are unpleasant to handle, create odours and without specialized soil-incorporation equipment can only be applied in small quantities. The most promising are the organic by-products of crops which are often available locally as wastes in large quantities. They can be successfully used to give temporary stability on road embankments and on construction sites in urban areas.

Chapter 10
MECHANICAL METHODS OF EROSION CONTROL

Mechanical field practices are used to control the movement of water and wind over the soil surface. A range of techniques is available and the decision on which to adopt depends on whether the objective is to reduce the velocity of runoff and wind, increase surface water storage capacity or safely dispose of excess water. Mechanical methods are normally employed in conjunction with agronomic measures.

10.1 CONTOURING

Carrying out ploughing, planting and cultivation on the contour can reduce soil loss from sloping land by up to 50 per cent compared with cultivation up-and-down the slope. The effectiveness of contour farming varies with slope steepness and slope length, for it is inadequate as the sole conservation measure for lengths greater than 180 m at 1° steepness. The allowable length declines with increasing steepness to 30 m at 5.5° and 20 m at 8.5°. Moreover the technique is only effective during storms of low rainfall intensity. Protection against more extreme storms is improved by supplementing contour farming with strip-cropping (section 8.3). The soil loss from contour strip-cropped fields is 25 to 45 per cent of that from fields managed by up-and-down tillage depending upon the slope steepness. A 50 per cent reduction in erosion was achieved on the Kamennaya steppe near Voronozezh, USSR, using contour strip-cropping with strips 50 to 100 m wide and alternating five fields of grains with three of grass and one with a legume (Tregubov, 1981).

On silty and fine sandy soils, erosion may be further reduced by storing water on the surface rather than allowing it to run off. Limited increases in storage capacity can be obtained by forming ridges, usually at a slight gradient of about 1:400 to the contour, at regular intervals determined by the slope steepness. Contour ridging is generally ineffective on its own as a soil conservation measure on slopes steeper than 4.5°. On a 5° slope with a shallow, highly erodible sandy soil, ridging increased annual soil loss from 3 to 9 kg m^{-2} under pineapples in the Eastern Cape Region of South Africa (McPhee, Hartmann and Kieck, 1983). However, there are many instances of the successful use of ridges. A system of alternating 1 m wide broadbeds and 0.5 m wide sunken furrows reduces annual soil loss to 0.16 kg m^{-2} on vertisols near Hyderabad, Andhra Pradesh, India, from 0.56 kg m^{-2} with conventional flat planting. It also allows crops to be grown during the rainy season instead of the land lying fallow so that two crops per year are obtained instead of one. The furrows are graded at between 1:125 and 1:250; steeper grades result in too much erosion whilst gentler grades do not provide sufficient drainage under wet conditions. The furrows discharge into grass waterways (Kampen, Hari Krishna and Pathak, 1981). The technique is particularly effective in rainstorms of 30 mm or more. The mean annual soil loss on vertisols over the period 1975–80 was 0.02 kg m^{-2} for these storms using graded broad beds and furrows compared with 0.13 kg m^{-2} with traditional flat planting. When used on alfisols the technique increased erosion compared with conventional practice because underlying less pervious clays were exposed in the furrows resulting in greater runoff (Pathak, Miranda and El-Swaify, 1985). Experiments carried out to investigate ways of reducing erosion under vines in the Tokaj area of Hungary showed that on an 18° slope the construction of a ridge every tenth row gave an annual soil loss of 0.30 kg m^{-2} compared with 0.09 kg m^{-2} with a ridge every fifth row, 0.006 kg m^{-2} with a ridge every row and 0.40 kg m^{-2} with no ridges (Pinczés, 1980; data are conversions assuming a bulk density for the soil of 1.0 Mg m^{-3}). Ridging is also used to control erosion on the chernozem soils of the USSR. By deep loosening the soil to 340 mm, a ridger or lister creates side bunds, 150 to 200 mm high, and furrows, 300 mm wide which, on the contour on a 3° slope, decrease annual soil loss to 1.4 kg m^{-2}, increase soil moisture by 9 per cent and increase grain yields (Tregubov, 1981).

Greater storage of water and more effective erosion control can be achieved by connecting the ridges with cross-ties over the intervening furrows, thereby forming a series of rectangular depressions which fill with water during rain. Because crop damage can occur if the water cannot soak into the soil within 48 h, this practice, known as tied-ridging, should only be used on well-drained soils. If it is applied to clay soils, waterlogging is likely to occur. When the practice was tried in Israel on wheat lands in Gaza, the soil loss over the 1980–81 winter was 15.6 g m^{-2} with 1.6 m wide ridges, 7.2 g m^{-2} with 0.6 m wide ridges and

29.3 g m^{-2} with flat planting. The wheat yield was highest on the 1.6 m wide ridges (Morin, Rawitz, Benyamini, Hoogmoed and Etkin, 1984). A similar technique, called range-pitting, is sometimes used on grazing land whereby a series of pits is dug, these being about 50 cm by 50 cm, 7.5 cm deep and 40 cm apart; variations in pit size are found (Neff and Wight, 1980). About 50 per cent of the storage capacity is lost after eight years and about 90 per cent after 28 years (Neff, 1973).

10.2 CONTOUR BUNDS

Contour bunds are earth banks, 1.5 to 2 m wide, thrown across the slope to act as a barrier to runoff, to form a water storage area on their upslope side and to break up a slope into segments shorter in length than is required to generate overland flow. They are suitable for slopes of 1° to 7° and are frequently used on smallholdings in the tropics where they form permanent buffers in a strip-cropping system, being planted with grasses or trees (Roose, 1966). The banks, spaced at 10 to 20 m intervals, are generally hand-constructed. There are no precise specifications for their design and deviations in their alignment of up to 10 per cent from the contour are permissible. Hurni (1984) calculated the effectiveness of contour bunds to control erosion in Wallo Province, Ethiopia, and showed that they would only reduce soil loss sufficiently on the lowest of the slopes examined (Table 10.1).

Table 10.1 Capacity of contour bunds to reduce erosion in Wallo Province, Ethiopia (after Hurni, 1984)

Bund form				
Slope	6°	14°	27°	33°
Height (m)	0.20	0.20	0.20	0.20
Width (m)	1.90	0.70	0.40	0.30
Storage capacity (m²)	0.19	0.07	0.04	0.03
Spacing (m)	20	15	10	8
Predicted soil loss (kg m^{-2} y^{-1})	3.0	11.5	11.5	12.5
Capacity of bunds to store soil (kg m^{-2})	11.4	5.9	4.8	4.5
Percentage of soil loss stored behind bunds in first and second year	100(1) 100(2)	51(1) 0(2)	42(1) 0(2)	36(1) 0(2)

10.3 TERRACES

Terraces are earth embankments constructed across the slope to intercept surface runoff and convey it to a stable outlet at a non-erosive velocity, and to shorten slope length. They thus perform similar functions to contour bunds. They differ from them by being larger and designed to more stringent specifications. Decisions are required on the spacing and length of the terraces, the location of terrace outlets, the gradient and dimensions of the terrace channel and the layout of the terrace system. (Tables 10.2 and 10.3).

Terraces can be classified into three main types: diversion, retention and bench (Table 10.4). The primary aim of diversion terraces is to intercept overland flow and channel it across the slope to a suitable outlet. They therefore run at a slight gradient, usually 1:250, to the contour. There are several varieties of diversion terrace. The Mangum terrace, formed by taking soil from both sides of the embankment, and the Nichols terrace, constructed by moving soil from the upslope side only, are broad-based with the embankment and channel occupying a width of about 15 m. Narrow-based terraces are only 3 to 4 m wide and consequently have steeper banks which cannot be cultivated. For cultivation to be possible, the banks should not exceed 14° slope if small machinery is used or 8.5° if large reaping machines are operated. Diversion terraces are not suitable for ground slopes greater than 7° because of the expense of construction and the close spacing which would be required.

Retention terraces are used where it is necessary to conserve water by storing it on the hillside. They are therefore ungraded or level and generally designed with the capacity to store runoff volume with a ten-year return period without overtopping. These terraces are normally recommended only for permeable soils on slopes of less than 4.5°.

Bench terraces consist of a series of alternating shelves and risers and are employed where steep slopes, up to 30°, need to be cultivated. The riser is vulnerable to erosion and is protected by a vegetation cover and sometimes faced with stones or concrete. There is no channel as such but a storage area is created by sloping the shelf into the hillside (Fig. 10.1). The basic bench terrace system can be modified according to the nature and value of the crops grown. Two kinds of system are used in Peninsular Malaysia (Williams and Joseph, 1970). Where tree crops are grown, the terraces are widely spaced, the shelves being wide enough for one row of plants, usually rubber or oil palm, and the long, relatively gentle riser banks being planted with grass or a ground creeper. With more valuable crops such as temperate vegetables grown in the highlands, the shelves are closely spaced and the steeply sloping risers frequently protected by masonry. Level bench terraces are used where water conservation is also a requirement, as in the loess areas of China (Fang, Zhou, Liu, Liu, Ren and Zhang, 1981) and in parts of Kenya (Barber, Thomas and Moore, 1981).

Table 10.2 Design lengths and grades for terrace channels (after Hudson, 1981*a*)

Maximum length:	normal	250 m (sandy soils) to 400 m (clay soils)
	absolute	400 m (sandy soils) to 450 m (clay soils)
Maximum grade:	first 100 m	1:1 000
	second 100 m	1:500
	third 100 m	1:330
	fourth 100 m	1:250
	where a constant grade is used, 1:250 is recommended	
Ground slopes:	diversion terraces	usable on slopes up to 7°; on steeper slopes the cost of construction is too great and the spacing too close to allow mechanized farming
	retention terraces	recommended only on slopes up to 4.5°
	bench terraces	recommended on slopes of 7 to 30°

Table 10.3 Formulae for determining spacing of terraces

Approach

Many formulae have been developed for determining the difference in height between two successive terraces; this height difference is known as the vertical interval (*VI*).

THEORETICAL FORMULA

For steady-state conditions, the runoff (Qw) at slope length (L) on a hillside can be expressed as:

$$Qw = (R - i) \, L \cos \theta$$

where R is the rainfall intensity, i is the infiltration capacity and θ is the slope angle.

From the Manning equation of flow velocity:

$$Qw = (R - i) \, L \cos \theta = \frac{r^{5/3} \sin^{\frac{1}{2}} \theta}{n}$$

The hydraulic radius (r) is expressed by:

$$r = \left(\frac{vn}{\sin^{\frac{1}{2}} \theta}\right)^{\frac{3}{2}}$$

Table 10.3 (*cont.*)

THEORETICAL FORMULA

Therefore:

$$(R - i) \, L \, \cos \theta = \left[\left(\frac{vn}{\sin^{\frac{1}{4}} \theta} \right)^{\frac{3}{2}} \right]^{5/3} \frac{\sin^{\frac{3}{4}} \theta}{n}$$

Rearranging for given values of R and i, say those for the one-hour rainfall with a ten-year return period, and for a preselected value of v, say the maximum permissible velocity for the soil (Table 10.7), gives a slope distance L which can be used as the distance between terraces down the slope:

$$L = \frac{v^{5/2} \, n^{3/2}}{(R - i) \sin^{\frac{3}{4}} \theta \cos \theta}$$

A value of $n = 0.01$ is recommended for bare soil. The vertical interval is obtained from:

$$VI = L \sin \theta$$

For example, if the peak rainfall excess $(R-i)$ on a sandy soil is 0.2 mms^{-1}, select a value for $v = 0.75$ m s^{-1}; then for a slope of 3°

$$L = \frac{0.75^{5/2} \times 0.20^{3/2}}{0.0002 \times 0.109\,4 \times 0.988\,6}$$

$$L = 22.55 \text{ m}$$
$$VI = 1.18 \text{ m}$$

EMPIRICAL FORMULAE

United States Soil Conservation Service	VI (ft) $= a\text{S} + b$	where a varies from 0.3 in the south to 0.6 in the north and b is 1 or 2 according to the erodibility of the soil
Zimbabwe	VI (ft) $= \dfrac{S + f}{2}$	where f varies from 3 to 6 according to the erodibility of the soil
South Africa	VI (ft) $= \dfrac{S}{a} + b$	where a varies from 1.5 for low rainfall areas to 4 for high rainfall areas and b varies from 1 to 3 according to the erodibility of the soil
Algeria	VI (m) $= \dfrac{S}{10} + 2$	

Table 10.3 (*cont.*)

EMPIRICAL FORMULAE

Israel	$VI \text{ (m)} = XS + Y$	where X varies from 0.25 to 0.3 according to the rainfall and Y is 1.5 or 2.0 according to the erodibility of the soil
Kenya	$VI \text{ (m)} = \dfrac{0.3\,(S + 2)}{4}$	
New South Wales	$HI \text{ (m)} = K\,S^{-0.5}$	where K varies from 1.0 to 1.4 according to the erodibility of the soil

Note It is recommended that three or more of the formulae be used and that design spacing be based on a consensus of the results.

SPECIAL FORMULAE FOR BENCH TERRACES

Algeria/Morocco	$VI \text{ (m)} = (260S)^{-0.3}$ $VI \text{ (m)} = (64S)^{-0.5}$	for slopes 10–25% for slopes over 25%
Taiwan/Jamaica	$VI \text{ (m)} = \dfrac{(S.Wb)}{100 - (S.U)}$	where Wb is the width of the shelf (m) and U is the slope of the riser (expressed as a ratio of horizontal distance to vertical rise and usually taken as 1.0 or 0.75)
China	$VI \text{ (m)} = \dfrac{Wb}{(\cos S - \cot \beta)}$	where β is the angle of slope of the riser (normally 70–75°)
Taiwan	$VI \text{ (m)} = \dfrac{(Wb.S) + (0.1S - U)}{100 - (S.U)}$	for inward sloping bench terraces

---

VI = vertical interval between terraces
HI = horizontal interval between terraces
S = slope (per cent)
After Gichungwa (1970); Fournier (1972); Charman (1978); Hudson (1981*a*); Sheng (1972*b*); Fang, Zhou, Liu, Liu, Ren and Zhang (1981); Bensalem (1977); Chan (1981).

Table 10.4 Types of terraces

Diversion terraces	Used to intercept overland flow on a hillside and channel it across slope to a suitable outlet, e.g. grass waterway or soak away to tile drain; built at slight downslope grade from contour.
– Mangum type	Formed by taking soil from both sides of embankment.
– Nichols type	Formed by taking soil from upslope side of embankment only.
– Broad-based type	Bank and channel occupy width of 15 m.
– Narrow-based type	Bank and channel occupy width of 3–4 m.
Retention terraces	Level terraces; used where water must be conserved by storage on the hillside.
Bench terraces	Alternating series of shelves and risers used to cultivate steep slopes. Riser often faced with stones or concrete. Various modifications to permit inward-sloping shelves for greater water storage or protection on very steep slopes (Fournier, 1972) or to allow cultivation of tree crops and market-garden crops.

Source: Morgan (1980).

Although bench terraces appear to be reasonably satisfactory as a conservation measure in Malaysia, they are not necessarily suited to all steeply sloping land. In the Uluguru Mountains in Tanzania, they are unsuitable because, according to Temple (1972*b*), the top soil is too thin so that their construction exposes the infertile subsoil, they require too high a labour input for construction and maintenance, and they hold back so much water on the hillsides that the soils become saturated and landsliding is induced. As an alternative conservation measure, the use of step or ladder terraces (*fanya juu*) is recommended. These consist of narrow shelves, similar in size to terracettes, cut by a hoe. Little subsoil is dug out and during cultivation vegetation and crop residue are spread over the shelves and covered with soil cut from the face of the terrace upslope. Only rarely do ladder terraces break down under heavy rain (Temple and Murray-Rust, 1972).

10.4 WATERWAYS

The purpose of waterways in a conservation system is to convey runoff at a non-erosive velocity to a suitable disposal point. A waterway must therefore be carefully designed. Normally its dimensions must provide sufficient capacity to confine the peak runoff from a storm with a ten-year return period. Three types of waterway can be incorporated in a complete surface water disposal system: diversion channels, terrace channels and grass waterways (Fig. 10.2). Diversions are placed upslope of areas of farmland to intercept water running off the slope above and divert it across the slope to a grass waterway. Terrace channels collect runoff from the inter-terraced areas and also convey it across the slope to a

DIVERSION TERRACE

Profile

Bank   Channel

5.5–14°   5.5–14°   Ground slope ≤ 7°

Construction

Earth
movement

Mangum terrace   Nichols terrace

Width

15 m   3–4 m

Broad-based   Narrow-based

RETENTION TERRACE

Bank   Channel   Ground slope ≤ 4.5°

7°   7°

Fig. 10.1 Terraces.

Soil Erosion and Conservation

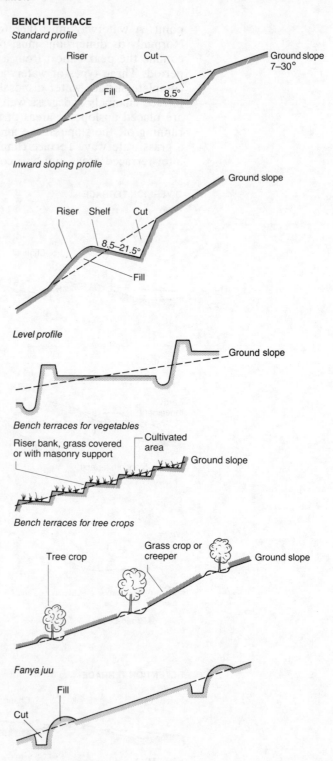

BENCH TERRACE

Standard profile

Riser

Cut

Ground slope 7–30°

Fill

8.5°

Inward sloping profile

Ground slope

Riser   Shelf   Cut

8.5–21.5°

Fill

Level profile

Ground slope

Bench terraces for vegetables

Riser bank, grass covered or with masonry support

Cultivated area

Ground slope

Bench terraces for tree crops

Tree crop

Grass crop or creeper

Ground slope

Fanya juu

Fill

Cut

Fig. 10.1 (*cont.*)

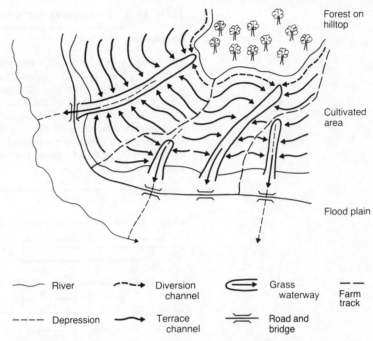

	River		Diversion channel		Grass waterway		Farm track
	Depression		Terrace channel		Road and bridge		

Fig. 10.2   Typical layout of waterways in a soil conservation scheme.

grass waterway. Grass waterways are therefore designed to transport downslope the runoff from these sources to empty into the natural river system (Table 10.5); they are located in natural depressions wherever possible but, occasionally, natural channels are reshaped to serve as grass waterways. Design procedures for waterways are described in Table 10.6. Grass waterways are recommended for slopes up to 11°; on steeper slopes the channels should be lined with stones, acceptable for slopes up to 15°, or concrete. On

Table 10.5   Types of waterway used in soil conservation systems

Diversion ditches	Placed upslope of areas where protection is required to intercept water from top of hillside; built across slope at slight grade so as to convey the intercepted runoff to a suitable outlet.
Terrace channels	Placed upslope of terrace bank to collect runoff from inter-terraced area; built across slope at slight grade so as to convey the runoff to a suitable outlet.
Grass waterways	Used as the outlet for diversions and terrace channels; run downslope, at grade of the sloping surface; empty into river system or other outlet; located in natural depressions on hillside.

Source: Morgan (1980).

Table 10.6 Procedures for waterway design

Approach

The design procedures are based on the principles of open-channel hydraulics. The method presented here represents an application of the Manning equation of flow velocity (equation 2.8). The cross-section of the waterway may be triangular, trapezoidal or parabolic. Triangular sections are not recommended because of the risk of scour at the lowest point. Since channels which are excavated as a trapezoidal section tend to become parabolic in time, the procedure described here is for a parabolic section.

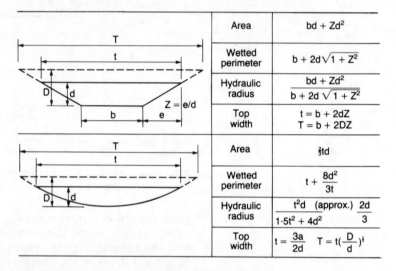

Area	$bd + Zd^2$
Wetted perimeter	$b + 2d\sqrt{1 + Z^2}$
Hydraulic radius	$\dfrac{bd + Zd^2}{b + 2d\sqrt{1 + Z^2}}$
Top width	$t = b + 2dZ$ $T = b + 2DZ$
Area	$\frac{2}{3}td$
Wetted perimeter	$t + \dfrac{8d^2}{3t}$
Hydraulic radius	$\dfrac{t^2d}{1\cdot5t^2 + 4d^2}$ (approx.) $\dfrac{2d}{3}$
Top width	$t = \dfrac{3a}{2d}$ $T = t(\dfrac{D}{d})^{\frac{1}{2}}$

Basic dimensions of common channel sections

The waterways used in soil conservation works on agricultural land are normally designed to convey the peak runoff expected with a ten-year return period without causing scour or fill. The peak runoff can be estimated using the method shown in Table 10.7. The design is based on conditions expected to prevail two years after installation. Although the waterway is therefore vulnerable to erosion during this period, providing a stable design for this time would result in overdesign for the rest of its life. It would also lead to an unnecessary reduction in the area which can be devoted to arable farming.

Design problem

Design a parabolic grass waterway to convey a peak flow of 6 m³ s⁻¹ on a 1 per cent slope over an erodible sandy soil with Bermuda grass vegetation in a good stand cut to a height of 60 mm.

Procedure

Discharge (Q)	= 6 m³ s⁻¹ (given)
Slope (s)	= 0.01 (given)

Table 10.6 (*cont.*)

Procedure	
Velocity (*v*)	select a maximum permissible velocity according to proposed vegetation cover and local soil $= 1.5$ m s^{-1}

Maximum safe velocities in channels

	Maximum velocity on cover expected after two seasons		
Material	*Bare*	*Medium grass cover*	*Very good grass cover*
	m/s	m/s	m/s
Very light silty sand	0.3	0.75	1.5
Light loose sand	0.5	0.9	1.5
Coarse sand	0.75	1.25	1.7
Sandy soil	0.75	1.5	2.0
Firm clay loam	1.0	1.7	2.3
Stiff clay or stiff gravelly soil	1.5	1.8	2.5
Coarse gravels	1.5	1.8	unlikely to form very good grass cover
Shale, hardpan, soft rock, etc.	1.8	2.1	
Hard cemented conglomerates	2.5	—	—
Intermediate values may be selected			

Roughness (*n*)	select a suitable value according to the vegetation retardance class (*CI*); the value of *CI* can be estimated knowing the length of the plant stems (*m*) and the density of the stems per unit area (*M*); the latter can be estimated in turn from the grass type, a qualitative description of the stand and the percentage cover. $m = 0.060$ m (given) $M = 5\,380$ stems m^{-2} (from table) $CI = 2.5\,(h\ \sqrt{M})^{\frac{1}{3}}$ (Temple, 1982) $CI = 2.5\,(0.060 \times \sqrt{5\,380})^{\frac{1}{3}}$ $CI = 6.75$

Properties of grass channel linings
Values apply to good uniform stands of each cover*

Cover group	Estimated cover factor, C_F	Covers tested	Reference stem density	
			Stems/ft^2	Stems/m^2
Creeping grasses	0.90	Bermuda grass	500	5 380
		Centipede grass	500	5 380

Table 10.6 (*cont.*)

Properties of grass channel linings
Values apply to good uniform stands of each cover*

Cover group	Estimated cover factor, C_F	Covers tested	Reference stem density	
			Stems/ft^2	Stems/m^2
Sod-forming grasses	0.87	Buffalo grass	400	4 300
		Kentucky bluegrass	350	3 770
		Blue grama	350	3 770
Bunch grasses	0.50	Weeping love grass	350	3 770
		Yellow blue stem	250	2 690
Legumes[†]	0.50	Alfalfa	500	5 380
		Lespedeza sericea	300	3 230
Annuals	0.50	Common *lespedeza*	150	1 610
		Sudan grass	50	538

* Multiply the stem densities given by 1/3, 2/3, 1, 4/3, and 5/3, for 'poor, fair, good, very good, and excellent' covers respectively. The equivalent adjustment to C_F remains a matter of engineering judgment until more data are obtained or a more analytical model is developed.

† For the legumes tested, the effective stem count for resistance (given) is approximately 5 times the actual count very close to the bed. Similar adjustment may be needed for other unusually large-stemmed and/or woody vegetation.

Values of Manning's n for vegetated channels

CI	Description	n
10.0	Very long dense grass (over 600 mm)	0.06–0.20
7.6	Long grass (250–600 mm)	0.04–0.15
5.6	Medium grass (150–200 mm)	0.03–0.08
4.4	Short grass (50–150 mm)	0.03–0.06
2.9	Very short grass (less than 50 mm)	0.02–0.04

Interpolating between the lowest of the values for n for CI of 5.6 and CI of 7.6, select a value for $CI = 6.75$, $n = 0.034$
Calculate the hydraulic radius (r) from the Manning equation:

$$r = \left(\frac{vn}{s^{0.5}}\right)^{1.5}$$

$$r = \left(\frac{1.5 \times 0.034}{0.01^{0.5}}\right)^{1.5}$$

$$r = 0.364 \text{ m}$$

Calculate the required cross-sectional area (A) of the channel:

$$A = \frac{Q}{v}$$

$$A = \frac{6}{1.5}$$

$$A = 4 \text{ m}^2$$

Calculate the design depth which for a parabolic section can be approximated by:

$$d = 1.5r$$
$$d = 1.5 \times 0.364$$
$$d = 0.55 \text{ m}$$

Table 10.6 (*cont.*)

Procedure

Calculate the top width which for a parabolic section is expressed by:

$$t = \frac{A}{0.67d}$$

$$t = \frac{4}{0.67 \times 0.55}$$

$$t = 10.86 \text{ m}$$

Check that the capacity given by the design criteria is adequate; for a parabolic section:

$$Q = Av = 0.67tdv$$
$$Q = 0.67 \times 10.86 \times 0.55 \times 1.5$$
$$Q = 6 \text{ m}^3 \text{ s}^{-1} \text{ which is adequate}$$

Add 20 per cent freeboard to design depth:

$$= 0.55 + 0.11 = 0.66$$

Final design criteria:

depth   = 0.66 m
top width = 10.86 m

After Schwab, Frevert, Edminster and Barnes (1966); Hudson (1981*a*); Temple (1982).
Notes: This procedure can be used for all waterways in a terrace and waterway system. With terrace channels and diversion channels, however, the slope is not predetermined by the ground slope but should be selected from guidelines given in Table 10.2. Terrace channels are usually unvegetated except with broad-based terraces where they may be cropped as part of the inter-terrace area. A value of $n = 0.02$ should be used for bare soil. When the above procedure is applied to small discharges, the design depths are sometimes greater than the design widths; since the channel then resembles a gully, it is undesirable. Also, the dimensions are too small for the channel to be easily constructed. To avoid these problems, a minimum size is recommended for terrace channels of 2.0 m wide and 0.5 m deep.

hillsides with alternating gentle and steep sections, a grass waterway with drop structures on the steeper slopes should be used. The selection of grasses for planting should take account of the local soil and climatic environment and the need to establish a dense cover very rapidly. Commonly used grasses are *Cynodon dactylon* (Bermuda grass), *Poa pratensis* (Kentucky bluegrass), *Bromus inermis* (smooth bromegrass) and *Pennisetum purpureum* (Napier grass). It is recommended, however, to seek local agronomic advice before making the final selection.

Grass waterways can be replaced in the water disposal system by tile drains. Diversion and terrace channels are graded to a soak-away, normally located in a natural depression, which provides the intake to the drain. The tile system is designed to remove surface water over a period not exceeding 48 h so that crop damage does not occur. Soil loss from tile-outlet terraces is much reduced because less than 5 per cent of the sediment delivered to the soak-aways passes into the drainage system (Laflen, Johnson and Reeve, 1972). The tile outlet consists of four parts: the inlet tube, the orifice plate, the conducting pipe and the outlet. The inlet tube is usually made of plastic and rises from a pipe below ground to a height which is 70 to 100 mm higher than

Table 10.7   Estimating the volume of peak runoff

Approach

Several methods have been developed for estimating the volume of peak runoff from small areas where no measured data exist. These include the rational formula and the United States Soil Conservation Service Curve Number. Both these require meteorological information which is often not readily obtainable. The procedure described here can be operated with the minimum of data. It has been developed by Hudson (1981*a*) for use in tropical Africa.

Problem

Estimate the volume of peak runoff for a roughly circular catchment of 50 ha of which (A) 10 ha comprises steeply sloping land with shallow rocky soils, (B) 15 ha is cultivated land with loamy soils and slopes of 6–9° and (C) 25 ha is flat land devoted to pasture on clay soils.

Procedure

The runoff generating characteristics for any catchment can be represented by an area-weighted score based on the vegetation, soil and slope conditions. Typical scores for each of these factors are shown in the table below.

Catchment characteristics

Cover		*Soil type and drainage*		*Slope*	
Heavy grass or forest	10	Deep, well drained soils, sands	10	Very flat to gentle (0–3°)	5
Scrub or medium grass	15	Deep, moderately pervious soil, silts	20	Moderate (3–6°)	10
Cultivated lands	20	Soils of fair permeability and depth, loams	25	Rolling (6–9°)	15
Bare or eroded	25	Shallow soils with impeded drainage	30	Hilly or steep	20
		Medium heavy clays or rocky surfaces	40	Mountainous	25
		Impervious surfaces and waterlogged soils	50		

The value of the catchment characteristic (*CC*) for the problem catchment is calculated as follows:

Region	*Factor values*			*Percentage area weighting*	*Total*
	Cover	*Soil*	*Slope*		
A	25 +	40 +	20 ×	0.20	17.0
B	20 +	25 +	10 ×	0.30	18.0
C	10 +	40 +	5 ×	0.50	27.5
Catchment characteristic (*CC*)				=	62.5

From table, read peak runoff with a ten-year return period for area (A) = 50 and *CC* = 62.5. Interpolating gives peak runoff = 9.25 m³ s⁻¹

Table 10.7 (*cont.*)

Peak runoff as a function of catchment characteristics and area

A \ CC	25	30	35	40	45	50	55	60	65	70	75	80
5	0.2	0.3	0.4	0.5	0.7	0.9	1.1	1.3	1.5	1.7	1.9	2.1
10	0.3	0.5	0.7	0.9	1.1	1.4	1.7	2.0	2.4	2.8	3.2	3.7
15	0.5	0.8	1.1	1.4	1.7	2.0	2.4	2.9	3.4	4.0	4.6	5.2
20	0.6	1.0	1.4	1.8	2.2	2.7	3.2	3.8	4.4	5.1	5.8	6.5
30	0.8	1.3	1.8	2.3	2.9	3.6	4.4	5.3	6.3	7.3	8.4	9.5
40	1.1	1.5	2.1	2.8	3.5	4.5	5.5	6.6	7.8	9.1	10.5	12.3
50	1.2	1.8	2.5	3.5	4.6	5.8	7.1	8.5	10.0	11.6	13.3	15.1
75	1.6	2.4	3.6	4.9	6.3	8.0	9.9	11.9	14.0	16.4	18.9	21.7
100	1.8	3.2	4.7	6.4	8.3	10.4	12.7	15.4	18.2	21.2	24.5	28.0
150	2.1	4.1	6.3	8.8	11.6	14.7	18.2	21.8	25.6	29.9	35.0	40.6
200	2.8	5.5	8.4	11.7	15.3	19.1	23.3	28.0	33.1	38.5	45.0	52.5
250	3.5	6.5	9.7	13.2	17.2	21.7	27.0	32.9	39.6	46.9	55.0	63.7
300	4.2	7.0	10.5	14.7	19.6	25.2	31.5	38.5	46.2	54.6	63.7	73.5
350	4.9	8.4	12.6	17.2	23.2	30.2	37.8	46.3	53.8	62.5	71.5	81.0
400	5.6	10.0	14.4	19.4	25.6	33.6	42.2	51.0	60.0	69.3	79.5	90.0
450	6.3	10.5	15.5	21.5	28.5	36.5	45.5	55.5	65.5	76.0	86.5	97.5
500	7.0	11.0	17.0	23.5	31.0	40.5	51.0	62.0	73.0	84.0	95.0	106.5

A is the area of the catchment in hectares, *CC* is the catchment characteristics from previous table, and the runoff (in cubic metres per second) is for a 10-year frequency.

Notes:
Adjustment factors to runoff values in table:

Rainfall intensity:	tropical (high)	multiply by 1.0
	temperate (low)	multiply by 0.75
Catchment shape:	long, narrow	multiply by 0.8
	square/circular	multiply by 1.0
	broad, short	multiply by 1.25
Return period:	2 years	multiply by 0.90
	5 years	multiply by 0.95
	10 years	multiply by 1.0
	25 years	multiply by 1.25
	50 years	multiply by 1.5

the adjacent terrace bank; the tube has holes or slots at regular intervals above ground level and a removable cap to prevent entry of debris and allow access. The orifice plate is positioned at the base of the tube where it connects with the conducting pipe; it regulates the downward flow of water. The conducting pipe, also of plastic, carries water from one or more inlet tubes to the outlet which is normally in a natural waterway. The terrace bank adjacent to the inlet must be level to reduce the risk of overtopping by ponded water. Although tile outlets are becoming more popular than grass waterways in the USA because they take up less crop land, they are more expensive. On a world-wide basis, grass waterways remain the cheapest and most effective form of terrace outlet. The design procedures for tile outlets are not described in this text, therefore, but they are similar in principle to those for tile drainage systems (Griessel and Beasley, 1971).

The effectiveness of terrace and waterway systems in reducing erosion can be illustrated by several studies of bench terracing (Sheng, 1981). On a clay loam soil with a 17° slope cropped to yams in Jamaica, annual soil loss was 1.7 kg m^{-2} compared with 13.3 kg m^{-2} without terraces. For a similar soil and slope, the soil loss under bananas was 1.7 kg m^{-2} with terracing and 18.3 kg m^{-2} without. On a 17° slope with loam to clay loam soils cropped to maize and beans in rotation in El Salvador, the annual soil loss was 3.0 kg m^{-2} with terracing and 10.0 kg m^{-2} without. The main reason for the reductions in erosion is the way the system manages the runoff. The terraces divide the hillside into inter-terrace areas which should be small enough in size to generate only small quantities of runoff. The grass waterway reduces the speed of flow because of the retardance effects of the vegetation. The arrangement of the waterway network gives a high tributary (diversion and terrace channels) to main channel (grass waterway) ratio and a catchment which is elongate in shape rather than square or circular; both attributes contribute to a reduction in peak flow.

A terrace and waterway system must be designed to give the most efficient layout possible in terms of farming operations. This can be achieved by following a systematic design procedure (Table 10.8) and then making adjustments within certain tolerance limits to take account of the local topography. Once a system has been constructed, regular maintenance is required to prevent it from deteriorating. This includes cutting the grass in the waterways to maintain it at the height on which the channel design is based; regular application of fertilizers to promote grass growth; closure of the waterways to animals and vehicles, especially when the soil is wet and damage could occur; and regular inspection and repair of breaks in the terrace banks. Although a terrace and waterway system will fail with the occurrence of a storm of much higher magnitude than that for which it is designed, by far the most common cause of failure is inadequate maintenance.

Table 10.8 Procedures for laying out terrace and waterway systems

1   Using aerial photographs, topographic maps and reconnaissance field surveys, determine the preliminary positions of the grass waterways. Locate the waterways in the natural depressions or drainage lines of the ground surface.

2   Locate the main breaks of slope and any badly eroded or gullied areas. Terrace banks should wherever possible be located to incorporate slope breaks and be positioned upslope of eroded lands.

3   Determine the spacing of the terraces (Table 10.3). The computed spacings may be varied by 25–30 per cent to allow for adjustments in position of the terraces to conform with slope breaks and avoid eroded areas.

Table 10.8 (*cont.*)

4   Determine terrace lengths (Table 10.2). Terraces must be limited in length to avoid dangerous accumulations of runoff and large cross-sectional areas to the terrace channels.

5   Adjust the positions of the grass waterways if necessary to avoid excessive terrace lengths.

6   Locate paths and farm roads along the divides between separate terrace and waterway systems (Fig. 10.2). The use of crest locations minimizes the catchment area contributing runoff to the road. Runoff may then be discharged into the surrounding land without the need for side drains. Crest locations also dispense with the need for bridges and culverts, avoid breaking up terraces to allow roads to cross them and keep vehicles away from grass waterways.

7   Using contour maps and aerial photographs, plan the layout of the system. Locate the grass waterways and diversion channels on the maps and photographs. Locate the top or key terrace and position the others in relation to it in accordance with the design spacings, lengths and gradients and in keeping with the location of slope breaks and eroded areas. Note that terraces often begin at a ridge or high point on a spur and run away from it before turning approximately parallel to it and running across the slope.

8   Examine the layout to see if it is practical for farming. Check whether the smallest inter-terrace areas can be worked with the proposed machinery, assuming contour cultivation and allowing room for turning at each end; if they cannot, the terrace network may need adjustment or the land involved will have to be taken out of cultivation. The terrace spacing should be adjusted to the nearest multiple of the width of the equipment to be used on the inter-terrace area.

9   On land of irregular topography, the terraces will converge in steeper sloping areas, resulting in many point rows during farming operations. This inconvenience can be minimized by the greater expense of installing a parallel terrace system. This involves cutting channels deeper on the spurs and filling in the depressions. With parallel layouts, the recommended terrace spacing is $0.67VI$. Locate the top or key terrace and, using this new spacing, draw in successive terraces parallel to it. Check each terrace in turn to see that it always has a downhill grade and that the grade is nowhere excessive. When a terrace line is unsatisfactory because it has an uphill section or the downhill grade is too steep, this line is eliminated and replaced by a new keyline. A new set of parallel terraces is located in relation to the second keyline.

10   Calculate the design dimensions of the grass waterways, terrace channels and diversion channels. It may be desirable to design the grass waterways in sections. This will allow adjustments to be made to the width and depth as slope steepness changes. It will also enable drop structures to be incorporated in the waterway on sections where the slope exceeds 11° and prevent excessively wide waterways being installed at the top of the slope where the runoff is less.

11   Stake out the waterway in the field and construct it by excavating soil from the centre and throwing it to each side to form the banks; check first, however, that the natural depression

Table 10.8 (*cont.*)

does not already meet the design depth and top width requirements. Seed the grass cover along with compost, fertilizer and mulch.

12   Stake out the positions of the diversion channels and terrace channels along the outlet or grass waterway to the appropriate vertical interval. From these positions, the terraces are pegged out across the slope according to the selected grade. The vertical intervals should be checked regularly. Begin with the diversion channel, then the top terrace and work downslope. Minor adjustments to the positions of the terrace channels can be made within a tolerance of ±50 mm *VI*. Mark the lines of the channels with a plough furrow.

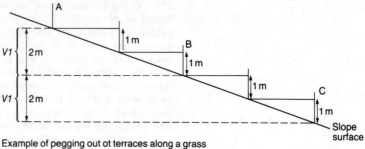

Example of pegging out ot terraces along a grass waterway for vertical interval of 2 m

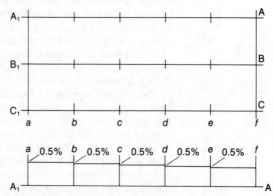

Example of pegging out across the slope at a grade of 1:200 or 0.5 per cent

13   Construct the diversion channel and then the terraces, beginning at the top and working downslope. This method of working is necessary because each terrace channel is designed to convey only the runoff from its inter-terrace area; it cannot cope with runoff from further upslope and so the protection works there must be in place prior to construction. If the top soil is thin, it should be scraped off first, stored and then returned to the inter-terrace area after the terraces are complete.

After Schwab, Frevert, Edminster and Barnes (1966); Troeh, Hobbs and Donahue (1980); Hudson (1981*a*); Wenner (1981).

10.5 STABILIZATION STRUCTURES

Stabilization structures play an important role in gully reclamation and gully erosion control. Small dams, usually 0.4 to 2.0 m in height, made from locally available materials such as earth, wooden planks, brushwood or loose rock, are built across gullies to trap sediment and thereby reduce channel depth and slope. These structures have a high risk of failure but provide temporary stability and are therefore used in association with agronomic treatment of the surrounding land where grasses, trees and shrubs are planted. If the agronomic measures successfully hold the soil and reduce runoff, the dams can be allowed to fall into disrepair. Even though they are temporary, the dams have to be carefully designed. They must be provided with a spillway to deal with overtopping during high flows and installed at a spacing appropriate to the slope of the channel. The spacing of the dams can be determined from the formula of Heede (1976):

$$\text{SPACING} = \frac{HE}{K \tan \theta \cos \theta} \qquad (10.1)$$

where HE is the dam height and K is a constant. $K = 0.3$ for $\tan \theta \leq 0.2$; $K = 0.5$ for $\tan \theta > 0.2$. The dam height is measured from the crest of the spillway to the gully floor. Based on the costs of construction, loose-rock dams are only economical with heights up to 0.45 m; single-fence dams are the most economical for dam heights of 0.45 to 0.75 m; and double-fence dams for heights of 0.75 to 1.7 m (Heede and Mufich, 1973). The gully depths for which these dam heights are recommended are up to 1.2, 1.2 to 1.5 and 1.5 to 2.1 m respectively. Keying a check dam into the sides and floor of the gully greatly improves its stability. This entails digging a trench, usually 0.6 m deep and wide, across the channel, but if the channel walls are deeply cracked and fissured, the trench should be increased in depth to 1.2 or even 1.8 m. Aprons must be installed on the gully floor downstream of the check dam to prevent flows from undercutting the structure. Where the slope of the gully floor is less than 8.5°, the length of the apron should be 1.5 times the height of the structure; for steeper slopes it should be 1.75 times its height. At the downstream end of the apron, a loose rock sill about 0.15 m high should be built to create a pool to help absorb the energy of the water falling over the spillway. The spillway should be designed to convey peak flows with a given return period, usually 25 years. It is recommended that the spillway be trapezoidal in cross-section with a bottom length (L) which is equal to the bottom width of the gully. A longer spillway is not desirable because water flowing over the spillway will strike the gully sides where protection against erosion is less. The depth of the spillway (D) is given by the equation

$$D = \left(\frac{Q}{1.65L}\right)^{\frac{2}{3}}$$ (10.2)

and, assuming the spillway sides are sloped at 1:1, the top length (Lt) is obtained from

$$Lt = L + D$$ (10.3)

(Heede, 1976). This approach assumes that the spillways approximate to a broad-crested weir.

Construction of a loose-rock dam (Fig. 10.3) begins by sloping back the tops of the banks. A trench is then dug across the floor of the gully and into the banks into which the large rocks are placed to form the toe of the structure. The dam is built upwards from the toe, using the flatter rocks on the downstream face. Rocks smaller than 100 mm diameter should not be used because they will be quickly washed out. A dam made of large rocks will leave large voids in the structure through which water jets may flow, weakening the dam. These jets will also carry sediment

Cross-section

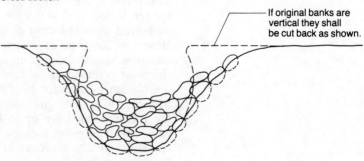

If original banks are vertical they shall be cut back as shown.

Side-section

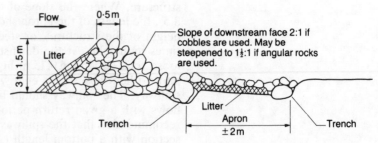

Flow

0·5 m

3 to 1.5 m

Litter

Slope of downstream face 2:1 if cobbles are used. May be steepened to 1½:1 if angular rocks are used.

Litter

Trench

Apron
±2 m

Trench

Fig. 10.3 Construction of a loose-rock dam (after Gray and Leiser, 1982).

through the dam instead of allowing it to accumulate on the upstream side. To avoid these effects, the dam should be made with a graded rock structure. An effective composition is 25 per cent of the rocks between 100 and 140 mm diameter, 20 per cent between 150 and 190 mm, 25 per cent between 200 and 300 mm, and 30 per cent between 310 and 450 mm (Heede, 1976). A second trench should be made to mark the downstream end of the apron and filled with heavy rocks. A 100 mm thick layer of litter, such as leaves, straw or fine twigs, is laid on the floor of the apron and covered with a solid pavement of rock. A thick layer of litter is also placed on the upstream face of the dam.

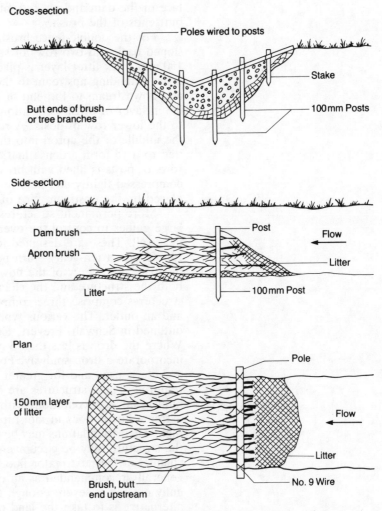

Fig. 10.4 Construction of a single-fence brush dam (after Gray and Leiser, 1982).

When building a single-fence brush dam, the gully banks are first sloped back and stout posts are then driven into the floor and banks of the gully to a depth of about 1 m below the surface and about 0.5 m apart (Fig. 10.4); willow is the recommended material. A 150 mm thick layer of litter is placed on the floor of the gully between the posts extending upstream to the proposed base of the dam and downstream to the end of the apron. Green tree branches or brush are laid on top of the litter, the longer ones at the bottom, with the butt ends upstream. Usually the gully is filled with brush which is trampled to compress it into a compact mass. Cross poles are fixed on the upstream side of the posts and the brush is tied to the structure with galvanized wire. A layer of litter is placed on the upstream face of the dam and packed into the openings between the butt ends of the brush.

For the double-fence brush dam, the gully banks are sloped back and two rows of stout posts are erected. A 150 mm thick litter layer is placed on the floor of the gully, again extending upstream to the proposed base of the dam and downstream to the end of the apron (Fig. 10.5). A 0.3 m layer of brush is positioned on the apron and attached to the lower row of posts. A row of stakes is driven through the middle of the apron into the gully floor and the brush tied to it to form a dense mat. The space between the two rows of posts is filled with brush laid across the gully; this is compressed tightly and held in position with wire. Litter is placed on the upstream face of the dam.

More permanent structures are sometimes required on large gullies to control the overfall of water on the headwall. These are designed to deal safely with the peak runoff with a ten-year return period. They must therefore dissipate the energy of the flow in a manner which protects both the structure and the channel downstream. The structures comprise three components: an inlet, a conduit and an outlet. The various types of each component are outlined in Schwab, Frevert, Edminster and Barnes (1966). Where the drop is less than 3 m, the structure should incorporate a drop spillway. For drops between 3 and 6 m, a chute is used and for greater drops a pipe spillway is required. These structures are expensive and, since they are built in adverse conditions with unstable soils subject to extreme fluctuations in moisture, their failure rate is also high. Their foundations may be undermined by animals and the structure may be circumvented if the gully cuts a new channel in the next major flood. Thus they cannot be generally recommended as an economic investment. If the gully erosion is severe enough to require them, a cheaper alternative is to take the land out of cultivation or grazing and allow it to revegetate either naturally or by reseeding. Their greatest value is where agricultural land in flatter

Cross-section (posts and litter only)

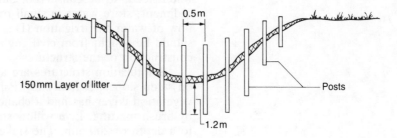

0.5 m

150 mm Layer of litter

Posts

1.2 m

Side-section

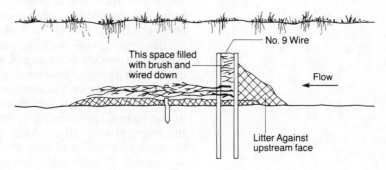

No. 9 Wire

This space filled
with brush and
wired down

Flow

Litter Against
upstream face

Plan

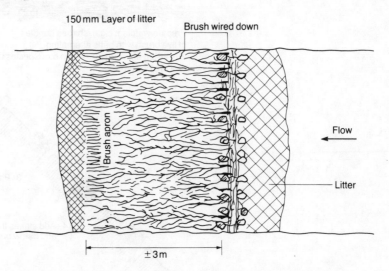

150 mm Layer of litter

Brush wired down

Brush apron

Flow

Litter

±3 m

Fig. 10.5   Construction of a double-fence brush dam (after
Gray and Leiser, 1982).

areas needs to be protected from channel erosion and where water needs to be conserved. Small dams are used to trap sediment, store water in small reservoirs and control the flow of water for irrigation (Das and Singh, 1981). Advice should be sought from civil engineers on the design and construction of the structures.

Stabilization structures are also used to control erosion on steep slopes. Stability for a short period until a dense vegetation cover has had a chance to grow can be achieved by brush matting. Live willow stakes are driven into the soil to a depth of 200 mm. The stakes are placed about 1 m apart to form a row along the contour with a distance of 10 to 20 m between the rows depending upon the steepness of the slope. Sprouting brushwood is spread over the slope, butt ends downslope, compressed to ensure no area is left uncovered, and tied to the stakes with galvanized wire. A similar technique is wattling which consists of placing bundles of woody plant stems, using species which will root easily such as *Salix, Leucaena, Baccharis* and *Tamarix*, in shallow trenches on the contour with rows spaced 1 to 6 m apart. The wattling is tied to stakes on the downslope side of the trench and secured by further stakes driven through the material (Fig. 10.6). After installation, the wattling is covered with soil until only about 10 per cent of the bundle is exposed. Grasses and trees can be planted between the wattles.

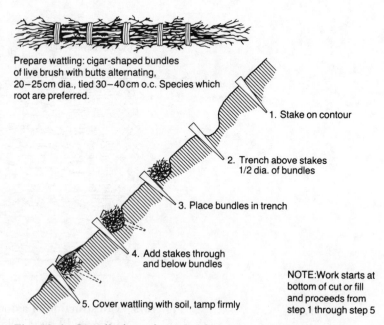

Prepare wattling: cigar-shaped bundles of live brush with butts alternating, 20–25 cm dia., tied 30–40 cm o.c. Species which root are preferred.

1. Stake on contour

2. Trench above stakes 1/2 dia. of bundles

3. Place bundles in trench

4. Add stakes through and below bundles

5. Cover wattling with soil, tamp firmly

NOTE: Work starts at bottom of cut or fill and proceeds from step 1 through step 5

Fig. 10.6   Installation of wattles for slope stabilization (after Gray and Leiser, 1982).

More permanent protection of banks and embankments can be achieved by facing them with a resistant material such as concrete. Better, however, is to construct retaining walls with gabions. These are rectangular steel wire-mesh baskets, packed tightly with stones, and they have the advantages of allowing seepage of water through the facing and of deforming by bending without loss of structural efficiency rather than by cracking. Gabions are supplied flat and then folded into their rectangular shape on site. They are placed in position and anchored before being filled with stones 125 to 200 mm in diameter. The gabion is filled to one-third of its depth after which two connecting wires or braces are inserted front to back to prevent bulging of the wire basket on further filling. The bracing is repeated when the basket is two-thirds full. The gabion is slightly overfilled to allow for settlement, the hinged lid is closed and wired to the sides. The simplest structure consists of one tier of gabions, 1 m high. A second tier can be positioned on top of the first, set back about 0.5 m. The addition of further tiers, however, requires bracing the structure against overturning and should not be attempted without civil engineering advice. Similar advice should be sought for other types of retaining walls and on the benching of long, steep slopes.

Control of surface and seepage water is often needed on steep slopes to minimize landslides and slumps. This can be achieved by drainage which will help to prevent the build-up of soil water. The principles are to construct a diversion channel to run at grade across the hillslope, upslope of the area of risk, and thereby reduce the amount of water coming into the area. Subsurface drains of 75 mm diameter PVC perforated pipe wrapped in a filter cloth to prevent blockage can also be installed to intercept subsurface flow. The area itself can be drained by rubble drains, excavated to a depth of 300 mm and a width of 500 mm and filled with rocks. Safe outlets must be provided for all components of the drainage system.

10.6 WINDBREAKS

Shelterbelts are placed at right angles to erosive winds to reduce wind velocity and, by spacing them at regular intervals, break up the length of open wind blow. Shelterbelts are strictly living windbreaks. Inert structures such as stone walls, slat and brush fences and cloth screens can be used to perform similar functions on a smaller scale.

A shelterbelt is designed so that it rises sharply on the windward side and provides both a barrier and a filter to wind movement. A complete belt consists of two tree rows and up to three shrub rows, one of which is placed on the windward side. The density of the belt should not be so great as to form an impermeable barrier nor so sparse that the belt is transparent. A belt of the correct density is best described as translucent. It should be possible to see the presence of objects on the other side of the barrier without being able to identify them. This density is equivalent to a porosity of 40 to 50 per cent. It gives the greatest overall reductions in windspeed over a distance 30 times the barrier height (Skidmore and Hagen, 1977). More open barriers do not reduce wind velocity sufficiently. With denser barriers there is a much greater reduction in windspeed close to but, since the velocity increases more rapidly with distance downwind than is the case for more porous barriers, they are effective for shorter distances. Using wind tunnel studies, Woodruff and Zingg (1952) developed the following equation for determining shelterbelt spacing:

$$L = 17H \ (V_t/V) \cos \alpha \qquad\qquad (10.4)$$

where L is the distance apart of the belt, H is the height of the belt, V is actual wind velocity measured at a height of 15 m above the ground surface, V_t is the threshold velocity for particle movement, taken as 34 km h^{-1}, and α is the angle of deviation of the prevailing wind from a line perpendicular to the belt. Effective protection in the field rarely reaches this theoretical level of $17H$, however, because of variable growth and poor maintenance of the trees. A distance of about 10 or 12 times the height of the belt is more realistic (Khimina, 1973; Sneesby, 1953). Where 5 to 7 m high hedges are used, the effective distance protected is about 30 times the barrier height but, because of their lower height, the absolute distance protected is much less. Belts of 6.7 m high trees protected for a distance of $20H$ near Youyu, Shaanxi, China (Li, 1984). Belt lengths should be about 24 times the barrier height. Widths of belt vary from about 9 m for a two-row tree belt with associated shrubs to about 3 m for hedge belts. These widths mean that belts can occupy about 3 per cent of the land area they are protecting.

Where there is a dominant erosive wind from a single direction, the best protection is obtained by aligning the shelterbelts in parallel rows at right angles to it. Where erosive winds come from several directions, grid or herringbone layouts may be necessary. The requirement is to provide maximum protection averaged over all wind directions and all wind velocities above the threshold level. This may be achieved by a scheme in which complete protection is not obtained from any single wind direction. The effectiveness of shelterbelt layouts can be evaluated using equation 3.7. This is first applied to obtain a measure

for wind erosivity with no protection. A measure is then
obtained for the shelterbelt layout by reducing the values of
$\bar{V}t$ by the ratio V_x/V_o, where V_x is the wind velocity at
distance x from the belt, with x measured in units of the
barrier height, and V_o is the wind velocity in the open field.
Values of V_x/V_o can be determined for a belt with 40 per
cent porosity by the equation:

$$V_x/V_o = 0.85 - 4e^{-0.2H'} + e^{-0.3H'} + 0.0002H'^2 \qquad (10.5)$$

where $H' = x/\sin \beta$ when β is the acute angle of incident
wind (Skidmore and Hagen, 1977).

The greatest effect of shelterbelts is found where, as a
result of farmer collaboration in a collective belt planting
scheme, a regional framework exists of hedges placed along
property boundaries in a coordinated way so that they form
a parallel series of main line barriers, 200 to 400 m apart.
Within this framework, individual farmers are free to plant
additional hedges. Collective shelterbelt schemes are
encouraged by Hedeselskabet (Danish Land Development
Service) to control erosion on the sandy soils of Jylland
(Olesen, 1979). Their effect can be seen from two west–east
transects showing reductions in wind velocities (Fig. 10.7).
Within a distance of 10 to 20 km from the coast, the wind
velocity is reduced by 50 per cent along the transect just
north of Esbjerg and that reduction is maintained to the east
coast; this transect has many shelterbelts and small
plantations. In contrast, along a transect with few
shelterbelts from Rømø to Åbenrå, an equivalent reduction
is not obtained for 60 km (Jensen, 1954).

The plant species selected for shelterbelts should be
rapid growing, tolerant of wind and light, and frost
resistant where necessary. Preference should be given to

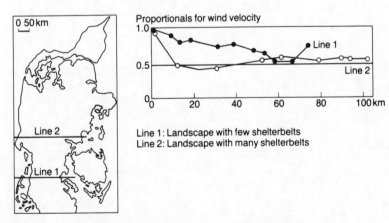

Fig. 10.7   Effects of shelterbelts on wind velocities in south
Jylland, Denmark (after Jensen, 1954).

local rather than imported species. The side-effects of shelterbelts are decreased evapotranspiration, higher soil temperatures in winter but lower in summer, and greater risk of weeds and pests.

10.7 GEOTEXTILES

Several types of netting woven from natural fibres such as jute or made from artificial fibres such as nylon are now manufactured commercially for use in erosion control. They are supplied in rolls, unrolled over the hillslope from the top and anchored with large pins or stapled. They are designed to give temporary stability on roadsides and on steep slopes not used for agriculture until such time as the vegetation cover grows. The thinner nets, comprising one layer of mesh, are generally unsatisfactory on their own and need to be combined with a mulch. Their success depends upon the area of contact between the soil and the net and on a firm attachment of the mesh to the ground (Reynolds, 1978). Because of this, meshes which are 10 to 20 mm thick and which are filled with soil after they are layed on the ground are more effective: they can reduce erosion to about 20 per cent of that on unprotected land. Netting is also made for use as windbreaks.

Chapter 11
CONCLUSION

The ultimate objective of research on soil erosion is to solve erosion problems by adopting suitable soil conservation measures. Suitability can be judged in various ways. The measures may reduce erosion to an acceptable level. They may be selected for their ability to deal with specific processes of erosion which have been shown to be important in a particular area. They may be appropriate to the local farming system in terms of their level of technology and compatibility with existing farming practices. They may be economically justifiable either by cost–benefit analysis in the short term or by retaining productive soils in the long term.

The economic and social issues affecting soil conservation have been briefly referred to in Chapter 6 and have been analysed by Shaxson (1981), Hudson (1981a; 1981b) and Eckholm (1976). A detailed treatment is beyond the scope of this book. Attention here has been focused on the need for the strategies of erosion control to be based on a proper diagnosis of the erosion problem in terms of its process and severity. An understanding is therefore required of the way in which the soil erosion processes operate and how different conservation measures interact with them. This in turn implies a knowledge of the range of conservation practices that are available. Given this background, the key issues to successful soil conservation design are how to furnish data on the nature of the erosion problem through erosion surveys and how to predict the effects of implementing soil conservation measures through erosion modelling.

The justification of carrying out erosion surveys in practice, prior to designing conservation works, and of continuing research into erosion survey techniques is that they perform the following tasks more effectively than any other method. First, they provide a focus for integrating research on erosion carried out by geomorphologists, hydrologists, pedologists and engineers. Second, they draw attention to the most relevant factors controlling erosion at different scales of study and, therefore, to those to which conservation measures need be directed. Third, they help identify the most important processes at work. This is vital for deciding whether anti-erosion measures should be concentrated on surface or subsurface erosion, on detachment or transport of soil particles, and on promoting infiltration of excess water or its removal over the land surface in waterways. Fourth, they point to the problem of selecting an appropriate figure as a target to which to reduce the erosion rate. There can be no universally applicable figure. It must be varied according to the rate of natural erosion, which in turn is related to the relief of the land and the frequency of moderate and high magnitude wind and rainstorms, and the size of the area being considered. Fifth, they provide a system of mapping the data required to develop predictive models.

Whilst the general principles and working methods for erosion survey have been established with sufficient flexibility to modify them to fit local conditions, the methods for assessing the effects of soil conservation practices on erosion are not so firmly developed. Some indication can be obtained from the comparative studies of erosion rates with and without particular practices cited in the last three chapters. If the effects of several measures operating together, combining, for example, agronomic practices, mechanical controls and soil management, are to be evaluated, recourse has to be made to some form of predictive model. Empirical models, such as the Universal Soil-Loss Equation which is widely used as a design tool, are only moderately satisfactory because they are poorly related to the mechanics of soil erosion and do not consider interactions between the controlling factors. Although the new generation of erosion models will undoubtedly do a better job, their development to a stage where they are widely and easily usable is some way off. Nevertheless, existing empirical models can be usefully applied, at least on a relative basis and, in areas similar in conditions to those where they were developed, in absolute terms as well. All designers of soil conservation strategies should adopt the discipline of subjecting their schemes to evaluation using one or more of these models. The percentage reduction in soil loss expected by each scheme should be assessed and stated. In addition to developing models which will be more applicable in an absolute sense, better methods need to be found for assessing soil loss tolerance so that model predictions can be compared with what is required for long-term sustained use of the land. At present, such comparisons can be made but only crudely.

Although the emphasis of this book has been placed, intentionally, on soil erosion, its philosophy has been to encourage better conservation practice and more acceptable conservation design. Improvements to conservation techniques are most likely to come from the research of agricultural engineers. Indeed, soil conservation is traditionally a preserve of agricultural engineering. It is hoped that this book has shown the valuable role, in supplementing and making more effective the work of the engineer, that the applied physical geographer can play.

REFERENCES

Adams, J. E., Richardson, C. W. and Burnett, E. (1978) 'Influence of row spacing of grain sorghum on ground cover, runoff and erosion', *Soil Sci. Soc. Am. J.* **42**, 959–62.

Ahnert, F. (1976) 'Brief description of a comprehensive three-dimensional process-response model of landform development', *Z. f. Geomorph. Suppl.* **25**, 29–49.

Aina, P. O. (1979) 'Soil changes resulting from long-term management practices in Western Nigeria', *Soil Sci. Soc. Am. J.* **43**, 173–7.

Aina, P. O., Lal, R. and Taylor, G. S. (1977) 'Soil and crop management in relation to soil erosion in the rainforest of western Nigeria', in *Soil erosion: prediction and control, Soil Conservation Society of America Spec. Publ. No.* **21**, 75–82.

Aina, P. O., Lal, R. and Taylor G. S. (1979) 'Effects of vegetal cover on soil erosion on an alfisol', in Lal, R. and Greenland, D. J. (eds), *Soil physical properties and crop production in the tropics*, Wiley, 501–8.

Alberts, E. E., Moldenhauer, W. C. and Foster, G. R. (1980) 'Soil aggregates and primary particles transported in rill and interrill flow', *Soil Sci. Soc. Am. J.* **44**, 590–5.

Aldon, E. F. (1976) 'Soil ripping treatments for runoff and erosion control', in *Proc. Fed. Inter-Agency Sediment Conf., Denver, Colo.*, **3**, 2-24–2-29.

Al-Durrah, M. M. and Bradford, J. M. (1982) 'Parameters for describing soil detachment due to single water drop impact', *Soil Sci. Soc. Am. J.* **46**, 836–40.

Ambar, S. and Wiersum, K. F. (1980) 'Comparison of different erodibility indices under various soil and land use conditions in west Java', *Indon. J. Geog.* **10**(39), 1–15.

André, J. E. and Anderson, H. W. (1961) 'Variation of soil erodibility with geology, geographic zone, elevation and vegetation type in northern California wildlands', *J. Geophys. Res.* **66**, 3351–8.

Arnalds, A. (1980) 'Lúpinurannsóknir' *Rannsóknastofnun Landbúnaðarins Report* **59**.

Arulanandan, K., Loganathan, P. and Krone, R. B. (1975) 'Pore and eroding fluid influences on the surface erosion of a soil', *J. Geotech. Engng. Div., ASCE* **101**, 53–66.

Astill, C. (1981) 'The use of soil stability aids', in *Proc. SAWMA Conf. Soil and crop loss: developments in erosion control*, Nat. Agr. Centre, Stoneleigh.

Ateshian, J. K. H. (1974) 'Estimation of rainfall erosion index', *J. Irrigation and Drainage Div. ASCE* **100**, 293–307.

Babu, R., Tejwani, K. G., Agarwal, M. P. and Bhushan, L. S. (1978) 'Distribution of erosion index and iso-erodent map of India', *Indian J. Soil Cons.* **6**(1), 1–12.

Baffoe-Bonnie, E. and Quansah, C. (1975) 'The effect of tillage on soil and water loss', *Ghana J. Agric. Sci.* **8**, 191–5.

Bagnold, R. A. (1937) 'The transport of sand by wind', *Geogr. J.* **89**, 409–38.

Bagnold, R. A. (1941) *The physics of blown sand and desert dunes*, Chapman and Hall, London.

Bagnold, R. A. (1979) 'Sediment transport by wind and water', *Nordic Hydrol*, **10**, 309–22.

Baker, C. F., Morgan, R. P. C., Brown I. W., Hawkes, D. E. and Ratcliffe, J. B. (1979) 'Soil erosion survey of Moel Famau Country Park', *Clwyd County Council Planning and Estates Dept., Country Park Research Report* **2**, Nat. Coll. Agric. Engng, Silsoe, Occasional Paper **7**.

Barber, R. G., Thomas, D. B. and Moore, T. R. (1981) 'Studies on soil erosion and runoff and proposed design procedures for terraces in the cultivated, semi-arid areas of Machakos District, Kenya', in Morgan, R. P. C. (ed.), *Soil conservation: problems and prospects*, Wiley, 219–37.

Barrow, G., Brotherton, D. I. and Maurice, O. C. (1973) 'Tarn Hows experimental restoration project', *Countryside Recreation News Suppl.* **9**, 13–18.

Bayfield, N. G. (1973) 'Use and deterioration of some Scottish hill paths', *J. Appl. Ecol.* **10**, 635–44.

Bazzoffi, P., Torri, D. and Zanchi, C. (1980) 'Stima dell'erodibilità dei suoli mediante simulazione di pioggia in laboratorio. Nota 1: simulatore di pioggia'. *Ann. Ist. Sperimentale Studio Difesa Suolo* **11**, 129–40.

Bennett, H. H. (1939) *Soil conservation*, McGraw-Hill.

Bennett, J. P. (1974) 'Concepts of mathematical modeling of sediment yield', *Water Resour. Res.* **10**, 485–92.

Bensalem, B. (1977) 'Examples of soil and water conservation practices in North African countries', *FAO Soils Bull.* **33**, 151–60.

Bergsma, E. (1974) 'Soil erosion sequences on aerial photographs', *ITC Journal* **1974-3**, 342–76.

Bergsma, E. and Valenzuela, C. R. (1981) 'Drop testing aggregate stability of some soils near Mérida, Spain', *Earth Surf. Proc. Landf.* **6**, 309–18.

Berry, L. (1970) 'Some erosional features due to piping and subsurface wash with special reference to the Sudan', *Geografiska Ann.* **52-A**, 113–19.

Berry, L. and Ruxton, B. P. (1960) 'The evolution of Hong Kong harbour basin', *Z. f. Geomorph*, **4**, 97–115.

Berry, M. J. (1956) 'Erosion control on Bukit Bakar, Kelantan', *Malay. Forester* **19**, 3–11.

Beschta, R. L. (1978) 'Long-term patterns of sediment production following road construction and logging in the Oregon Coast Range', *Water Resour. Res.* **14**, 1011–16.

Bie, S. W. and Beckett, P. H. T. (1971) 'Quality control in soil survey. II. The cost of soil survey', *J. Soil Sci.* **22**, 453–65.

Bishop, D. M. and Stevens, M. E. (1964) 'Landslides on logged areas in southeast Alaska', *USDA Forest Research Service Paper* **NOR-1**.

Blong, R. J. (1970) 'The development of discontinuous gullies in a pumice catchment', *Am. J. Sci.* **268**, 369–83.

Bocharov, A. P. (1984) *A description of devices used in the study of wind erosion of soils*, Balkema.

Bollinne, A. (1975) 'La mesure de l'intensité du splash sur sol limoneux. Mise au point d'une technique de terrain et premiers résultats, *Pédologie* **25**, 199–210.

Bollinne, A. (1977) 'La vitesse de l'érosion sous culture en région limoneuse', *Pédologie* **27**, 191–206.

Bollinne, A. (1978) 'Study of the importance of splash and wash on cultivated loamy soils of Hesbaye (Belgium)', *Earth Surf. Proc.* **3**, 71–84.

Bonell, M. and Gilmour, D. A. (1978) 'The development of overland flow in a tropical rain forest catchment', *J. Hydrol.* **39**, 365–82.

Bonsu, M. (1981) 'Assessment of erosion under different cultural practices on a savanna soil in the Northern Region of Ghana', in Morgan, R. P. C. (ed.), *Soil conservation: problems and prospects*, Wiley, 247–53.

Bonsu, M. and Obeng, H. B. (1979) 'Effects of cultural practices on soil erosion and maize production in the semi-deciduous rain forest and forest-savanna transitional zones of Ghana', in Lal,

R. and Greenland, D. J. (eds), *Soil physical properties and crop production in the tropics,* Wiley, 509–19.

Boon, W. and Savat, J. (1981) 'A nomogram for the prediction of rill erosion', in Morgan, R. P. C. (ed.), *Soil conservation: problems and prospects,* Wiley, 303–19.

Bork, H. R. and Rohdenburg, H. (1981) 'Rainfall simulation in southeast Spain: analysis of overland flow and infiltration', in Morgan, R. P. C. (ed.), *Soil conservation: problems and prospects,* Wiley, 293–302.

Borst, H. L. and Woodburn, R. (1942) 'The effect of mulching and methods of cultivation on runoff and erosion from Muskingum silt loam', *Agric. Engng.* **23**, 19–22.

Borsy, Z. (1972) 'Studies on wind erosion in the wind-blown sand areas of Hungary', *Acta Geographica Debrecina* **10**, 123–32.

Bouyoucos, G. J. (1935) 'The clay ratio as a criterion of susceptibility of soils to erosion', *J. Am. Soc. Agron.* **27**, 738–41.

Brady, N. C (1974) *The nature and properties of soils,* Macmillan.

Brice, J. C. (1966) 'Erosion and deposition in the loess-mantled Great Plains, Medicine Creek drainage basin, Nebraska', *USGS Prof. Paper* **352–H**, 255–339.

Brierley, J. S. (1976) 'Kitchen gardens in the West Indies with a contemporary study from Grenada', *J. Trop. Geog.* **43**, 30–40.

Brown, L. R. (1981) *Building a sustainable society,* Norton.

Browning, G. M., Norton, R. A., McCall, A. G. and Bell, F. G. (1948) 'Investigation in erosion control and the reclamation of eroded land at the Missouri Valley Loess Conservation Experiment Station, Clarinda, Iowa', *USDA Tech. Bull.* **959**.

Bruce-Okine, E. and Lal, R. (1975) 'Soil erodibility as determined by raindrop technique', *Soil Sci.* **119**, 149–57.

Bryan, R. B. (1968) 'The development, use and efficiency of indices of soil erodibility', *Geoderma* **2**, 5–26.

Bryan, R. B. (1969) 'The relative erodibility of soils developed in the Peak District of Derbyshire', *Geografiska Ann.* **51–A**, 145–59.

Bryan, R. B. and De Ploey, J. (1983) 'Comparability of soil erosion measurements with different laboratory rainfall simulators', *Catena Suppl.* **4**, 33–56.

Bubenzer, G. D. (1979) 'Rainfall characteristics important for simulation', *Proc. Rainfall Simulator Workshop, Tucson, Ariz, USDA–SEA, Agric. Reviews and Manuals* **ARM–W–10**, 22–34.

Buckham, A. F. and Cockfield, W. E. (1950) 'Gullies formed by sinking of the ground', *Am. J. Sci.* **248**, 137–41.

Bučko, Š. (1975) 'Investigation of normal and accelerated water erosion in Slovakia', *Studia Geomorphologica Carpatho-Balcanica* **4**, 27–38.

Buol, S. W., Hole, F. D. and McCracken, R. J. (1973) *Soil genesis and classification*, Iowa State Univ. Press.

Burgess, P. F. (1971) 'The effect of logging on hill dipterocarp forest', *Malay. Nat. J.* **24**, 231–7.

Burrough, P. A., Beckett, P. H. T. and Jarvis, M. G. (1971) 'The relation between cost and utility in soil survey (I–III)', *J. Soil Sci.* **22**, 359–94.

Burykin, A. M. (1957) 'O vnutripochvennom stoke v gornykh usloviyakh vlazhnykh subtropikov', *Pochvovedenie* **12**, Engl. transl. in *Water regime and erosion*, Israel Program for Scientific Translation, Nat. Sci. Foundation and Dept. Agric. Washington, D.C.

Butler, B. E. (1959) 'Periodic phenomena in landscapes as a basis for soil studies', *CSIRO Aust. Soil Publ.* **14**.

Butler, B. E. (1967) 'Soil periodicity in relation to landform development in southeastern Australia', in Mabbutt, J. A. and Jennings, J. N. (eds), *Landform studies from Australia and New Guinea*, ANU Press, 231–66.

Carson, M. A. and Kirkby, M. J. (1972) *Hillslope form and process*, Cambridge University Press.

Carter, C. E., Greer, J. D., Braud, H. J. and Floyd, J. M. (1974) 'Raindrop characteristics in south central United States', *Trans. Am. Soc. Agric. Engnrs.* **17**, 1033–7.

Central Soil and Water Conservation Research and Training Institute (1977) *Annual Report*, Dehra Dun, India.

Chan, C. C. (1981) 'Conservation measures on the cultivated slopelands of Taiwan', *Food and Fertilizer Technology Center Taipei, Extension Bull.* **157**.

Chapman, G. (1948) 'Size of raindrops and their striking force at the soil surface in a red pine plantation', *Trans. Am. Geophys. Un.* **29**, 664–70.

Charman, P. E. V. (1970) 'The influence of sodium salts on soils with reference to tunnel erosion in coastal districts. Part II. Grafton area', *J. Soil Conserv. Serv. NSW* **26**, 71–86.

Charman, P. E. V. (1978) 'Soils of New South Wales: their characterisation, classification and conservation', *NSW Soil Conserv. Serv. Tech. Handbook* **1**.

Charreau, C. (1972) 'Problèmes poses par l'utilization agricole des sols tropicaux par des cultures annuelles', *Tropical Soil Research Symp.*, IITA, Ibadan.

Cheng, N. Z. (1984) 'Experiment on green manure crops on fallow land in summer', *Soil and Water Conserv. China* **28**, 17–20 (in Chinese with English summary).

Chepil, W. S. (1945) 'Dynamics of wind erosion. III. Transport capacity of the wind', *Soil Sci.* **60**, 475–80.

Chepil, W. S. (1946) 'Dynamics of wind erosion. VI. Sorting of soil material by wind', *Soil Sci.* **61**, 331–40.

Chepil, W. S. (1950) 'Properties of soil which influence wind erosion. II. Dry aggregate structure as an index of erodibility', *Soil Sci.* **69**, 403–14.

Chepil, W. S. (1960) 'Conversion of relative field erodibility to annual soil loss by wind', *Soil Sci. Soc. Am. Proc.* **24**, 143–5.

Chepil, W. S. and Woodruff, N. P. (1963) 'The physics of wind erosion and its control', *Advances in Agronomy* **15**, 211–302.

Chepil, W. S., Siddoway, F. H. and Armbrust, D. V. (1964) 'Wind erodibility of knolly terrain', *J. Soil and Water Conserv.* **19**, 179–81.

Chepil, W. S., Woodruff, N. P. and Zingg, A. W. (1955) 'Field study of wind erosion in western Texas', *USDA Soil Conserv. Serv. Tech. Paper* **SCS–TP–125**.

Childs, E. C. (1969) *An introduction to the physical basis of soil water phenomena*, Wiley.

Chisci, G. and Zanchi, C. (1981) 'The influence of different tillage systems and different crops on soil losses on hilly silty-clayey soil', in Morgan, R. P. C. (ed.), *Soil conservation: problems and prospects'*, Wiley, 211–17.

Chisci, G., Lorenzi, G. and Piccolo, L. (1978) 'Effects of a ferric conditioner on clay soils', in Emerson, W. W., Bond, R. D. and Dexter, A. R. (eds), *Modification of soil structure*, Wiley, 309–14.

Chorley, R. J (1959) 'The geomorphic significance of some Oxford soils', *Am. J. Sci.* **257**, 503–15.

Cogo, N. P., Moldenhauer, W. C. and Foster, G. R. (1984) 'Soil loss reductions from conservation tillage practices', *Soil Sci. Soc. Am J.* **48**, 368–73.

Colclough, J. D. (1965) 'Soil conservation and soil erosion control in Tasmania: tunnel erosion', *Tasman. J. Agr.* **36**, 7–12.

Coleman, R. (1981) 'Footpath erosion in the English Lake District', *Appl. Geog.* **1**, 121–31.

Combeau, A. and Monnier, G. (1961) 'A method for the study of structural stability: application to tropical soils', *African Soils* **6**, 33–52.

Cooke, R. U. and Doornkamp, J. C. (1974) *Geomorphology in environmental management*, Oxford University Press.

Coutts, J. R. H., Kandil, M. F., Nowland, J. L. and Tinsley, J. (1968) 'Use of radioactive ^{59}Fe for tracing soil particle movement. I. Field studies of splash erosion', *J. Soil Sci.* **19**, 311–24.

Crouch, R. J. (1978) 'Variation in the structural stability of soil in a tunnel-eroding area', in Emerson, W. W., Bond, R. D. and Dexter, A. R. (eds), *Modification of soil structure*, Wiley, 267–74.

Cruse, R. M. and Larson, W. E. (1977) 'Effect of soil shear strength on soil detachment due to raindrop impact', *Soil Sci. Soc. Am. J.* **41**, 777–81.

Das, D. C. (1977) 'Soil conservation practices and erosion control in India: a case study', *FAO Soils Bull.* **33**, 11–50.

Das, D. C. and Singh, S. (1981) 'Small storage works for erosion control and catchment improvement: mini case studies', in Morgan, R. P. C. (ed.), *Soil conservation: problems and prospects*, Wiley, 425–47.

David, W. P. and Beer, C. E. (1975) 'Simulation of soil erosion – Part 1. Development of a mathematical erosion model', *Trans. Am. Soc. Agr. Engnrs.* **18**, 126–9, 133.

Davidson, J. L. and Quirk, J. P. (1961) 'The influence of dissolved gypsum on pasture establishment on irrigated sodic clays', *Aust. J. Agric. Ros.* **12**, 100–10.

De Kesel, M. and De Vleeschauwer, D. (1981) 'Sand dune fixation in Tunisia by means of polyurea polyalkylene oxide (Uresol)', in Lal, R. and Russell, E. W. (eds), *Tropical agricultural hydrology,* Wiley, 273–81.

De Meester, T. and Jungerius, P. D. (1978) 'The relationship between the soil erodibility factor K (Universal Soil Loss Equation), aggregate stability and micromorphological properties of soils in the Hornos area, S. Spain', *Earth Surf. Proc.* **3**, 379–91.

Demek, J. (1971) *Manual of detailed geomorphological mapping,* Czechoslovak Academy of Science, Institute of Geography, Brno.

De Ploey, J. (1969) 'L'érosion pluviale: expériences à l'aide de sables traceurs et bilans morphogéniques', *Acta Geographica Lovaniensia* **7**, 1–28.

De Ploey, J. (1974) 'Mechanical properties of hillslopes and their relation to gullying in central semi-arid Tunisia', *Z. f. Geomorph. Suppl.* **21**, 177–90.

De Ploey, J. (1977) 'Some experimental data on slopewash and wind action with reference to Quaternary morphogenesis in Belgium', *Earth Surf. Proc.* **2**, 101–15.

De Ploey, J. (1981*a*) 'Crusting and time-dependent rainwash mechanisms on loamy soil', in Morgan, R. P. C. (ed.), *Soil conservation: problems and prospects,* Wiley, 139–52.

De Ploey, J. (1981*b*) 'The ambivalent effects of some factors of erosion', *Mém. Inst. Géol. Univ. Louvain* **31**, 171–81.

De Ploey, J. and Cruz, O. (1979) 'Landslides in the Serra do Mar, Brazil', *Catena* **6**, 111–22.

De Ploey, J. and Gabriels, D. (1980) 'Measuring soil loss and experimental studies', in Kirkby, M. J. and Morgan, R. P. C. (eds), *Soil erosion*, Wiley, 63–108.

De Ploey, J., Savat, J. and Moeyersons, J. (1976) 'The differential impact of some soil factors on flow, runoff creep and rainwash', *Earth Surf. Proc.* **1**, 151–61.

De Vleeschauwer, D., Lal, R. and De Boodt, M. (1979) 'Influence of soil conditioners on water movement through some tropical soils', in Lal, R. and Greenland, D. J. (eds), *Soil physical properties and crop production in the tropics*, Wiley, 149–50.

Diaconu, C. (1969) 'Résultats de l'étude de l'écoulement des alluvions en suspension des rivières de la Roumanie', *Bull. Assoc. Scient. Hydrol.* **14**, 51–89.

Dixon, R. M. and Simanton, J. R. (1980) 'Land imprinting for better watershed management', in *Symp. Watershed Management*, Am. Soc. Civil Engnrs, 809–26.

Dolgilevich, M. I., Sofronova, A. A. and Mayevskaya, L. L. (1973) 'Klassifikatsia pochv zapadnoy Sibiri, severnogo Kazakhstana po stepeniy podatlivosti k vetrovoy eroziy', *Bull. VNIIA* **12**.

Douglas, I. (1967*a*) 'Natural and man-made erosion in the humid tropics of Australia, Malaysia and Singapore', *Int. Assoc. Scient. Hydrol. Pub.* **75**, 17–30.

Douglas, I. (1967*b*) 'Man, vegetation and sediment yield of rivers, *Nature* **215**, 925–8.

Douglas, I. (1968) 'Sediment sources and causes in the humid tropics of northeast Queensland', in Harvey, A. M. (ed.), *Geomorphology in a tropical environment*, British Geomorphological Research Group Occasional Paper **5**, 27–39.

Douglas, I. (1972) *The environment game*, Inaugural lecture, University of New England, Armidale.

Douglas, I. (1976) 'Erosion rates and climate: geomorphological implications', in Derbyshire, E. (ed.), *Geomorphology and climate*, Wiley, 269–87.

Douglas, I. (1978) 'The impact of urbanisation of fluvial geomorphology in the humid tropics', *Géo-Eco-Trop.* **2**, 239–42.

Douglas, J. T. and Goss, M. J. (1982) 'Stability and organic matter content of surface soil aggregates under different methods of cultivation and in grassland', *Soil and Tillage Research* **2**, 155–76.

Downes, R. G. (1946) 'Tunnelling erosion in northeastern Victoria', *J. Counc. Scient. Indus. Res.* **19**, 283–92.

Drainage and Irrigation Department (1970) *Rainfall records for West Malaysia, 1959–1965*, Kuala Lumpur.

D'Souza, V. P. C. and Morgan, R. P. C. (1976) 'A laboratory study of the effect of slope steepness and curvature on soil erosion', *J. Agric. Engng. Res.* **21**, 21–31.

Dunne, T. (1979) 'Sediment yield and land use in tropical catchments', *J. Hydrol.* **42**, 281–300.

Dunne, T. and Black, R. D. (1970) 'Partial area contributions to storm runoff in a small New England watershed', *Water Resour. Res.* **6**, 1296–1311.

Dunne, T., Dietrich, W. E. and Brunengo, M. J. (1978) 'Recent and past erosion rates in semi-arid Kenya', *Z. f. Geomorph. Suppl.* **29**, 130–40.

Dyrness, C. T. (1975) 'Grass–legume mixtures for erosion control along forest roads in western Oregon', *J. Soil and Wat. Conserv.* **30**, 169–73.

Eckholm, E. P. (1976) *Losing ground*, Norton.

Ellison, W. D. (1944) 'Two devices for measuring soil erosion', *Agric. Engng.* **25**, 53–5.

Ellison, W. D. (1947) 'Soil erosion studies. II. Soil detachment hazard by raindrop splash', *Agric. Engng.* **28**, 197–201.

El-Swaify, S. A., Dangler, E. W. and Armstrong, C. L. (1982) *Soil erosion by water in the tropics*, College of Tropical Agriculture and Human Resources, Univ. Hawaii.

Elwell, H. A. (1981) 'A soil loss estimation technique for southern Africa', in Morgan, R. P. C. (ed.), *Soil conservation: problems and prospects*, Wiley, 281–92.

Elwell, H. A. and Stockings, M. A. (1976) 'Vegetal cover to estimate soil erosion hazard in Rhodesia', *Geoderma* **15**, 61–70.

Emmett, W. W. (1970) 'The hydraulics of overland flow on hillslopes', *USGS Prof. Paper* **662–A**.

Evans, A. C. (1948) 'Studies on the relationships between earthworms and soil fertility. II. Some effects of earthworms and soil structure', *Appl. Biol.* **35**, 1–13.

Evans, R. (1977) 'Overgrazing and soil erosion on hill pastures with particular reference to the Peak district', *J. Br. Grassl. Soc.* **32**, 65–76.

Evans, R. (1980) 'Mechanics of water erosion and their spatial and temporal controls: an empirical viewpoint', in Kirkby, M. J. and Morgan, R. P. C. (eds), *Soil erosion*, Wiley, 109–28.

Evans, R. (1981) 'Potential soil and crop losses by erosion', in *Proc. SAWMA Conf. Soil and crop loss: developments in erosion control*, Nat. Agr. Centre, Stoneleigh.

Evans, R. and Morgan, R. P. C. (1974) 'Water erosion of arable land', *Area* **6**, 221–5.

Eyles, R. J. (1966) 'Stream representation on Malayan maps', *J. Trop. Geog.* **22**, 1–9.

Eyles, R. J. (1967) 'Laterite at Kerdau, Pahang, Malaya', *J. Trop. Geog.* **25**, 18–23.

Eyles, R. J. (1968*a*) 'Morphometric explanation: a case study', *Geographica* (*University of Malaya*) **4**, 17–23.

Eyles, R. J. (1968*b*) 'Stream net ratios in West Malaysia', *Bull. Geol. Soc. Am.* **79**, 701–12.

Eyles, R. J. (1968*c*) *A morphometric analysis of West Malaysia*, unpub. PhD thesis, University of Malaya.

Eyles, R. J. (1970) 'Physiographic implications of laterite', *Bull. Geol. Soc. Malay.* **3**, 1–7.

Fang, Z. S., Zhou, P. H., Liu, Q. D., Liu, B. H., Ren, L. T. and Zhang, H. X. (1981) 'Terraces in the loess plateau of China', in Morgan, R. P. C. (ed.), *Soil conservation: problems and prospects*, Wiley, 481–513.

FAO (1965) *Soil erosion by water*, Rome.

Farmer, E. E. (1973) 'Relative detachability of soil particles by simulated rainfall', *Soil Sci. Soc. Am. Proc.* **37**, 629–33.

Farres, P. (1978) 'The role of time and aggregate size in the crusting process', *Earth Surf. Proc.* **3**, 243–54.

Felipe-Morales, F., Meyer, R., Alegre, C. and Vittorelli, C. (1979) 'Losses of water and soil under different cultivation systems in two Peruvian locations, Santa Ana (Central Highlands) and San Ramon (Central High Jungle), 1975–1976', in Lal, R. and Greenland, D. J. (eds), *Soil physical properties and crop production in the tropics*, Wiley, 489–99.

Fenster, C. R. and McCalla, T. M. (1970) 'Tillage practices in western Nebraska with a wheat–fallow rotation', *Nebr. Agr. Sta., Lincoln, Bull.* **597**.

Fenster, C. R. and Wicks, G. A. (1977) 'Minimum tillage fallow systems for reducing wind erosion', *Trans. Am. Soc. Agric. Engnrs.* **20**, 906–10.

Fenton, E. W. (1937) 'The influence of sheep on the vegetation of hill grazings in Scotland', *J. Ecol.* **25**, 424–30.

Finkel, H. J. (1959) 'The barchans in southern Peru', *J. Geol.* **67**, 614–47.

Finney, H. J. (1984) 'The effect of crop covers on rainfall characteristics and splash detachment', *J. Agric. Engng. Res.* **29**, 337–43.

Fleming, G. (1983) *River basin model for water and sediment resource* assessment. *User Guide Volume 2. The sediment erosion transport deposition model and flow routing.* University of Strathclyde, Glasgow.

Fleming, G. and Fattorelli, S. (1981) 'Data requirements for sediment, erosion and transport simulation', *Int. Ass. Scient. Hydrol. Pub.* **133**, 321–7.

Fleming, G. and Fattorelli, S. (1984) 'Simulation of sediment yield from Alpine watersheds', *Proc. Workshop on Prediction of agricultural nonpoint source pollution: model selection and application, Venezia,* Univ. Padova, L1–L24.

Floyd, E. J. (1974) 'Tunnel erosion: a field study in the Riverina', *J. Soil Conserv. Serv. NSW* **30**, 145–56.

Foster, G. R. (1982) 'Modeling the erosion process', in Haan, C. T., Johnson, H. P. and Brakensiek, D. L. (eds), *Hydrologic modeling of small watersheds,* Am. Soc. Agric. Engnrs. Monograph **No. 5**, 297–380.

Foster, G. R. and Lane, L. J. (1981) 'Simulation of erosion and sediment yield from field-sized areas', in Lal, R. and Russell, E. W. (eds), *Tropical agricultural hydrology,* Wiley, 375–94.

Foster, G. R. and Meyer, L. D. (1972) 'A closed-form soil erosion equation for upland areas', in Shen, H. W. (ed.), *Sedimentation,* Dept. Civil Engng, Colorado State Univ., Fort Collins, Colo., 12-1–12-19.

Foster, G. R. and Meyer, L. D. (1975) 'Mathematical simulation of upland erosion by fundamental erosion mechanics', in *Present and prospective technology for predicting sediment yields and sources,* USDA Agr. Res. Serv. Pub. **ARS-S-40**, 190–207.

Foster, G. R., Johnson, C. B. and Moldenhauer, W. C. (1982) 'Hydraulics of failure of unanchored cornstalk and wheat straw mulches for erosion control', *Trans. Am. Soc. Agric. Engnrs,* **25**, 940–7.

Foster, G. R., Meyer, L. D. and Onstad, C. A. (1973) 'Erosion equations derived from modeling principles', *ASAE Paper No. 73–2550,* Am. Soc. Agric. Engnrs, St Joseph, Mich.

Foster, G. R., Lane, L. J., Nowlin, J. D., Laflen, J. M. and Young, R. A. (1981) 'Estimating erosion and sediment yield on field-sized areas', *Trans. Am. Soc. Agric. Engnrs.* **24**, 1253–63.

Fournier, F. (1960) *Climat et érosion: la relation entre l'érosion du sol par l'eau et les précipitations atmosphériques,* Presses Universitaires de France.

Fournier, F. (1972) *Soil conservation,* Nature and Environment Series, Council of Europe.

Fredén, C. and Furuholm, L. (1978) 'The Säterberget Gully at Brattforsheden, Värmland', *Geologiska Föreningens i Stockholm Förhandlingar* **100**, 231–5.

Free, G. R. (1960) 'Erosion characteristics of rainfall', *Agric. Engng.* **41**, 447–9, 455.

Fryrear, D. W. (1984) 'Soil ridges–clods and wind erosion', *Trans. Am. Soc. Agric. Engnrs.* **27**, 445–8.

Gabriels, D. and De Boodt, M. (1978) 'Evaluation of soil conditioners for water erosion control and sand stabilization', in Emerson, W. W., Bond, R. D. and Dexter, A. R. (eds) *Modification of soil structure*, Wiley, 341–8.

Gabriels, D., Pauwels, J. M. and De Boodt, M. (1975) 'The slope gradient as it affects the amounts and size distribution of soil loss material from runoff on silt loam aggregates', *Med. Fac. Landbouww. Rijksuniv. Gent.* **40**, 1333–8.

Gabriels, D., Pauwels, J. M. and De Boodt, M. (1977) 'A quantitative rill erosion study on a loamy sand in the hilly region of Flanders', *Earth Surf. Proc.* **2**, 257–9.

Gabriels, D., Maene, L., Lenvain, J. and De Boodt, M. (1977) 'Possibilities of using soil conditioners for soil erosion control', in Greenland, D. J. and Lal, R. (eds), *Soil conservation and management in the humid tropics*, Wiley, 99–108.

Gerlach, T. (1966) 'Współczesny rozwój stoków w dorzeczu górnego Grajcarka (Beskid Wysoki-Karpaty Zachodnie)', *Prace Geogr. IG PAN* **52** (with French summary).

Gerlach, T. (1967) 'Evolutions actuelles des versants dans les Carpathes, d'après l'exemple d'observations fixes', in Macar, P. (ed.), *L'évolution des versants*, University of Liège, 129–38.

Gerlach, T. and Niemirowski, M. (1968) 'Charakterystyka geomorfologiczna dolin Jaszcze i Jamne', *Zak. Ochr. Przyrody Polsk. Ak. Nauk, Studia Naturae, Seria A* **2**, 11–22.

Getahun, A. (1983) 'The role of agroforestry in soil and water conservation in the tropics', in Thomas, D. B. and Senga, W. M. (eds), *Soil and water conservation in Kenya*, Inst. Dev. Studies and Fac. Agr., Univ. Nairobi, Occasional Paper **No. 42**, 338–49.

Ghadiri, H. and Payne, D. (1977) 'Raindrop impact stress and the breakdown of soil crumbs', *J. Soil Sci.* **28**, 247–58.

Ghadiri, H. and Payne, D. (1979) 'Raindrop impact and soil splash', in Lal, R. and Greenland, D. J. (eds), *Soil physical properties and crop production in the tropics*, Wiley, 95–104.

Gichungwa, J. K. (1970) *Soil conservation in Central Province (Kenya)*, Ministry of Agriculture, Nairobi.

Gifford, G. F. (1976) 'Applicability of some infiltration formulae to rangeland infiltrometer data', *J. Hydrol.* **28**, 1–11.

Gilmour, D. A. (1977) 'Logging and the environment with particular reference to soil and stream protection in tropical rainforest situations', in FAO, *Guidelines for watershed management, Conservation Guide* 1, Rome.

Godwin, R. J. and Spoor, G. (1977) 'Soil failure with narrow tines', *J. Agric. Engng. Res.* **22**, 213–28.

Gong, S. Y. and Jiang, D. Q. (1977) 'Soil erosion and its control in small gully watersheds in the rolling loess area on the middle reaches of the Yellow River', *Paris Symp. Erosion and soil matter transport in inland waters*, preprint.

González, M. H. (1971) '¿Que es condición de pastizal?', *Boletín Pastizales* **2**, 8–10.

Gorchichko, G. K. (1977) 'Device for determining the amount of soil splashed by raindrops', *Soviet Soil Sci.* **8**, 610–13.

Gosh, R. L., Kaul, O. N. and Subba-Rao, B. K. (1978) 'Some aspects of water relations and nutrition in *Eucalyptus* plantations', *Indian Forester* **104**, 517–24.

Graf, W. L. (1979) 'The development of montane arroyos and gullies', *Earth Surf. Proc.* **4**, 1–14.

Gray, D. H. and Leiser, A. T. (1982) *Biotechnical slope protection and erosion control*, Van Nostrand Reinhold.

Gregory, K. J. and Gardiner, V. (1975) 'Drainage density and climate', *Z. f. Geomorph.* **19**, 287–98.

Gregory, K. J. and Walling, D. E. (1973) *Drainage basin form and process,* Edward Arnold.

Grierson, I. T. (1978) 'Gypsum and red-brown earths', in Emerson, W. W., Bond, R. D. and Dexter, A. R. (eds), *Modification of soil structure*, Wiley, 315–24.

Griessel, O. and Beasley, R. P. (1971) 'Design criteria for underground terrace outlets', *Univ. Missouri Ext. Div. Sci. and Tech. Guide* **1525**.

Grissinger, E. H. (1966) 'Resistance of selected clay systems to erosion by water', *Water Resour. Res.* **2**, 131–8.

Grissinger, E. H. and Asmussen, L. E. (1963) 'Discussion of channel stability in undisturbed cohesive soils by E. M. Flaxman', *J. Hydraul. Div. ASCE* **89**, 529–64.

Guðmunsson, Ó. (1980) 'Approaches, materials and methods', in Guðmunsson, Ó., Arnalds, A. (eds), *Consultancy reports for the Project on utilization and conservation of grassland resources in Iceland*, Rannsóknastofnun Landbúnaðarins Report **61**, 3–33.

Gupta, A. (1982) 'Observations on the effects of urbanization on runoff and sediment production in Singapore', *Sing. J. Trop. Geog.* **3**, 137–46.

Hack, J. T. and Goodlett, J. C. (1960) 'Geomorphology and forest ecology of a mountain region in the central Appalachians', *USGS Prof. Paper* **347**.

Hall, A. D. (1945) *The soil*, John Murray.

Hall, G. F., Daniels, R. B. and Foss, J. E. (1979) 'Soil formation and renewal rates in the US', *Symp. Determinants of soil loss tolerance*, Soil Sci. Soc. Am. Annual Meeting, Fort Collins, Colo.

Hall, M. J. (1970) 'A critique of methods of simulating rainfall', *Water Resour. Res.* **6**, 1104–14.

Hannam, I. D. (1979) 'Urban soil erosion: an extreme phase in the Stewart subdivision, West Bathurst', *J. Soil Conserv. Serv. NSW* **35**, 19–25.

Hannam, I. D. and Hicks, R. W. (1980) 'Soil conservation and urban land use planning', *J. Soil Conserv. Serv. NSW* **36**, 134–45.

Hardan, A. and Al-Ani, A. N. (1978) 'Improvement of soil structure by using date and sugar beet waste products', in Emerson, W. W., Bond, R. D. and Dexter, A. R. (eds), *Modification of soil structure*, Wiley, 305–8.

Hazelhoff, L., van Hoof, P., Imeson, A. C. and Kwaad, F. J. P. M. (1981) 'The exposure of forest soil to erosion by earthworms', *Earth Surf. Proc. Landf.* **6**, 235–50.

Hedfors, L. (1983) 'Evaluation and economic appraisal of soil conservation in a pilot area: a summarised report', in Thomas, D. B. and Senga, W. M. (eds), *Soil and water conservation in Kenya*, Inst. Dev. Studies and Fac. Agr. Univ. Nairobi, Occasional Paper **42**, 257–62.

Heede, B. H. (1971) 'Characteristics and processes of soil piping in gullies', *USDA Forest Service Research Paper* **RM-68**, Rocky Mountain Forest and Range Experiment Station, Fort Collins, Colo.

Heede, B. H. (1975*a*) 'Watershed indicators of landform development', in *Proc. Hydrol. Water Resour. in Ariz. and the Southwest, Vol. 5*, Ariz. Sect. Am. Water Resour. Assoc. and Hydrol. Sect. Ariz. Acad. Sci., 43–6.

Heede, B. H. (1975*b*) 'Stages of development of gullies in the west', in *Present and prospective technology for predicting sediment yields and sources*, USDA Agric. Res. Serv. Pub. **ARS-S-40**, 155–61.

Heede, B. H. (1976) 'Gully development and control: the status of our knowledge', *USDA Forest Service Research Paper* **RM-169**. Rocky Mountain Forest and Range Experiment Station, Fort Collins, Colo.

Heede, B. H. and Mufich, J. G. (1973) 'Functional relationships and a computer program for structural gully control', *J. Environmental Management* **1**, 321–44.

Hénin, S. G., Monnier, G. and Combeau, A. (1958) 'Méthode pour l'étude de la stabilité structural des sols', *Ann. Agron.* **9**, 73–92.

Hesp, P. (1979) 'Sand trapping ability of culms of marram grass (*Ammophila Arenaria*)', *J. Soil Conserv. Serv. NSW* **35**, 156–60.

Heusch, B. (1970) 'L'érosion du Pré-Rif. Une étude quantitative de l'érosion hydraulique dans les collines marneuses du Pré-Rif occidental', *Ann. Rech. Fores. Maroc* **12**, 9–176.

Hibbert, A. R., Davis, E. A. and Brown, T. C. (1975) 'Managing chaparral for water and other resources in Arizona', in *Proc. Watershed management symp.*, ASCE Irrig. and Drain. Div., 445–68.

Higginson, F. R. (1973) 'Soil erosion of land systems within the Hunter Valley', *J. Soil Conserv. Serv. NSW* **29**, 103–10.

Hillel, D. (1960) 'Crust formation in loessial soils', *Trans. VIIth Int. Soil Sci. Congr. Madison, WI*, 330–7.

Hillel, D. (1971) *Soil and water. Physical principles and processes*, Academic Press.

Hills, R. C. (1970) 'The determination of the infiltration capacity of field soils using the cylinder infiltrometer', *British Geomorphological Research Group Technical Bulletin* **5**.

Hjulström, F. (1935) 'Studies of the morphological activity of rivers as illustrated by the River Fyries', *Bull. Geol. Inst. Univ. Uppsala* **25**, 221–527.

Hollis, G. E. (1974) 'The effect of urbanization on floods in the Canon's Brook, Harlow, Essex', in Gregory, K. J. and Walling, D. E. (eds), *Fluvial processes in instrumented watersheds*, Inst. Br. Geogr. Spec. Pub. **6**, 123–40.

Holý, M., Svetlosanov, V., Handová, Z., Kos, Z., Váska, J. and Vrána, K. (1982) 'Procedures, numerical parameters and coefficients of the CREAMS model: application and verification in Czechoslovakia', *Int. Inst. Appl. Syst. Anal. Collaborative Paper* **CP-82-23**.

Hoogmoed, W. B. and Stroosnijder, L. (1984) 'Crust formation on sandy soils in the Sahel. I. Rainfall and infiltration', *Soil and Tillage Research* **4**, 5–24.

Horikawa, K. and Shen, H. W. (1960) 'Sand movement by wind (on the characteristics of sand traps)', *US Beach Erosion Board Tech. Mem.* **119**.

Horton, R. E. (1945) 'Erosional development of streams and their drainage basins: a hydrophysical approach to quantitative morphology', *Bull. Geol. Soc. Am.* **56**, 275–370.

Horváth, V. and Erödi, B. (1962) 'Determination of natural slope category limits by functional identity of erosion intensity', *Int. Assoc. Scient. Hydrol. Pub.* **59**, 131–43.

Hsu, S. A. (1973) 'Computing eolian sand transport from shear velocity measurements', *J. Geol.* **81**, 739–43.

Huang, C., Bradford, J. M. and Cushman, J. H. (1982) 'A numerical study of raindrop impact phenomena: the rigid case', *Soil Sci. Soc. Am. J.* **46**, 14–19.

Hudson, N. W. (1957) 'The design of field experiments on soil erosion', *J. Agric. Engng. Res.* **2**, 56–65.

Hudson, N. W. (1961) 'An introduction to the mechanics of soil erosion under conditions of sub-tropical rainfall', *Proc. and Trans. Rhod. Scient. Assoc.* **49**, 15–25.

Hudson, N. W. (1963) 'Raindrop size distribution in high intensity storms', *Rhod. J. Agric. Res.* **1**, 6–11.

Hudson, N. W. (1965) *The influence of rainfall on the mechanics of soil erosion with particular reference to Southern Rhodesia*, unpub. MSc thesis, University of Cape Town.

Hudson, N. W. (1981*a*) *Soil conservation*, Batsford.

Hudson, N. W. (1981*b*) 'Non technical constraints on soil conservation', in Tingsanchali, T. and Eggers, H. (eds), *Southeast Asian regional symposium on problems of soil erosion and sedimentation*, Asian Institute of Technology, 15–26.

Hudson, N. W. and Jackson, D. C. (1959) 'Results achieved in the measurement of erosion and runoff in Southern Rhodesia', *Proc. Third Inter-African Soils Conference*, Dalaba, 575–83.

Hurni, H. (1981) 'Soil erosion in Huai Thung Choa, northern Thailand: concerns and constraints', *Highland–lowland interactive systems project, scientific report*, United Nations Univ. and Univ. Bern.

Hurni, H. (1983) *Soil conservation research project Ethiopia. Volume 3. Second Progress Report (Year 1982)*, Univ. Bern and United Nations Univ.

Hurni, H. (1984) *Soil conservation research project Ethiopia. Volume 4. Third Progress Report (Year 1983)*, Univ. Bern and United Nations Univ.

Hussein, M. H. and Laflen, J. M. (1982) 'Effects of crop canopy and residue on rill and interrill soil erosion', *Trans. Am. Soc. Agric. Engnrs.* **25**, 1310–15.

Iana, S. (1972) 'Considérations sur la protection des versants en Dobroudgea', *Acta Geographica Debrecina* **10**, 51–5.

Imeson, A. C. (1971) 'Heather burning and soil erosion on the North Yorkshire Moors', *J. Appl. Ecol.* **8**, 537–42.

Imeson, A. C. (1976) 'Some effects of burrowing animals on slope processes in the Luxembourg Ardennes: Part 1. The excavation of animal mounds in experimental plots', *Geografiska Ann.* **58-A**, 115–25.

Iverson, R. M. (1980) 'Processes of accelerated pluvial erosion on desert hillslopes modified by vehicular traffic', *Earth Surf. Proc.* **5**, 369–88.

Jackson, S. J. (1984) *The role of slope form on soil erosion at different scales as a possible link between soil erosion surveys and soil erosion models*, unpub. PhD thesis, Cranfield Institute of Technology.

Jensen, M. (1954) *The shelter effect*, Danish Technical Press.

Jiang, D. Q., Qi, L. D. and Tan, J. S. (1981) 'Soil erosion and conservation in the Wuding River Valley, China', in Morgan, R. P. C. (ed.), *Soil conservation: problems and prospects*, Wiley, 461–79.

Jóhannesson, B. (1960) 'The soils of Iceland', *Univ. Res. Inst, Dept. Agr. Reports Series B* **13**.

Johnson, C. B. and Moldenhauer, W. C. (1979) 'Effect of chisel versus moldboard plowing on soil erosion by water', *Soil Sci. Soc. Am. J.* **43**, 177–9.

Johnston, A. E. (1982) 'The effects of farming systems on the amount of soil organic matter and its effect on yield at Rothamsted and Woburn', in Boels, D., Davies, D. B. and Johnston, A. E. (eds), *Soil degradation*, Balkema, 187–202.

Jones, M. J. (1971) 'The maintenance of soil organic matter under continuous cultivation at Samaru, Nigeria', *J. Agric. Sci. Camb.* **77**, 473–82.

Jones, R. G. B. and Keech, M. A. (1966) 'Identifying and assessing problem areas in soil erosion surveys using aerial photographs', *Photogrammetric Record* **5/27**, 189–97.

Josué Martinez, T. G. and González, M. H. (1971) 'Influencia de la condición de pastizal en la infiltración de agua en el suelo', *Boletín Pastizales* **2**(2), 2–5.

Jovanović, S. and Vukčević, M. (1958) 'Suspended sediment regimen on some watercourses in Yugoslavia and analysis of erosion processes', *Int. Assoc. Scient. Hydrol. Pub.* **43**, 337–59.

Kairiukstis, L. and Golubev, G. (1982) 'Application of the CREAMS model as part of an overall system for optimizing environmental management in Lithuania, USSR: first experiments', in Svetlosanov, V. and Knisel, W. G. (eds), *European and United States case studies in application of the CREAMS model*, Int. Inst. Appl. Syst. Anal. Collaborative Proceedings Series **CP-82-S11**, 99–119.

Kalesnik, S. V. (1961) 'The present state of landscape studies', *Soviet Geog.* **2**(2), 24–33.

Kampen, J., Hari Krishna, J. and Pathak, P. (1981) 'Rainy season cropping on deep vertisols in the semi-arid tropics: effects on hydrology and soil erosion', in Lal, R. and Russell, E. W. (eds), *Tropical agricultural hydrology*, Wiley, 257–71.

Keech, M. A. (1969) 'Mondaro Tribal Trust Land. Determination of trend using air photo analysis', *Rhod. Agric. J.* **66**, 3–10.

Kellman, M. C. (1969) 'Some environmental components of shifting cultivation in upland Mindanao', *J. Trop. Geog.* **28**, 40–56.

Kemper, B. and Derpsch, R. (1981) 'Results of studies made in 1978 and 1979 to control erosion by cover crops and no-tillage techniques in Paraná, Brazil', *Soil and Tillage Research* **1**, 253–68.

Kermack, K. A. and Haldane, J. B. S. (1950) 'Organic correlation and allometry', *Biometrika* **37**, 30–41.

Khimina, N. T. (1973) 'Protideflatsionnay effektivnosti sistem lesiyikh polos na peschaiyi zemlyakh', *Bull. VNIIALM* **12**, 26–8.

Kirkby, A. V. T. and Kirkby, M. J. (1974) 'Surface wash at the semi-arid break in slope', *Z. f. Geomorph. Suppl.* **21**, 151–76.

Kirkby, M. J. (1969*a*) 'Infiltration, throughflow and overland flow', in Chorley, R. J. (ed.), *Water, earth and man*, Methuen, 215–27.

Kirkby, M. J. (1969*b*) 'Erosion by water on hillslopes', in Chorley, R. J. (ed.), *Water, earth and man*, Methuen, 229–38.

Kirkby, M. J. (1971) 'Hillslope process-response models based on the continuity equation', in Brunsden, D. (ed.), *Slopes: form and process,* Inst. Br. Georgr. Spec. Pub. **3**, 15–30.

Kirkby, M. J. (1976) 'Hydrological slope models: the influence of climate', in Derbyshire, E. (ed.), *Geomorphology and climate*, Wiley, 247–67.

Kirkby, M. J. (1980) 'The problem', in Kirkby, M. J. and Morgan, R. P. C. (eds), *Soil erosion*, Wiley, 1–16.

Klingebiel, A. A. and Montgomery, P. H. (1966) 'Land capability classification', *USDA Soil Conserv. Serv. Agric. Handbook* **210**.

Knapp, B. J. (1978) 'Infiltration and storage of soil water', in Kirkby, M. J. (ed.), *Hillslope hydrology*, Wiley, 43–72.

Knisel, W. G. (1980) 'CREAMS: a field scale model for chemicals, runoff and erosion from agricultural management systems', *USDA Conserv. Res. Report* **26**.

Knisel, W. G. and Svetlosanov. V. (1982) 'Review of case studies of CREAMS model application', in Svetlosanov, V. and Knisel, W. G. (eds), *European and United States case studies in application of the CREAMS model*, Int. Inst. Appl. Syst. Anal. Collaborative Proceedings Series **CP-82-S11**, 121–35.

Knottnerus, D. J. C. (1976) 'Stabilisation of wind erodible land by an intermediate crop', *Med. Fac. Landbouww. Rijksuniv. Gent.* **41**, 73–9.

Knottnerus, D. J. C. (1979) *Wind erosion research by means of a wind tunnel. Measures to control wind erosion of soil and other materials for reasons of economy and health*, Inst. Bodemvruchtbaarheid, Haren (Gr).

Kohnke, H. and Bertrand, A. R. (1959) *Soil conservation*, McGraw-Hill.

Kolenbrander, G. J. (1974) 'Efficiency of organic manure in increasing soil organic matter content', *Trans. 10th Int. Congr. Soil Sci.* **2**, 129–36.

Komura, S. (1976) 'Hydraulics of slope erosion by overland flow', *J. Hydraul. Div. ASCE* **102**, 1573–86.

Konuche, P. K. A. (1983) 'Effects of forest management practices on soil and water conservation in Kenya forests', in Thomas, D. B. and Senga, W. M. (eds), *Soil and water conservation in Kenya*, Inst. Dev. Studies and Fac. Agr. Univ. Nairobi, Occasional Paper **42**, 350–9.

Kowal, J. M. and Kassam, A. H. (1976) 'Energy load and instantaneous intensity of rainstorms at Samaru, northern Nigeria', *Trop. Agric.* **53**, 185–97.

Kwaad, F. J. P. M. (1977) 'Measurements of rainsplash erosion and the formation of colluvium beneath deciduous woodland in the Luxembourg Ardennes', *Earth Surf. Proc.* **2**, 161–73.

Laflen, J. M. and Colvin, T. S. (1981) 'Effect of crop residue on soil loss from continuous row cropping', *Trans. Am. Soc. Agric. Engnrs.* **24**, 605–9.

Laflen, J. M and Moldenhauer, W. C. (1979) 'Soil and water losses from corn–soybean rotations', *Soil Sci. Soc. Am. J.* **43**, 1213–15.

Laflen, J. M., Johnson, H. P. and Reeve, R. C. (1972) 'Soil loss from tile-outlet terraces', *J. Soil and Wat. Conserv.* **27**, 74–7.

Laing, I. A. F. (1978) 'Soil surface treatment for runoff inducement', in Emerson, W. W., Bond, R. D. and Dexter, A. R. (eds), *Modification of soil structure*, Wiley, 249–56.

Lal, R. (1976) 'Soil erosion problems on an alfisol in western Nigeria and their control', *IITA Monograph* **1**.

Lal, R. (1977*a*) 'Soil-conserving versus soil-degrading crops and soil management for erosion control', in Greenland, D. J. and Lal, R. (eds), *Soil conservation and management in the humid tropics*, Wiley, 81–6.

Lal, R. (1977*b*) 'Soil management systems and erosion control', in Greenland, D. J. and Lal, R. (eds), *Soil conservation and management in the humid tropics*, Wiley, 93–7.

Lal, R. (1981*a*) 'Soil conservation: preventive and control measures', in Morgan, R. P. C. (ed.), *Soil conservation: problems and prospects*, Wiley, 175–81.

Lal, R. (1981*b*) 'Deforestation of tropical rainforest and hydrological problems', in Lal, R. and Russell, E. W. (eds), *Tropical agricultural hydrology*, Wiley, 131–40.

Lang, R. D. and McCaffrey, L. A. H. (1984) 'Ground cover: its effects on soil loss from grazed runoff plots, Gunnedah', *J. Soil Conserv. Serv. NSW* **40**, 56–61.

Langbein, W. B. and Schumm, S. A. (1958) 'Yield of sediment in relation to mean annual precipitation', *Trans. Am. Geophys. Un.* **39**, 1076–84.

Lattanzi, A. R., Meyer, L. D. and Baumgardner, M. F. (1974) 'Influence of mulch rate and slope steepness on interrill erosion', *Soil Sci. Soc. Am. Proc.* **38**, 946–50.

Laws, J. O. and Parsons, D. A. (1943) 'The relationship of raindrop size to intensity', *Trans. Am. Geophys. Un.* **24**, 452–60.

Leaf, C. F. (1970) 'Sediment yields from central Colorado snow Zone', *J. Hydraul. Div. ASCE* **96**, 87–93.

Lee, J. and Diamond, S. (1972) 'The potential of Irish land for livestock production', *Nat. Soil Surv. Ireland, Soil Surv. Bull.* **26**.

Leigh, C. (1982*a*) 'Sediment transport by surface wash and throughflow at the Pasoh Forest Reserve, Negri Sembilan, Peninsular Malaysia', *Geografiska Ann.* **64–A**, 171–80.

Leigh, C. H. (1982*b*) 'Urban development and soil erosion in Kuala Lumpur, Malaysia', *J. Environmental Management* **15**, 35–45.

Leopold, L. B., Wolman, M. G. and Miller, J. P. (1964) *Fluvial processes in geomorphology*, Freeman.

Li, J. H. (1984) 'Benefits drawn from network of shelter belts in farmland of Pengwa Production Brigade, Youyu Country', *Soil and Wat. Conserv. China* **22**, 24–5 (in Chinese with English summary).

Liddle, M. J. (1973) *The effects of trampling and vehicles on natural vegetation*, unpub. PhD thesis, Univ. Coll. N. Wales, Bangor.

Lindsay, J. I. and Gumbs, F. A. (1982) 'Erodibility indices compared to measured values of selected Trinidad soils', *Soil Sci. Soc. Am. J.* **46**, 393–5.

Logie, M. (1982) 'Influence of roughness elements and soil moisture on the resistance of sand to wind erosion', *Catena Suppl* **1**, 161–73.

Low, F. K. (1967) 'Estimating potential erosion in developing countries', *J. Soil and Wat. Conserv.* **22**, 147–8.

Low, K. S. and Goh, K. C. (1972) 'The water balance of five catchments in Selangor, West Malaysia', *J. Trop. Geog.* **35**, 60–6.

Lugo-Lopez, M. A. (1969) 'Prediction of the erosiveness of Puerto Rican soils on a basis of the percentage of particles of silt and clay when aggregated', *J. Agric. Univ. Puerto Rico* **53**, 187–90.

Luk, S. H. (1981) 'Variability of rainwash erosion within small sample areas', in *Proc. Twelfth Binghampton Geomorphology Symp.*, Allen and Unwin 243–68.

Luk, S. H. and Morgan, C. (1981) 'Spatial variations of rainwash and runoff within apparently homogenous areas', *Catena* **8**, 383–402.

Lundgren, B. and Nair, P. K. R. (1985) 'Agroforesty for soil conservation', in El-Swaify, S. A., Moldenhauer, W. C. and Lo, A. (eds), *Soil erosion and conservation*', Soil Conserv. Soc. Am. 703–711.

Lundgren, L. (1978) 'Studies of soil and vegetation development on fresh landslide scars in the Mgeta Valley, western Uluguru Mountains, Tanzania', *Geografiska Ann.* **60-A**, 91–127.

Lundgren, L. and Rapp, A. (1974) 'A complex landslide with destructive effects on the water supply of Morogoro town, Tanzania', *Geografiska Ann.* **56-A**, 251–60.

Lyles, L. and Allison, B. E. (1976) 'Wind erosion: the protective role of simulated standing stubble', *Trans. Am. Soc. Agric. Engnrs.* **19**, 61–4.

Lyles, L. and Allison, B. E. (1980) 'Range grasses and their small grain equivalents for wind erosion control', *J. Range Management* **33**, 143–6.

Lyles, L. and Allison, B. E. (1981) 'Equivalent wind erosion protection from selected crop residues', *Trans. Am. Soc. Agric. Engnrs.* **24**, 405–9.

Lyles, L., Dickerson, J. D. and Schmeidler, M. F. (1974) 'Soil detachment from clods by rainfall: effects of wind, mulch cover and initial soil moisture', *Trans. Am. Soc. Agric. Engnrs.* **17**, 697–700.

McCormack, D. E. and Young, K. K. (1981) 'Technical and societal implications of soil loss tolerance', in Morgan, R. P. C. (ed.), *Soil conservation: problems and prospects*, Wiley, 365–76.

McCormack, R. J. (1971) 'The Canada Land Use Inventory: a basis for landuse planning', *J. Soil and Wat. Conserv.* **26**, 141–6.

McGregor, J. C. and Mutchler, C. K. (1978) 'The effect of crop canopy on raindrop size distribution and energy', *USDA Sedimentation Lab. Annual Report*, Oxford MS.

McPhee, P. J., Hartmann, M. O. and Kieck, N. F. (1983) 'Soil erodibility and crop management factors of soils under pineapple production', *ASAE Paper No. 83-2073*, Am. Soc. Agric. Engnrs, St Joseph, Mich.

Maene, L. M. and Chong, S. P. (1979) 'Drop size distribution and erosivity of tropical rainstorms under the oil palm canopy', *Lapuran Penyelidikan Jabatan Sains Tanah 1977–78*, Universiti Pertanian Malaysia, 81–93.

Maene, L. M., Thong, K. C. Ong, T. S. and Mokhtaruddin, A. M. (1979) 'Surface wash under mature oil palm', in Pushparajah, E. (ed.), *Proc. Symp. Water in Malaysian agriculture*, Malay, Soc. Soil. Sci., 203–16.

Maner, S. B. (1958) 'Factors affecting sediment delivery rates in the Red Hills physiographic area', *Trans. Am. Geophys. Un.* **39**, 669–75.

Mannering, J. V. and Johnson, C.B. (1969) 'Effect of row crop spacing on erosion and infiltration', *Agron. J.* **61**, 902–5.

Marston, D. and Hird, C. (1978) 'Effect of stubble management on the structure of black cracking clays', in Emerson, W.'W., Bond, R. D. and Dexter, A. R. (eds), *Modification of soil structure*, Wiley, 411–17.

Marston, D. and Perrens, S. J. (1981) 'Effect of stubble on erosion of a black earth soil', in Tingsanchali, T. and Eggers, H. (eds), *Southeast Asian regional symposium on problems of soil erosion and sedimentation*, Asian Institute of Technology, 289–300.

Martin, L. and Morgan, R. P. C. (1980) 'Soil erosion in mid-Bedfordshire', in Doornkamp, J. C., Gregory, K. J. and Burn, A. S. (eds), *Atlas of drought in Britain, 1975–76*, Inst. Br. Geogr., 47.

Mason, B. J. and Andrews, J. B. (1960) 'Drop size distributions from various types of rain', *Quart. J. Roy. Met. Soc* **86**, 346–53.

Mazurak, A. P., Chesnin, L. and Tiarks, A. E. (1975) 'Detachment of soil aggregates by simulated rainfall from heavily manured soils in eastern Nebraska', *Soil Sci. Soc. Am. Proc.* **39**, 732–6.

Megahan, W. F. and Molitor, D. C. (1975) 'Erosional effects of wildfire and logging in Idaho', in *Proc. Watershed management symp.*, ASCE Irrig. and Drain. Div., 423–44.

Mein, R. G. and Larson, C. L. (1973) 'Modeling infiltration during a steady rain', *Water Resour. Res.* **9**, 384–94.

Merritt, E. (1984) 'The identification of four stages during microrill development', *Earth Surf. Proc. Landf.* **9**, 493–6.

Meyer, L. D. (1965) 'Mathematical relationships governing soil erosion by water', *J. Soil and Wat. Conserv.* **20**, 149–50.

Meyer, L. D. (1979) 'Methods for attaining desired rainfall characteristics in rainfall simulators', *Proc. Rainfall Simulator Workshop, Tucson, Ariz., USDA-SEA Agric. Reviews and Manuals* **ARM-W-10**, 35–44.

Meyer, L. D. (1981*a*) 'How rain intensity affects interrill erosion', *Trans. Am. Soc. Agric. Engnrs.* **24**, 1472–5.

Meyer, L. D. (1981*b*) 'Modelling conservation practices', in Morgan, R. P. C. (ed.), *Soil conservation: problems and prospects*, Wiley, 31–44.

Meyer, L. D. and Harmon, W. C. (1979) 'Multiple-intensity rainfall simulator for erosion research on row sideslopes', *Trans. Am. Soc. Agric. Engnrs.* **22**, 100–3.

Meyer, L. D. and Wischmeier, W. H. (1969) 'Mathematical simulation of the process of soil erosion by water', *Trans. Am. Soc. Agric. Engnrs.* **12**, 754–8, 762.

Meyer, L. D., Foster, G. R. and Nikolov, S. (1975) 'Effect of flow rate and canopy on rill erosion', *Trans. Am. Soc. Agric. Engnrs.* **18**, 905–11.

Middleton, H. E. (1930) 'Properties of soils which influence soil erosion', *USDA Tech. Bull.* **178.**

Midriak, R. (1965) 'Poškodenie pôdy eróziou pri prietrži mračien v oblasti Kendic pri Prešove', *Polnohospodárstvo* **9**, 696–707.

Mikhailov, D. Ya (1949) 'Osnovbiye cherti eroziy pochv Tyan-Shanya', *Trudy yub. sessii. posv. stoletiyu so dnya rozhdeniya V. V. Dokuchayeva*, Izd. Akad. Nauk SSSR, Moscow.

Mikhailov. T. (1972) 'Certaines particularités des processes d'érosion contemporains en Bulgarie', *Acta Geographica Debrecina* **60**, 41–50.

Miller, C. R., Woodburn, R. and Turner, H. R. (1962) 'Upland gully sediment production', *Int. Assoc. Scient. Hydrol. Pub.* **59**, 83–104.

Mitchell, J. K. and Gunther, R. W. (1976) 'The effects of manure applications on runoff, erosion and nitrate losses', *Trans. Am. Soc. Agric. Engnrs.* **19**, 1104–6.

Mitchell, J. K., Mostaghimi, S. and Pond, M. C. (1983) 'Primary particle and aggregate size distribution of eroded soil from sequenced rainfall events', *Trans. Am. Soc. Agric. Engnrs.* **26**, 1771–7.

Moeyersons, J. (1983) 'Measurements of splash-saltation fluxes under oblique rain', *Catena Suppl.* **4**, 19–31.

Moeyersons, J. and De Ploey, J. (1976) 'Quantitative data on splash erosion simulated on unvegetated slopes', *Z. f. Geomorph. Suppl.* **25**, 120–31.

Mokhtaruddin, A. M. and Maene, L. M. (1970) 'Soil erosion under different crops and management practices', *Int. Conf. Agricultural Engineering in National Development, Universiti Pertanian Malaysia Paper No. 79–53.*

Moldenhauer, W. C. (1965) 'Procedure for studying soil characteristics using disturbed samples and simulated rainfall', *Trans. Am. Soc. Agric. Engnrs.* **8**, 74–5.

Moldenhauer, W. C. and Foster, G. R. (1981) 'Empirical studies of soil conservation. Techniques and design procedures', in Morgan, R. P. C. (ed.), *Soil conservation: problems and prospects*, Wiley, 13–29.

Moldenhauer, W. C. and Onstad, C. A. (1975) 'Achieving specified soil loss levels', *J. Soil and Wat. Conserv.* **30**, 166–8.

Moore, I. D. and Eigel, J. D. (1981) 'Infiltration into two-layered soil profiles', *Trans. Am. Soc. Agric. Engnrs.* **24**, 1496–503.

Morgan, R. P. C. (1971) 'Rainfall of West Malaysia: a preliminary regionalization using principal components analysis', *Area* **3**, 222–7.

Morgan, R. P. C. (1972) 'Observations on factors affecting the behaviour of a first-order stream', *Trans. Inst. Br. Geogr.* **56**, 171–85.

Morgan, R. P. C. (1973*a*) 'The influence of scale in climatic geomorphology: a case study of drainage density in West Malaysia', *Geografiska Ann.* **55-A**, 107–15.

Morgan, R. P. C. (1973*b*) 'Soil-slope relationships in the lowlands of Selangor and Negri Sembilan, West Malaysia', *Z. f. Geomorph.* **17**, 139–55.

Morgan, R. P. C. (1974) 'Estimating regional variations in soil erosion hazard in Peninsular Malaysia', *Malay. Nat. J.* **28**, 94–106.

Morgan, R. P. C. (1976) 'The role of climate in the denudation system: a case study from West Malaysia', in Derbyshire, E. (ed.), *Climate and geomorphology*, Wiley, 317–43.

Morgan, R. P. C (1977) 'Soil erosion in the United Kingdom: field studies in the Silsoe area, 1973–75', *Nat. Coll. Agric. Engng. Silsoe Occasional Paper* **4**.

Morgan, R. P. C. (1978) 'Field studies of rainsplash erosion', *Earth Surf. Proc.* **3**, 295–9.

Morgan, R. P. C. (1980*a*) 'Field studies of sediment transport by overland flow', *Earth Surf. Proc.* **5**, 307–16.

Morgan, R. P. C. (1980*b*) 'Soil erosion and conservation in Britain', *Progress in Physical Geography* **4**, 24–47.

Morgan, R. P. C. (1980*c*) 'Preliminary testing of the CREAMS erosion sub-model with field data from Silsoe, Bedfordshire, England', *Int. Inst. Appl. Syst. Anal. Collaborative Paper* **CP-80-21**.

Morgan, R. P. C. (1980*d*) 'Implications', in Kirkby, M. J. and Morgan, R. P. C. (eds), *Soil erosion*, Wiley, 253–301.

Morgan, R. P. C. (1981*a*) 'Soil erosion in the UK', *Final Report to Natural Environment Research Council* **GR3/1997**.

Morgan, R. P. C. (1981*b*) 'Field measurement of splash erosion', *Int. Assoc. Scient. Hydrol. Pub.* **133**, 373–82.

Morgan, R. P. C. (1985*a*) 'Effect of corn and soybean canopy on soil detachment by rainfall', *Trans. Am. Soc. Agric. Engnrs.* **28**, 1135–40.

Morgan, R. P. C. (1985*b*) 'Assessment of soil erosion risk in England and Wales', *Soil use and management*, **1**, in press.

Morgan, R. P. C. and Finney, H. J. (1985) 'Drag coefficients of single crop rows and their implications for wind erosion control', *Paper to Int. Conf. British Geomorphological Research Group*, Manchester.

Morgan, R. P. C., Hatch, T. and Sulaiman, W. (1982) 'A simple procedure for assessing soil erosion risk: a case study for Malaysia', *Z. f. Geomorph. Suppl.* **44**, 69–89.

Morgan, R. P. C., Martin, L. and Noble, C. A. (1986) 'Soil erosion in the United Kingdom: a case study from mid-Bedfordshire', in preparation.

Morgan, R. P. C., Morgan, D. D. V. and Finney, H. J. (1982) 'Stability of agricultural ecosystems: documentation of a simple model for soil erosion assessment', *Int. Inst. Appl. Syst. Anal. Collaborative Paper* **CP-82-50**.

Morgan, R. P. C., Morgan, D. D. V. and Finney, H. J. (1984) 'A predictive model for the assessment of soil erosion risk', *J. Agric. Engng. Res.*, **30**, 245–253.

Morgan, R. P. C., Morgan, D. D. V. and Finney, H. J. (1985) 'Predicting hillslope runoff and erosion in the Silsoe area of Bedfordshire, England using the CREAMS model', Paper presented at *4th Int. Conf. Soil Conservation*, Maracay, Venezuela.

Morin, J., Benyamini, Y. and Michaeli, A. (1981) 'The effect of raindrop impact on the dynamics of soil surface crusting and water movement in the profile', *J. Hydrol.* **52**, 321–36.

Morin, J., Goldberg, D. and Seginer, I. (1967) 'A rainfall simulator with a rotating disk', *Trans. Am. Soc. Agric. Engnrs.* **10**, 74–7, 79.

Morin, J., Rawitz, E., Benyamini, Y., Hoogmoed, W. B. and Etkin, H. (1984) 'Tillage practices for soil and water conservation in the semi-arid zone. II. Development of the basin tillage system in wheat fields', *Soil and Tillage Research* **4**, 155–64.

Mosley, M. P. (1973) 'Rainsplash and the convexity of badland divides', *Z. f. Geomorph. Suppl.* **18**, 10–25.

Mosley, M. P. (1982) 'The effect of a New Zealand beech forest canopy on the kinetic energy of water drops and on surface erosion', *Earth Surf. Proc. Landf.* **7**, 103–7.

Moss, A. J. and Walker, P. H. (1978) 'Particle transport by continental water flows in relation to erosion, deposition, soils and human activities', *Sedimentary Geol.* **20**, 81–139.

Moss, A. J., Green, P. and Hutka, J. (1982) 'Small channels: their formation, nature and significance', *Earth Surf. Proc. Landf.* **7**, 401–15.

Mou, J. and Xiong, G. (1980) 'Prediction of sediment yield and evaluation of silt detention by measures of soil conservation in small watersheds of north Shaanxi', *Int. Symp. River Sedimentation, Beijing*, preprint (in Chinese with English summary).

Murgatroyd, A. L. and Ternan, J. L. (1983) 'The impact of afforestation on stream bank erosion and channel form', *Earth Surf. Proc. Landf.* **8**, 357–69.

Musgrave, G. W. (1947) 'The quantitative evaluation of factors in water erosion: a first approximation', *J. Soil and Wat. Conserv.* **2**, 133–8.

Mutchler, C. K. and Young, R. A. (1975) 'Soil detachment by raindrops', in *Present and prospective technology for predicting sediment yields and sources*, USDA Agr. Res. Serv. Pub. **ARS-S-40**, 113–17.

Nassif, S. H. and Wilson, E. M. (1975) 'The influence of slope and rain intensity on runoff and infiltration', *Hydrol. Sci. Bull.* **20**, 539–53.

Natural Environment Research Council (1975) *Flood studies report. II. Meteorological studies*, London.

Neff, E. L. (1973) 'Water storage capacity of contour furrows in Montana', *J. Range Management* **26**, 298–301.

Neff, E. L. and Wight, J. R. (1980) 'Contour furrowing as a range management practice', in *Symp. Watershed management*, Am. Soc. Civil Engnrs, 827–35.

Negev, M. (1967) 'A sediment model on a digital computer', *Stanford Univ. Dept. Civil Engng. Tech. Report* **76**.

Nepali, S. B. (1981) 'Soil erosion and traditional know-how', in Tingsanchali, T. and Eggers, H. (eds), *Southeast Asian regional symposium on problems of soil erosion and sedimentation*, Asian Institute of Technology, 365–79.

Newbould, P. (1982) 'Losses and accumulation of organic matter in soils', in Boels, D., Davies, D. B. and Johnston, A. E. (eds), *Soil degradation*, Balkema, 107–31.

Newson, M. (1980) 'The erosion of drainage ditches and its effect on bed-load yields in mid-Wales: reconnaissance case studies', *Earth Surf. Proc.* **3**, 275–90.

Ng, S. K. (1969) 'Soil resources in Malaya', in Stone, B. C. (ed.), *Natural resources in Malaysia and Singapore*, Kuala Lumpur, 141–51.

Noble, C. A. and Morgan, R. P. C. (1983) 'Rainfall interception and splash detachment with a Brussels sprouts plant: a laboratory simulation', *Earth Surf. Proc. Landf.* **8**, 569–77.

Nossin, J. J. (1964) 'Geomorphology of the surroundings of Kuantan (Eastern Malaya)', *Geol Mijnb*, **43**, 157–82.

Okigbo, B. N. (1977) 'Farming systems and soil erosion in West Africa', in Greenland, D. J. and Lal, R. (eds), *Soil conservation and management in the humid tropics*, Wiley, 151–63.

Okigbo, B. N. and Lal, R. (1977) 'Role of cover crops in soil and water conservation', *FAO Soils Bull.* **33**, 97–108.

Olesen, F. (1979) *Collective shelterbelt planting*, Hedeselskabet, Viborg.

Olofin, E. A. (1972) *Landform analysis of the Ulu Langat District, Selangor: a case study in map compilation for planning purposes*, unpub. MSc thesis, University of Malaya.

Olofin, E. A. (1974) 'Classification of slope angles for land planning purposes', *J. Trop. Geog.* **39**, 72–7.

Ologe, K. O. (1972) 'Gulies in the Zaria area. A preliminary study of headscarp recession', *Savanna* **1**, 55–66.

O'Loughlin, C. L. (1974) 'A study of tree root strength deterioration following clearfelling'; *Can. J. Forest Res.* **4**, 107–113.

O'Loughlin, C. L. and Watson, A. (1979) 'Root-wood strength deterioration in radiata pine after clearfelling', *N.Z.J. Forestry Sci.* **9**, 284–293.

Osuji, G. E., Babalola, O. and Aboaba, F. O. (1980) 'Rainfall erosivity and tillage practices affecting soil and water loss on a tropical soil in Nigeria', *J. Environmental Management* **10**, 207–17.

Othieno, C. O. and Laycock, D. H. (1977) 'Factors affecting soil erosion within tea fields', *Trop. Agric.* **54**, 323–30.

Palmer, R. S. (1964) 'The influence of a thin water layer on water-drop impact forces', *Int. Assoc. Scient. Hydrol. Pub.* **65**, 141–8.

Pálsson, H. and Stefánsson, Ó. E. (1968) *Farming in Iceland*, Búnaðarfélag Íslands, Reykjavík.

Pandey, K. K. (1981) 'Fodder trees and conservation of cultivated lands in Nepal', in Tingsanchali, T. and Eggers, H. (eds), *Southeast Asian regional symposium on problems of soil erosion and sedimentation*, Asian Institute of Technology, 233–40.

Panton, W. P. (1969) 'Land capability classification programme for

West Malaysia', in Stone, B. C. (ed.), *Natural resources in Malaysia and Singapore*, Kuala Lumpur, 152–60.

Parsons, D. A., Apmann, R. P. and Decker, G. H. (1964) 'The determination of sediment yields from flood water sampling', *Int. Assoc. Scient. Hydrol. Pub.* **65**, 7–15.

Pathak, P., Miranda, S. M. and El-Swaify, S. A. (1975) 'Improved rainfed farming for semi-arid tropics: implications for soil and water conservation, in El-Swaify, S.A., Moldenhauer, W.C. and Lo, A. (eds), *Soil erosion and conservation*, Soil Conserv. Soc. Am., 338–354.

Pearce, A. J. (1976) 'Magnitude and frequency of erosion by Hortonian overland flow', *J. Geol.* **84**, 65–80.

Perrens, S. J. and Trustrum, N. A. (1984) 'Assessment and evaluation for soil conservation policy', *East–West Environment and Policy Institute, Workshop Report*, Honolulu, HI.

Philip, J. R. (1957) 'The theory of infiltration. I. The infiltration equation and its solution', *Soil Sci.* **83**, 345–57.

Pidgeon, J. D. and Soane, B. D. (1978) 'Soil structure and strength relations following tillage, zero tillage and wheel traffic in Scotland', in Emerson, W. W., Bond, R. D. and Dexter, A. R. (eds), *Modification of soil structure*, Wiley, 371–8.

Piest, R. F., Bradford, J. M. and Spomer, R. G. (1975) 'Mechanisms of erosion and sediment movement from gullies', in *Present and prospective technology for predicting sediment yields and sources*, USDA Agr. Res. Serv. Pub. **ARS–40**, 162–76.

Pihan, J. (1979) 'Risques climatiques d'érosion hydrique des sols en France', in Vogt, H. and Vogt, Th. (eds), *Colloque sur l'érosion agricole des sols en milieu tempéré non Mediterranéen*, Univ. Louis Pasteur, Strasbourg, 13–18.

Pinczés Z. (1980) 'A müvelési ágak és módok hatása a talajerózióra', *Földr. Közl.* **28**, 357–79.

Pla, I. (1977) 'Aggregate size and erosion control on sloping land treated with hydrophobic bitumen emulsion', in Greenland, D. J. and Lal, R. (eds), *Soil conservation and management in the humid tropics*, Wiley, 109–15.

Poesen, J. (1981) 'Rainwash experiments on the erodibility of loose sediments', *Earth Surf. Proc. Landf.* **6**, 285–307.

Poesen, J. and Savat, J. (1981) 'Detachment and transportation of loose sediments by raindrop splash. II. Detachability and transportability measurements', *Catena* **8**, 19–41.

Pope, A. and Harper, J. J. (1966) *Low-speed wind tunnel testing*, Wiley.

Quansah, C. (1981) 'The effect of soil type, slope, rain intensity and their interactions on splash detachment and transport', *J. Soil Sci.* **32**, 215–24.

Quansah, C. (1982) *Laboratory experimentation for the statistical derivation of equations for soil erosion modelling and soil conservation design*, unpub. PhD thesis, Cranfield Institute of Technology.

Quansah, C. and Baffoe-Bonnie, E. (1981) 'The effect of soil management systems on soil loss, runoff and fertility erosion in Ghana', in Tingsanchali, T. and Eggers, H. (eds), *Southeast Asian regional symposium on problems of soil erosion and sedimentation*, Asian Institute of Technology, 207–17.

Quinn, N. W. and Laflen, J. M. (1983) 'Characteristics of raindrop throughfall under corn canopy', *Trans. Am. Soc. Agric. Engnrs.* **26**, 1445–50.

Quinn, N. W., Morgan, R. P. C. and Smith, A. J. (1980) 'Simulation of soil erosion induced by human trampling', *J. Environmental Management* **10**, 155–65.

Ramaswamy, S. D., Aziz, M. A. and Narayanan, N. (1981) 'Some methods of control of erosion of natural slopes in urbanized areas', in Tingsanchali, T. and Eggers, H. (eds), *Southeast Asian regional symposium on problems of soil erosion and sedimentation*, Asian Institute of Technology, 327–39.

Rao, D. P. (1975) 'Applied geomorphological mapping for erosion surveys: the example of the Oliva basin, Calabria', *ITC Journal* **1975–3**, 341–50.

Rao, Y. P. (1981) 'Evaluation of cropping management factor in Universal Soil Loss Equation under natural rainfall conditions of Kharagpur, India', in Tingsanchali, T and Eggers, H. (eds), *Southeast Asian regional symposium on problems of soil erosion and sedimentation*, Asian Institute of Technology, 241–53.

Rapp, A., Axelsson, V., Berry, L. and Murray-Rust, D. H. (1972) 'Soil erosion and sediment transport in the Morogoro river catchment, Tanzania', *Geografiska Ann.* **54-A**, 125–55.

Reid, I. (1979) 'Seasonal changes in microtopography and surface depression storage of arable soils', in Hollis, G. E. (ed.), *Man's impact on the hydrological cycle in the United Kingdom*, Geo Books, Norwich, 19–30.

Renfro, G. W. (1975) 'Use of erosion equations and sediment-delivery ratios for predicting sediment yield', in *Present and prospective technology for predicting sediment yields and sources*, USDA Agr. Res. Serv. Pub. **ARS-S-40**, 33–45.

Reynolds, K. C. (1978) 'Synthetic meshes for soil conservation use on black earths', *J. Soil Conserv. Serv. NSW.* **34**, 145–60.

Reynolds, S. G. (1975) 'Soil property variability in slope studies: suggested sampling schemes and typical required sample sizes', *Z. f. Geomorph.* **19**, 191–208.

Rice, R. M. and Krammes, J. S. (1970) 'Mass-wasting processes in watershed management', *Proc. Symp. Interdisciplinary aspects of watershed management*, Am. Soc. Civil Engnrs, 231–60.

Rich, L. R. (1972) 'Managing a ponderosa pine forest to increase water yield', *Water Resour. Res.* **8**, 422–8.

Richter, G. (1980) 'On the soil erosion problem in the temperate humid area of central Europe', *GeoJournal* **4**, 279–87.

Richter, G. and Negendank, J. F. W. (1977) 'Soil erosion processes and their measurement in the German area of the Moselle river', *Earth Surf. Proc.* **2**, 261–78.

Rickson, R. J. (1985) 'Small plot field studies of soil erodibility using a rainfall simulator', Paper presented at *4th Int. Conf. Soil Conservation*, Maracay, Venezuela.

Ripley, E. A. and Redmann, R. E. (1976) 'Grassland', in Monteith, J. L. (ed.), *Vegetation and the atmosphere. Vol. 2. Case studies*, Academic Press, 349–98.

Robinson, M. and Blyth, K. (1982) 'The effect of forestry drainage operations on upland sediment yields: a case study', *Earth Surf. Proc. Landf.* **7**, 85–90.

Roche, L. (1974) 'The practice of agri-silviculture in the tropics with special reference to Nigeria', *FAO Soils Bull.* **24**, 179–90.

Roehl, J. W. (1962) 'Sediment source areas, delivery ratios and influencing morphological factors', *Int. Assoc. Scient. Hydrol. Pub.* **59**, 202–13.

Roels, J. M. and Jonker, P. J. (1985) 'Representativity and accuracy of measurements of soil loss from runoff plots', *Trans. Am. Soc. Agric. Engnrs.* **28**, in press.

Rogers, N. W. and Selby, M. J. (1980) 'Mechanisms of shallow translational landsliding during summer rainstorms: North Island, New Zealand', *Geografiska Ann.* **62-A**, 11–21.

Roose, E. J. (1966) *Etude de la méthode des bandes d'arrêt pour la conservation de l'eau et des sols*, Cyclo. ORSTOM, Adiopodoumé, Ivory Coast.

Roose, E. J. (1967) 'Dix années de mesure de l'érosion et du ruissellement au Sénégal', *L'Agron. Trop.* **22**, 123–52.

Roose, E. J. (1970) 'Importance relative de l'érosion, du drainage oblique et vertical dans la pédogenèse actuelle d'un sol ferrallitique de moyenne Côte d'Ivoire', *Cah. ORSTOM, sér. Pédol.* **8**, 469–82.

Roose, E. J. (1971) *Influence des modifications du milieu naturel sur l'érosion: le bilan hydrique et chimique suite à la mise en culture sous climat tropical*, Cyclo. ORSTOM, Adiopodoumé, Ivory Coast.

Roose, E. J. (1975a) *Erosion et ruissellement en Afrique de l'ouest: vingt années de mesures en petites parcelles expérimentales*, Cyclo. ORSTOM, Adiopodoumé, Ivory Coast.

Roose, E. J. (1975*b*) 'Natural mulch or chemical conditioners for reducing soil erosion in humid tropical areas', in *Soil conditioners*, Soil Sci. Soc. Am. Spec. Pub. **7**, 131–8.

Roose, E. J. (1976) 'Contribution à l'étude de l'influence de la mésofaune sur la pédogenèse actuelle en milieu tropical', *Rapp. ORSTOM*, Abidjan, 2–23.

Roose, E. J. (1977) 'Application of the Universal Soil Loss Equation of Wischmeier and Smith in West Africa', in Greenland, D. J. and Lal, R. (eds), *Soil conservation and management in the humid tropics*, Wiley, 177–87.

Rooseboom, A. and Annandale, G. W. (1981) 'Techniques applied in determining sediment loads in South African rivers', *Int. Assoc. Scient. Hydrol. Pub.* **133**, 219–24.

Rosewell, C. J. (1970) 'Investigations into the control of earth-work tunnelling', *J. Soil Cons. Serv. NSW* **26**, 188–203.

Rougerie, G. (1967) 'Facteurs climatiques et facteurs édaphiques dans la différentiation des teneurs des eaux de drainage en substances dissoutes', in Macar, P. (ed.), *L'évolution des versants*, University of Liège, 259–70.

Rowntree, K. M. (1983) 'Rainfall erosivity in Kenya: some preliminary considerations', in Thomas, D. B. and Senga, W. M. (eds), *Soil and water conservation in Kenya*, Inst. Dev. Studies and Fac. Agr. Univ. Nairobi Occasional Paper **42**, 1–19.

Rozhkov, A. G. (1973) 'Intensivnost' rosta ovragov v Moldaviy', in *Eroziya pochv i roosloviye protsessi*, *Vol.* 3, Izd. Moskovskogo Universiteta, 87–104.

Sánchez Muñoz, A. and Valdés Reyna, J. (1975) 'Infiltración de agua en dos tipos vegetativos relacionando suelo-vegetación', *Boletín Pastizales* **6**(5), 2–6.

Savat, J. (1975) 'Discharge velocities and total erosion of a calcareous loess: a comparison between pluvial and terminal runoff', *Rev. Géom. Dyn.* **24**, 113–22.

Savat, J. (1977) 'The hydraulics of sheet flow on a smooth surface and the effect of simulated rainfall', *Earth Surf. Proc.* **2**, 125–40.

Savat, J. (1979) 'Laboratory experiments on erosion and deposition of loess by laminar sheet flow and turbulent rill flow', in Vogt, H. and Vogt, Th. (eds), *Colloque sur l'érosion agricole des sols en milieu tempéré non Mediterranéen*, Univ. Louis Pasteur, Strasbourg, 139–43.

Savat, J. (1981) 'Work done by splash: laboratory experiments', *Earth Surf. Proc. Landf.* **6**, 275–83.

Savat, J. (1982) 'Common and uncommon selectivity in the process of fluid transportation: field observations and laboratory experiments on bare surfaces'. *Catena Suppl.* **1**, 139–160.

Savat, J. and Poesen, J. (1977) 'Splash and discontinuous runoff as creators of fine sandy lag deposits with Kalahari Sands', *Catena* **4**, 321–32.

Schertz, D. L. (1983) 'The basis for soil loss tolerance', *J. Soil and Wat. Conserv.* **38**, 10–14.

Schumm, S. A. (1979) 'Geomorphic thresholds: the concept and its applications', *Trans. Inst. Br. Geogr.* **4**, 485–515.

Schwab, G. O., Frevert, R. K., Edminster, T. W. and Barnes, K. K. (1966) *Soil and water conservation engineering*, Wiley.

Scoging, H. M. and Thornes, J. B. (1979) 'Infiltration characteristics in a semi-arid environment', *Int. Assoc. Scient. Hydrol. Pub.* **128**, 159–68.

Shallow, P. G. D. (1956) 'River flow in the Cameron Highlands', *Central Electricity Board, Hydro-electric Technical Memorandum*, **3**, Kuala Lumpur.

Sharpe, C. F. S. (1938) *Landslides and related phenomena*, Columbia University Press, New York.

Shaxson, T. F. (1981) 'Reconciling social and technical needs in conservation work on village farmlands', in Morgan, R. P. C. (ed.), *Soil conservation: problems and prospects*, Wiley, 385–97.

Sheng, T. C. (1972a) 'A treatment-oriented land capability classification scheme for hilly marginal lands in the humid tropics', *J. Scient. Res. Counc. Jamaica* **3**, 93–112.

Sheng, T. C. (1972b) 'Bench terracing', *J. Scient. Res. Counc. Jamaica* **3**, 113–27.

Sheng, T. C. (1981) 'The need for soil conservation structures for steep cultivated slopes in the humid tropics', in Lal, R. and Russell, E. W. (eds), *Tropical agricultural hydrology*, Wiley, 357–72.

Shiyatyy, Ye. I., Lavrovsky, A. B. and Khmolenko, M. I. (1972) 'Effect of texture on the cohesion and wind resistance of soil clods', *Soviet Soil Sci.* **4**, 105–12.

Siemens, J. C. and Oschwald, W. R. (1978) 'Corn–soybean tillage systems: erosion control, effects on crop production, costs', *Trans. Am. Soc. Agric. Engnrs.* **21**, 293–302.

Sigurbjörnsson, B. (1980) 'Foreword', in Guðmunsson, Ó, and Arnalds, A. (eds), *Consultancy reports for the project on utilization and conservation of grassland resources in Iceland*, Rannsóknastofnun Landbúnaðarins Report **61**, 1–2.

Singer, M. J. and Blackard, J. (1978) 'Effect of mulching on sediment in runoff from simulated rainfall', *Soil Sci. Soc. Am. J.* **42**, 481–6.

Skempton, A. W. and Hutchinson, J. N. (1969) 'Stability of natural slopes and embankment sections', *Proc. 7th Int. Conf. Soil Mech. Fdn. Engng*, 291–340.

Skidmore, E. L. and Hagen, L. J. (1977) 'Reducing wind erosion with barriers', *Trans. Am. Soc. Agric. Engnrs.* **20**, 911–15.

Skidmore, E. L. and Woodruff, N. P. (1968) 'Wind erosion forces in the United States and their use in predicting soil loss', *USDA Agr. Res. Serv. Agr. Handbook* **346**.

Skidmore, E. L., Nossaman, N. L. and Woodruff, N. P. (1966) 'Wind erosion as influenced by row spacing, row direction and grain sorghum population', *Soil Sci. Soc. Am. Proc.* **30**, 505–9.

Slack, D. C. and Larson, C. L. (1981) 'Modelling infiltration: the key process in water management, runoff and erosion', in Lal, R. and Russell, E. W. (eds), *Tropical agricultural hydrology*, Wiley, 433–50.

Smalley, I. J. (1970) 'Cohesion of soil particles and the intrinsic resistance of simple soil systems to wind erosion', *J. Soil Sci.* **21**, 154–61.

Smith, D. D. (1958) 'Factors affecting rainfall erosion and their evaluation', *Int. Assoc. Scient. Hydrol. Pub.* **43**, 97–107.

Smithen, A. A. and Schulze, R. E. (1982) 'The spatial distribution in southern Africa of rainfall erosivity for use in the Universal Soil Loss Equation', *Water SA*, **8**, 74–8, 165–7.

Sneesby, N. J. (1953) 'Wind erosion and the value of shelterbelts', *Agriculture* **60**, 263–71.

So, H. B., Tayler, D. W., Yates, W. J. and McGarity, J. W. (1978) 'Amelioration of structurally unstable grey and brown clays', in Emerson, W. W., Bond, R. D. and Dexter, A. R. (eds), *Modification of soil structure*, Wiley, 325–33.

Soane, B. D. and Pidgeon, J. D. (1975) 'Tillage requirement in relation to soil physical properties', *Soil Sci.* **119**, 376–84.

Soil Survey of England and Wales (1979) *Land use capability: England and Wales*, 1:1 000 000 map sheet.

Soil Survey of England and Wales (1983) *Soil Map of England and Wales*. 1:250 000.

Soong, N. K. (1979) 'The prospects of using natural rubber for conditioning tropical soils', in Lal, R. and Greenland, D. J. (eds), *Soil physical properties and crop production in the tropics*, Wiley, 105–10.

Soons, J. M. and Rainer, J. N. (1968) 'Micro-climate and erosion processes in the Southern Alps, New Zealand', *Geografiska Ann.* **50-A**, 1–15.

Spoor, G. and Godwin, R. J. (1979) 'Soil deformation and shear strength characteristics of some clay soils at different moisture contents', *J. Soil Sci.* **30**, 483–98.

Spoor, G., Leeds-Harrison, P. B. and Godwin, R. J. (1982) 'Potential role of soil density and clay mineralogy in assessing the suitability of soils for mole drainage', *J. Soil Sci.* **33**, 427–41.

Sreenivas, L., Johnston, J. R. and Hill, H. O. (1947) 'Some relationships of vegetation and soil detachment in the erosion process', *Soil Sci. Soc. Am. Proc.* **11**, 471–4.

Stallings, J. H. (1957) *Soil conservation*, Prentice-Hall.

Starkel, L. (1972) 'The role of catastrophic rainfall in the shaping of the relief of the Lower Himalaya (Darjeeling Hills)', *Geogr. Polonica* **21**, 103–47.

Starkel, L. (1976) 'The role of extreme (catastrophic) meteorological events in contemporary evolution of slopes', in Derbyshire, E. (ed.), *Geomorphology and climate*, Wiley, 203–46.

Stehlík, O. (1975) 'Potenciálni eroze pûdy proudícî vodou na území CSR', *Studia Geographica* **42**, Brno.

Steindórsson, S. (1980) 'Flokkun gróðurs í gróðurfélög', *Íslenzkar Landbúnaðarrannsóknir* **12**(2), 11–52.

Stevens, J. H. (1974) 'Stabilization of eolian sands in Saudi Arabia's Al Hasa oasis', *J. Soil and Wat. Conserv.* **29**, 129–33.

Stocking, M. A. (1980) 'Examination of the factors controlling gully growth', in De Boodt, M. and Gabriels, D. (eds), *Assessment of erosion*, Wiley, 505–20.

Stocking, M. A. and Elwell, H. A. (1973a) 'Prediction of subtropical storm soil losses from field plot studies', *Agric. Met.* **12**, 193–201.

Stocking, M. A. and Elwell, H. A. (1973b) 'Soil erosion hazard in Rhodesia', *Rhod. Agric. J.* **70**, 93–101.

Stocking, M. A. and Elwell, H. A. (1976) 'Rainfall erosivity over Rhodesia', *Trans. Inst. Br. Geogr.* **1**, 231–45.

Stredňanský, J. (1977) 'Kritické rýchlosti vetra z hladiska erodovatelnosti pôd na južnom Slovensku', *Vysoká škola polnohospodárska*, Nitra.

Streeter, D. T. (1977) 'Gully restoration on Box Hill', *Countryside Recreation Review* **2**, 38–40.

Stuttard, M. J. (1984) 'Effect of tillage on clod stability to rainfall: laboratory simulation', *J. Agric. Engng. Res.* **30**, 141–7.

Subrahmanyam, M. S., Lee, L. C. and Lee, S. C. (1981) 'Use of rice husk ash for soil stabilization', *Buletin Persatuan Geologi Malaysia* **14**, 143–51.

Sulaiman, W., Maene, L. M. and Mokhtaruddin, A. M. (1981) 'Runoff, soil and nutrient losses from an ultisol under different legumes', in Tingsanchali, T. and Eggers, H. (eds), *Southeast Asian regional symposium on problems of soil erosion and sedimentation*, Asian Institute of Technology, 275–86.

Sveinbjörnsson, H. (1979) *Soil conservation in Iceland*, State Soil Conservation Service, Gunnarsholt.

Swan, S. B. St. C. (1970) 'Piedmont slope studies in a humid tropical region, Johor, southern Malaya', *Z. f. Geomorph. Suppl.* **10**, 30–9.

Swanson, F. J. and Dyrness, C. T. (1975) 'Impact of clearcutting and road construction on soil erosion by landslides in the West Cascade Range, Oregon', *Geology* **3**, 393–6.

Swanson, N. P. (1965) 'Rotating-boom rainfall simulator', *Trans. Am. Soc. Agric. Engnrs.* **8**, 71–2.

Tackett, J. L. and Pearson, R. W. (1965) 'Some characteristics of soil crust formed by simulated rainfall', *Soil Sci.* **99**, 407–13.

Talsma, T. (1969) '*In situ* measurement of sorptivity', *Aust. J. Soil Res.* **17**, 269–76.

Tejwani, K. G. (1981) 'Watershed management as a basis for land development and management in India', in Lal, R. and Russell, E. W. (eds), *Tropical agricultural hydrology*, Wiley, 239–55.

Tejwani, K. G., Srinivasan, V. and Mistry, M. S. (1961) 'Gujarat can still save its ravine lands', *Indian Farming* **11**(8), 20–1.

Temple, D. M. (1982) 'Flow retardance of submerged grass channel linings', *Trans. Am. Soc. Agric. Engnrs.* **25**, 1300–3.

Temple, P. H. (1972a) 'Measurements of runoff and soil erosion at an erosion plot scale with particular reference to Tanzania', *Geografiska Ann.* **54-A**, 203–20.

Temple, P. H. (1972b) 'Soil and water conservation policies in the Uluguru Mountains, Tanzania', *Geografiska Ann.* **54-A**, 110–23.

Temple, P. H. and Murray-Rust, D. H. (1972) 'Sheet wash measurements on erosion plots at Mfumbwe, eastern Uluguru Mountains, Tanzania', *Geografiska Ann.* **54-A** 195–202.

Temple, P. H. and Rapp, A. (1972) 'Landslides in the Mgeta area, western Uluguru Mountains, Tanzania', *Geografiska Ann.* **54-A**, 157–93.

Thórarinsson, S. (1958) 'The Öraefajökull eruption of 1362', *Acta Naturalia Islandica II.* No. **2**, Reykjavík.

Thornes, J. B. (1976) 'Semi-arid erosion systems: case studies from Spain', *London School of Economics Geogr. Papers* **7**.

Thornes, J. B. (1979) 'Fluvial processes', in Embleton, C. and Thornes, J. (eds), *Process in geomorphology*, Edward Arnold, 213–271.

Thornes, J. B. (1980) 'Erosional processes of running water and their spatial and temporal controls: a theoretical viewpoint', in Kirkby, M. J. and Morgan, R. P. C. (eds), *Soil erosion*, Wiley, 129–82.

Thorp, J. (1949) 'Effect of certain animals that live in soils', *Science Monthly* **68**, 180–91.

Thorsteinsson, I. (1980*a*) 'Gróðurskilyrði, gróðurfar, uppskera gróðurlenda og plöntuval búfjár', *Íslenzkar Landbúnaðarransóknir* **12**(2), 85–99.

Thorsteinsson, I. (1980*b*) 'Nýting úthaga: beitarthungi', *Íslenzkar Landbúnaðarrannsóknir* **12**(2), 113–22.

Thorsteinsson, I. (1980*c*) 'Beitagildi gróðurlenda', *Íslenzkar Landbúnaðarrannsóknir* **12**(2), 123–5.

Thorsteinsson, I., Ólafsson, G. and van Dyne, G. M. (1971) 'Range resources of Iceland', *J. Range Management* **24**, 86–93.

Till, R. (1973) 'The use of linear regression in geomorphology', *Area* **5**, 303–8.

Tisdall, J. M. and Oades, J. M. (1982) 'Organic matter and water stable aggregates in soils', *J. Soil Sci.* **33**, 141–64.

Torri, D. and Sfalanga, M. (1984) 'Some problems on soil erosion modelling', *Proc. Workshop on Prediction of agricultural nonpoint source pollution: model selection and application, Venezia*, Univ. Padova. B1–B10.

Tregubov, P. S. (1981) 'Effective erosion control in the USSR', in Morgan, R. P. C. (ed.), *Soil conservation: problems and prospects*, Wiley, 451–9.

Tricart, J. (1961) 'Méchanismes normaux et phénomènes catastrophiques dans l'évolution des versants du bassin du Guil (Hautes-Alpes, France)', *Z. f. Geomorph.* **5**, 277–301.

Tricart, J. (1972) *Landforms of the humid tropics, forests and savannas*, transl. de Jonge, C. J. K. Longman.

Troeh, F. R., Hobbs, J. A. and Donahue, R. L. (1980) *Soil and water conservation for productitivy and environmental protection*, Prentice-Hall.

Trustrum, N. A., Thomas, V. J. and Lambert, M. G. (1984) 'Soil slip erosion as a constraint to hill country pasture production', *Proc. N.Z. Grassland Assoc.* **45**, 66–76.

Tuckfield, C. G. (1964) 'Gully erosion in the New Forest, Hampshire', *Am. J. Sci.* **262**, 759–807.

Uchijima, Z. (1976) 'Maize and rice', in Monteith, J. L. (ed.), *Vegetation and the atmosphere*, Academic Press, 33–64.

United States Department of Agriculture (1979) 'Field manual for research in agricultural hydrology', *USDA Agr. Handbook* **224**.

van Asch, Th. W. J. (1980) 'Water erosion on slopes and landsliding in a Mediterranean landscape', *Utrechtse Geografische Studies* **20**.

van Asch, Th. W. J. (1983) 'Water erosion on slopes in some land units in a Mediterranean area', *Catena Suppl.* **4**, 129–40.

van Asch, Th. W. J. and Epema, G. F. (1983) 'The power of detachment and the erosivity of low intensity rains', *Pédologie* **33**, 17–27.

van Genderen, J. L. (1970) 'The morphodynamics of the Crati River basin, Calabria, *ITC Publications, Series B* **56**, Delft.

van Wambeke, A. R. (1962) 'Criteria for classifying tropical soils by age', *J. Soil Sci.* **13**, 124–32.

Verstappen, H. Th. and van Zuidam, R. A. (1968) *ITC system of geomorphological survey*, ITC.

Vink, A. P. A. (1968) 'Aerial photographs and the soil sciences', in *Aerial surveys and integrated studies*, UNESCO 127–31.

Vink, A. P. A. (1975) *Landuse in advancing agriculture*, Springer-Verlag.

Vittorini, S. (1972) 'The effects of soil erosion in an experimental station in the Pliocene clay of the Val d'Era (Tuscany) and its influence on the evolution of the slopes', *Acta Geographica Debrecina* **10**, 71–81.

Voetberg, K. S. (1970) *Erosion on agricultural lands*, Agricultural University, Wageningen.

Voorhees, W. B. and Lindstrom, M. J. (1984) 'Long-term effects of tillage method on soil tilth independent of wheel traffic compaction', *Soil Sci. Soc. Am. J.* **48**, 152–5.

Voroney, R. P., van Veen, J. A. and Paul, E. A. (1981) 'Organic carbon dynamics in grassland soils. II. Model validation and simulation of the long-term effects of cultivation and rainfall erosion', *Can. J. Soil Sci.* **61**, 211–24.

Voznesensky, A. S. and Artsruui, A. B. (1940) 'Laboratoriya metod opretseleniy protivoerozionnoy ustoychivosti pochv', in *Voprosi protivoerozionnoy ustoychivosti pochv*, Izd. Zakavk. NIIVKH, Tbilisi.

Vuillaume, G. (1969) 'Analyse quantitative du rôle du milieu physicoclimatique sur le ruissellement et l'érosion à l'issue de bassins de quelques hectares en zone sahélienne (Bassin du Kountkouzout, Niger)', *Cah. ORSTOM, sér. Hydrol.* **6**, 87–132.

Walling, D. E. (1974a) 'Suspended sediment and solute yields from a small catchment prior to urbanisation', in Gregory, K. J. and Walling, D. E. (eds), *Fluvial processes in instrumented watersheds*, Inst. Br. Geogr. Spec. Pub. **6**, 169–92.

Walling, D. E. (1974b) 'Suspended sediment production and building activity in a small British basin', *Int. Assoc. Scient. Hydrol. Pub.* **113**, 137–44.

Walling, D. E. and Webb, B. W. (1983) 'Patterns of sediment yield', in Gregory, K. J. (ed.), *Background to palaeohydrology*, Wiley, 69–100.

Weaver, T. and Dale, D. (1978) 'Trampling effects of hikers, motor cycles and horses in meadows and forests', *J. Appl. Ecol.* **15**, 451–7.

Wenner, C. G. (1981) *Soil conservation in Kenya*, Ministry of Agriculture, Nairobi.

Whitmore, T. C. and Burnham, C. P. (1969) 'The altitudinal sequence of forests and soils on granite near Kuala Lumpur', *Malay. Nat. J.* **22**, 99–118.

Wicks, G. A. and Smika, D. E. (1973) 'Chemical fallow in a winter wheat–fallow rotation', *Weed Sci.* **21**, 97–102.

Wiersum, K. F. (1985) 'Effects of various vegetation layers of an *Acacia auriculiformis* forest plantation on surface erosion in Java, Indonesia', in El-Swaify, S. A., Moldenhauer, W. C. and Lo, A. (eds), *Soil erosion and conservation*, Soil Sci. Soc. Am., 79–89.

Wiersum, K. F., Budirijanto, P. and Rhomdoni, D. (1979) 'Influence of forests on erosion. Seminar on the erosion problem in the Jatiluhur area', *Inst. Ecol. Padjadjaran Univ. Bandung, Report* **3**.

Wiggins, S. L. (1981) 'The economics of soil conservation in the Acelhuate River Basin, El Salvador', in Morgan, R. P. C. (ed.), *Soil conservation: problems and prospects*, Wiley, 399–417.

Williams, A. R. and Morgan, R. P. C. (1976) 'Geomorphological mapping applied to soil erosion evaluation', *J. Soil and Wat. Conserv.* **31**, 164–8.

Williams, C. N. and Joseph, K. T. (1970) *Climate, soil and crop production in the humid tropics*, Oxford University Press.

Williams, J. R., Dyke, P. T. and Jones, C. A. (1982) 'EPIC: a model for assessing the effects of erosion on soil productivity', *Proc. Third Int. Conf. State-of-the-art in ecological modelling*, Elsevier.

Wischmeier, W. H. (1973) 'Conservation tillage to control water erosion', in *Proc. Natl. Conserv. Tillage Conf.*, Soil Conserv. Soc. Am., 133–41.

Wischmeier, W. H. (1975) 'Estimating the soil loss equation's cover and management factor for undisturbed areas', in *Present and prospective technology for predicting sediment yields and sources*, Agr. Res. Serv. Pub. **ARS-S-40**, 118–24.

Wischmeier, W. H. (1978) 'Use and misuse of the Universal Soil Loss Equation', *J. Soil and Wat. Conserv.* **31**, 5–9.

Wischmeier, W. H. and Mannering, J. V. (1969) 'Relation of soil properties to its erodibility', *Soil Sci. Soc. Am. Proc.* **23**, 131–7.

Wischmeier, W. H. and Smith, D. D. (1958) 'Rainfall energy and its relationship to soil loss', *Trans. Am. Geophys. Un.* **39**, 285–91.

Wischmeier, W. H. and Smith, D. D. (1962) 'Soil loss estimation as a tool in soil and water management planning', *Int. Assoc. Scient. Hydrol. Pub.* **59**, 148–59.

Wischmeier, W. H. and Smith, D. D. (1978) 'Predicting rainfall erosion losses', *USDA Agr. Res. Serv. Handbook* **537**.

Wischmeier, W. H., Johnson, C. B. and Cross, B. V. (1971) 'A soil erodibility nomograph for farmland and construction sites', *J. Soil and Wat. Conserv.* **26**, 189–93.

Withers, B. and Vipond, S. (1974) *Irrigation: design and practice*, Batsford.

Wolman, M. G. (1967) 'A cycle of sedimentation and erosion in urban river channels', *Geografiska Ann.* **49-A**, 385–95.

Wolman, M. G. and Miller, J. P. (1960) 'Magnitude and frequency of forces in geomorphic processes', *J. Geol.* **68**, 54–74.

Woodburn, R. and Kozachyn, J. (1956) 'A study of relative erodibility of a group of Mississippi gully soils', *Trans. Am. Geophys. Un.* **37**, 749–53.

Woodruff, N. P. and Siddoway, F. H. (1965) 'A wind erosion equation', *Soil Sci. Soc. Am. Proc.* **29**, 602–8.

Woodruff, N. P. and Zingg, A. W. (1952) 'Wind-tunnel studies of fundamental problems related to windbreaks', *US Soil Conserv. Serv. Pub.* **SCS-TP-112**.

Woodruff, N. P. and Zingg, A. W. (1953) 'Wind tunnel studies of shelterbelt models' *J. Fores.* **51**, 173–8.

Woodruff, N. P. and Zingg, A. W. (1955) 'A comparative analysis of wind-tunnel and atmospheric air-flow patterns about single and successive barriers', *Trans. Am. Geophys. Un.* **36**, 203–8.

Woodruff, N. P., Chepil, W. S. and Lynch, R. D. (1957) 'Emergency chiseling to control wind erosion', *Kansas Agr. Exp. Sta. Tech. Bull.* **90**.

Woodruff, N. P., Fryrear, D. W. and Lyles, L. (1963) 'Engineering similitude and momentum transfer principles applied to shelterbelt studies', *Trans. Am. Soc. Agric. Engnrs* **6**, 41–7.

Wright, J. L. and Brown, K. W. (1967) 'Comparison of momentum and energy balance methods of computing vertical transfer within a crop', *Agron. J.* **59**, 427–32.

Yair, A. (1972) 'Observations sur les effets d'un ruissellement dirigé selon la pente des interfluves dans une région semi-aride d'Israel', *Rev. Géogr. Phys. Géol. Dyn.* **14**, 537–48.

Yair, A. and Rutin, J. (1981) 'Some aspects of the regional variation in the amount of available sediment produced by isopods and porcupines, northern Negev, Israel', *Earth Surf. Proc. Landf.* **6**, 221–34.

Yalin, Y. S. (1963) 'An expression for bedload transportation', *J. Hydraul. Div. ASCE* **89**, 221–50.

Yariv, S. (1976) 'Comments on the mechanism of soil detachment by rainfall', *Geoderma* **15**, 393–9.

Yorke, T. H. and Davis, W. J. (1971) 'Effects of urbanization on sediment transport in Bel Pre Creek Basin, Maryland', *USGS Prof. Paper* **750-B**, B128–B223.

Young, A. (1969) 'Present rate of land erosion', *Nature* **224**, 851–2.

Young, A. (1972) *Slopes*, Oliver and Boyd.

Young, A. (1973) 'Soil survey procedure in land development planning', *Geogr. J.* **139**, 53–64.

Young, A. (1976) *Tropical soils and soil survey*, Cambridge University Press.

Yu, Z. Y. (1984) 'Technique of afforestation in Taihang Mountains', *Soil and Wat. Conserv. China* **28**, 26–9 (in Chinese with English summary).

Zaborski, B. (1972) 'On the origin of gullies in loess', *Acta Geographica Debrecina* **10**, 109–11.

Zachar, D. (1970) *Erózia pôdy*, SAV Bratislava.

Zachar, D. (1982) *Soil erosion*, Elsevier.

Zanchi, C. and Torri, D. (1980) 'Evaluation of rainfall energy in central Italy', in De Boodt, M. and Gabriels, D. (eds), *Assessment of erosion*, Wiley, 133–42.

Zanchi, C., Bazzoffi, P., D'Egidio, G. and Nistri, L. (1981) 'Field rainfall simulator', in *Field excursion guide, Proc. Florence Symp. Int. Assoc. Scient. Hydrol.* 46–9.

Zaruba, Q. and Mencl, V. (1969) *Landslides and their control*, Elsevier.

Zaslavsky, D. and Sinai, G. (1981) 'Surface hydrology: V. In-surface transient flow', *J. Hydraul. Div. ASCE* **107**, 65–93.

Zhao, B. L. (1984) 'Obvious effects of closing hillside for vegetative recovery in Baisongling Mountain in Qingyang County, Henan Province', *Soil and Wat. Conserv. China* **24**, 42–3 (in Chinese with English summary).

Zhao, R. H. (1984) 'Mixed forest of pines and oaks is an excellent type of mixed plantation in areas of soil and water losses in W. Liaoning', *Soil and Wat. Conserv. China* **23**, 15–16 (in Chinese with English summary).

Zingg, A. W. (1940) 'Degree and length of land slope as it affects soil loss in runoff', *Agric. Engng.* **21**, 59–64.

Zingg, A. W. (1951) 'A portable wind tunnel and dust collector developed to evaluate the erodibility of field surfaces', *Agron. J.* **43**, 189–91.

Zingg, A. W. (1953) 'Wind tunnel studies of the movement of sedimentary material', *Proc. 5th Hydraulic Conf. Iowa State Univ. Bull.* **34**, 111–35.

INDEX